Dreams of Africa in Alabama

Dreams of Africa in Alabama

The Slave Ship *Clotilda* and the Story
of the Last Africans Brought to America

SYLVIANE A. DIOUF

OXFORD
UNIVERSITY PRESS

Oxford University Press, Inc., publishes works that
further Oxford University's objective of excellence
in research, scholarship, and education.

Oxford New York
Auckland Cape Town Dar es Salaam Hong Kong Karachi
Kuala Lumpur Madrid Melbourne Mexico City Nairobi
New Delhi Shanghai Taipei Toronto

With offices in
Argentina Austria Brazil Chile Czech Republic France Greece
Guatemala Hungary Italy Japan Poland Portugal Singapore
South Korea Switzerland Thailand Turkey Ukraine Vietnam

Published by Oxford University Press, Inc.
198 Madison Avenue, New York, NY 10016

www.oup.com

First issued as an Oxford University Press paperback, 2009

Oxford is a registered trademark of Oxford University Press

Library of Congress Cataloging-in-Publication Data
Diouf, Sylviane A. (Sylviane Anna), 1952–
Dreams of Africa in Alabama : the slave ship Clotilda and the story of the
last Africans brought to America / Sylviane A. Diouf.
p. cm.
Includes bibliographical references and index.
ISBN 978-0-19-538293-8 (pbk.)
1. Slaves—Alabama—History—19th century. 2. West Africans—Alabama—History—
19th century. 3. Slaves—Alabama—Biography. 4. West Africans—Alabama—Biography.
5. Slavery—Alabama—History—19th century. 6. Clotilda (Ship). 7. Slave trade—Alabama—
Mobile—History—19th century. 8. Slave trade—United States—History—19th century.
9. Mobile (Ala.)—Social conditions—19th century. 10. Mobile (Ala.)—Race relations—
History—19th century. I. Title.
E445.A3D56 2007   306.3'620899660761—dc22   2006053153

Printed in the United States of America
on acid-free paper

To the People of African Town,
Past, Present, and Future

To Sény F. and Mariam M. Kamara

I goes back to Africa every night, in my dreams.

—Ossa Keeby

Contents

7

African Town 151

8

Between Two Worlds 182

9

Going Back Home 207

Acknowledgments

I FIRST CAME ACROSS THE STORY of the young people brought to Mobile on the *Clotilda* in 1996. As I worked on other projects over the years, I kept it in the back of my mind. Until one day I found myself in Africatown, going over tombstones in deadly heat, and looking for records in the middle of a hurricane.

As I researched and wrote this book in New York, Africatown, Mobile, Washington, and all over Bénin, I spent much time with great people and I am grateful for the assistance, encouragement, and support they gave me. I owe a huge debt of gratitude to my friend, historian Elisée Soumonni in Cotonou, for his wonderful hospitality and invaluable help, from translations to providing sources, from exciting discussions to critique. I benefited immensely from Léon Degny's research and knowledge, and from Roger N'Tia's humor and scholarship. My gratitude goes to all the informants who answered, patiently, a tremendous amount of questions.

In Mobile, I am indebted to Michael V. Thomason, former Director of the University of South Alabama Archives, where treasures are kept and shared with enthusiasm. He has been a most knowledgeable and generous host, guide, scholar, and archivist. Thanks also to archivist Carol Ellis, and to Thomas Ashby. At the Mobile County Probate Court, the wonderful Collette King went out of her way, even scouring the attic, with extraordinary warmth and passion, to help me find precious records, and I am deeply grateful to her.

Henry C. Williams, Sr., shared his memories of Cudjo Lewis and his knowledge of Africatown. Lorna Woods and Dr. Dorothy Ford, both direct descendants of the *Clotilda* Africans, contributed their time, research, and recollections. I appreciate all the help I got from Charles J. Torrey III of The Museum of Mobile, Nancy Dupree of the Alabama Department of Archives and History, and Pamela Major of the Mobile Municipal Archives.

Curator Joellen P. ElBashir, at the Manuscript Division of the Moorland-Spingarn Research Center, Howard University in Washington, D.C., has been superbly gracious and obliging. I have also been greatly helped by her colleague,

Ida E. Jones, Senior Manuscript Librarian. My thanks to Walter B. Hill Jr., Senior Archivist at the National Archives and Records Administration; to Laurel A. Clark, who assisted with research at NARA, and to cartographer Mike Siegel of Rutgers University.

I did most of my research at the Schomburg Center for Research in Black Culture of The New York Public Library, where the amount and diversity of materials is a daily amazement. For his constant and effective support, his encouragements and understanding, I am deeply grateful to its chief, Howard Dodson.

Elisée Soumonni, Michael V. Thomason, Henry M. McKiven Jr., and Robin Law have critiqued various parts of my manuscript and I cannot thank them enough for their insightful comments. But it goes without saying that inadequacies are entirely mine.

Jennifer Gates believed in this project from the start and never ceased to encourage me; and in the beginning, when it really mattered, Rev. Holly Morales, former Deputy Director of the Mobile Public Library, put my research in the right direction. I owe them much.

I have the deepest appreciation for my editor Susan Ferber's skillful comments and suggestions. My thanks also to Joellyn M. Ausanka at Oxford; Rick Delaney; Benoît Sognonvi, President of the Alliance of Beninese in New York, New Jersey, and Connecticut; Robert Battles, Director of Africatown Community Mobilization Project, Inc.; Delores S. Dees, President of the African-American Archives and Museum in Mobile; and Israel Lewis III.

Finally, I am greatly appreciative of my family's support. Mariam, Martine, Alain, and Maman: un grand merci. Love, and much more than thanks, go to my best friend, my son Sény.

Dreams of Africa
in Alabama

Introduction

O N A JANUARY NIGHT IN 2002, a truck backed up to a statue in front of Union Missionary Baptist Church, north of Mobile, Alabama. One or two people got out, cut through parts of the heavy bronze bust, ripped it from its brick base, and disappeared with their loot. The theft shocked and angered the congregation of pastor A. J. Crawford, Sr. They had just celebrated the New Year and were preparing to commemorate, the following month, the 130th anniversary of the church. Unlike those of the Virgin Mary or George Washington, this statue was the only one of its kind in the country. The theft struck at the very core of a community that will never have any equivalent in North America. Determined to bring the statue back home, the congregation established a reward fund. In case the bust was not found, the money would be used to cast a new one. The wooden model, carved fifty years earlier, was still in town.

The statue dated back to 1959, when a steel shaft was sunk 100 feet into the earth in front of the church, to commemorate the one hundred years that had passed since the honored man and his companions had set foot on Alabama soil.[1] The bust and the shaft were the symbols of an exceptional tale.

In the summer of 1860, less than a year before the outbreak of the Civil War, one hundred and ten young men, women, and children were brought to the Alabama River, north of Mobile. They had just spent six weeks onboard the *Clotilda*, a fast schooner that had brought them from a world away. They were the last recorded group of captive Africans brought to the United States. Acting for Timothy Meaher, one of the most prominent businessmen in Mobile, Captain William Foster had smuggled them in under cover of night. He had to be careful because decades earlier, on January 1, 1808, the country had abolished the international slave trade. Although tens of thousands of Africans had since landed, the slavers could, in theory, be hanged.

After emancipation, the young people tried to get back home but, unable to do so, they eventually bought land and founded their own town. One of their first major enterprises was the construction of a church. Cudjo Lewis used to ring the bell. One hundred and thirty years later, it was his bronze bust that was stolen from in front of the brick building that had replaced the white clapboard church erected by the men and women of the *Clotilda*. Cudjo did not belong to a distant past: he lived through World War I, Garvey's Back to Africa Movement, the Great Migration, and the Great Depression. He died in 1935, the last survivor of the last slave ship.

Cudjo and his companions were part of a tiny group of people born in Africa who witnessed the Civil War, Reconstruction, and the early decades of the twentieth century. To these men and women in their eighties and nineties living in the Jim Crow South, the Middle Passage was still a painfully vivid memory.

They have been all but forgotten today, but those who arrived on the *Clotilda* have also been denied. Their very existence was disregarded by President James Buchanan, who assured the country that the last slave ship had landed in 1858. W. E. B. Du Bois did not include their voyage in his celebrated book *The Suppression of the African Slave-Trade*. Warren S. Howard and Hugh Thomas dismissed it as a hoax in their extensive studies of the transatlantic slave trade. And up to the present day, historians and writers tout the *Wanderer* as the last slave ship to the United States, even though her trip had ended eighteen months earlier than the *Clotilda*'s.[2]

If the date of their awful journey has been contested or even refuted, more importantly, these Africans' singular experience has not generated much attention, although they realized more in America than many other groups of immigrants. In the heart of the Deep South, in Plateau and Magazine Point, three miles north of Mobile, they created a small town, the first continuously controlled by blacks, the only one run by Africans. And unlike most post-Reconstruction black settlements, theirs has endured, and is home to hundreds of their descendants, who, in turn, form the only African American community whose members can all identify their African ancestors.

Their story started in West Africa, in the Bight of Benin, a region known, ominously, as the Slave Coast. From small towns in the countries that are today Benin and Nigeria, young adults, teenagers, and children were brought to the coast and locked up in a slave pen, a *barracoon*, in Ouidah. They had names like Kossola, Abache, Abile, Omolabi, Kupollee, Kêhounco, and Arzuma. They were farmers, fishermen, and traders; they followed Islam, Vodun, or the Orisa. Some had been married, others were too young to have gone through initiation.

The largest group was made up of prisoners of war captured by the Dahomian army during a dawn attack on their town. The rest of their companions were victims of kidnappings or slave raids. They spoke various languages, had lived in different parts of the region, and had different cultures and experiences. But in the *barracoon* and on the *Clotilda*, they created a strong, tight-knit community.

The man at the origin of their dreadful journey, Timothy Meaher, owned a plantation and, with his brothers James and Burns, a shipyard and several steamers. As some people in the South were agitating for the reopening of the international slave trade, he had bet a large sum that he could bring "a shipful of niggers" to Mobile and not be caught. His accomplice in the scheme, William Foster, was the builder of the *Clotilda*. With his schooner disguised as an innocuous cargo ship, Foster sailed to Ouidah in March 1860. There, in a *barracoon* near the beach, he selected nineteen-year-old Kossola—who became Cudjo Lewis; Kêhounco, a young girl who had been kidnapped; Arzuma, a Muslim woman from the North; and dozens of their companions.

Brought to America and enslaved for almost five years on plantations and steamboats, the young Africans formed a bloc, distinct from everyone else, and ready to stand up forcefully to anybody, white or black, they perceived as a threat. Once free again, they regrouped, and put their energy into finding a way to go back to their families in Africa. When their plan failed, they decided to do the next best thing: recreate Africa where they were. They shared all they had, saved money, built each other's houses, and solved problems collectively. Despite the hardships, their sense of unity and kinship made their "African Town" a success. Conversing in a common West African language, they ruled their settlement according to their laws. Gumpa, a nobleman from Dahomey who had fallen from grace, was their chief; and they appointed two young men to be their judges.

Within this African enclave, they raised their children, teaching them the languages and values they had learned from their families and brought from the homelands they cherished. Long after their deportation, they still hoped the interviews they gave to curious strangers would somehow get word to their relatives that they were still alive.

Their arrival on the *Clotilda* had been widely reported in the newspapers, and over the course of sixty-five years, the Africans of Mobile talked to journalists and writers, from obscure people to a Pulitzer Prize winner, and the future novelist Zora Neale Hurston. *Harper's Weekly* published an interview of Cudjo and his wife, Abile, in 1887. Henry Romeyn, an officer with the Fourteenth U.S. Colored Infantry regiment, wrote about them, as did Mary McNeil Scott, the famous Mobile poetess and wife of renowned Japanese art expert Ernest Francisco Fenollosa. Samuel Hawkins Marshall Byers, the poet, diplomat, and author who composed the song *Sherman's March to the Sea* visited them in 1903, and published a long article in *Harper's Monthly*. Alabama-born former slave, activist, and educator Booker T. Washington also paid a visit, in 1909; and Emma Langdon Roche, a Mobile illustrator, published a book about their story in 1914.

In the summer of 1928, Zora Neale Hurston spent two months gathering detailed information from Cudjo Lewis for a book. He told her about his youth and capture, the Middle Passage, enslavement, and life in African Town. Hurston finished the last draft of her manuscript, titled *Barracoon*, in April 1931.[3] She had produced an invaluable document on the lives of a group of people with a unique experience in American history. She sent it to publishers, but it never found a taker, and has still not been published.

From what Abache, Cudjo, and the others said to outsiders and to their own children and grandchildren, from court documents, and from photographs, a clear enough picture of their lives, with a few shady spots, has emerged. Very little of the experience of Africans deported to and enslaved in the West has come to light, and it has generally been through the autobiographies or biographies of a handful of successful men such as Olaudah Equiano, Ottobah Cugoano, or Venture Smith.[4] Next to nothing is known about the lives and aspirations of ordinary people, particularly of women. But precious information can be found in the *Clotilda* Africans' own words, those of the Americans who met them or lived among them, and the words of their descendants.

Their story provides an exceptional perspective on the slave trade. For the first time, the same events can be presented from the points of view of the slave captain and the victims, since they all shared their thoughts about what happened in the *barracoon* and during the Middle Passage. It also offers insight into the type of cultural survival techniques the young people—ages five to twenty-eight—devised. Many of them had not gone through or completed initiation, but they still carried on parts of their cultural heritage on the plantations. In addition, their concerns, hopes, and objectives shed light on what other Africans' preoccupations may have been.

Most slave narratives and former slaves' interviews revolve around life in servitude, but this story has a larger scope: it is concerned not only with slavery, but also with freedom, and life in the twentieth century. The Africans in Mobile represent a unique group of people who grew up free, spent the majority of their years of bondage during the Civil War, and soon became free again. Their transition from freedom to servitude and back to freedom highlights the aspects of their cultures that were most useful to them as individuals and as members of a free community. Their experience offers a unique view into what practices Africans retained, those they adapted, and those they adopted.

Their life story touches on several important issues in African, African American, and American history, and incorporates much of the larger history of deported Africans and of African Americans in the nineteenth century: life in the *barracoons*, the Middle Passage, the domestic slave trade, the illegal slave trade, the reopening of the international slave trade, slavery, African social and cultural "retentions," conversion to Christianity, Reconstruction, Freedmen's politics and education, African American life after Emancipation, convict labor, and reparations for ex-slaves.

Their often tense relations with some African Americans showcase the complexity of the black community at the time. These early frictions, during slavery, hint at prejudice, issues of balance of power based on numbers, and perhaps fears of disruption of the negotiated status quo within the native black population. They help explain why the Africans, once free, chose to self-segregate and create their own town, even though several married African Americans. One, James Dennison, uprooted as a child from South Carolina by the domestic slave trade, met them on the day of their arrival and became a significant member of their community.

Keeping themselves at a distance from their neighbors, oriented toward their homelands, the young Africans built a future for themselves and their descendants rooted in Alabama soil. Willingly, and sometimes unwillingly, they became an integral part of African American and Southern history. They were forced to work for the Confederacy, put money in the Freedman's Bank, voted in one decisive election, and were closely familiar with the justice system.

Their legacy has endured. Thousands of their descendants now reside all over the country, but know that African Town, now called Africatown, is their homeplace. Many, in the fifth generation, still live on the land their ancestors bought and developed, their sturdy houses having replaced the founders' wooden homes. But what has not changed is their sense of being "different" and their determination to preserve a peculiar heritage.

Beyond statistics on the number of people deported from Africa, which do matter, what matters more is the men, women, and children they represent. The story of those who arrived on the *Clotilda* is about the lives and experiences in Africa and America of a select group of young people of various cultural backgrounds, who found themselves in a dreadful situation and joined together to survive on their own terms.

They had the same dream as twelve and a half million Africans sent against their will to the Americas: returning home to their families. Like almost all of them, they did not realize it. But they tried to recreate their own Africa on the soil of Alabama.

Known Africans Deported to Mobile on the *Clotilda*

American Name	"African" name in Mobile/ original name	Origin
Adams, Phily		
Africa, John		
Africa, Lancer		
Allen, Pollee	Pollee/Kupollee	Yoruba
Allen, Rose		
Auro, Ernes?		
Auro, John	Oroh or Wouro	Edo or Dendi
Brunston, Ardassa	Adissa	Yoruba
Cooper, Katie	Monabee/Omolabi	Yoruba
Dennison, Lottie	Kanko/Kêhounco	Yoruba
Johnson, Samuel		
Keeby, Anna		
Keeby, Ossa		Hausa
Lee, Josephina		
Lee, Peter	Gumpa	Fon
Lewis, America/Maggie		
Lewis, Celia	Abila/Abile	Yoruba
Lewis, Charles	Oloualay/Oluale	Yoruba
Lewis, Cudjo	Kazoola/Kossola	Yoruba
Livingstone, Zuma	Ar-Zuma	Nupe
Nichol, Lillie		
Shade, Jaybee, Jaba	Jaba/Jabi/Jabar	Jaba/Jabi/Muslim?
Shade, Polly		
Thomas, Anthony		
Turner, Clara	Abache	Yoruba
Wigfall, Shamba	Shamba	?/Shamba?
Williams, Allie		
	Ahdabi	Yoruba
	Ajemo	
	Ajua	Mina/Ewe
	Alloko	Yoruba
	Bossah	Yoruba
	Koloko	Yoruba
	Cooyaka	
	Cozaloo/Gossalo	Holli?
	Deza	
	Esso	
	Fabumi	Yoruba
	Foloroah	
	Gockilago	
	Gohoby	Yoruba
	Goobee	
	Iyouha	
	Lahla	
	Luwe	
	Messa/Meïssa	Muslim
	Ojo Facha	Yoruba
	Okégbalê	Yoruba
	Sakaru	Yoruba
	Sanalowa	
	Somee	

U.S. Federal Censuses, 1870, 1880, 1900; "Religion of Dahomans"; Emma Langdon Roche, *Historic Sketches of the South*; Zora Neale Hurston, *Barracoon*; informants: Aroua Adénlé, Deen Badarou, Léon F. Degny, Oba Onitako Oyiguin Adedounloye, Salimata Orou, Elisée Soumonni.

CHAPTER ONE

Mobile and the Slave Trades

A T THE TIME OF THE YOUNG AFRICANS' ARRIVAL, Mobile, their future home, was Cotton City. And it is cotton that brought them there in a tale of two slave trades, one over land, and the other over sea. A tale of migrations, it is the story of white men attracted by fabled economic opportunities; and of black men and women transported against their will. Blacks and whites were two sides of the same story, one group uprooted and exploited so that the other might prosper. And on a particular day in 1859, many fates were sealed on a steamer named *Roger B. Taney* going up the Mobile River.

Cotton City, the second-largest exporter of white gold in the country after New Orleans, was a place where, according to Hiram Fuller, a Massachusetts journalist who visited it in the 1850s, "people live in cotton houses and ride in cotton carriages. They buy cotton, they sell cotton, think cotton, eat cotton, drink cotton, and dream cotton. They marry cotton wives, and unto them are born cotton children. In enumerating the charms of a fair widow, they begin by saying she makes so many bales of cotton. It is the great staple—the sum and substance of Alabama. It has made Mobile, and all its citizens."[1] Between 1817, when Alabama became a territory, and 1861, the port would ship more than thirteen million bales of cotton, most of which was cultivated, picked, packed, and loaded by hundreds of thousands of black men and women. Some of the pickers, packers, and loaders worked for Captain Timothy E. Meaher, a wealthy and well-respected planter, lumber-mill owner, and ship builder.

Meaher was not a native son, but a Yankee, the son of a foreigner. His father, James O'Meagher, was born in 1784 in a small town in the county of Kilkenny in southeast Ireland, the son of Thiege O'Meagher, a rich country gentleman. The American saga of the O'Meagher family started when James, an engineer who had a passion for the sea, was asked to join the English army. He refused, as he put it, "to wear a red coat," arguing that no man in his family had ever done so. To avoid being impressed into service, he clandestinely boarded his uncle's ship and migrated to Newfoundland. He remained in Canada for a few years before deciding to try his luck in the United States. After settling in Maine, he started a career as a stonemason, quite a step down from his training as an engineer. In 1809, in the town of Bowdoinham, the twenty-five-year-old immigrant married seventeen-year-old Susannah Flanders Millay, the daughter of a migrant from Kilkenny turned American patriot, and his wife, Abigail Eastman, whose family was among the first Europeans to settle in Maine.[2] The young couple, who now went by the name Meagher, lived in Boston for a while, but returned to Maine and made their home in Whitefield, Lincoln County, a town founded in the 1770s by people just like them, Irish Catholics.[3] James continued to work as a mason until he lost a leg in an accident while building a Catholic church. He took on farming to continue sustaining his family. During fifty-eight years of marriage, the Meaghers had eight children. The eldest was James Millay, born in 1810. Then came Timothy, born in 1812. He was followed by William, Mary, Patrick Burns, John Cheverus, Dennis Ryan, and Abigail Ann.[4]

In 1835, Timothy and James bade farewell to the family and moved to Mobile. To entrepreneurial young men in their twenties, Alabama was an appealing destination. It was still a frontier state where money could be made in a few years, and Mobile was booming. Industry was in full expansion. Gold, coal, and the production of turpentine were growing. Sawmills turned pines into planks that made boats and furniture, and a third of its lumber was profitably exported to Cuba, Mexico, and Europe. With rivers all around to facilitate trade, rivers with exotic names like Black Warrior, Coosa, Tallapoosa, and Cahaba, there were all kinds of ship jobs available, and anyone could start as a deckhand. At the higher end of the maritime professions, boatbuilding and piloting had become the most glamorous and the most prestigious occupations. Alabama boys did not dream of becoming president, but captain or pilot on a riverboat.[5] Timothy was no longer a boy, but he dreamed that dream, too. James, on the other hand, was not taken by Mobile and, after a few months, he returned to Maine.

IF THE RIVERS WERE THE PRIDE of the state, cotton was its sustenance. Alabama, in the 1830s, was living in flush times. "Alabama Fever" had spread throughout the South after the War of 1812 and brought white settlers by the tens of thousands. They entered the Alabama heartland, where they met fierce resistance from the Upper Creeks, who were then defeated during the Creek War of 1813–1814. More Indian land was lost as Choctaw, Chickasaw, and Cherokee, even though they had fought alongside the United States against the British, were also forced to relocate westward to Indian Territory after the Treaty of Dancing Rabbit Creek in 1830. With large numbers of Native Americans pushed out, throngs of settlers left the Carolinas, Tennessee, Georgia, and Virginia and their over-exploited farms, "all going into cotton mightily."[6] They quickly drove the price of land to unprecedented heights and as swiftly the cotton output of the entire nation tripled. Some of the Southern newcomers to the Gulf States were rough, uncouth men and women, who often lacked education, money, and economic opportunities in the Old South. In Alabama, many could become prosperous like the people they looked up to or envied back home—usually first-generation "old money" themselves—but could not become. By 1860, several planters were worth a quarter of a million dollars in land, slaves, and stock, and raked in $10,000 to $15,000 a year (in today's dollars, the equivalent of $205,000 to $308,000.)[7] Besides the Southerners, Alabama also attracted Northern men and women, like Timothy Meagher, and foreigners, mostly Irish and Germans. A large part of the Alabamian population had thus arrived there recently and by 1850, some 45 percent of the residents had come from another state, or from a foreign country.[8]

Mobile was the busy, elegant commercial center of the state and its only port. Three local banks and sixteen insurance companies that insured boats, crops, and bondpeople were doing brisk business. Sixteen foreign nations that imported Alabama goods had opened consulates in the city, including Switzerland, Norway, Russia, and Belgium. There were foundries, mills, factories, and cotton presses. Cotton had created a rich class of merchants, planters, middlemen, and steamship captains, but even among the wealthy, most Mobilians were far from polished.[9] Amid the large male population, drunkenness that led to violence was an acute problem. Timothy, stocky, rawboned, rough, with a disdainful mouth (described once as "a very Celtic mouth of the Kerry type") was probably a regular visitor to the saloons rather than the salons.[10]

When he got to town, the young Yankee, who became known as Maher, Meagher, and finally Meaher, must have been in for a major culture shock. Long before he was born, Maine had abolished slavery. He may not even have seen any black person growing up, since there were less than 1,400 in the entire state when he left. But more than 43 percent of Alabamians, over 255,000, were black. In 1840, Mobile counted 12,672 inhabitants, and 3,069 of them were black and enslaved. The city was also home to the largest community of free people of color in the state, albeit a paltry 541.[11] Meaher did not own anybody. Unskilled, and so like many of the traditional Irish immigrants to the South—rather than the skilled Northern workmen, or the German or British nationals—he had signed up in 1835 as a deckhand on a steamboat, the *Wanderer*. He was ambitious and he rapidly worked his way up to mate, serving on nine ships before building a large sawmill on Chickasaw Bogue north of town in the early 1840s. Soon after, he had his first steamboat, the *William Bradstreet*, constructed in New Albany, Indiana.[12]

As his good fortune grew, Timothy called on his brothers to join him and share in the riches of Alabama river life. William and Dennis Ryan were the first to respond. William, four years younger than Timothy, became a steamboat captain, plying the river between Mobile and Montgomery. Dennis, still in his teens, worked as a clerk for his brothers until he died in 1845 at age eighteen. William did not enjoy Alabama for long, either; in 1850, the thirty-four-year-old captain passed away, leaving no family behind. Then Patrick Burns, twenty-eight, made the move. He worked with Timothy as a mate before becoming a captain in his own right. Meanwhile, James had been doing well following his relocation to Maine: he owned a large grocery store in Gardiner, after having taught school for a few years. But, perhaps because of William's death, the businessman packed his bags and moved his wife and three children to Mobile. John Cheverus followed suit and he too went to work on the river. But by 1853, at twenty-eight, he too was dead. Young sister Abby joined her brothers and lived with Timothy until 1853, when she married a very rich San Francisco banker, John Parrott, in Montgomery. Of the seven Meahers who had made it their home only James, Tim, Burns, and Abby had survived the move to Alabama. After having seen three of his brothers die, James had also lost his wife, Alice Landers, who had passed at twenty-eight, shortly after moving to Mobile. He had remarried in 1854, to a Maine girl named Sarah. Burns had also settled down and married Helen, a former schoolteacher from Albany, New York.[13] Finally, in 1855 Timothy married Mary C. Waters, a niece of Edward Kavanagh, a lawyer, secretary of state, commissioner, congressman, chargé d'affaires in Portugal, and governor of Maine.[14]

With his brothers in business, Timothy, the family pioneer, could greatly expand. Following the *William Bradstreet*, he had built the *Orline St. John*, a steamer named after a young woman he had fallen in love with in his young days. The ship was to meet a tragic end. Among the brothers' other ships was the *William G. Jones, Jr.*, the first steamboat of its kind built in Mobile, a very fast ship that bore the name of a family friend, the district circuit judge. Other Meaher creations were the *William R. Hallett*; the *Roger B. Taney*; the *Czar* (the last two closely associated with the story of the Africans); the *Waverly*; the schooner *Sarah E. Meaher*, named for James's wife and seized in an international incident in 1855; and the *Southern Republic*, the largest steamer to cruise the Alabama River, which later distinguished itself during the Civil War.[15] James was much involved in the part of the brothers' business that consisted of shipping pine and cypress timber to the West Indies. In later years he would be named president of the Mobile Trade Company. Burns, who in the early days was a mate under Timothy's supervision, became the captain of the *Czar* and the proprietor of a plantation in Grove Hill, the seat of Clarke County. In 1859, the *Advertiser* reported that "The Messrs. Meaher, at their mill near the city, have sawed 2,000,000 feet of lumber, and 1,209,000 shingles during the year, and are preparing to build another large steamer."[16] The three brothers had plantations, sawmills, timberlands, and steamboats. They owned everything they worked with: the timber and the boats; the enslaved men and women who cut the wood, made the planks, built the boats, loaded and unloaded them, and grew the cotton transported on the ships; and the food that fed them all.

Like 10 percent of the white families in the city, the brothers were slave-holders. The city of 30,000 kept a quarter of its population in chains.[17] In the summer of 1860, Burns held nineteen people in bondage, nine adults and ten children under fifteen. Only five were, in plantocracy terminology, "prime hands," men and women in their twenties. Before the addition of the *Clotilda* Africans, Burns was one of about 2,100 Alabamians who owned between fifteen and twenty people. To qualify as a planter one had to own twenty slaves, and after the *Clotilda* sailed in, this Meaher indeed became one. His real estate wealth was estimated at $1,850. It was very comfortable, but not much compared to one of his neighbors, Lorenzo James, a planter originally from South Carolina whose real estate value was $45,000 and whose personal property reached $164,150, mostly invested in his 103 workers.[18] Burns's personal estate—men, women, and children, along with his share in the brothers' shipping and milling business—was worth $19,750.

James Meaher had twenty-two slaves. Eighteen were men between sixteen and fifty-five years old, and more than 70 percent of those were "prime men." The four women he owned were of childbearing age, although at least two did not have any children. Specificities about James's wealth are not known since his net worth was not reported in the 1860 census, but it certainly was larger than his brother's since he owned more people whose value was higher. What about Timothy? How many people had he enslaved? Strangely enough, there is no documentation on that matter except, one would imagine, in his personal papers that his family has strenuously refused to make public. His name is not listed in the Slave Schedules of 1860 or 1850. Timothy Meaher, the most famous of the brothers, turned out to be the most elusive. In December 1850, he appeared in the Federal Census in Mobile under the name Meher, as a boatman living with his sister Abby; but a few months earlier, in August, the siblings had also been counted in the Maine census as residents of Whitefield, along with brothers James, William, Burns, John, and sister Mary. They might have gathered there for a family affair such as a wedding, baptism, or funeral. Timothy had thus been counted twice in the federal census of 1850; but it would take another twenty years for him to be enumerated again. In October 1850, when the Alabama Slave Schedules were compiled, he may still have been in Maine, although his brother James was back in Mobile. Whatever the case may be, Timothy's name did not appear as one of the state's slave owners in 1850. The same was true in 1860. He should have been paying taxes on his slaves, which would indicate how many he owned, but the Mobile tax records only show three people enslaved by the brothers' company, JM & T Meaher, in 1860 and four in 1861.[19] Given the fact that Burns and James owned around twenty people each, one can imagine Timothy's "holdings" before the *Clotilda* at perhaps the same number. It cannot be excluded that several or most laborers were hired from other slaveholders, as was the case with his cook, which could help explain why he did not appear in the Slave Schedules.

Some of the Meaher brothers' friends who became part of the *Clotilda* plan were men who, like the Maine natives, had come from somewhere else in search of land and money, or more land and more money. Thomas Buford, fifty-seven, who lived close to Timothy and James and became the owner of several Africans, had migrated from Kentucky with his Virginian-born wife, Amanda, in the early 1840s. As a landlord and farmer, his real estate was worth $10,000 ($205,000 today) in 1860. His personal property, which included his enslaved labor, was almost double that amount. In 1850, he owned nineteen people, seven males and twelve females ranging in age from two to sixty-six. Ten years later, his property included twenty-four men, women, and children. John M. Dabney, forty-one, who would come to play a significant role in the Africans' ordeal, had arrived in 1850 from King William County, Virginia, with his wife, Elizabeth, and several bondpeople. He was representative of a well-off class of migrants from the Upper South, who had pulled into town with a following of shackled men and women.[20]

DURING THE NINETEENTH CENTURY, hundreds of thousands of African Americans from the Old South, like those owned by Dabney, were displaced in an unprecedented forced migration.[21] Mostly by foot, but also by ship and train, they followed their owners reaching for the cotton and sugar lands of the Deep South. The miserable caravans were all over the countryside, the cities, and the small towns. "In the course of the day," recounted an English traveler, "we met a great many families of planters emigrating to Alabama and Mississippi to take up cotton plantations—their slaves tramping through the waxy ground on foot, and the heavy wagons containing the black women and children slowly dragging on, and frequently breaking down. . . . We passed at least 1000 negro slaves all trudging on foot, and worn down with fatigue."[22] When the big rush was over, about 400,000 black men, women, and children, according to some estimates, had been forced by their owners deep into the South.[23]

The Meahers had not come to the Gulf with bondpeople in tow, so they had had to buy them. South Carolinian James Dunwoody Brownson De Bow, superintendent of the Census Bureau in 1850, and founder and editor of the very influential *De Bow's Review*, could have been talking about the brothers when he described the nouveaux slave owners of the Gulf States:

> All over the new States of the Southwest enormous estates are in the hands of men who began life as overseers or city clerks, traders and merchants. Often the overseer marries the widow. Cheap lands, abundant harvests, high prices, give the poor man soon a negro. His ten bales of cotton bring him another, a second crop increases his purchases, and so he goes on, opening land and adding labor, until in a few years his draft for $20,000 upon his merchant becomes a very marketable commodity.[24]

The Meahers were in the right place to acquire laborers. In the 1850s, Mobile was the slave-trading emporium of Alabama, attracting traders and planters from as far away as Mississippi. With the development of southwestern cotton and sugar land, enslaved labor was in huge demand. But there were not enough hands in the state. In the eighteenth century, the solution had been simple: bring in Africans. But after the abolition of the international slave trade in 1808 enslaved people had to be transferred at a high price from Virginia, Delaware, Maryland, and the Carolinas, where tobacco and cotton were in decline and the plantations required fewer laborers. As many as 1.2 million men, women, and children—including free people kidnapped into slavery— were forced, between 1790 and the 1860s, into an internal migration twice as large as the transatlantic slave trade to the United States. It was facilitated by the significant natural increase—compared with the rest of the Americas—in the enslaved population that, although consistently lower than the white rate, was still important.[25] The half a million men and women who had been introduced into the country from Africa had become 2.3 million in 1830, 3.6 million in 1850, and almost 4.5 million in 1860. Selling people to the Deep South was quite lucrative. It was the largest source of income in the South, after plantation slavery itself; and the rate of return on capital invested in the slave trade between 1830 and 1860 was consistently higher than in slaveholding.[26]

Meanwhile, in "the quarters," to be "sold down the river" had become a collective nightmare. In slave narratives and interviews, testimonies abound of men, women, and children torn apart from their loved ones.[27] Comparing it to the now illegal international slave trade, the black newspaper *Freedom's Journal* stated that the suppression of the internal trade was of more pressing concern:

> In our humble opinion, the thousands which are annually appropriated for the suppression of the foreign slave trade, is to be considered but a secondary object, while our domestic slave trade is suffered to be carried on from one State to another. We may declaim as much as we please upon the horrors of the foreign slave trade, but we would ask, are the horrors of the internal trade less—are the relations of life less endearing in this country than in Africa— are the Wood folks of the South less cruel than the slavers on the coast?[28]

International and domestic slave trades were intrinsically linked. For the black population, the abolition of the international trade, deemed inhuman, should have signified the end of the internal trade, since they were both based on the same premises. And those who defended the African trade clamored that it had to be re-authorized since it was not different from the legally sanctioned internal trade.

Before the *Clotilda* sailed back to Mobile, the Meahers probably bought bondpeople at the King and Forman Negro Mart on Royal and State Streets. King had come from Richmond and had contacts in Virginia, who sent him coffles by land and sea. His market had two large yards that could hold several hundred people.²⁹ Dirty and exhausted, the new arrivals were fed, clothed, their skin greased to make them look healthier. The brothers may have also frequented John Ragland's mart on Royal and St. Anthony, or done business on the curb of the sidewalk at northeast Dauphin and Royal Street. But, like most slaveholders, they likely acquired a large part of their human property outside the markets. Every few weeks, cloth and trinket peddlers, horse traders, and speculators came calling at the plantations where most of the sales took place. In addition, there were advantages to being a steamship captain when it came to buying: after 1850, some speculators took their coffles to New Orleans on steamboats, then to Mobile, and from there up the Alabama and Tombigbee to the more active markets of Montgomery and Selma. When they went to board the Meahers' ships, the brothers could have had first pick. The Meahers, the traders, and the enslaved, they certainly all had heard the song that accompanied the coffles on the river.

> Up an' down de Mobile Ribber
> Two speckelaters for one po' lil nigger.³⁰

James, for one, must have heard it many times. A young man enslaved by Burns Meaher who was to play a significant part in the Africans' lives, he had been a victim of the domestic slave trade too. Born in Charleston in 1840, he was sold as a boy with his aunt Amy to Burns. Over the years, James had become a boat pilot, transporting to Mobile the products of the plantation: bales of cotton, turpentine, chickens and eggs, molasses, rice, beef, pork, and bread. On his return trip, he brought groceries, fertilizers, fruits, and alcohol. At twenty, in 1860, he was a dashing figure, five feet, eight inches tall, with two long plaits he had inherited from his Indian side of the family.³¹ Noah, another protagonist of the Africans' saga, had been sold down the river from North Carolina. He would work many years for Timothy, and spend the rest of his life far from his family back East.

With the uprooting of people like James and Noah, the forced migration had almost achieved the planters' objectives of a larger manpower to till the land and work the boats, but not quite. In 1790, the Lower South accounted for 21 percent of the enslaved population, but in 1860, the percentage had increased to 59. Maryland and Virginia, which in 1790 had 60 percent of the nation's unfree labor, only retained 18 percent in 1860. The 47,500 black men and women who lived in Alabama in 1820 had become 437,770 forty years later. Sixty percent had come from somewhere else, mostly from Virginia, Georgia, and the Carolinas. And of those who were born in the state, the great majority were the children of those Virginians, Georgians, and Carolinians. The white population had increased too, but by a smaller percentage. Whereas the black population had been multiplied by ten, whites had seen their numbers increase only sixfold. The rate of increase of the black population had been significantly higher than the white rate throughout the Deep South.[32] There were now more hands to hoe, plow, ditch, chop, and pick, but the human landscape had been dramatically transformed at enormous costs. By far the highest price was paid in blood, terror, and tears by black men, women, and children, those who had been sold down the river and those who had seen them go. There was also the price paid in bills, coins, and bank drafts on the tabs of the Gulf Coast planters. The acquisition of more than a million bondpeople had cost them close to a billion dollars. Most thought that Eastern Negroes had become far too expensive.

On July 20, 1860, less than two weeks after the *Clotilda* had returned to Mobile, the auctioneers Betts & Gregory of Franklin Street in Richmond estimated the price of a prime male at $1,550 to $1,620, while a "second rate or ordinary" man fetched between $1,100 and $1,200. Prime girls could reach $1,450 and the ordinary "wench" $900 to $1,100. In Mobile, the same men were acquired for more than $2,400 (about $49,000 in today's dollars). Already the year before, the *Mobile Register* of January 19, 1859, had called the prices "exorbitant." In the previous ten years, the cost of land and enslaved labor had increased nearly 100 percent.[33] Never in the history of the South had bondpeople been so expensive. The old commercial rule that linked their price to the price of cotton no longer applied, as one commentator deplored:

> The old rule of pricing a negro by the price of cotton by the pound—that is to say, if cotton is worth twelve cents, a negro man is worth twelve hundred dollars, if at fifteen cents, then fifteen hundred dollars—does not seem to be regarded. Negroes are twenty-five per cent higher now, with cotton at ten and a half cents, than they were two or three years ago, when it was worth fifteen and sixteen cents. Men are demented upon the subject. A reverse will surely come.[34]

THE MASSIVE DISPLACEMENT of African Americans to the Gulf States was exposing a regional fracture in the slaveholding South between sellers and buyers, and a potentially explosive class fissure between those who could afford to pay top prices and those who could not.

The domestic trade had not entirely lived up to the buyers' expectations. They needed more workers, and at cheaper prices. When most slaveholders living in the 1860s were born, the legal transatlantic slave trade was but a memory.[35] Only the oldest knew what it was like to walk to a boat full of Africans in broad daylight and buy them at affordable prices. But if the trade was now illegal, its victims were not. There were ways of making them above-board as soon as they arrived. The 1833 Alabama code, for example, stated that illegally "brought or imported" Africans were to be sold, lawfully, to the highest bidder at public auction. Following the federal Act of 1818 that rewarded informers who denounced the slavers, half the proceeds went to the collector of customs, but if there had been an informant the money had to be shared equally between him and the official. The rest went to the territorial treasury.[36] In other words, slaveholders could still get African laborers legally; the only losers, in theory, were the shippers, who forfeited their expected benefits and had to pay taxes on each individual they had introduced. Yet, they could still make fortunes. James Bowie, the Alamo "hero" and his brother Rezin, who invented the bowie knife, had perfected the scheme, as one of their accomplices explained:

> As the country improved and land property became enhanced in value James sold out his land on the bayou and used the means thus obtained in speculat-ing in the purchase of Africans from Jean LaFitte, the pirate, who brought them to Galveston for sale. James, Rezin (another of Jim's older brothers), and myself fitted out some small boats at the mouth of the Calcasieu, and went into the trade on shares. Our plan was as follows: First we purchased forty Negroes from LaFitte at the rate of one dollar per pound, or an average of $140 for each Negro; we then brought them into the limits of the United States, delivered them to the customs house officer, and ourselves became the inform-ers. The law gave the informer half the value of the Negroes, which were put up and sold in the United States. We continued to follow this business until we had made $65,000, then we quit and soon spent all our earnings.[37]

When illegal dealings were uncovered, the traffickers, who supposedly risked their heads, were not worried. A presidential pardon was de rigueur. Thomas Jefferson, James Madison, James Monroe, John Quincy Adams, and Andrew Jackson all pardoned slavers caught red-handed.[38] To many slaveholders it all smacked of hypocrisy. Why not be honest about it, they complained, and simply reopen the international slave trade that would bring them as much cheap labor as they needed?

The idea had started to gain strength in the early 1850s and was first pro-moted by Leonidas W. Spratt, the editor of the Charleston Standard. Although it would definitely remain a minority view, within a few years it had reached the Houses of Representatives in the Southern states, the Southern Commer-cial Conventions, and the Congress of the United States. Among its most out-spoken advocates were Robert Barnwell Rhett of the Charleston Mercury; James Hopkins Adams, governor of South Carolina; William Lowndes Yancey, a former U.S. senator from Alabama; and James De Bow. They did not, how-ever, all share the same ultimate objective. For some, it was mostly a question of needed labor, but for others, it was a political matter first and foremost. Then–Mississippi senator Jefferson Davis exemplified the ambiguity: he was a proponent of the revival but limited only to Texas and the western territories; he was firmly against the introduction of Africans in his state. There were enough enslaved people there, he believed, although a better distribution system was needed.[39]

To its political advocates, the reopening of the international slave trade was a simple proposition. The United States, they alleged, was at an economic disadvantage because of a dearth of plantation workers, especially in the Deep

South. The nation was losing the competition with Great Britain and France, which had abolished slavery in 1834 and 1848, respectively. Those two countries had resolved their own shortages by settling tens of thousands of Africans liberated from the slave ships in their Caribbean colonies; and by bringing in close to 58,000 African indentured workers as so-called apprentices who could never find a boat to go back home after their contract had expired, along with Indian laborers.[40] But the issue of concern was actually more regional than national. International slave trade advocates claimed that the South was losing political power within the nation, due in part to a strong demographic increase in the North fed by European immigration, while the South was cut off from its traditional supply of manpower. Spratt calculated that for every 50,000 Africans introduced, the South would gain 30,000 federal votes, according to the 1787 Three-Fifths Compromise.[41] In addition, Southern expansionism was at stake. The free states were expanding, while the South could not claim new lands due, according to the revivalists, to the scarcity of enslaved people to work them.[42] Of course, purely economic issues were far from forgotten, even if they were not always presented as crucial. Daniel Lee, editor of the *Southern Cultivator* and a university professor, wrote in the Georgia *Constitutionalist* that if one million men and women "now worthless in Africa" were put to work, the Southern mines would "pay a good interest on a thousand million dollars, and the muscles of these savages [would] pay a fair interest on a thousand or five hundred dollars each." In one year, the "savages" would have paid for their transportation, the cost of buying them, and, at $500 apiece, they would add a $500 million value to the South.[43]

But even among political supporters, objectives could be diametrically opposed. Some, like pamphleteer and sociologist George Fitzhugh of Virginia, thought that the reopening would save the Union by pushing a revitalized South to remain in it. Others, such as Spratt, made it clear that since the North would refuse to reopen, agitating around the question was a positive step toward secession.[44] In May 1858, when the Southern Commercial Convention met in Montgomery, Alabama, the majority report recommended the adoption of firm motions in favor of reopening the trade and advocated the creation of a committee to study its feasibility. But the debate was so fierce with opponents from the Border States that the question was left for further discussion at the following convention in Vicksburg, Mississippi. Meanwhile, the Louisiana House of Representatives took matters into its own hands and authorized the introduction of 2,500 free Africans to work as apprentices for at least fifteen years.[45] It was little more than grandstanding because in many states blacks were compelled to leave once they became free, so the immigration of free Africans was in contradiction with their laws. In Alabama, for example, free blacks who had settled after February 1832, were liable to two years in the penitentiary if they did not leave the state after notification by the authorities. If they were still around one month after their release, they were to be sent to prison for five years. As for those who had been emancipated in the state, they were to be sold as slaves if they had not left Alabama within six months.[46] In 1859, undaunted by the collapse of the Louisiana scheme after the State Senate refused to pass the bill on apprentices, the revival activists moved a step further: they launched the African Labor Supply Association with headquarters at Vicksburg, Virginia.

The association's president, James De Bow, alleged he had nothing but the welfare of the Africans in mind when he advocated their massive introduction, "From the teeming millions, the barbarian hosts, crushed, oppressed, benighted, of that father-land [of our present labor system], cannot a few more subjects be spared to civilization?"[47] The founders of African Town would discover soon enough that the image of the savage African was going to haunt them and their descendants for a long time. And it sometimes came from quite unexpected quarters.

Besides hastening the prospect of secession for the radical political wing, the popularity of the international slave trade rested, for those preoccupied with cheaper labor, on what they saw as the price gouging that accompanied the domestic trade. According to a Louisiana revivalist, "the price of negroes has already reached that point which is beyond the means of small planters, and they cannot afford to invest their small amounts of spare capital in a species of property that may be swept away by the diseases of the climate—perhaps, the very next week after its purchase—and thus, in the loss of one negro fellow, a three years' saving is gone with him."[48]

The populist appeals to the small planters were paralleled by propaganda aimed at the poor, those who would never be able to afford enslaved labor anyway. According to the revival propagandists in search of a solid white front across social classes, even the destitute could become slaveholders, and the reopening of the international slave trade, with its prospective vast influx of inexpensive enslaved labor, could only bolster their prospects. With more Africans available, more people could have slaves, they argued with utmost demagoguery, and the peculiar institution would have more supporters.[49]

The growing immigration of Europeans also entered the revival debate. Although many went south, the vast majority chose the North—hence increasing its demographic, political, and economic power—because there they did not have to compete with the cheapest manpower available, enslaved labor. If it became cheap, the advocates alleged, immigrants could buy Africans and would support slavery. The big planters too, according to De Bow, should favor the reopening for the common good because, even if they saw their net worth drop, "the basis of slavery will be enlarged, and be brought to embrace in a direct and tangible interest, every member of the community, and its area at the same time be widened by the introduction of new States."[50] Finally, the revivalists argued, if slavery was good and just, then why was the international slave trade banished? By reviving it, the stain would be lifted from the institution.

On the other side of the debate, the large planters in the Border States were fiercely opposed to reopening the international slave trade. According to abolitionist newspaper *The National Era*, their hostility came from the fact that they were "competitors with Congo and Dahomey in the production of negroes for the Southern market."[51] But there was also ambivalence in their midst and some of their colleagues in the Deep South supported them. In Louisiana, some threatened to leave if the trade was revived; and in South Carolina, many large planters were for the revival, while nonplanters were against.[52] Just as the domestic slave trade revealed regional and class fractures, the agitation for the African trade revival exposed geographic, social, political, economic, and class divisions within the South. The black press rejoiced, "Criminal as this effort to revive the slave trade is, we expect much good to result from it. It must necessarily divide the South, and give rise to issues between Southern men which may become fatal to the system of Slavery."[53]

Some wealthy slaveholders feared that "low-cost" Africans would dramatically decrease the value of the bondpeople already in the country. In 1860, two million Southerners belonged to slaveholding families and kept in servitude 3,950,000 men, women, and children. A small group, less than 8,000, which represented 2 percent of the slaveholders, monopolized almost one million men, women, and children, or close to a quarter of the country's "holdings."[54] These planters had what today would be millions of dollars invested in black men and women. A significant drop in their price, and the slaveholders' fortunes would vastly diminish. To rally support, they couched their argument in a populist language palatable to the masses. Just as the revivalists claimed they only had the Africans and the poor whites in mind, the opponents presented themselves as only concerned with the welfare of those less fortunate. The influx of poorly qualified Africans, they argued, would impede development; poor whites would find even less work and therefore would never be able to save enough to acquire even cheap enslaved labor. For good measure, they inserted a catastrophic political scenario into the debate. The seller states, seeing their slaveholding value reduced to nothing, would be forced to abolish slavery, thereby increasing the number of free states, they predicted.[55] To this frightening perspective they added a line about the insecurity that a flood of "cannibals," "heathen and worthless men," and "black rascals" would bring to the country. President James Buchanan sympathized, and in a message to Congress in December 1859, he asserted:

> Reopen the trade, and it would be difficult to determine whether the effect would be more deleterious on the interests of the master or on those of the native born slave. Of the evils to the master, the one most to be dreaded would be the introduction of wild, heathen, and ignorant barbarians among the sober, orderly, and quiet slaves, whose ancestors have been on the soil for several generations. This might tend to barbarize, demoralize, and exasperate the whole mass, and produce the most deplorable circumstances. The effect upon the existing slaves would, if possible, be still more deplorable.[56]

The revival issue had made strange bedfellows, as the black press exposed. "The large slaveholder, the commercial and manufacturing classes, and the men of integrity and humanity, will take sides against [it], which the demagogues, appealing to the masses, will demand, in the name of the species of equality which is implied in the motto, 'Every citizen a slaveholder.'"[57]

In Mobile, the Meaher brothers were surely following the diatribes of the pro-reopening advocates sympathetically reported in the *Register*. The newspaper, edited by John Forsyth, a former ambassador to Mexico, proclaimed that slavery was "the beneficent source and wholesome foundation of our civilization" and, although he believed that "the time is not ripe for making [the reopening] a political and party issue," he nevertheless announced that the *Register* would try to hasten that time by "developing and elucidating the question." Shortly after his famous editorial, he was elected to the state legislature.[58] However, Alabama politicians had considerably cooled their support to a cause that had never rallied the South as a unified block. Secession was looming and a cohesive South was crucial to its success. Alabama Governor Andrew B. Moore had declared in mid-1859 that it would be desirable to repeal the law that made slave trading an act of piracy, but "neither this nor any other question should be permitted to divide the South in the crisis of the next year."[59]

But Timothy Meaher believed that the reopening was still part of the debate, and that illegally bringing in Africans was a logical, feasible, and rewarding enterprise. It all started on one of his regular packets that linked Mobile to Montgomery. The steamboat was the *Roger B. Taney*, named in honor of the scion of a Maryland tobacco family who had been the fifth chief justice of the U.S. Supreme Court since 1836. In 1857, Taney had rendered the majority decision in the famous *Dred Scott* case that had broadened the political gap between South and North. Dred Scott had been taken by his owner, Dr. Emerson from Missouri, to the free state of Illinois and the territory of Wisconsin. When the Army sent Emerson back to Missouri in 1842, Scott and his wife Harriett returned to the slave state and four years later petitioned for their freedom on the basis that they had lived on free soil for several years and were thus free, according to the 1824 Missouri Supreme Court decision "once free, always free." In March 1857, Scott lost his case in front of the Supreme Court by a seven-to-two decision, which said that Negroes could "claim none of the rights and privileges which [the Constitution] provides for and secures to citizens of the United States."

THE *ROGER B. TANEY* WAS THUS a most propitious place to hatch a scheme that was going to deprive a group of Africans of their rights. On that momentous day, between Mobile and Montgomery, Meaher and some of the men on board got into a discussion about the latest attempt by Congress to suppress the international slave trade. According to one rendition of the events, one of the men, a New Yorker, thought that the smugglers should be killed. "Yes, hanging the worst of them will scare the rest off," he said. Captain Meaher replied, "Nonsense! They'll hang nobody—they'll scare nobody." A clueless Mr. Ayers, from back East, "famous as a manufacturer of pills," claimed that it was impossible to introduce Africans anywhere in the United States. Mr. Matthews, a planter from Louisiana, retorted that it was indeed very feasible. Coming from a state where many Africans had recently disembarked under cover of night, he knew what he was talking about. And he was so confident that he placed a $100 bet that it could be done. As the discussion continued, Timothy Meaher himself bet "a large sum," according to one source; or more precisely as reported by another, "a thousand dollars that inside two years I myself can bring a shipful of niggers right into Mobile Bay under the officers' noses."[60]

The newspapers were replete with stories of Africans introduced as illegally as easily. They were often the expression of Southern bravado meant to embarrass the federal authorities and keep the cruisers traveling to remote areas.[61] On May 14, 1859, for example, the Texas *Richmond Reporter* had published an ad for four hundred "likely AFRICAN NEGROES, lately landed upon the Coast of Texas." Two hundred Africans were allegedly transported by train to Mobile the same year, and according to one testimony, eight hundred more were expected. In July 1859, the Mobile *Mercury* had run a piece saying, "We heard a gentleman who is 'up to snuff' say yesterday that another cargo of Africans had been landed upon the Gulf Coast, within a few days, and that the captain of the craft who brought them was in our city—he had seen and talked with him." Newspapers claimed that six hundred Africans had landed in August 1859 near Tampa, Florida. When the federal marshal got to the spot where they had disembarked, all he found, it was reported, was a burnt-out ship. There were sightings—some real, other imaginary—of just-landed Africans throughout the South.[62]

But the big headline of the day was the very authentic story of the *Wanderer*. The voyage originated in 1858 in New York City, the hub of the illegal slave trade—by then all nations had declared it unlawful—to Cuba, Brazil, and the South. The slavers had a good friend in high places. Judge Samuel Rossiter Betts who, in contradiction to judges in other port cities, and to the "Equipment Clause" that the U.S. Squadron had been instructed to enforce in 1849, had ruled that the presence of shackles, too much water and food for the crew, enormous pots to prepare food for many more people than the sailors, and lumber in abundance—to build shelves for the captives to lie on—were not sufficient evidence of a project to introduce African captives.[63] He let many slavers just sail away.

The *Wanderer*, owned by Charles Lamar and captained by William C. Corrie of Charleston, was sent to Port Jefferson on Long Island to be transformed into a slave ship. One of the main tasks was to set up tanks or casks capable of holding 15,000 gallons of water. Once the ship had been turned into a slaver and then disguised as a regular ship, she encountered a few suspicious authorities, but in the end, she entered the Congo River on September 16, 1858, after fifty-five days at sea. U.S. officials saw her sail upriver but, as had generally been the case for the past decades, they were either incompetent or turned a blind eye toward the obvious objective of the operation. In addition, officers of the British Navy charged with repressing the illegal slave trade never suspected its intentions. Within a few hours, more than four hundred people, mostly boys and young men, were brought aboard. On November 28, they reached Jekyll Island, Georgia. Four days later, half the group boarded the *Lamar* and traveled another sixteen miles past Savannah, where about 170 people were later picked up and taken to cotton plantations in the Edgefield area. The captives who had remained at Jekyll Island were dispatched by land to other estates. About forty were put on a train and they passed through Atlanta in December on their way to Alabama. But the authorities had caught wind of the affair and the ship had been seized. The captain, the crew, and the owner of the *Wanderer* were prosecuted, but their cases were either dismissed or the sentences were light. Lamar was fined $500 and was condemned to a month in jail that he actually spent confined at home. He had become a hero.[64]

In Alabama, the Congolese were attracting much attention. They were "in the hands of speculators" and put aboard the steamer *St. Nicholas* of Cox, Brainard & Company to go down the Alabama River."[65] A man who saw thirty-eight of them when they traveled through Montgomery thought they were "dull, sleepy, obtuse looking negroes, having no curiosity about anything. Many of them seemed to be laboring under a cutaneous affection which kept them upon the 'scratch' all the time." They were an advertisement for servitude. "When contrasted to our own negroes, who have descended from the same stock," continued the observer, "they show how much the breed is improved by the Southern mode of treatment—being made to do healthful work, well fed, well clothed, attended to when sick, and well taken care of generally."[66] The captives were going for about $850, up to eight times what the captain had paid for them.[67] The Federal courts knew some of the buyers and could have found where the young men and women were held. In 1860, an action was brought against Horatio N. Gould of Mobile. A bookkeeper originally from Connecticut, he had twenty-one slaves and was accused of buying some of the Congolese. But he escaped punishment under the 1820 piracy law because "an indictment which only charges that the accused, within this state, did hold, sell, or otherwise dispose of a negro or a slave who had previously been unlawfully imported by some other persons, without alleging that the accused did participate, aid or abet in the unlawful importation, is fatally defective." Cases were opened against other men in Georgia accused of "holding African Negroes," but no attempt was made to find, free, or repatriate the deportees.[68]

The *Wanderer* expedition had, at least in theory, made it slightly more difficult for the slavers, and there is little doubt that Meaher and friends knew it. In September 1859 the administration gave instructions to increase to eight the number of ships of the African Squadron whose mission was to discourage slave trading and, if unsuccessful at dissuasion, to catch the slavers. Moreover, three were steamers and thus faster than sailing ships. Another four steamers were assigned to Cuban waters. These new directives notwithstanding, the *Wanderer* incident had everything to inspire Timothy Meaher, his brothers, and their friends. The protagonists had been caught, indeed, but Southern justice, Northern complicity, and Federal apathy had conspired to make the venture a success after all.

Convinced that he too could effectively smuggle in Africans, Captain Meaher went around town talking to trusted friends about his plan. In short order he found a number of takers. He then set out to find the pièce de résistance of his new endeavor, a fast ship. He called on an old friend and associate, William Foster, thirty-seven, a skinny, bearded man from Pictou in Nova Scotia, Canada. Called the "Birthplace of New Scotland," Pictou had been settled in the eighteenth century by Scots, and after the Revolutionary War, by soldiers from the United States. Then came other immigrants from England and Ireland. Among them were William Foster's parents, both English. Foster had likely been familiar—even if vaguely—with African Americans, since several thousands had settled in Nova Scotia after the Revolutionary War and the War of 1812. But, contrary to those who lived in Alabama, they were free people who had gained their liberty by fighting alongside the British.

Foster had immigrated to Alabama around 1843. Heir to a long line of seafarers and boat builders, he had learned ship carpentering. In 1860, his real estate worth was estimated at $500 and his personal riches at $200.[69] Those were paltry sums. He was a boarder at Jacob Vanderslice's home, near Timothy Meaher's settlement. The young man had been Meaher's associate in other projects. A boat they both had interests in, the *Susan*, built by Foster, had just been through a high adventure. On December 9, 1858, more than a hundred men led by Harry Maury had boarded the ship at Mobile to go on a mission to Nicaragua to support General William Walker. A major actor in the slavery expansionism movement that flourished in the South in the 1850s and was closely linked to the reopening of the international slave trade, Walker wanted to conquer Central America and turn it into a slave state. He had first invaded Mexico's Baja California and tried to seize Sonora, and had proclaimed himself president of the Republic of Lower California before retreating. Arrested in California, he was tried and acquitted in a few minutes. He then entered Nicaragua as a mercenary during a civil war and proclaimed himself president there, too. Expelled, he went back to the United States in 1857. But his forces were bent on reclaiming "their" country. One week after they left Mobile on the *Susan* for their *reconquista*, the ship ran into a coral reef near Belize, and the filibusters had to go back home on a British boat. The *Susan* was lost.[70]

This time around, to go to the African coast Meaher and Foster chose the *Clotilda*, a schooner Foster had built a few years earlier. The ship's birth had not gone unnoticed. On October 17, 1855, a Mobile newspaper published news of the vessel:

> The Clotilda. Such is the name of a beautiful schooner built by Mr. Foster at his shipyard opposite the city, and which is now receiving her rigging at the foot of St. Anthony Street. This vessel in model and fastning does great credit to her builder, and afford another evidence of the capacity of our city for successful and economical shipbuilding. She is light and commodious, draws thirty inches forward and forty-two inches aft, and is intended for the Texas trade. Her tonnage is 137, Custom House measure, and her model is of that graceful turn which confers assurance that she will prove a fast sailor.[71]

Foster had registered the *Clotilda* on April 19 with the Customs Service. Her length was eighty-six feet; her breadth, twenty-three; and she had two masts and one deck. Her tonnage was given as 120 81/91 tons.[72] The ship had not been intended for the slave trade but she was capable of carrying about 190 people, as the average number of captives per ton in the Atlantic trade was 1.6.[73] The venture would thus be nothing like the average Cuban or Brazilian slaving operations of the day that transported anywhere from four hundred to more than a thousand Africans.

But was Meaher primarily interested in money? Charles Lamar, several months before the landing of the *Wanderer*, had acknowledged, "I have been in for grandeur, and been fighting for a principle. Now I am in for the dollars."[74] The Georgian had had time to reflect and reorganize his priorities but Meaher was new to the business. He was doubtless a man of action, but was he only that? He has been made to appear as an impulsive gambler, a man who was just in it for the bet. But he was more likely moved to act by his fierce convictions. His support of General Walker for the extension of slavery to Central America was a clear illustration of his strong political stance. He was the kind of man who put his money and assets to the service of his cause. Even Meaher's reason for ultimately retiring from his job as a ship captain was linked to his deeply felt, unwavering principles. And it seems safe to conclude from his actions that the enslavement, and later discrimination against and segregation of black people powerfully motivated him. In defense of slavery, its expansion, and its continuation, he was willing to take financial and personal risks.

Timothy Meaher said he paid $35,000 for the *Clotilda*.[75] Since the schooner had not been built for the slave trade, she needed a thorough makeover. Foster started the work of transforming her into "a low craft with tall masts, long spars, and broad sails like the wings of a yachting racer."[76] Meaher sent some of his men to work on the vessel in great secrecy. They loaded the ground tier with 125 barrels of water. On top of the water, they stacked 25 casks of rice, 30 casks of beef, 40 pounds of pork, 3 barrels of sugar, 25 barrels of flour,

4 barrels of bread, and 4 of molasses.[77] It was enough food, it was hoped, to accommodate a twelve-man crew for four months, and perhaps a hundred and thirty Africans for eight weeks. Then the trade goods were put on board. Eighty casks of *aguardiente rum*—as Foster put it erroneously, since *aguardiente* and rum were two different beverages—or rather *cachaca*, called "nigger rum," and twenty-five cases of "dry goods and sundries" found their way to the hold.[78]

It was an assortment of items that the two accomplices knew would be of interest to the coastal sellers. The merchandise was worth about $3,500, but it was just a complement to the most important item in the planned acquisition of about 125 captives: $9,000 (about $185,000 today) in gold.

A boat with enough food for a regiment, mammoth pots, too many barrels, and a provision of nigger rum that clearly indicated who its future consumers would be was far too obvious to officials, so the *Clotilda* underwent still another makeover. The tier full of compromising goods was covered with lumber that hid it from casual inspection and would be used later on to build platforms and partitions: the Africans' "beds." This was no elaborate camouflage compared to what was going on in the illegal slaving world at the time. To avoid detection, slavers had become experts at disguising the purpose of their trips. They had perfected several ploys. One was to load the water, food, and goods on several ships that sailed from different American ports. None, therefore, had enough slave-related paraphernalia to raise suspicion. Later, on the high sea and far from the cruisers, the cargo was unloaded from some of the vessels and redistributed to the two or three making the African voyage. The "cache of gold" was another ruse. The captain of a slaver would hide a bag of gold, anywhere from $2,500 to $4,000, in a place that the authorities would be certain to search. Once the compromising gold that would allegedly be used to buy the Africans was discovered, it was immediately confiscated. The investigation ended there. Since without the gold the purchases would be impossible, it was argued, the ship was cleared. The inspectors kept the money, and the slavers sailed away. It was easy to remake the loss: the benefits on the sale of four or five African men would make up for the bribe. Another ploy was to ship the lumber necessary for the construction of the platforms on another ship engaged in legitimate trade. Once on the African coast the planks were transshipped and the slaver's carpenter sawed them to the desired lengths. Even the huge water tanks could be built with lumber in Africa.[79] But the *Clotilda* was not a habitual slave ship with a savvy captain. It was Foster and Meaher's first slaving adventure, and they kept it simple.

Besides the goods and the gold, there was certainly something else on board. Like any other slave captain, Foster must have carried enough fetters, whips, knives, and guns to face a possible uprising. And since his ship risked being chased by men-of-war (naval vessels engaged in the repression of the slave trade), she was doubtless equipped with cannons that would help make a fast escape, although Foster did not mention any. A typical slave ship at the time took several cannons on the trip, "four six-pounders, two long brass 18-pounders, and four brass 12-pounders, besides small arms."[80] Foster acknowledged he had duplicate papers—and probably a collection of flags of various countries—handy to be presented upon demand, depending on the nationality of the man-of-war whose captain asked questions.

OF ALL POSSIBLE PLACES along the African coasts where captives could be bought, Foster and Meaher had settled on Ouidah in Dahomey, on the appropriately named Slave Coast. Angola and Congo, which had been providing hundreds of thousands of cheaper laborers to Cuba and Brazil, were much farther south, which meant more time and more risks. To recoup the cost of an enterprise there, a much bigger boat, capable of holding at least three hundred people, would be needed. But as the *Clotilda* was a small vessel, and the whole operation a small-scale endeavor, it made sense to do business in West Africa. Author Emma Langdon Roche believed that what prompted Meaher to launch an operation in Dahomey was an article on November 9, 1858, in the Mobile *Register* that stated, "The quarreling of the tribes on Sierra Leone River rendered the aspect of things very unsatisfactory. The King of Dahomey was driving a brisk trade in slaves, at from $50 to $60 each, at Wydah. Immense numbers of Negroes were collected along the coast for export."[81]

When the boat had been loaded with supplies, and all traces of the purpose of the voyage concealed, it was time to hire the crew. Seamen generally loathed slave-trading work, and were reluctant to go on these expeditions, but usually not on moral grounds. The pay was poor, mistreatment rampant, the work of cleaning up a slave ship and her captives was sordid, the possibility of revolts a reality, and crew mortality was high. A large proportion of the 300,000 to 350,000 men who worked on British and American slave ships between 1750 and 1807 had been tricked, kidnapped, or otherwise forced into naval service. After 1808, it was a given not to tell the sailors the purpose of the trip, because legal risks were now involved. Some sailors had been brought back to the United States and indicted. Others, intercepted on the high sea, had been dismissed in Sierra Leone or at the next port of call in Africa, while those captured near the beach were just left to fend for themselves. Crews whose mutinies failed were often detained in the same forts that held the African captives and they could be locked up for a year before being sent back home. As for the sick and the shipwrecked, they were abandoned in the coastal cities. The African coast had its share of discharged sailors who had embarked on what they thought was a legitimate trade trip to the Caribbean, and found themselves stranded between Senegal and Angola.[82]

Foster's men were in the dark as to what they had really signed up for. The first mate, George Duncan, a thirty-nine-year-old master mariner, and the second mate, J. B. Northrop, were Northerners from Rhode Island who like the rest of the crew had been picked up in Mobile and other Gulf ports from among the regular assortment of hard-drinking, rough-edged seamen.[83]

Foster wanted to take his future brother-in-law, William Vanderslice, along, but he was not back from a trip when the *Clotilda* left.[84]

On the night of March 3, 1860, Captain Foster left Jacob Vanderslice's house and walked through the woods to the Chickasaw Bogue, where the *Clotilda* was anchored. The bag of gold hung over his shoulder. He climbed aboard the ship, pulled out a piece of the cabin bulkhead, and hid the bag behind.[85] Soon his crew of eleven men boarded the vessel. The *Clotilda*, now a low ship with tall masts, long booms and broad sails, left Mobile Bay on the fourth with papers stating that she was taking a cargo of lumber to the island of Saint Thomas, in the Danish Virgin Islands.[86] Ship and crew sailed through the Gulf of Mexico without a hitch. In a little more than three days, they were near Cuba.

But when they reached the Atlantic, according to the captain, a major problem arose. The ship was drifting away. She was veering off course, and Foster was unable to put her back in the right direction. Each night, as he looked at the stars, he could see he was not going where he was supposed to. Then, it hit him: the bag of gold he had hidden was too close to the compass and was throwing off its reading. In the middle of the night, he walked discreetly to the bulkhead, removed the gold, and the needle immediately went back to the right position.[87] But it was not the end of the problems. On March 17, about sixty miles north of Bermuda, a violent storm hit. For nine days, the *Clotilda* was pounded by terrible winds. The gales were so powerful that they swept away everything on deck. The rudder head was split in three. Only two lifeboats had been saved. In the middle of the storm, a Portuguese man-of-war chased the ship for ten hours. There were "squalls all day and about dark our fore sail went out of the boli-rope in splinters: the most exciting race I ever saw."[88] Foster could reminisce with excitement (or embellish) thirty years after the event, but the fact is that the first leg of the voyage was a disaster.

Finally on April 14, forty days into the trip, the captain and his crew came in view of the Cape Verde Islands, the Portuguese-controlled archipelago off the coast of Senegal. It was one of the very first areas—once uninhabited—to which the Portuguese sailors had deported and enslaved Africans in the 1500s. It was the place where they repaired their ships, and the island had been heavily deforested as a result. Once again, a vessel in distress was coming to shore. But just as the crew was preparing to land at the island of Fogo, early in the morning they sighted another Portuguese man-of-war, sailing toward the *Clotilda*. Foster changed course, "to get away from her not wishing to be boarded so early on the voyage, as he would have followed us for capture."[89] Finally, the Portuguese ship disappeared, and the *Clotilda* entered the harbor of Praia.

The damage done by the storm was too serious to ignore. The ship had to undergo major repairs. Foster knew he was taking risks, because work being done on the lower deck might reveal the true purpose of the voyage. As they started to take off the lumber that covered the barrels of pork and the casks of rum, the crew finally realized they were on a slave ship. They had few choices. If they decided to leave the boat altogether, they would be stranded in Cape Verde. And as one sailor whose colleagues had discovered only in the Congo what they had signed up for put it, "nobody liked to be put out on the coast of Guinea alone."[90] Foster's men decided to mutiny. The mutiny turned into black-mail: they demanded more money or they would inform the Portuguese. In similar cases, things did not come to that: the captain would immediately pro-pose a raise and sometimes add as an incentive something few sailors would refuse, one or two Africans each they could sell upon arrival.[91] Foster had no choice; he agreed to pay them double.[92]

While the crew worked on the ship "cheerfully," as he stressed, their cap-tain befriended the Portuguese officials and the American consul. To put them on his side, he graciously offered their wives shawls and jewelry brought from Mobile.[93] Something else may have changed hands, too. It was the rule, during the illegal slave trade, to have a stash of money earmarked for kickbacks. What-ever the case may be, Foster benefited from the representatives' understand-ing. He noted, "I did not have any trouble with the American Consul notwithstanding his tact at guessing as to my whither bound: but he gave me clearance to trade on the coast of Africa and recommended me to go to the island of 'Anabow' [Annobon in Equatorial Guinea] and sell my cargo, as there was famine on the island."[94] With a wink, the American consul let the slaver do his job. Foster was lucky. Just a few months before, the naval depot of the African Squadron had been moved from Praia to Loango, just south of the Congo River, where most of the slaving activities were taking place. But then again, given the laissez-faire attitude of the African Squadron, it is quite pos-sible that, just like the consul, the men in charge of stopping the slave trade would have looked the other way. In a letter dated April 15, 1860—just as Foster was nearing Cape Verde—George Hamilton Perkins, commodore of the U.S. Navy, explained how, in the Congo, the captain of the *Sumter* had let go two ships with "their slave decks all laid and everything ready for the cargo." They had immediately been filled with captives and sailed away.[95]

Once they left Cape Verde, with the diplomat's benediction and advice, Foster and his crew ran into yet another man-of-war, the third in two months. It was, he claimed, a closer call than the two previous encounters. There was a moment of fear as the captain thought the vessel might shoot at them. But the breeze was good and his ship was soon out of reach of the cannons.[96] Foster did not mention the nationality of this particular man-of-war, but the first two were, according to him, Portuguese. British, American, Spanish, and Portu-guese naval patrols were cruising the Brazilian, African, and Caribbean waters in search of slavers and Foster had seen, he claimed, menacing ships in the two latter locations. The U.S. African Squadron had always been lackadaisical, if not an outright accomplice of the slavers, while the Royal Navy—which had seized 1,600 ships since 1807—was more vigilant. Portugal, on the other hand, was not active in the repression. Its squadron "was no more than a token," and it is a bit strange that the *Clotilda* was chased by her navy at least two times out of three.[97] One cannot exclude the possibility that the captain embellished the story with descriptions of suspenseful and dangerous close encounters on the high sea.

After having survived a devastating storm and successfully fended off attacks, the *Clotilda* reached the Slave Coast. Two and a half months after they had left Mobile, Foster and his crew anchored in the port of Ouidah.

CHAPTER TWO

West African Origins

*E*IGHTEEN-SIXTY WAS A GOOD YEAR to buy captives in Ouidah. The previous three years had been a boon for slave dealing in Dahomey. Such activity had not been seen for a long time, because, since the early 1850s, when it got involved in the legitimate commerce in palm oil, the kingdom had reduced its slave-trading activities. King Ghezo had been firmly encouraged down this new path by Great Britain, and, parallel to diplomatic exhortation, London had blockaded the Dahomian ports for six months in 1851–1852 when it had become apparent that the kingdom had not renounced the transatlantic slave trade. Finally, on January 13, 1852, Ghezo had reluctantly agreed to sign a treaty abolishing the "export of slaves to foreign countries" and promising to punish severely any person who broke the law. Deprived of the revenues brought by the trade in people, the kingdom was to receive instead the income generated by the export of oil needed by the European industries. Great Britain believed that palm and slave trades were incompatible, reasoning that since workers would be needed in the country to cultivate the palm and produce and transport the oil—the domestic slave trade had increased for these very reasons—the deportation of labor would thus be impractical and counterproductive. But Ghezo envisioned the palm oil trade not as a substitute for, but rather as a supplement to, the slave trade, which was a crucial part of the royal tradition of Dahomey.[1] Additionally, the revenues the palm oil generated were not comparable to what the slave trade had brought in, in part because its price on the world market and to the producers had started to decline in the mid-1850s.[2] Treaty or no treaty, by 1857 an overt resumption of the international slave trade looked like a seductive option to Ghezo, and soon slavers were back in large-scale business in the Bight of Benin.

Two main factors had contributed to the revitalization of the slave trade in Dahomey. One was the French "free immigrants" scheme. The government of Emperor Napoleon III had given a contract to the trade firm of Victor Régis for the recruitment of thousands of free people to be sent to Martinique and

Guadeloupe following the abolition of slavery in 1848. As nobody was interested in going, the plan was to buy captives, "free" them, and send them on their way. In Ouidah, Régis' agent, anticipating large shipments, had negotiated for the acquisition of people at $50 each, or $30 less than the current price. But the scheme had not only boosted demand, it had also attracted a lot of attention overseas. Slavers had flocked to the coast ready to pay $80 per person in order to get hold of the hundreds of captives Régis thought he had secured. In the United States, Southern opponents of the slave trade revival denounced the French arrangement, noting that since Africans could not be made to emigrate, the apprentices were in reality captives taken during slave raids.[3]

But the key factor was the resurgence of the Cuban slave trade, mostly carried on by American slavers, since the British Navy was not allowed to search their ships. In July 1857, while the revival of the international slave trade was agitating the South, the American brig *W. D. Miller* had taken captives on board near Ouidah. The *Vesta*, which had sailed from New Orleans, and the *Virginia Pearce* from New York were cruising around looking for opportunities. In September, the *James Buchanan* had embarked three hundred people. They all had evaded the British Squadron, but the *Abbot Deverieux* was seized with 270 people on board, and the *Jupiter* with 100 individuals out of an expected group of 250.[4]

When the *Mobile Register* announced on November 9, 1858, that the King of Dahomey was driving a brisk trade at Ouidah, its information—said to have attracted Timothy Meaher to the area—was quite accurate. But it would be Ghezo' s swan song. That same month, as he was coming back from a military campaign, he was wounded by a sniper at Ekpo, and later died of his wounds. According to Benjamin Campbell, British Consul in Lagos, the army of Dahomey killed and captured more than 1,400 people to avenge the king.[5] When the news of Ghezo's death finally reached the United States more than a year later, and three months after the Congolese from the *Wanderer* had been seen all over the South, *The New York Times* rejoiced, "The news . . . is fraught with evil tidings for the American advocates of the African Slave-trade. The only Sovereign in all the world who sympathized with their objects and would have actively furthered their designs, is no more."[6] However, contrary to the newspaper's optimistic view, the king's death, far from ushering in a new era of peace and stability, signaled the resumption of full-scale slave raiding.

One of Ghezo's sons, Badohun, succeeded him, taking the strong name Glèlè. He had two primary reasons for intensifying the raiding campaigns. One was the Dahomian practice of sacrificing prisoners of war during the huge festival in honor of the ancestors—the annual Customs—and the Grand Customs that marked a king's death. Since major Grand Customs were due to honor the late Ghezo, hundreds of future victims were expected in the capital, Abomey.[7] The other reason for a resumption of raiding was the Cuban demand for captives that had not abated and went practically unchecked. In 1859, British intelligence claimed that the island had introduced more than 30,000 Africans.[8] As he assumed power, Glèlè turned his military machine toward the hinterland, while independent traders continued to move caravans of captives throughout the area, including from Nigeria in the east. Prisoners of war, refugees, and victims of kidnapping were arriving on the coast from all directions. Such was the case of the 110 men, women, and children who were deported to Alabama. They came from various regions, bringing their own different cultures, histories, religions, and languages.

Several people were originally from Atakora. One woman mentioned in the 1890s that she was from "A'tarko" and came "long way from Dahomey." But more generally, their presence is attested to by several rites seen in Mobile before 1865 that were associated only with populations from this region.[9] Atakora is a mountainous area in northwest Benin that perhaps as early as the fifteenth century had been a refuge from conquerors, raiders, and pillagers for peoples coming from Togo in the west. The Batammariba, Berba, Besorube, Kabye, Lamba, Lokpa, Natemba, Niende, Soruba, Taneka, Tangamba, Waaba, and Yowa who settled there share many cultural traits, including the fact that they live in stateless societies.[10] Political and social organizations are not distinct, and authority lies with the lineage chief, the oldest man within a group of families who descends from the same ancestor. With no rulers, no castes, no professional or social differences, and no slavery, the system is based on gender and age class, which define everyone's status within the family. Culturally integrated and faced with a common adversary, the various populations of Atakora had established tight relations. Their economies were interdependent: some produced iron, while others transformed it into tools and weapons; those in the mountainous areas cultivated cereals, part of which they exchanged for the yams and rice grown by the men of the valleys. Exchanges also concerned poultry, goats, sheep, and cows, pottery, and baskets.[11]

Many deportees in Mobile had scarifications on the face and/or the body, and those who came from Atakora had gotten them in a particular manner. As they passed from one age class to the other their bodies indicated where they stood in the hierarchy. They received scarifications around the navel, then on the belly, and finally on the chest. Those on the face, numerous and very fine, barely visible, had been done much earlier, when they were two or three years old. The teenagers also got their upper teeth filed with small stones in the form of spikes.[12] At each stage of their ascension toward the highest status, young men were allowed to take part in certain activities: first, hunt and collective work, then war, and thereafter marriage. Young women followed a similar path as they grew up, with various scarifications, teeth-filing, and age appropriate activities. As girls, they helped their mothers in the domestic sphere and kept an eye on the younger children. In their teenage years, they took part in water and wood collecting, and in the transport of agricultural products. Every four or ten years (depending on the population) during the rainy season, initiation took place in the sacred forests and lasted from three to four days. Only after they had completed the rites were young men and women allowed to get married, the average age being eighteen for females and twenty for males.

One of the most remarkable features of the Atakora populations is their architecture. Their round adobe dwellings with two stories and terraces are connected together by solid walls that resemble fortresses.[13] Defense was a major concern in the region because although isolated, the people of Atakora were vulnerable to the attacks of the populations that had settled on the lower terrain, the Gulmanceba, Baatonu (or Bariba), and Tyokossy (or Anufo), who conducted a regular trade in prisoners for their own use and for sale. Dahomey never campaigned in the Atakora because it did not have to; it acquired captives from the Baatonu and Wangara traders, who in turn had bought them from the raiders. As they moved south along 370 miles of trade routes, the captives could be sold several times before they reached Ouidah.

OTHER DEPORTEES WERE ORIGINALLY from Dahomey itself.[14] Some may have been Mahi and/or Yoruba enslaved by the kingdom and settled within its borders. In that case, they had probably been convicted of a crime, as it was rare for people domestically enslaved to be sold overseas. But at least one man was Fon. As a rule, Dahomey did not sell its own people, the *danxomenù* ("property of Dahomey"). However, some free people convicted of crimes could be enslaved and deported as a punishment. Oral tradition reports that following a devastating fire in Ouidah, Ghezo sold overseas more than a thousand people from the neighborhood where the blaze had started. The Dahomian crown also got rid of political opponents or distrusted prominent people by thrusting them into the Atlantic trade.[15] One Fon, named Gumpa, was among the *Clotilda* deportees; he was a nobleman reputed to be related to a family member of Glèlè. As such he was an *ahovi*, the top of the social hierarchy in Dahomey that also consisted of *anato* or *danxomenù*, i.e., free men and women, and two categories of slaves: the *kannumon* (prisoners of war and raids, and people bought from the traders) and *ganto* (convicts condemned to enslavement). Emma Langdon Roche, who must have gotten the details from Adalaide Foster—since only her husband could have described the episode—reported the circumstances that led to Gumpa's deportation. According to the story, Akodé, the prince who supervised the sale of the captives in Ouidah, asked the captain to pick one person as a gift, the one Foster's "superior wisdom and exalted taste"—supposedly in the prince's words—designated as the finest. Foster, who wanted to flatter him, chose Gumpa, who was "nearly related" to him.[16] The motivation behind this offering is perplexing. Perhaps it was the man's dreadful way of asserting his absolute power over everyone in the room. Another possibility is that Akodé showed Foster some men he wanted to get rid of for any number of reasons, and asked him to choose from among them.

Another group of deportees were Yoruba traders on their way to Porto-Novo when they were ambushed by a party of Dahomians on the road between Abeokuta and Ketu.[17] They may have been the victims of a band of marauders, but much larger events were unfolding in the area at the time of their abduction. In mid-February 1860, the army of Dahomey had marched to Ketu (Ketou/Iketu)—about fifty miles east of Abomey—and camped close by. Glèlè had dispatched a messenger to the walled city to inform the *Alaketu* (king of Ketu) that he was about to attack Abeokuta much further east. The army left and was not heard from for several days as it lay in wait between the towns of Idigni and Meko. Their intention, it was learned, was to destroy Meko, but according to a contemporary testimony, the guides made a mistake and Glèlè then attacked Idigni.[18] It may be in these circumstances that the traders were caught.

The ethnic background of one woman, Zuma, if not her occupation, was reported fifty years after her arrival in Alabama. According to Roche, she was a "Tarkbar." The Tarkbar do not exist, but the actual ethnic group she was referring to is easily discernable under the approximate rendition of its name. Zuma was a Nupe, or a Takpa, as the Yoruba call her compatriots. The heart of Nupeland, *Kin Nupe*, lies in Nigeria in the basin of the Niger and Kaduna Rivers. Through various migrations the Nupe scattered over several regions of Nigeria and to northern Benin where they settled in multiethnic Borgu. Zuma said she was from "Loandi," which may be Louanzi in northeastern Borgu near the border with Nigeria.[19] The Nupe/Takpa are overwhelmingly Muslims and one of the names they—along with other Muslim populations in West Africa—give to their daughters is Arzuma. It is reserved to girls born on Friday, *Juma'a* in Arabic. Growing up, Zuma might have gone to Qur'anic school at around age seven, to learn to recite the Qur'an and write it in Arabic. As she got older, her life would have followed the traditional pattern. Nupe females are not involved in farming, but they process and sell agricultural products. Some work in crafts such as pottery, indigo-dyeing, and weaving.[20] Given her age when she arrived in Mobile, about twenty-three, there is no question that Zuma had already been married for several years. Contrary to the Fon, the Yoruba, or the women of Atakora, who usually married after eighteen due to lengthy initiation, Nupe girls did so around fifteen or sixteen. Zuma was married to an African while enslaved in Alabama, and it cannot be excluded that this man was actually her first husband. It is also highly probable that she had children, like a majority of the women caught up in the transatlantic slave trade. Being single is not an option in Africa—it is rare even today—because it goes contrary to the most fundamental African values of community and family, as well as Islamic principles. Since most captives in the transatlantic slave trade were between the ages of fifteen and thirty, it follows that married women with children represented a very high percentage of the female deportees.[21] The circumstances that led Zuma to a *barracoon* are not known. She said she had been captured by what former officer Henry Romeyn understood as being

"L'Ascotha." It is unclear whom this referred to. Before she left Ouidah, she had already been sold twice.[22] She may have changed owners along the close to 450 miles between Louanzi and Ouidah, or she could have been first enslaved domestically and been sold again to traders who took her to the coast.

Another young woman who embarked on the *Clotilda* had grown up far away from Borgu, and she and Zuma shared neither a language, a religion, nor an ethnicity. Her name, spelled Kanko in Mobile, was likely Kêhounco, a female Yoruba name that indicates the bearer was born after her parents had gone through a long period of infertility. Her family's oral history asserts that she said there had been a war between Dahomey and Lagos.[23] No such event happened even though tensions and even talks of war were common between Dahomey and the British established at Lagos since December 1851. The identification of the town as Lagos is also problematic, since Kanko would have known it as Eko. She passed on the story to her descendants in the 1910s and it was written down more than seventy years later, so there is room for errors. For example, Kanko was also said to have told her family that Dahomey was separated from the Congo by the Nile River. It is therefore possible that Lagos was a name added later by her descendants. There had been a war in March 1851 between Dahomey and Abeokuta, a center of Christianization supported and armed by the British Consulate at Lagos. This may be the war to which Kanko referred. She would have been about seven at the time. That she remembered or knew of the conflict would imply that she witnessed it or was sufficiently close to it to have heard of it. She told her descendants that where she lived traders left their merchandise at the market and went back home, and buyers helped themselves and deposited the money at the point of purchase. This was a widespread custom for petty trade in Yorubaland that relied on trust between buyer and seller and on public honesty.[24] She also mentioned the existence of the shilling (*shile* in Yoruba). The shilling, converted into cowry shells, was used all over the Bight of Benin from Ouidah to Lagos and does not indicate a specific area. Although a few clues point to Nigeria, Kanko herself indicated that she came from Dahomey.[25] A possible explanation is that at some point, she and her family were refugees in Dahomey following the numerous population movements that had resulted from the long history of conflicts between the kingdom and Yorubaland. They might also have been captives, deported from the east to Dahomey.

Contrary to most of her future *Clotilda* companions, she was not captured during a raid. She had been sent on an errand by her mother and cautioned not to take a certain path because slave catchers had been seen in the vicinity. She disobeyed and out of curiosity ventured to the coast to see what was going on. Obviously, she lived near the ocean if she believed her escapade could go unnoticed. She was kidnapped.[26] Abductions linked to the transatlantic slave trade were a common occurrence, and at least eight deported Africans—they were overrepresented—who wrote autobiographies or related their experience had been kidnapped.[27] Abductions were orchestrated by whites hunting for captives, local bandits in search of victims to sell to the traders, or desperate parents. In the latter case, relatives were looking to exchange the stranger they had snatched for the release of their children held in a *barracoon* on the coast.

At least two people among the *Clotilda* group, a man, Gossalow or Cozaloo, and his future wife had also been kidnapped. They were said to come from Whinney, which could be Weme, a kingdom on the Weme River, but may also be Ouinhi, a town about twenty-five miles east of Abomey.[28] It is located in a region, Hollidjé, settled by Holli (the name they were given by the Yoruba and Fon) or, as they call themselves, Dje. They speak a language related to Yoruba. The Holli—who filed their teeth—formed slaveless societies, and their families lived scattered but still under the supreme authority of the eldest man. They were frequently raided by Abomey.[29]

Among the captives was also a group of people who might have been Dendi speakers. Their presence can be deduced by their use, on Timothy Meaher's plantation, of a specific word. Granted, a single word is very little to trace a people's origin and circumspection is required, but this word is also quite particular. Noah, the young man from North Carolina who lived with and observed them closely, heard some of the Africans call water "la-lie or something lak dat."[30] As far as can be ascertained, only one population in the Benin/Nigeria area uses a term that sounds like "la-lie." It is "hari," which is pronounced with a rolled "r" that makes it sound as an "l." Along with Zarma (Niger), Dendi is a dialect of Songhay, a language that has no close relative, which explains the uniqueness of "hari" in the region.[31] The original Dendi homeland lies in southern Niger and in Borgu, in the extreme north of Benin. Dendi, which means "south" or "downstream," designates a region, a language, and an ethnicity that is essentially a mix of various populations: Songhay, Tchanga, Gulmanceba, Kumate, Kanuri, and Hausa. Nevertheless, there is a Dendi linguistic and cultural unity, and the various components act as clans within a larger, encompassing Dendi identity. Largely Sufi, of the Qadiriya brotherhood, the Dendi contributed to the spread of Islam in the region. They have three scarifications on each side of the face, from the forehead to the chin, but they do not have tattoos or scarifications on the body. Dendi are found in Borgu (in the Nigerian part as well), in Kebbi State (Nigeria), and Dendi traders have been present in Atakora at least as early as the seventeenth century.[32]

One man called himself Ossa Keeby in Mobile (also rendered as Keebe or Keebie) and explained that it was the name of a river in his homeland. According to Booker T. Washington, Keeby told him that he was from the upland of Dahomey, seven days from the sea, a description that fits the Banté region of Benin and would indicate that he came from there.[33] Washington's account seems straightforward, but because of numerous mistakes, various interpretations, and transcriptions, everything concerning the origins of the *Clotilda* Africans has to be scrutinized. It is possible that Keeby was referring to the homeland of the vast majority of his companions, not necessarily his own. If he had been the only one from his region and everybody else came from another, it would have been a logical thing to do. Roche's claim that the last survivors—with the exception of Zuma—were Tarkars cannot be taken at face value either. Kanko, for example, was not one of them. It is therefore possible that Keeby, part of the "Tarkar" community in Mobile, in fact came from somewhere else.

There is an Osse River in southwest Nigeria, but no Ossa River. No Keeby River exists in Benin, and although it is not impossible that there was one once, it is rare that a river would change names. But there is a Kebbi River: a confluent of the Niger, it runs about two hundred miles in the northwest part of Nigeria. Kebbi gave its name to a region and its inhabitants, the Kebbawa, a subgroup of the Hausa, whose language they speak and whose religion, Islam, they follow. Another clue as to Keeby's origin may lie in the very word "Hausa." Augustine Meaher, Timothy's son, wrote down Keeby's name as Aussy Kebba, a kind of dyslexic way of saying "Aussa Keeby." A deed written between the Meahers and Keeby bears the name Ossa, as does a list of some of the Africans' names written by one of their contemporaries. Although Ossa became Orsey to Roche and Osia to his descendants, Keeby's first name was Ossa and it may have been a deformation of "Hausa."[34]

KEBBI WAS A MARTIAL KINGDOM. In the sixteenth century, after taking its independence from Songhay, it became an empire and a dominant polity in western Hausaland, whose influence extended south to Oyo and Ibadan. But the kingdom declined in the eighteenth century, and in the second year of his *jihad*, in 1805, Shaykh Usman dan Fodio seized it. After the takeover of their old capital and center of foreign trade, Birnin Kebbi, the Kebbawa established a new one in Argungu from which one faction repeatedly attacked the occupiers. Heinrich Barth, the German explorer who visited Kebbi in 1854, recounted, "Several times during my stay [in Gwandu] the alarm was given that the enemy was approaching; and the whole political state of the place was plunged into the most terrible disorder, the enemy being established in several strong places at scarcely half a day's journey distance."[35]

When Ossa Keeby explained his last name in Mobile, he did not refer to the kingdom. The fact that he only mentioned the river seems to indicate that he attached a strong value to it. This in turn gives a clue about what his life and occupation could have been before he was deported. Along the Kebbi River, Kebbawa are mostly fishermen—they are called Serkawa—and are reputed for their talents. There is reason to believe that Keeby was a fisherman, and an additional clue seems to confirm it: in Mobile, during his free time, he fished.[36] How could a Serkawa find himself in Ouidah? The end of the 1850s saw several political and territorial conflicts between Gwandu and Kebbi that resulted

in prisoners of war on both sides. Since captives brought more money the farther they were from their point of seizure, as the risk of running away decreased when they found themselves in unknown territory, dealers took them
south to the coast, or north across the Sahara.[37] The southern market was still
strong because of the development of the trade in palm oil, which fueled the
domestic slave trade for the plantations. Once on the coast, some captives were
kept locally, while others were thrust into the transatlantic slave trade, changing hands as they moved south and west, past Lagos, Badagry, and Porto-Novo
to end up in Ouidah.

Some of Keeby's companions left a tenuous trail. A woman called Shamba
in Mobile may have come originally from Tchamba in the Kamboli region of
Togo and have named herself after her town. Another possibility is that she
was a Chamba from eastern Nigeria. In that case, she might have been named
so by her companions. Another woman was called Ardassa. Although the name
recalls the Dassa region of Benin, Dassa is a French colonial deformation of
Idaisa (pronounced Idaisha). The most likely origin for Ardassa is Adissa, a
Yoruba first name.

The geographical origin of a man variously called Jaba, Jabbar, Jaybee,
Jabez (an American name), and J. B. in Mobile is, like many others, difficult to
locate due to the different versions of his name. For example, if he were indeed
Jaba, he may have been a Jaba, a small non-Muslim (and now mostly Christian)
ethnic group living in the predominantly Muslim Kaduna State. But there are
also cities named Jabba in Kano and Nassarawa States. On the other hand, if
Jabbar (from *al-jabbar*, the Powerful, the Irresistible, an attribute of God), he
would have been a Muslim and may have come from Northern Benin or Northern Nigeria. If Jaybee, he might have been from Jabi, which is the name of several towns in Central Nigeria. Whatever his origin, what was significant was the
crucial skill he brought with him. He was the doctor, the man who knew better
than the others the herbal remedies that cured or helped recovery.[38]

Noah mentioned that the Africans on Timothy Meaher's plantation did
not call their homeland Africa, as he expected, but "some cuyus sof' soundin' ·
name lak 'Owa-ha-la'."[39] He had wrongly concluded that everyone came from
the same place and spoke the same language, but probably only a few were
from "Owahala." One candidate might be Owagala, Nigeria, south of the
confluence of the Niger and the Benue, in Igala country. The Igala, mostly
farmers, also raised cattle, sheep, and goats, while their craftsmen produced
weapons, cloth, and leatherwork. Igala women did not work in agriculture, but
were petty traders, and some were involved in large-scale trading.[40] Starting in
the 1850s, the Fulani invasions had led to a reconfiguration of the human landscape in the region with large numbers of people taken captive, others fleeing
their homes, and refugees relocating on safer grounds. The Igala polity that
had been involved in slave raiding and marketing had become the victim of

slaving. It could be in this context of Fulani raids that people from Owagala were taken to the coast and marched west to Ouidah.

However, an alternative hypothesis is possible. *Wahala*, meaning "troubles," affliction, is widely used in Yoruba and Hausa, but not as a proper noun. Perhaps people in Mobile referred to troubles—war, raid, kidnapping—at home, which led to Noah's misunderstanding. Here again, whether it was Owagala, *wahala*, or perhaps even something else, explanations are tentative because fragmentary information—in this case just one word—was relayed by one foreigner, Noah, to another, Mary McNeil Scott, both ignorant of the original language, thirty years after Noah had heard the word.

MUSLIMS AND NON-MUSLIMS; farmers, traders, and fishermen; victims of kidnapping, raids, and wars, thus formed part of the group that was to board the *Clotilda*. In their diversity, as well as in the manner in which they were captured, they were representative of the Africans deported over the Atlantic. But most of their companions originated in just one town from yet another geographic and cultural area. Henry Romeyn believed they were Tekki. Byers mentioned they came from Ataka.[41] For Emma Langdon Roche, and everybody after her, they were Tarkars, even though there is no such ethnicity. Zora Neale Hurston understood the name as Takkoi, which she identified not with a population but with a town about forty miles north of Porto-Novo, whose original name is Itakon, and official name, Takon. She based her assertion on the fact that Richard Francis Burton, the British adventurer and linguist, had seen in 1863 in Abomey the skull of the chief of Attako or Taccow "which was destroyed about three years ago."[42] It seemed a reasonable origin for the group, but Hurston was stretching the truth to make it fit the written record. Throughout her manuscript *Barracoon*, she faithfully and with great accuracy transcribed the foreign names and words Cudjo gave her, and she always used the same method, which consisted of breaking down the word into syllables linked by dashes. But there is one word, and one word only, that she wrote in another way: Akia'on, the name of the supposed king of Takkoi. Logically, if she had heard it from Cudjo, she should have spelled it Aki-a-on. However, she used Burton's spelling. Convinced she had found Cudjo's town in Burton's book, which she referenced in a note, she was less than candid when she wrote down Akia'on because Cudjo could not have told her it was his king's name. As a matter of fact, several clues indicate that Takon could not be his hometown. Recently, in *Ouidah*, historian Robin Law also suggested that Takon was "the" town based on Burton's account. But the campaign Burton mentioned took place in all likelihood during the dry season of 1860, which is actually the beginning of 1861. The attack would have occurred after the army of Dahomey, on its way to Abeokuta, had to turn back following an outbreak of smallpox.[43] Unable to reach their intended destination, the Dahomians would have raided Takon instead.

Moreover, some of what is known about the people's place of origin does not match Takon's geography, history, and culture. According to them, their town was "many days from the water" or "seven days" from the sea, north of Dahomey in a region that had hills; it was surrounded by a wall with eight gates; had round houses; and *oro*, a secret male society, officiated there.[44] Takon is located south of Dahomey, in a flat zone about two and a half walking days from the sea, a distance which for rural, nineteenth-century Africans used to walking over vast expanses could not qualify as being "many days" away. In addition, it was never surrounded by a wall.[45] In Southern Benin, including in Takon, houses—whether Yoruba or Adja-Fon—are rectangular, not round.[46] And finally, there is no *oro* in town and there has never been. The very name Itakon is said, by its present king and his court, to mean "we refuse the oro" (*Ita* = *oro*; *ko* = to refuse). According to Itakon oral tradition, a woman who came from Ilaro (Nigeria) with her twin brother founded the town after she decided to leave two others, Sakete and Yoko, because of *oro*.[47]

A map drawn by Cudjo, although highly problematic and unreliable, indicates that his hometown was northeast of Dahomey, which eliminates Takon, but could apply to the hills of Dassa.[48] As in Takon, however, houses there are rectangular, and the lack of towns whose names resemble Ataka, Tarkar, or Takkoi adds to the improbability of this location. Togon—two or three miles south of Dassa-Zoume—has been pinpointed as a possible place of origin. However, it was a village without a market, the latter a major feature of Cudjo's hometown.[49]

From words and names passed on by the Africans in Mobile, it is evident that the core group was Yoruba. But the language has several dialectical variations and some names or words are only found among a particular group. These words, added to geography, specific architecture, defense systems, *oro*, and other cultural elements, point toward Banté, a hilly area north of Dahomey, about eight days from the sea. Linguistic data help substantiate the assumption of Banté origin. One hint relates to Cudjo's name at birth, which was rendered as Kazoola in Mobile but is most likely Kossola. Yoruba in Takon and other areas of Benin do not recognize the name and cannot translate it, but it is immediately decipherable to one group of Yoruba, those called Isha, who live in Banté and have a town named Kossola. Oral tradition recounts that it was founded by chief Balagbaro and a group of people who came with him from the west. They had changed locations several times and in the last, Djiin, the chief's children died. He decided to migrate once again in order to find a place where his offspring would live. When he did, he gave grace to God, and said Kossola. *Ko* means "not"; *so*, "fruitful"; and *la*, "loss." The meaning of Kossola is thus "I do not lose my fruits any more," or "my children do not die any more."[50] Cudjo stressed that this name was given to him by his mother, and perhaps she did so after having lost other children.

Another linguistic clue that places the town in the region can be found in Roche's account that the people called the spirit of good *Ahla-ahra*, and the spirit of evil *ahla-bady-oleelay*. Among the Isha of Banté, something bad is called *n'bady* and whatever is good is called *dara*. *Ahla* means dream. Therefore, for the Isha, the spirit of evil is *ahla bady*, which means bad dreams caused by bad spirits, while the spirit of good is *ahla dara*.[51] *Dara* exists in what is today called standard Yoruba and in various dialectal forms of the language spoken in Benin, but *n'bady* is an Isha term. In the domain of the occult, Cudjo mentioned that it was a crime for people to take the mustaches of the leopards they killed because they were reserved for the king and intended to make "medicine," which is to be used in the occult. Such a custom existed in Banté, where the whiskers were supposed to give power to the king.[52] As for *oro*, it is an integral part of Isha social life.

Roche stated that the town's chief industry was the production of palm oil, which would indicate a more southern location. However, she did not claim it was their main activity, only the main industry. Palm oil was indeed extracted in Banté, and although it was not the main production, it was the chief *industry*. Banté architecture also meshes with what Cudjo and his companions described. Yoruba houses, whether in Nigeria or Benin, are distinctly rectangular, but among the Isha, they are still round.[53]

The defense system found in the area also conforms to the Africans' account. Protective walls of two types surrounded Isha towns. In some, ditches eight to ten yards deep by four to five yards wide were doubled by a wide and tall wall. Others had no ditch but were circled by a two-yard-high thick enclosure, upon which hedges of dense, thorny bushes were planted. In both cases at least one emergency exit seconded the main gate. The group's town had eight, which was rare. In the area, according to oral tradition, there were eight at N'Koko, which was attacked by Abomey.[54] Traditional African genealogies do not provide dates, but one of the chiefs of N'Koko, whose place in the lineage corresponds to the mid-1800s, was named Tchacon Amoussou, which may have given the various King of Takon, Ataka, Takkoi, Tekki, and Tarkar relayed by the Americans in Mobile. There are other possibilities. In contrast to other areas, several towns in the region have names that resemble what Americans understood, such as Atakou, Akatakou, Ataké Osho, and Ataké Oshe. *Ataké* means "elevation," and other towns that used the word as part of their name may have disappeared like several others following an epidemic or a particularly brutal slave raid.[55]

BANTÉ IS THE ISHA CRADLE IN BENIN. The first Isha came originally from Ile-Isha ("the town of the Isha," or Ilesha) in Nigeria. According to oral tradition, the movement occurred in the sixteenth century, in the wake of raids organized by Oyo against Ilesha and Ile Ife, and took the populations west to Togo.

Unable to resist Asante pressure from further west, they moved back east in the eighteenth century and settled in Banté, founding villages and towns such as Kossola and N'Koko. Other groups arrived later from Ile Ife and Oyo. Wherever these populations had come from, they had several things in common: they were fleeing wars and slave raids, had identical social and religious practices, and spoke the same language with some variations. The various groups established several towns and villages, and maintained peaceful relations with one another in the new Isha land they had created.[56]

Contrary to what has been said and published, the main group in Mobile did not come from a village, let alone the "jungle," but from a town. The definition of a town in Africa depends on specific criteria that are different from those used in the West, where number of inhabitants, and proportion of workers in the primary, secondary, and tertiary sectors are among the main standards. The first element that defines the group's place of origin as a town is the presence of a king. The fortifications with a central door and numerous exits indicate that the place had a significant political, as well as police and military, function and was thus in need of particular security. The fact that it had a market—probably located in front of the king's compound—shows it filled an important economic role in the area; and so does the central door, because it was there that traders and strangers were taxed.[57] Villages lack all these elements. Thus, whatever the size of their town, the people who grew up there were urban dwellers, not villagers. The town, especially through its market, was a place of economic and cultural exchange, attracting people from far away who brought in goods and an opening on the outside world.

CUDJO HAS DESCRIBED HIS EARLY LIFE—and, by extension, the other young men's experiences—in some detail. He insisted quite strenuously that he came from a modest family, although he also said his grandfather was an officer who had land, cattle, sheep, and goats and had several wives and children. The family was free and the grandfather owned at least a few slaves. The manner in which he chastised them is worthy of note. According to his grandson, he threatened to—but never did—sell them to the Portuguese for tobacco.[58] The fact that he made these specific threats is revealing of the fear that the overseas deportation was known to induce in the captives. Throughout the 1850s, during the palm oil alternative, traders on the coast purchased people ostensibly as domestics but shipped them out discreetly. One outcome was that many escaped from Ouidah when they understood their intended destination.[59] The grandfather's threat was thus similar to that made by East Coast slaveholders who threatened to sell their bondpeople to the Deep South. In both cases, the owner played on the fear of losing one's family and leaving for an unknown land that everyone agreed was far worse than the known world, bad as it was. The reference to the Portuguese slave trader and the tobacco is also significant, as it shows how some of what was going on along the coast was known in the hinterland. Cudjo's grandfather was referring to the Brazilian merchants who had settled in Ouidah in the nineteenth century, and probably to the most famous, Francisco Felix de Souza, known as Chacha. Cudjo said his grandfather died when he was still a boy, which would be in the late 1840s. Chacha passed away in 1849, so there is reason to believe that he was indeed talking about him. As for the tobacco—cultivated by enslaved Africans—it represented the main trade item that Brazil exchanged for captives in the Bight of Benin.[60]

Cudjo's father was named O-lo-loo-ay (Hurston's transcription), that is, Oluwale or Oluale. *Olu* designates a king or a chief, and the name is normally reserved to men of the royal family, which was not the case of Cudjo's father. His mother's name was Ny-fond-lo-loo.[61] Among the Isha, Fondlolu indicates that the woman who bears this name was a devotee of a particular *orisa* (deity) and had been initiated in a convent.[62] She was her husband's second wife, and Cudjo was her second child. She had four more after him. The first co-wife had nine children, and the third had three. It was a fairly typical family. When still young, Cudjo received a light scarification, a bent line on the right cheek, and had six of his upper and lower teeth on one side chipped so as to form a circle when his mouth was closed. A young woman named Abache, who was deported along with him, had slight tattoos, and six of her upper front teeth had been chipped away in the form of a convex opening. Tooth filing, like scarifications and tattoos, was linked to family or aesthetics. The people in Mobile could be identified readily by those who knew how to decipher these signs.[63]

Cudjo had a happy and active childhood playing with his siblings, climbing up trees, playing the drum. At fourteen, he started to train as a soldier by learning how to track, hunt, camp, shoot arrows, and throw spears. The training lasted several years, although, he insisted, the goal was not to actually make war, but to be impressive enough so as to deter any attack. However, if someone struck, the men were ready. A major element of their defensive and offensive strategy was the gates. Cudjo called it the secret of the gates. When an enemy attacked, people would run out and hide in the forest. The assailants, finding an empty town, would leave. The townsmen would then come out of hiding and assault them from behind. In Banté, the village doors were by tradition guarded by young men.[64]

During his adolescence, Cudjo got initiated into *oro*, the Yoruba secret male society, which is in charge of controlling and policing society. Some of the men's duties are to find out and dispose of criminals, accused sorcerers, and witches; to administer justice; and conjure evil for the protection of the village or town. American missionary Thomas Jefferson Bowen, who lived in Nigeria in the 1850s, described *oro* as "the personification of the executive or vindictive power of the government." A witness of the society's actions, Bowen saw *oro* whip a man convicted of adultery. Another, condemned to death for murder, was hung in the woods.[65]

When *oro* is out, women and non-initiates have to stay indoors—a taboo that persists today—and in the old days, they were killed if caught. William H. Clarke, a Southern Baptist missionary colleague of Bowen, described how "the streets present a most desolate appearance, the markets are closed, the cooks have all vacated their stands, the people have disappeared as if by magic and stillness reigns almost supreme."[66] Of his *oro* days Cudjo recalled that from the initiation house he heard roaring right outside and was told to find the source of the noise. When he got to the door, the roaring sounded far away. He was told to go find it in the forest. After he had vainly looked for the animal, the men explained to him the secret of the stick and string that roars like a lion or a bull. These sticks, bull-roarers or rhombos, have a string at one end, from six to eight feet, and they are rotated horizontally. According to the velocity and the size, they produce different kinds of sounds. Cudjo explained, "One de call it de 'he' one de 'she' and one dey call it de dog 'cause dey make it bark day a way."[67] Called *igbe oro* or the voice of *oro*, the rhombos symbolize the secret initiation society and serve as warning sign for women and non-initiates to get indoors. The big stick is called *agba hu hu*, the small ones used for youngsters are *aja oro*, or *oro*'s dogs, which is also the name given to the young initiates like Cudjo.[68] *Oro* holds an annual ceremony during which the initiates meet in the woods for seven to nine days. It is likely during one of these ceremonies that Cudjo entered the society. Afterward, he was offered a meal with roast meat and palm wine during which he was taught to keep secrets and given a peacock feather. At nineteen, he was spotted showing an interest in a young woman, and his father decided it was time for him to start another phase of initiation. In African cultures that practice it, marriage cannot occur before initiation is completed. But Cudjo's life was interrupted by Dahomey, and he never finished his training.

ONE YOUNG MAN NAMED KUPOLLEE (*ku* means death in Yoruba), who was known as Pollee in Mobile, had a different experience. Among his distinctive marks were his two upper front teeth that had been pecked off to form an inverted V.[69] But it is the earrings he had gotten in his young days and continued to wear in Alabama—one small hoop in each ear—that reveal who he was and what he did. They indicate that he had been initiated into the religion of the *orisa*.

Kupollee was not a simple follower, but a servant of the gods. In the Yoruba religion, some people are designated by priests and priestesses for dedication to a particular god, or *orisa*. They spend several months (usually nine for males) in the sacred forest and the *ile-orisa*, the "house of the God." The objective of the novices' training is to change their personality. Once they enter the "convent," they are entirely shaved, receive new clothes, a new name, and the ritual scarifications or tattoos of their respective *orisa* on the face, the neck, and the shoulders. They also learn a new language, known only to the initiates. Their parents bring food, which is gathered and eaten by the whole convent, but they are not allowed to see their sons or daughters until the end of their seclusion. When their religious initiation is completed, the devotees come out, wearing elaborate raffia costumes, and sing and dance for their community of relatives and friends. As they go back to their families, they respond only to their new names. In the past people who insisted on using their old one could be killed. Besides their specific tattoos, what signals the convent initiates is a bracelet of cowry shells sometimes doubled by a row of black beads, or an earring.[70]

What can be said about the young man is that Kupollee was his initiate name, not his birth name. It is no longer possible to know of what *orisa* he was a devotee, but what is certain is that he had an in-depth knowledge of his religion. The earrings show that he had finished his religious initiation and was thus allowed to marry. Kupollee had also gone through a ritual that in retrospect must have seemed eerie to him. A week after the coming-out and dance, the initiates are symbolically redeemed: they pretend they are prisoners from a foreign country put up for sale. Their parents act as if they were looking for the best captive and choose their relative, offering a small gift. The initiates in turn give them a cowry and follow them home. For several months, they continue to pretend they are prisoners, exchanged for the true son or daughter of the family who lives in exile.[71]

Kupollee's town was mostly Isha, but it had regular visitors, attracted by the market.[72] They were Fulani, Gambari, Nupe, and Ijesha. The Ijesha are Yoruba from southern Nigeria, related to the Isha. Gambari—the name given in Benin to the Hausa—were traders, engaged in selling cloth, spices, and kola nuts.[73] The Nupe or Takpa were also traders; and the Fulani tended and sold cattle to the local butchers. The itinerant occupations of these groups took them all over the region, and although they did not live permanently in most Banté villages and towns, they spent time there. It is not clear if some of those captured during the raid and brought to Ouidah ended up in Alabama. Of the original names that have survived, none seems to belong to these particular ethnicities—except for Zuma—which does not mean, however, that they were not present in Alabama, as most names have not been documented.

EACH AND EVERY MILITARY CAMPAIGN of Dahomey has not been recorded, but Glèlè was reputed to have led fourteen between his father's death in 1858 and mid-1860. The first was on Doume, Kanahoun, and Doyissa in Isha country.[74] The raiding "season" took place during the main dry months, between November and March. The raid on Idigni—during which the Yoruba traders who were deported to Mobile may have been captured—occurred on or about February 16, 1860. The army did not immediately go back to Abomey. According to British intelligence, the Dahomians were still east of the Okpara River on March 6.[75] Finally, a dispatch of April 9 signaled that they no longer were in the region. The British Consul at Abeokuta reported on that day, "It is now ascertained that Guelélé has returned to Abomey, and, although there have been rumours of his having taken the field a second time to obtain more victims for his ensuing sacrifices, yet at this advanced period, the season of the rains being close at hand, there is no chance of his venturing far from his barbarous capital." [76] There was thus talk of another campaign, and even though the consul dismissed its practicality due to the approaching rains, there is evidence that it did take place.

With a return to Abomey sometime in late March or early April, there was time for the army to launch a new attack and have the captives delivered to Ouidah the first week of May. No written documentation of the incident has surfaced, and the only known sources are the people who lived through the event and recounted their story in Mobile. According to them, the reason for Dahomey's attack was their king's refusal to share their cattle and corn with Abomey, as emissaries from Glèlè had demanded. He had presumably replied to the envoys that the crops belonged to his people, not to him, and that the king should stop his slave hunts and have his people grow food instead, a common insult hurled at Abomey.[77]

In a twist that may have been true, but may also have been a rationalization for Abomey's victory, the people in Mobile said that a man who had been banished by their king for some bad deed had gone to Dahomey and revealed the secret of the gates. What is known about Dahomey's tactics gives some credence to the claim. Generally, *agbadjigbeto*, spies who dealt in the occult and the secular, were sent to the "enemies" to weaken their protective *vodun* and, it was believed, to draw a map of their town, including the location of its gates. A traitor would have filled the role of *agbadjigbeto* even better. Abomey's strategy when attacking a village or town has been well documented.[78] The army slept during the day and marched at night; it did not approach a target directly but made detours. One of its favorite tactics was to pass a town, and then, when the relieved population had lowered its guard, turn around and attack it. To avoid detection, scouts went ahead and kidnapped the people found outside the town, so that they would not give the alert.

Cudjo's account of the assault on his town represents one of only four such narratives by deported Africans.[79] It is more detailed than the others. Not only did he describe what happened to him, but also what he saw, and what befell the king.

On the eve of the attack, the troops of Dahomey marched during the night and camped several miles away. By early dawn, they walked toward the town. There were already a few men working in the fields outside the gates. They were killed on the spot. Without a sound, the soldiers surrounded the town. According to Cudjo, "All night they march. Some go on one side. They hide, lay low down in de woods. Others go on other side, they lay low in de woods. All around they go."[80] People were fast asleep when the soldiers started yelling and breaking down the great gate with axes. Others, having climbed the walls in silence, were already inside; they were armed with French guns, and knives. As people staggered from their homes to flee, the soldiers grabbed them, cut off their heads, and twisted their necks to detach them from their bodies; sometimes they hacked off their jaws. Like his neighbors, Cudjo ran to one of the eight gates to get out, but soldiers were posted at each exit. He finally saw a door that he thought was not guarded and made a dash for the bush. He passed through the gate, but just outside he was seized by a group of men. He begged them to let him go back to his mother but they tied him up. Wherever he turned, he saw the wounded, the prisoners, and the headless bodies. The king finally walked out of one door and was brought to Glèlè. He asked him why the soldiers of Dahomey did not fight like men, in broad daylight, Cudjo asserted. In the Yoruba tradition of military honor, the shame was on the victors who had won through ruse instead of valor. Glèlè made no excuse for his longstanding tactics and, talking through an interpreter, told him he was going to send him to a *barracoon* and sell him. The man's response was that he had been a king in his land, like his father and his ancestors before him, and he was not going to Dahomey. He said he would die a king rather than become a slave. A Yoruba chief's honor usually required him to kill himself after a defeat, although it was not set in stone.[81] To be reduced to slavery and sold overseas was the utmost disgrace, and the king's honor and posterity were visibly more precious to him than life. Glèlè made a sign, and an Amazon beheaded him. When he saw the king dead, Cudjo once again tried to escape, but he was overpowered. He called for his mother, but he did not see any relative.[82]

A typical Dahomian attack on a sleeping town or village did not last more than thirty minutes. By sunrise, the army and the captives were far away. Indeed, Cudjo stressed that by the time the coffle was ready to go, the sun was just rising. Only the elderly, the wounded, and those who had found good hiding places were left behind. The march to the sea is another important episode that few Africans, besides Cudjo, have recounted. With the prisoners tied one to the other, the cortege started walking south, with severed heads dangling from the soldiers' belts. During the journey, Glèlè and his dignitaries were carried on hammocks. The first night, the captives slept on the ground, which demoralized Cudjo, who was not used to such conditions. The thought of his loved ones, of whom he had no news, greatly depressed him. Nobody from his family was among the captives. The conclusion was clear: if they had not been able to flee, they had been killed. Despondent, he had not eaten that day, just drank some water. He cried the whole night. As the soldiers and their coffle moved on, he noticed something that has not been recorded elsewhere. One town they passed had a red flag, so Glèlè sent a delegation, and the town's chief soon arrived in his hammock with a supply of yams and corn. The red flag went down, and a white one went up. The soldiers roasted the gift and had dinner. The scenario repeated itself at each town and Cudjo figured out what the flags meant. According to his analysis, a red one signified that the village or town refused to pay taxes to Dahomey and was ready to fight (unless coerced by Glèlè not to do so, as had happened in the first case). People who displayed a white flag were disposed to give whatever Glèlè asked for. If the king was dead the flag was black.[83]

After three days, the heads the army carried started to decompose. The smell was so strong that it made Cudjo sick. To the absolute horror of the prisoners, the soldiers stopped to smoke them on sticks. The column remained in that spot for nine days before continuing on to Dahomey. At this point, Cudjo's narratives contradict each other and become murky. According to Hurston, he said they had passed many towns whose names he did not recall, but two he distinctly remembered were "eko (Meko) and Ahfahshay." Then they were taken to "Lomey" and "Dwydah."[84] Eko and Meko are two different cities. Eko is Lagos and Meko, also located in Nigeria, lies about one hundred miles northwest of it. It is unclear what exactly Cudjo said—Eko or Meko, or something else that sounded similar. What likely happened is that Hurston could not locate Eko on a map because it is the local name of the city. She certainly could, however, locate Meko, and must have concluded that Cudjo meant Meko, not Eko. As for Ahfahshay, it is Ajachè, the name the Yoruba give to Porto-Novo. In this version the route followed by Cudjo and his companions was through their hometown, then through Lagos, Porto-Novo, Abomey, Badagry, and Ouidah. The army, the king, and their cortege of prisoners would thus have gone south to the coast, then east, then west, then north, then back to the coast, east again, and west.

To further complicate things, another version of the route had been given to Emma Langdon Roche. The map Cudjo had drawn for her traced a line from the hometown to Eko, "Budigree," "Adaché" and on directly to "Why-dah," which, she stressed, he and his companions sometimes called Gréfé (Glehwe or Grehwe means plantation house and is the Fon name of Ouidah). There was no stop in Abomey. Cudjo's map indicates that he and his companions knew the location of the cities quite well, but their route is as problematic as the one Cudjo gave Hurston. The army of Dahomey could not have marched through Lagos or Badagry, territories it had not conquered. In addition, Glèlè could not have taken this road because Dahomey kings never traveled by the sea; it was an absolute taboo. Finally, the army always went back to Abomey or Cana to dispose of its prisoners. It is thus impossible to envision any circumstances under which Glèlè and his troops would make useless, time-consuming, tortuous detours through hostile areas or not go back to Abomey. The two accounts cannot be reconciled, and none of them fits historical reality, but some confusion may be dispelled.

Some people captured in Nigeria (in Kebbi and Igala country for example) would have taken the Lagos–Badagry–Porto-Novo–Ouidah route. They would not have gone to Abomey because they had not been seized by Dahomey. The

Yoruba traders would have gone from Ketu to Porto-Novo to Ouidah, if kid-napped by marauders; but they would have gone to Abomey if captured by the army. But there is only one possible route for the core group, and it is from their hometown to Abomey, and then to Ouidah. The confusion can be ex-plained by at least two factors: people coming from different regions took dif-ferent routes that somehow got conflated when they recounted their march to the sea several decades later; and fading recollections. Although Cudjo had an excellent memory, it is one thing to vividly remember indelible events such as the raid, the march, or the *barracoon*; it is another to recall the names of towns one had never seen before, especially under such circumstances.

IN ROCHE'S ACCOUNT, there is no stop in Abomey and only the mention of a Dahomian village, which had fresh heads and skulls on sticks.[85] But, in Hurston's *Barracoon*, once the group arrived in Abomey, the city where the king got his house, as Cudjo called it, the unfolding of events becomes clear again. There, Glèlè and his army were welcomed back with much drumming and display of old and fresh skulls on sticks. Cudjo said that the palace seemed as if it were made of skulls; he added he knew it was not, but it looked that way.[86] His observation was accurate. When Francisco Borghero, an Italian Catholic mis-sionary, visited the forty-hectare site of the royal palaces the following year, he saw that they were surrounded by a "large adobe wall on which human skulls are set every five meter, held by iron picks. . . . The king's houses are decorated [with skulls] everywhere."[87] The wall was sixteen to twenty-six feet high and almost two miles long, protected by a ditch and a barricade of thorns. The skulls from slain kings and chiefs, prisoners of war and sacrificed victims, were not a decoration, but a symbol of power designed to carry a dramatic message to whoever came to the city about the authority and supremacy of Dahomey. To the captives, the wall was a grisly foresight of what lay in store for their loved ones. Upon arrival, they were locked up in a stockade and lightly fed for three days. Cudjo described what happened there. "Our women weep and beg to go home. Our men beg to go home and promise to give the yams. Dahomey's men beat us and show us the heads of our fadders and mudders."[88]

On the fourth day, a feast was held with singing, dancing, and drumming, most likely to celebrate the triumphal return of the king and his contingent of prisoners of war, and to "sell" them. It was the custom for Dahomian kings to buy from their soldiers the captives and heads they had brought back. It has been argued that the objective of this symbolic purchase, called "the washing of hand," was to protect the king from the supernatural vengeance of the pris-oners. By buying them, he was supposed to show that he had had nothing to do with their capture.[89] Just three years after Cudjo and his companions arrived in Abomey, Richard F. Burton witnessed the ceremony:

Shouts and thrills announced that cowries and cloth were being brought from the palace. Each owner of a skull received for it a head of shells. . . . All the captives "with names" advanced on their knees up a lane leading towards the King. . . . Their cords were held by their captors, who sold them to the Crown. The minimum price was one head and two fathoms of cloth.[90]

After the sale, the prisoners went through two other routines, although no one mentioned them to Roche or Hurston, who would most likely have reported them, had they known. The first was the triage. Abomey functioned as a sorting center. After each campaign, the chief craftspeople were invited by the king to inspect the prisoners. Divided according to gender, they stood in line while each was interrogated as to his or her skills and prior occupation. Those deemed valuable to the kingdom, such as tailors, pottery makers (all females), hatmakers, shoemakers, and musicians, were retained and integrated into the crafts guilds. They received new names, which were the patronyms of the specific craft families they were now part of. Another category of specialists was retained: the spiritual leaders. The acquisition of the occult powers of other populations, through their spiritual experts, was an integral part of the war bounty, considered one of the most desired assets.[91] Particular farmers and hunters were also retained and put to work for the kingdom, while the king gave other prisoners to his favorites. The men and women who had no special usefulness were again divided. Some would be sacrificed during the customs, the others sold to traders.

Before the people slated for Ouidah left, another ritual that has not been reported in written sources was held. Each captive threw a stone on a pile that is today located within the perimeter of a high school (Lycée Houffon). There are two explanations for the existence of this ten-foot-high mound, which has not been touched, presumably, since the end of the slave trade.[92] The first one, confirmed by historian Elisée Soumonni and by the curator of the Historical Museums of Abomey, is that the stones represented a type of census. With each one deposited, the kingdom had a sense of the magnitude of its trade in captives. Oral tradition has a different but not contradictory explanation. It says that the stone mound was a spiritual spot, and it is so designated by the local repertory of sites linked to the slave trade. According to this version, by throwing a stone the captives symbolically expressed that they had forgotten their origins and were entering a new world. They then circled the heap three times. In both accounts, the quantity of stones is an indicator of the number of men, women, and children who left Abomey for the coastal markets and ultimately the Americas.

A few days after they had entered Abomey, Cudjo, Polle, Abache, and their companions were rounded up and marched more than sixty miles to the sea. The first halt on the so-called slave route was Zogbodome, where prisoners underwent a medical exam and were treated, if necessary. Next, the caravans stopped at Toffo to rest, before a third stop at Allada. The final stop was Savi, about eight miles northeast of Ouidah.[93] The captives who had come from the east, Kebbi and Owagala, for instance, were taken by pirogue, dug-out canoe, to the ports of Abomey-Calavi or Jakin, on the lagoon, and either continued the journey on the water or were dispatched by foot to Ouidah.[94]

WHEREVER THEY WERE COMING FROM, the prisoners arrived in a city whose main function had been the deportation of people, most of whom, like themselves, had not been judged of any value to the maintenance and expansion of Dahomey. With 272,500 identified captives embarked on 763 ships, Ouidah had deported over 51 percent of the known prisoners who transited through the Bight of Benin. Of the more than sixty main slave ports of the Atlantic, it was outpaced only by Bonny in Nigeria with 384,000 identified departures, and Cabinda in Angola with 272,800.[95] Once again, the people from Banté were locked up in a stockade and fed some rice. The main foreign slave traders had built their own *barracoons* after the French, Portuguese, and English forts that had held captives until the 1840s—when they were converted to palm oil warehouses—were no longer used as jails. In the mid-1840s, six large factories were in operation.[96] One was called Zomaï, which means "where the fire does not go," and was the slave dealer Chacha Francisco de Souza's compound and *barracoon* in town.[97] But oral tradition recalls another Zomaï not in the city, but south of it in Zoungbodji ("little plateau" in Fon). The location of a *barracoon* at Zoungbodji has not been corroborated in written sources. But Cudjo's account seems to confirm its existence. He and his companions were detained in a place from which they could see the ships on the sea. The ocean would not have been visible from a *barracoon* in Ouidah, but it would have been from Zoungbodji, midway between the city and the beach. The stockade was located behind a white house "on the river-bank."[98] The riverbank, actually a lagoon, is not in Ouidah but just south of Zoungbodji. Moreover, it appears from Cudjo's account that this house was associated with the slaving business. He thought Foster went there after he left the *barracoon* following his purchase. It may have been the customhouse or ferry-house mentioned a few years earlier by Scottish traveler John Duncan, which was occupied by the inspector for passes and permits that the merchants in Ouidah gave to individuals leaving the port. The passes specified the number of persons supposed to depart in an effort to prevent smuggling, and Foster would thus have had to go there.[99] Oral tradition from the other side of the Atlantic gives credence to what some people in Ouidah asserted.

Descriptions of life in the *captiveries* by people who survived them are as rare as they are precious, and none are detailed. Samuel Ajayi Crowther, detained in a *barracoon* at Lagos for four months in 1822, recalled, "Men and boys were at first chained together, with a chain of about six fathoms in length, thrust through an iron fetter on the neck of every individual, and fastened at both ends with padlocks." Although males were not chained at all times, Joseph Wright, an Egba of Nigeria, held two months by the Portuguese in Lagos in the late 1820s, also insisted on the chains and ropes. Ottobah Cugoano of Ghana was quite succinct, "I was soon conducted to a prison, for three days, where I heard the groans and cries of many, and saw some of my fellow-captives."[100]

When Cudjo talked about the *barracoon* in Ouidah, instead of focusing on the horror of the experience, the confinement, the overcrowding, the diseases, the despair, the bad treatment, and the filth, he recalled people hollering from pen to pen to know where the others were from. He also remembered that after a while the sadness had subsided. They were young, he recalled, and "play game and climb up de side de barracoon so we see whut goin' on outside."[101] It cannot be said that time had softened his memories because other incidents that happened at the same time left him distraught more than seventy-five years later. There is no reason either to doubt what he described. Amid the horror of the *barracoon*, some people still found the inner resource to "play game." Far from being questionable, Cudjo's unique account is an illustration of the captives' resilience that had not previously surfaced; and it gives more depth and accuracy to what we know about their experience.

In all its abysmal abjection, the factory could also be a place of hope. It was there that some prisoners were freed by their families or friends for everyone else to see. The redemption of captives was a difficult, complicated, but not uncommon endeavor that has been well documented.[102] In some circumstances, people could go to the factories or the ships and free their relatives. In most cases, the slavers refused money and demanded a more desirable individual or several people as substitutes. The chances of redeeming a loved one grew with one's hometown's proximity to the coast. But for those from far away, the search could be futile. Captives were sold all along the routes and there was no sure way of finding where they had been taken. People seized during raids had sometimes lost the family members who could have ransomed them. Those who, like Kanko, had been abducted often stood little chance of being found as many hours or even days—if they had been traveling—could pass before anyone realized they were gone. Given the closeness of African families—and simple humanity—it is certain that the people who were in a position to do so did attempt to redeem their relatives and friends; some even tried to locate their loved ones long after the ships had sailed away. Others made the ultimate sacrifice, and offered themselves in exchange for a family member. By the same token, there is no doubt that the captives knew their families would be looking for them. Even people who had seen part of their families destroyed counted on the ones they hoped had survived: "I know they hunt for me," Cudjo said.[103] As they saw some of their companions led out of the *barracoons*, the captives could keep the faith. But in the vast majority of cases, the expectation was ultimately crushed.

The *barracoon* was also a space of encounters, the origin of strong friendships that would be reinforced on the slave ships. Each nation, according to Cudjo's recollection, was housed in a separate building. But what is known about the recruitment of the *Clotilda*'s group, which included people from different regions and ethnicities, shows that individuals who formed groups too small to be held separately were simply added to larger communities. The widespread notion that ethnic groups were systematically mixed as a sort of guarantee against revolts proves to be unfounded, once again. Among the various known languages spoken by the group of people who boarded the *Clotilda*, few were reciprocally intelligible. Dendi is in a class by itself, Yoruba and Fon have only a few words in common, the languages of the Atakora are not related to Fon or Yoruba, let alone Hausa or Nupe. However, as usual in Africa, some people would have been bilingual or trilingual, or have known many more languages and dialects. Hausa and Dendi were trade languages spoken by non-Hausa and non-Dendi traders. Traders also spoke the tongues of the populations they were in contact with; intermarriages resulted in children learning both their parents' languages; and migrations as well as multi-ethnic towns or neighborhoods led to people being fluent in more than one language. As has always been done in Africa, the multilingual individuals acted as interpreters so that communication in the *barracoon* would not be hampered.

Besides encountering people from other parts of the region, the captives from the hinterland also discovered the Europeans. For the first time, Cudjo saw white men. He and his companions had heard of them while growing up, but none had ever been to their town. He did not elaborate about what he thought of them, but other Africans did. To an unknown West African Muslim enslaved in South Carolina, the whites appeared "the ugliest creatures in the world." Gaspard Theodore Mollien, who traveled through Senegal and Guinea in 1818, recalled how people overtly made fun of him, his long nose, and his tight pants. Olaudah Equiano described them as "white men with horrible looks, red faces, and loose hair."[104] But there was something about the foreigners that was infinitely more sinister than their looks; some people believed they were cannibals. A young girl named Abile ("second born" in Yoruba), who was about fifteen when deported, later confessed that she starved herself in Mobile because she was scared the whites would eat her.[105] The myth had had a long life. When she heard it, it had been floating around in Africa for more than four hundred years. Its first recorded expression goes back to 1456. Italian navigator Alvise Ca' da Mosto heard the accusation on the Gambia River, as his three ships were surrounded by men in pirogues. Being outnumbered and poorly armed, the Portuguese asked for a truce and tried to open a friendly dialogue. They were rebuffed as the men replied, "they had had news of our coming and of our trade with the negroes of Senegal who, if they sought our friendship could not but be bad men, for they firmly believed that we Christians ate human flesh, and that we only bought negroes to eat them, that for their part they did not want our friendship on any terms, but sought to slaughter us all."

European traders, officials, and explorers had all heard the stories, as had German physician Paul Erdman Isert, who founded an agricultural colony in the Gold Coast and knew variations on the theme. "I was once asked by a slave, in complete earnest," he wrote, "if the shoes I was wearing had been made of Black skin, since he had observed that they were the same colour as his skin. Others say that we eat the Blacks and make gunpowder of their bones." In some cases these tales were spread by the Europeans themselves. The Révérend Père Labat, for example, was convinced that Dutch, English, and Portuguese traders had been spreading tales about French cannibals out of envy for their success in the trade. During the illegal slave trade, a Portuguese crew presented the British as cannibals so that the captives on board would not try to signal their presence to the navy.[106]

The tale had definitive allegorical value, since whites did indeed consume Africans in the Americas, but it was not its objective. It has been argued that Africans were prompt to paint Europeans as cannibals because they often accused their own far-away neighbors of anthropophagy.[107] Another reading of the myth is that the supposed cannibalism was only metaphorical and that Africans related it to witchcraft. In any event, the assumption is that "Africans" believed it. What people said at the time of first contact in the fifteenth century may have reflected their beliefs, but they may also have been simply insulting the Portuguese. Centuries later, the deported Africans' narratives that mentioned white cannibalism made quite clear that the stories circulated mostly in the interior, and particularly among children. Equiano reported the tale, but stated adults said it was not true. Augustino, a young man who had been deported to Brazil in 1830, testified that several *children* had jumped from the slave ship because they were afraid they were being fattened to be eaten. He did not mention any adults committing suicide for the same reason. Ottobah Cugoano wrote, "I saw several white people, which made me afraid that they would eat me, according to our notion, as children, in the inland parts of the country." He was a child when kidnapped, and stated plainly that it was children from the hinterland who believed the tale. Joseph Wright had heard that the Portuguese were going to eat him when he got to their country. He was still a boy. Samuel Ajayi Crowther and his friends thought for a while that parts of a hog hanging on a British ship were human flesh.[108] Crowther was fifteen.

Based on the deportees' accounts, it seems that the white cannibal myth can be explained rather prosaically as part of the array of strategies Africans had elaborated to protect their families. By painting whites as cannibals, the ultimate monstrosity in most African cultures, the adults tried to ensure that their children would not venture away, go where they were not supposed to, at a time when kidnappings linked to the Atlantic slave trade were widespread. The fact that white men were not found in the interior reinforces the argument, because it was evident to children on the coast that they were not involved in anthropophagy; only youngsters who had never seen them could believe the story.

As Gossalow, Abile, Zuma, Cudjo, and Pollee were discovering the white men they had heard about in various ways, the men they called *yovo*, *anasara*, *bature*, or *oyinbo*, one of them, William Foster, was about to enter their world.

CHAPTER THREE

Ouidah

HE *CLOTILDA* WEIGHED ANCHOR a mile and a half from shore at Ouidah on May 15. At 4 P.M., a man in a canoe came alongside the ship and asked what the captain's business was. The American responded that he wanted "to exchange commodities" and wished to see the "prince and officials." He was ready to go ashore but the sea was rolling "at a fearful height." A large pirogue, sixty feet long, manned by twenty rowers who made a game of the high waves, took Foster in and landed him on the beach, where an interpreter assigned three men to take care of him. Since the city was located three miles from the shore, north of a lagoon, through woods, and at the end of a bad road, visitors and dignitaries were carried there. Hammocks were the favorite mode of portage for the elite. A ten-foot net was hung to a long bamboo post carried on its ends on the heads of two men. A canopy protected the passenger from the sun. This is how William Foster entered Ouidah.[1]

With its Aja and Fon population, an influx of Yoruba from the east who had taken refuge in the region after the fall of Oyo, freedmen and -women returned from Bahia, merchants from Brazil, Saro—Yoruba liberated from the slave ships by the British Navy and settled in Sierra Leone, who had then migrated to Dahomey—and Europeans dealing in captives or in palm products, in the nineteenth century Ouidah was a more cosmopolitan city than Mobile. Foster, who probably thought he would find a large village with primitive lodging, was shocked. He marveled at the level of comfort. "Upon arrival, I found splendid accommodations for traders," he noted. The following morning, after breakfast, the interpreter picked him up to show him the city and introduce him to the "ebony Prince" in charge of the "exchange of commodities." His name was Akodé, he was a nephew of Glèlè, and he wore the title Chodaton, meaning "the king owns everything." Father Francesco Borghero, the Catholic missionary, met him several times in 1861 and thought "Tchiudato" was "one of the personalities the most intimate with the king." Richard Burton described him in 1863 as "a young man, tall and well made, of coaly complexion, broadfaced, and with a prepossessing expression," who wore a green silk tunic and smoked a Brazilian cigar.[2] To Foster, he simply appeared hefty, weighing about 250 pounds. The fifty officials at the meeting kneeled when the Chodaton, a former trader, entered the room. His presence is significant because when Foster made his acquaintance, he had just been appointed to "assist" the *yovogan*, the man in charge of dealing with the whites (*yovo* in Fon). His new position was first reported by the British in April 1860, and he had probably assumed it recently, which not only reinforces the authenticity of Foster's account, but also the sometimes disputed date of his voyage. Akodé's appointment was part of King Glèlè's effort to better control the trade in Ouidah, as well as to balance the older officials appointed by his father, whose loyalty he was not sure of.[3]

After a few drinks, Foster stated his business. He wanted to buy 125 people at $100 each, and would pay with $9,000 in gold and merchandise. As a newcomer to the business, he thought the operation would be fast and that he would be quickly on his way back to Mobile. But negotiations between traders and officials took time. For the next eight days, he did not really know what was going on and thought he was being held hostage. In the meantime, he went with the interpreter to visit "the place of worship," where he saw "a large square of ground with a wall ten ft. high upon which was covered with snakes. Trees in there were loaded with the repulsive things, reveling in their deified relation: Devotees attending had them swarmed around their necks and waists." The site—which still exists—was dedicated to the *vodun* Dangbe, a python.[4]

Finally, the American was brought back to see Chodaton Akodé and seal the deal. Then came the intriguing episode of Gumpa's sale, not mentioned in Foster's manuscript. The captain, "Having agreeably transacted affairs with the Prince," was led by two men to a *barracoon* to make his selection. The slaver's surgeon was usually in charge of the examination to determine the selected captives' age and health, but since Foster had none on board, he had to take care of the task himself. The place, according to his estimate, held four thousand people, all in "a state of nudity."[5] It is true that the people captured by Dahomey during predawn raids were not dressed in the same manner as they would have been during the day, but they were far from being naked. What Foster and other Europeans and Americans saw in Africa were not naked people, but people Western culture considered naked. To the men and women Foster chose in the *barracoon*, the clothes they had on, torn and filthy as they must have been after their march to the sea, were of extreme importance.

The selection process, so immensely critical to the captives, was of little interest to Foster. It was only worth a few words on a page—"they gave me liberty to select one hundred and twenty five." Foster's manuscript and Cudjo and his companions' various interviews allow us for the first time to look at the same events from the perspective of the slave captain and the standpoint of the deportees. As expected, what they saw, lived, were interested in, and noticed are quite different. What happened in the factory was a defining moment to the men, women, and children who had been held for several weeks—about three weeks for those from Banté—not knowing what their future was going to be. They recalled that after Foster and the two men from Dahomey had entered the place, the interpreter told them to form circles of ten men and circles of ten women. Foster, in the middle of each ring, inspected every individual closely. He looked at their skin, their hands, and their feet, he felt their legs and arms, and he opened their mouths to inspect their teeth.[6] Although Cudjo and his companions, probably out of a sense of decency, did not elaborate, it is almost certain that they underwent a more intrusive assessment. Generally, venereal diseases were feared and the private parts of both men and women were inspected.

Each time Foster saw somebody he wanted, he pointed at him or her, and the person selected was taken out of the circle. According to Cudjo, the final count was sixty-five men and sixty-five women, but Foster stated he had bought one hundred and twenty-five. After the sale, one routine scrupulously observed was to shave the prisoners to avoid lice. The captives of the *Clotilda* did not report it, but there is little question that they were indeed shaved. Although it may seem the most innocuous measure of all, from an African perspective, it was a serious violation. Africans have traditionally used their hair as a marker of identity and a major component of their aesthetic. The high value they placed on elaborate hairdos caught the European travelers' attention as they noted the myriad styles they encountered on both men and women.[7] Hair was sculpted, partly shaved, twisted, braided, rolled, woven, and adorned with beads, gold, silver, feathers, grass, combs, pins, fibers, seeds, and shells. It was a means of communication identifying the bearers' ethnicity, family, social status, or profession. When Mahommah Gardo Baquaqua—a young man who had been deported from Djougou, in northeast Benin, around 1844—had arrived on the coast, a man from Djougou knew who he was through his hairdo.[8] Hair also signaled the enslaved. Shaved heads—under certain circumstances—or short or unkempt hair identified someone as nonfree. This was a logical consequence of enslavement, because the captives had lost their former status and their familial, ethnic, and professional identity. Their new hairstyles had to reflect their current condition, the cutting off of past affiliations, a sort of virtual death that would engender, usually at the second generation, a brand-new identity, sometimes including a new ethnic one. Symbolically, the shaving imposed by the Westerners severed, if only momentarily, the identities represented by the elaborate hairstyles of the captives. Sulayman Diallo from Senegal had been incensed when the people who had kidnapped him cut his hair to make him look like a prisoner of war.[9] This outrage at being shaved is a key indication of how the Africans continued to perceive themselves as free even as they were being sold and bought.

Another customary practice of the slavers was the branding. Baquaqua described how the captives were "placed with our backs to the fire, and ordered not to look about us, and to insure obedience, a man was placed in front with a whip . . . another man then went round with a hot iron, and branded us the same as they would the heads of barrels or any other inanimate goods or merchandize."[10] Foster forbade the operation, he wrote, "peremptorily."[11] Interestingly, this is the only direct reference he made to the "cargo of negroes" he had bought, a self-serving allusion to what he likely thought was proof of his compassion.

His mission accomplished, the captain made plans to leave the following day. He asked his interpreter to send the group to the warehouse on the beach in the morning, and to have them on board and ready to leave by 10 A.M.[12] He then went back to the traders' quarters for his last night in Ouidah, after eight days in the city, likely content at the prospect of going back home, even if apprehensive about the voyage. For the people he had picked, this same last night was a heartbreak: their selection put a brutal end to weeks of doubt and hope. For those who still had family members in the entrepot, it was the final confirmation of leaving them behind. It meant the certainty of never returning to one's hometown and loved ones. The factory was appalling, but the prospect of leaving it was dreadful. On the eve of departure, it was customary for future deportees to be fed a big meal that served the dual purpose of cheering them up and strengthening them for the trip ahead. There is little chance that it ever achieved any of these objectives. Nothing could cheer up people who saw overseas deportation as worse than death. As for sending people out to sea for the first time in their lives with a stomach full of palm oil and rice, it was actually a rather poor idea. Baquaqua did not know his own big meal would be his last on African soil, and his case was not exceptional. John Duncan saw a large group of cheerful young men and children marching in chains to the beach, on their way to the slave ship, believing they were going out on their daily walk.[13]

But Cudjo and his companions were well aware it was the end. The people who had brought them their big meal had told them so. They spent the night in misery, tears, and anxiety. "Den we cry, we sad cause we doan want to leave de rest of our people in de barracoon. We all lonesome for our home. We doan know whut goin' become of us, we doan want to be put apart from one another."[14] Even though a large group from the same town had been chosen, most were left behind: children, husbands, wives, brothers and sisters, friends, and neighbors. Scholars have stressed the mortality that accompanied each phase of a group's journey, from the "collateral damage" of people killed in war or raid, to those who died on the march, in the factory, on the ship, and upon arrival. But what the deaths and the sales represented to the survivors has not been addressed. Their journey was a tragic succession of separations. When a town or village was raided, the first severance came between the dead and the living; the second between those who were too old, too weak, too young, too sick, or too injured to leave and the young and healthy. Along the way, some relatives, friends, and neighbors were sold and others died, severing connections that had become even more precious. For the people sorted at Abomey came another phase in the separation cycle; some stayed, others were going to be killed, and the rest deported. The selection, as well as deaths by epidemics or other means in the *barracoons*, led to the ultimate parting on African soil. By the time they walked to the ships, Africans, for whom family and community are particularly critical, had already gone through several highly traumatic separations. And the journey was far from over. On the last night, the immediacy of the separation was unbearable; relatives and friends knew they would never see one another again and would always wonder what had happened to their loved ones. It was a personal disaster for all, whether they were going to leave or stay for another week, another month, another ship. Leaving the coast also meant the irrevocable loss of family and home; it was the certitude of never going back. To the millions of Africans about to embark on the Middle Passage, the last moments on land were an all-encompassing agony.

THAT NIGHT IN OUIDAH the town crier warned the population to stay home and not go out. The curfew was customary when captives were ready to be embarked in the morning. There was always the possibility of an attack on the coffle or the ship by relatives trying to free their loved ones.[15] The next day, Cudjo, Abile, Ossa, Zuma, Abache, and their companions were chained one to the other and lead out of the enclosure, past the white house, where Foster had gone after concluding the sale. They could see several ships and white men in conversation with Dahomian officials. Foster was there too. When he saw them he got into his hammock, and was carried across the lagoon. They walked behind, wading in the neck-high water. They feared they were going to drown.[16] None of that or what followed immediately was of any significance to Foster. His only concern was the commercial transaction, "I went on board at 6 A.M. and had my cargo thrown overboard in water tight casks. And they sent their surf men who swam the casks ashore safely."[17] To the captives, however, everything that took place that day was immensely memorable.

On the beach, the canoe men were waiting, ready to transport them to the *Clotilda*. The group gathered on the beach was intently observing what was going on. It was their future they were trying to decipher by scrutinizing every detail. They watched the canoe men transport merchandise and people to the ships, going back and forth. Some were whites, others were "po' Affican."[18] This characterization indicates that they were not traders or officials, but people Cudjo identified with, men and women who were in the same predicament. This of course would mean that other ships were taking up captives. Another witness, Kanko, mentioned that three ships with guns ready were loading up people.[19] It is not clear if she included the *Clotilda*, but she and Cudjo agreed that theirs was not the only group being deported. Foster did not mention anything, nor did British intelligence. Nevertheless, the possibility exists that several hundred people were forced onto slave ships that morning.

On one of their trips back and forth, the canoe men took Foster to his vessel.[20] He ordered the crew to throw his trade goods overboard and, when the merchandise arrived on shore, the captives were unchained and led to the pirogues, whose headboards had the word "Slave" painted in large letters.[21] No record of their reactions and feelings as they were about to leave land and sail away was left behind, which is not surprising since very few accounts exist as to any African's state of mind. Ottobah Cugoano, deported from Ghana, explained that "when a vessel arrived to conduct us away to the ship, it was a most horrible scene; there was nothing to be heard but the rattling of chains, smacking of whips, and the groans and cries of our fellow-men. Some would not stir from the ground, when they were lashed and beat in the most horrible manner." But beyond the description of some people's physical reaction, Baquaqua expressed how that moment could never be articulated: "At length, when we reached the beach, and stood on the sand, oh! how I wished that the sand would open and swallow me up. My wretchedness I cannot describe. It was beyond description. The reader may imagine, but anything like an outline of my feelings would fall very short of the mark, indeed."[22]

THE BRIEF CANOE RIDE to the ship was dangerous. The coast at Ouidah and east and west of it is bordered by a sandbar and a high triple surf that can make pirogues jump up to an almost ninety-degree angle. Fishermen ride the waves fearlessly, but to the people who had never seen the sea—arguably the majority of the deportees—as well as all those who had but had never been on a canoe (only fishermen do), the journey was nothing short of terrifying, and it could be lethal. It was not unusual for the pirogues to roll over, sending their passengers to drown or be eaten by sharks. When the canoe that preceded Baquaqua's capsized, about thirty people lost their lives. Just before he embarked, Joseph Wright saw a canoe go under and half the captives on board die. And three months after the *Clotilda* sailed away, on August 12, a steamer had embarked 1,200 people at Ouidah, and 25 drowned in their chains when a pirogue turned over on the surf.[23] It was a sight that petrified the people still on the beach and provided hope to those who wanted to die.

As they left the pirogues to climb on board the *Clotilda*, the canoe men forced everyone to take off their clothes. They resisted, but it was to no avail. "You go where you can get plenty of clothes," the men said.[24] As a rule of the trade, captives were transported naked over the Atlantic. The famous rendition of the slave ship *Brookes*, with her men and women wearing white loincloths, was a Puritanical version of what really transpired on the slave ships. Black bodies were dressed and undressed in white imagination as Europeans and Americans saw fit: savage Africans went about naked in their homelands, but the general public believed they were dressed on the slave ships. About ship nudity, however, Africans and European slavers agreed. "The people of the great vessel were wicked," stressed Ali Eisami Gazirmabe, a Kanuri from Bornu deported from Porto-Norvo in 1818: "when we had been shipped, they took away all the small pieces of cloth which were on our bodies, and threw them into the water." Augustino of Brazil testified that "The clothes of all the negroes going on board ship were stripped off them, even to the last rag." Slave dealers were blunt about the practice. "Once alongside, their clothes are taken off and they are shipped on board in perfect nakedness; this is done without distinction of sex," explained Theophilus Conneau, a famous captain of the illegal slave trade. "This precaution is necessary to keep them free from vermin. . . . As they are kept in total nudity the whole voyage, cleanliness is preserved with little trouble."[25] Whatever the motivation, to the Africans, being deprived of their clothes was a signal not that their status had changed to slavery, since people enslaved in Africa were not denuded, but that whites considered them not human. To those who believed in European cannibalism, it was a bad omen; and to all it was an ultimate degradation. Adults, "fathers and mothers of families," as they are called in Africa, had their honor stripped from them along with their clothes. Honor is a cardinal virtue in Africa, and physical modesty is so important that in traditional societies spouses never see each other naked. Decades later, the men and women who had boarded the *Clotilda* still spoke of the profound humiliation they felt when their clothes were torn off. Besides the fury at being handled as if they were nonhumans, and the shame of being seen naked by friends, they later were also offended by what the episode signified in America. Their native-born neighbors in Alabama made fun of them and Africans in general who, they believed, used to go around naked. "I so shame!" Cudjo lamented: "We come in de 'Merica soil naked and de people say we naked savage. . . . Dey doan know de [canoe men] snatch our clothes 'way from us."[26] He expressed what other Africans experienced in the Americas in relation to nakedness: they were publicly subjected to it at the hands of Europeans and Americans, but were presented as never having had clothes in the first place, more clear proof of their need for Christian modesty and Western civilization that could only be acquired through enslavement.

After seventy-five people had climbed on board, the captain and his crew had "an alarming surprise." The sailor with the looking glass yelled, "Sail ho, steamer to leeward ten miles." Two steamers were approaching, intent, Foster thought, on capturing the ship. Once again the crew attempted to mutiny. Afraid of being arrested for slave smuggling, they wanted to take the ship rowboats to get to shore. If successful, they would have been part of the sorry contingent of deceived sailors who ended their slaving trip on the coast, waiting for another ship to take them home. Foster had to come up with something believable to say to keep his crew on board. He told them they would not make it to shore because of the surf. They then realized their only chance of escaping the steamers was to hurry up the loading, but there was still the equivalent of a pirogue full of people on the beach. Meanwhile, two canoes were approaching with thirty-five more men, women, and children.[27] Cudjo always claimed he was in the last one, and almost did not make it. He might have been among those whose future is not known, those Foster left behind. How he found himself in that situation is not clear. Two versions of the event exist. Emma Langdon Roche reported that after Foster had selected him, Cudjo was stolen by a man from Dahomey and hidden under the white house for reasons unknown. At any rate, he told Roche that being from inland, he had never seen the sea, and he was a curious nineteen years old. So he climbed up a fence to look at the surf. "I hear the noise of the sea on shore, an' I wanta see what maka dat noise, an' how dat water worka—how it fell on shore an' went back again. I saw some of my people in a little boat and I holler to them. Then Captain Foster spied me, an' he say, 'Oh hee! Oh hee!' an' pulla me down. An' I was the last to go."[28] If this was the case, then the incident took place early on, when the group was leaving the *barracoon*, and Foster was still around. Hurston's version is fairly different. According to her, Cudjo was one of the last on the beach and was almost left there when he saw his friend Ossa Keeby in a canoe and decided he wanted to go with him.[29] Why Cudjo would want to follow a friend, under the circumstances, is puzzling. Whatever the case might really have been, in both versions, he was one of the last to leave and he was embarked because he had made himself conspicuous by calling out to his friends.

Once everyone was on board, Foster ordered his crew to pull up the anchor. The *Clotilda* sailed away with 110 men, women, and children, leaving 15 or 20 on the beach. Foster had just lost about 10 percent of Meaher's investment, but the schooner had lived up to her reputation. She outran the steamers. Within four hours, she was out of sight of the land and the ships. Kanko told her descendants that the British Navy was nearby and she asserted that one of the slave ships that had been at Ouidah that day was seized.[30] It is not clear how she could have witnessed the incident, unless it happened just before she got into the *Clotilda*.

FOR KANKO AND HER COMPANIONS in the hold, in complete darkness, the Middle Passage had just begun. The first days of absolute confinement in the *Clotilda* must have been among the worst. On some boats, the heat could reach 120 to 130 degrees, leading people to faint. A slave captain acknowledged that sometimes the steam from their bodies came up the gratings like a furnace.[31] Below deck, remembered Baquaqua, "day and night were the same to us, sleep being denied us from the confined position of our bodies, and we became desperate through suffering and fatigue." He added: "I suffered, and so did the rest of us, very much from sea sickness at first, but that did not cause our brutal owners any trouble." The lockdown was a time of immense suffering. Seasickness made people vomit, they had open sores from skin rubbing on rough planks. Dr. Joseph Cliffe, an American involved in the illegal slave trade, said people bruised when they were put on board, but after a while they became so skinny and light that the bruising was "very trifling." The men's heavy shackles produced blisters and wounds around their ankles. When the surf was high, the strong pitches of the boats sent bodies violently bumping into one another. An African enslaved in Virginia told his grandson that during storms, some people hit their heads against the iron bars and died.[32]

The unfamiliar, creaking noises of the *Clotilda*, the loud banging of the water, the thunderous wind in the sails sounded like "a thousand beasts" in the bush. The waves made people feel like the ship was way up in the sky, and then suddenly at the bottom of the sea. Below the *Clotilda*'s deck, the ceiling was low, but the shortest people could stand up, which was rarely the case on other ships.[33] They remained confined, Cudjo and his companions said, for thirteen days. The captives and the captain's calendars and recollections coincided. They did not know why they were locked up for so long, but it was a safe precaution on Foster's part to avoid detection. His narrative of the voyage, replete with his observations on the direction of the winds, the speed of the ship, and the hide-and-seek game with the men-of-war, revealed that on the twelfth day, near Cape Palmas (Liberia), he did encounter a man-of-war. If the boat had been seized, the entire crew would have been put on the cruiser along with the captives. But this time the fetters would be on the white men. When it had happened to the sailors who had transported Samuel Ajayi Crowther, he had taken his revenge on the Portuguese captain now in chains and had struck him on the head. Unfortunately for Cudjo, Pollee, Zuma, and the others, a heavy squall pushed the *Clotilda* away. "We were safe," Foster wrote.[34] The people he transported would have begged to differ. If the British Navy had seized the ship, they would have been sent to Sierra Leone, from where, as Gumpa knew, they could have made their way back to their homelands. Ouidah, Porto-Novo, Abeokuta, Badagry, and Lagos all had neighborhoods settled by thousands of Saro. If caught by the Americans, the companions would have been dispatched to Liberia, where they would have started a new life, free, among some of their compatriots.

The next day, they were led on deck for the first time. Unable to stand up after having been lying down for so long, they had to be carried by the crew and walked around the deck like invalids. For the first time in their life, they saw the high sea. Cudjo summed up their feelings of helplessness and shock at being thrust into the middle of nowhere and not knowing where they were going, "We looka, an' looka, an looka'—nothin' but sky and water. Whar we com' from, we do not know—whar we go, we do not know." After the first thirteen days, they spent much time on deck, contrary to what was the norm during the illegal slave trade. They had very little to eat, but what affected them most, just as it had other Africans who related their Middle Passage experience, was the lack of water. They received only a small quantity twice a day, and it tasted like vinegar. "They geeve us leetle water—one swallow twice each day. They geeve it in a leetle can. When we swallow they snatch it way and geeve it to the next man," is how Cudjo described their ordeal.[35] They were thankful when it rained because they could catch the water in their hands and mouths. Many decades later, Abache talked with much anguish of the heat and the lack of water.[36] Grabaung, one of the *Amistad* captives, also recalled that thirst was tormenting him and his companions on the voyage from Sierra Leone. Augustino, the young man deported to Brazil, stated, "In consequence of having a very insufficient supply of water, their thirst became so intense that many, from absolute suffocation, from the want of drink, died." Baquaqua and his shipmates were also tortured by thirst: "A pint a day was all that was allowed, and no more; and a great many slaves died upon the passage. There was one poor fellow became so very desperate for want of water, that he attempted to snatch a knife from the white man who brought in the water, when he was taken up on deck and I never knew what became of him. I supposed he was thrown overboard." Whatever the daily per-person regulations were—twenty-four ounces on Danish ships, three pints on Portuguese, two quarts on British ships—the Africans' testimonies concurred that they never received enough water.[37] And as if the warm water that had been sitting in wooden barrels for weeks did not taste bad enough, it was often filtrated through a woolen blanket to eliminate insects and other impurities and then treated with vinegar.

Apart from the want of water, the people of the *Clotilda* told Roche and Hurston they were not mistreated and that nobody got sick.[38] It was just as well, because the ship did not have a physician. Foster had taken a risk with Timothy Meaher's investment. It is doubtful that the shipbuilder had any medical skills, and his assortment of sailors tricked into a slaving voyage that seemed to have been their first were probably as ignorant as he was. Nor did anyone die, according to these accounts. But Cudjo was reported a few years later as saying that they did get sick and that two people died.[39] Given these contradictory statements, what really transpired is impossible to know. But one way or another, Foster's boat was an anomaly. The nineteenth century witnessed one of the highest mortality rates of the entire slave trade era. It had peaked to about 27 percent in the 1600s and declined to 10 percent at the beginning of the nineteenth century, but had picked up again after 1850, when it had reached on average 16 percent, which would have translated into seventeen dead on the *Clotilda*. Several factors made the last years some of the worst. The repression of the illegal slave trade was, paradoxically, the main culprit. Captives were locked up in congested and insalubrious *barracoons* for longer periods of time, as slave dealers and captains waited for the coast to clear of the navy ships that patrolled the oceans. As a consequence, as soon as they saw an opening, hundreds of people were rushed to the slavers and embarked in record time without much of a screening for diseases, including those that could be contagious. The extraordinary overcrowding of the ships themselves, the "tight-packing" that was a direct result of the fight against the slave trade, was also a factor, albeit not the main one.[40]

The documented violence that plagued the other vessels also makes Foster's boat one of the exceptions. But it was different in other regards as well. The people on board were roughly equally divided between men, women, girls, and boys. Each group was a little over twenty-five strong. Whereas in the seventeenth century, children under fifteen represented 10 to 12 percent of the deported Africans, their numbers reached 41 to 43 percent from 1801 to 1850, and 36 percent afterwards. The *Clotilda*'s number—50 percent—was thus well above average, especially for a vessel originating in the Bight of Benin. After 1851, no more than 19 percent of the captives from this area were children.[41] Overall, the proportion of youngsters had dramatically increased during the illegal slave trade. Since it had become more difficult and risky to introduce Africans into the United States, slavers felt they might as well make sure that they got people who had long working and reproductive lives ahead of them. As they were expressing, through this strategy, their pessimism as to the longevity of the international slave trade, they were also showing how optimistic they were about the survival of slavery itself. How the children made the trip on the *Clotilda* is not known, but in general, they were packed in the steerage, which may have been the worst part of the ship because of its small size and unbearable heat. Usually, the boys were allowed an individual space of about five feet by fourteen inches and the girls, four feet by twelve inches. Since they were harmless, youngsters were allowed on deck for longer periods than the adults.

The *Clotilda*'s fifty-fifty ratio of females to males was also inconsistent with nineteenth-century patterns. Until 1850, about 31 percent of the captives were females. Between 1851 and 1867, however, they were less than 25 percent, although almost 28 percent in the vessels that came from the Bight of Benin. The overall decline in the proportion of females (the share of girls increased), which reached its peak before 1800, has not yet been explained. Although women and girls were not shackled like the men and could move about, they had to face unique worries. Sexual abuse was rampant on slave ships, as slavers themselves acknowledged. Ottobah Cugoano recalled, "it was common for the dirty filthy sailors to take the African women and lie upon their bodies."[42] Just what occurred on the *Clotilda* is a matter of conjecture, but nothing was ever said about any kind of sexual abuse. If something did happen, it is quite doubtful that the Africans would have mentioned it to their children and their interviewers. It is one thing to talk about the mistreatment of anonymous women— as Ottobah did—and quite another to refer to one's own rape or those of easily identifiable wives and friends. As for Foster, he obviously had no compelling reason to report rapes, if they ever took place.

Of the dozen deported Africans who left testimonies of their lives, only Equiano, Baquaqua, and Cugoano referred to the Middle Passage. The silence or elusiveness of the others was not an aberration, nor was it a coincidence. It rested on solid African cultural ground. Talking publicly about anything of a personal nature is frowned upon in traditional African cultures, in which people are comfortable with secrecy (a central part of initiation), where the untold and the unexplained have their place, and where reserve and discretion are considered fundamental virtues. Most Africans, including the people of the *Clotilda*, did not leave detailed descriptions of the Middle Passage because they did not want to. Even though they had lived in the West longer than in their homelands, they were still Africans. As a result, what is known about the journey is mostly its mechanics, its awful routine, explained by the slavers themselves and Western witnesses.

MORE INTERESTING IS TO TRY to understand what occupied the people's thoughts and what they did outside of the slavers' control. Scholars, attempting to decipher their state of mind, have insisted on fear. Fear, terror, apprehensiveness, bewilderment, and fright are words they use repeatedly to describe what the captives supposedly felt from the beginning of their voyage to the end. Although fright was certainly present at the onset, nothing indicates that it was a permanent state. After a few days, once the routine had been established, and the movements of the ship understood, there was no reason why the Africans would have been terrified. They would abhor the lockdown, hate jumping up and down naked in a parody of dancing that offended their honor, be enraged at the conditions they were forced to live in, be infuriated at the violence, and be depressed. But except when specific dreadful events occurred, or they could not tell what gesture, look, or deed would bring down the whip, terror was likely not the dominant sentiment. What seems to have occupied their mind is what had preoccupied them on land, and they expressed it in various ways. On the ship that took him from Cameroon to Cuba, William Thomas recalled, "All cried very much at going away from their home and friends, some of them saying they would kill themselves."[43] Dr. Trotter, a slave ship surgeon, testified:

> they showed signs of *extreme distress and despair, from a feeling of their situation at being torn from their friends and connections*. Many retain those impressions a long time. In proof of which, the slaves, on board his ship, being often heard in the night making a howling melancholy noise, expressive of extreme anguish; he repeatedly ordered the woman, who had been his interpreter, to enquire into the cause. She discovered it to be owing to their having dreamt they were *in their own country again*, and finding themselves, when awake, in *the hold of a slave-ship*. This exquisite sensibility was particularly observable among the women; many of whom, on such occasions, he found in hysteric fits.[44]

A Mr. Town revealed that the men had revolted on his ship because, they told him, "*what business he had to carry them from their country. They had wives and children, whom they wanted to be with.*" He thought that the people fell "sick, sometimes owing to their crowded state, but *mostly* to *grief for being carried away from their country and friends.*" Men and women also sang about these separations in their own words. Ephraim's grandfather in Virginia told him that often one person sang and the other hummed. "What dey sing?" he said: "Nobody don' know. It's not ou' ah words. Dey sing language what dey learn in Africa when dey was free!" Because Africans often turn their sadness, pain, and grief into songs, those on board the slave ships had especial reason to sing; and even the Europeans, who had a different cultural relation to singing, understood that they were not witnessing expressions of joy. Ecroyde Claxton, a ship surgeon, testified, "they were songs of sad lamentations . . . they were all sick, and by and by they should be no more; they also sung songs expressive of their fears of being beaten, of their want of victuals, particularly the want of their native food, and of their never returning to their own country."[45] James Towne, who had made several trips on slave ships, asked the British Parliament, "Have you ever heard the Slaves singing and have you been acquainted with the subject of their songs? I have. I never found it any thing joyous, but lamentations. . . . [I]t was complaints for having been taken away from their friends and relations."[46]

As it had been all along, the loss of family and home was what weighed most heavily on people's mind. To find oneself cut off from family was to be reduced to an individual; and individuality, let alone individualism, are loathed in African cultures. It is essential to understand African societies' high degree of integration in order to try to comprehend the mindset of the deportees and, by extension, the particular institution they created on the ships. African families are large but also close and unified. This unity and closeness are constantly affirmed and reinforced through duties, exchanges of services and gifts, visits, participation in ceremonies, name-giving (giving the name of a family member to a newborn), family councils, placement of a child with a relative, and countless other daily gestures and long-term collective activities. Within the community, this effort at unification is expressed in the powerful age classes that structure society, irrespective of caste or social status, and demand loyalty and dedication from their members throughout their lives. At a still higher level the widespread and very important "joking relationships" or "joking kinships" link various groups through conventional humor, based on interethnic clan and family name correspondences that go back centuries. They allow individuals from different ethnicities to tease one another regardless of age, gender, or social status. They bond strangers instantly through laughter and deflect tensions. All these links that, in Africa, make a human being a person were not entirely severed on the ships when people from the same town or region found themselves together; but for others the loss was far-reaching. Cudjo, Pollee, and Abache, for example, came from the same town; Ossa Keeby may have been completely on his own. Africans lost more than relatives and friends when they were deported; they lost a part of who they were, of their very identity as people whose sense of self comes from their connections to others, not their individuality. The re-creation of a surrogate community was therefore a vital process for the deportees, which started in the *barracoon* and continued on the ship.

Even though the Middle Passage had nothing in common with initiation, an eagerly anticipated time of integration, the fact that people withstood physical pain together was not unlike their experience of communal suffering during initiation. This special connection led to the creation of a new defined group, the shipmates, *bâtiments* (Haiti, French for ship), *malungo* (Brazil), *malongue* (Trinidad), *mati* or *sippi* (Surinam). This ship community brought together people of different ethnicities, languages, religions, gender, and former status. The solidarity, dedication, and mutual support of the shipmates did not end with the journey, but remained strong, sometimes through several generations in the Americas.[47] Although they do not seem to have used any particular word to describe their companions—such as shipmate—the people on the *Clotilda* did form such a tightly knit community and maintained it vigorously.

DURING THEIR AWFUL VOYAGE, because they did not know what to expect, they scrutinized everything intently for what could be useful information, or help them understand or take advantage of a situation. They observed the horizon, the crew, and the sea. On other ships, this type of analysis was what enabled uprisings to take place. People observed the routine of the crew, located where the weapons were held, and looked for opportunities. On the *Clotilda*, the shipmates, who had never been on the high sea, noticed changes in the color of the water; it had been blue at the beginning of the trip, then green, and at some point it looked as red as blood. It was different still as they approached some islands.[48]

On the twentieth day, according to their count, they found Foster agitated. He was constantly looking through his binoculars. He climbed up the mast and looked around for a long time. He then rushed back down, and instructed the crew to put down the sail and anchor the ship. Then the Africans were ordered to go back to the hold. The *Clotilda* did not move until night. What had happened? Foster did not mention this incident. But on June 30, near the Bahamas, the ship almost ran into a sunken vessel. According to the captain, she was ten feet away.[49] It would have been the best news for the passengers, provided they could have been rescued. As a British colony, the Bahamas had abolished slavery in 1834, and had they come on land, they would have been freed. Near Tortuga, Foster said the crew spotted two men-of-war.

The cruisers did not bother them because the sailors had taken down the ship's square sail and the foretopmast: the *Clotilda* now looked like an innocuous ship that was doing business along the coast. Foster thus claimed to have outrun or outwitted five men-of-war on his way back. Even though it may seem inflated, it is not implausible. The first encounter was at Ouidah, a notorious point of embarkation; the second off Liberia, an area that was regularly patrolled; and the last in the Caribbean, the other zone under surveillance where the U.S. Navy had joined the British the year before. These efforts notwithstanding, the British had little success—the United States even less—and Foster's trip was emblematic of their general failure. Between the 1810s and the 1860s, the Royal Navy liberated 160,000 Africans—out of more than 3.4 million who were deported—and seized 1,600 ships.[50] From the Captain's perspective, the failed patrols had made the lengthy voyage exciting.

How long was the Middle Passage? Cudjo claimed repeatedly that it lasted seventy days.[51] Some shipmates said they were fifty-five days at sea.[52] Foster's recollection was that he sailed from Mobile on March 4 and arrived in Ouidah on May 15. He probably departed around the twenty-fourth. According to British records, four ships left Ouidah in 1860—there may have been others that were not documented, including those mentioned by Cudjo and Kanko—and transported a total of about 2,500 persons, 1,200 of whom left on a single steamer bound for Cuba, which was reached, allegedly, in eighteen days. The *Clotilda* was not mentioned by name, but a "schooner under American colors" was reported to have embarked 101 people on May 11.[53] The *Clotilda* was indeed a schooner, the number of captives is close to what Foster acknowledged, and the month is right. The British at Lagos got their information secondhand through their spies, and it is not surprising that the date may have been off by a few days. But by and large, their intelligence meshes with Foster's account and with what transpired upon arrival in Alabama. By July 8, the *Clotilda* was sailing into the Gulf of Mexico. Thus the Middle Passage would have lasted forty-five days. This duration is corroborated by the latest research. Between 1851 and 1867, it took ships forty-five days to sail from the Bight of Benin to the United States.[54] In the mid-1800s, the only people who were en route for more than seventy days came all the way from Mozambique and Madagascar. There is no question that the conditions the *Clotilda's* passengers endured were likely to have led Cudjo to feel as if the journey was much longer, but there is also little doubt that it did last about forty-five days, as Foster claimed.

The day before the ship entered the Gulf, Ossa, Zuma, Omolabi, and their companions had seen the color of the water change, and spotted land at a distance. They were ordered back into the hold. The sailors came down to tell them to keep quiet and showed them leafy branches to make them understand they were near land.[55]

THEIR JOURNEY WAS ALMOST OVER and they were still free, in the sense that mattered to them most: free as opposed to enslaved. Even if to Europeans and Americans the slave trade was a trade in slaves, to the Africans it was a deportation of free people followed by their enslavement. They considered themselves prisoners until they were effectively enslaved by someone. One of the clearest illustrations of this conviction can be found in some men's comments after a rebellion they had organized on a ship had failed (they launched a second one later). They told William Snelgrave that he was a great rogue to have bought them to carry them away from their country, and they were resolved to regain their liberty if possible. They still thought of themselves as free men who were prisoners, a view that was the opposite of Snelgrave's, as he told them they had forfeited their freedom before he bought them, either as criminals or prisoners of war. They were his property, he contented, but in their own eyes they were free men held against their will.

Similarly, Abubakar al-Siddiq, born in Timbuktu and deported to Jamaica in 1805, made abundantly clear when he wrote about his life that he had become a slave only in the West Indies. After three months on the ship, he "came on shore in the land of Jamaica. This was the beginning of my slavery until this day. I tasted the bitterness of slavery from them, and its oppressiveness." King Adinkra's army had made him a prisoner; the Christians—as a Muslim he categorized people in religious terms—to whom he was sold on the Gold Coast had had no impact on his status. He had arrived a free man in Jamaica but "they" had made him a slave. Cugoano wrote that he had been in "horrible slavery" for about eight or nine months, that is after he had arrived in Grenada. When he landed in Brazil, Baquaqua stressed, "I cared but little then that I was a slave, having escaped the ship was all I thought about." He mentioned that he was enslaved only when he reached land, not when he was on the ship. Similarly, the people of the *Clotilda* talked of themselves as slaves only in Alabama. During the march and in the *barracoon*, they cried for their families, but in America, in addition, they cried because they were enslaved. And when Cudjo talked about his and his companions' time in slavery, he dated it from the moment they worked for their owners, not before.[56] What this shows, and contrary to what has been said and written about the Middle Passage, is that in the Africans' minds the journey, with all its gruesomeness, was probably not the defining experience that changed everything. The abject degradation, the humiliation, the daily assaults on their dignity, the nakedness, the lying in filth, the torture, and the vile bashing of their honor did not seem to have altered their sense of identity as freeborn men and women who found themselves prisoners. To the crew, the captain, and the prospective buyers, in contrast, they had been slaves long before they had even set foot on the ships. From the whites' perspective, traders on the coast had sold them slaves, not men and women, and the American and Caribbean planters were about to buy chattel bound to that condition by virtue of their racial inferiority.

All that the people held under deck knew is that they had gone through a dramatic reversal of fortune. They would have been stunned at the notion that their new condition was due not to God's will, war, or trickery, but to inferiority. They had changed during the journey, yet their belief in their worth as free human beings had not. But, as they were about to touch land, they were going to definitely lose their confiscated liberty, and they were going to become Africans.

CHAPTER FOUR

Arrival in Mobile

T HE *CLOTILDA* ENTERED THE MISSISSIPPI SOUND on Sunday, July 8, 1860. The crew anchored off Point-of-Pines in Grand Bay. There were a few things for the captain to do: according to his account, William Foster had to meet Timothy Meaher, who would have the crew's pay; tug the *Clotilda* up the Alabama River; and lastly, go to the discreet spot already selected to land the Africans. Foster knew exactly what to do because he and Timothy Meaher had put together an elaborate plan four months earlier. Every detail had been taken care of. Once the Africans had landed and Meaher had paid the crew, he and his men were to sail further south to Tampico, a port on the Pánuco River in Mexico.[1] There, the *Clotilda* was to reinvent herself one more time. The once innocuous schooner that had crossed the ocean as a slave ship would turn back into an innocent vessel. Foster would see to it that all traces of the jail it had been for six weeks were scrubbed away. The masts, the sails, and the boom would be altered once again. The *Clotilda* would be no more. She would change her name. Money would pass from one hand to another, and someone would give her legitimate papers and clearance to sail to New Orleans. Louisiana made a brisk business with Tampico, sending in food and prefabricated wooden houses, thus making good cover for the ship.

But "Captain Timothy and party," as Foster called them, were not there when the ship arrived. Foster had to calm his men, who expected to be paid upon arrival. Whatever he told them, the crew was not convinced, and they mutinied once again. The tension was high; they were now in American waters, pirates with a full load of "contraband" that could be detected any minute. Foster proposed a solution: he would go on shore, get the money, and come back. The sailors were not swayed; they were even more determined than they had been in Cape Verde and Ouidah. Foster claimed they threatened to kill him if he tried to "take the negroes ashore without their money." But they relented, and he went looking for a tugboat to take the *Clotilda* up to Spanish River, far from the wide-open Mississippi Sound. He found what he needed and hurried back on board. The men were furious. Foster, obsessed with taking the ship out of sight, had not tried to find the money to pay them. Exasperated, they started their fourth mutiny. This time, they had the upper hand; they refused to harness the ship to the tugboat. The captain was cornered. There was nothing else for him to do but pay them. He rowed to shore again and gave a driver with a horse and buggy a whopping $25 to take him to Mobile. He then sent an envoy to his partner. The man was one of the sentinels that Meaher, who knew he was being watched, had posted around Mobile Bay and the Mississippi Sound with instructions to let him know immediately when the *Clotilda* sailed in.[2] Obviously, the system had not worked. Nobody had seen the ship when she first arrived. The messenger jumped on his horse, and headed north.

Meaher was at home, sitting on the gallery of his house on Telegraph Road. Noah, the "house boy" from North Carolina, recalled this particular day: "Ole Marse wuz settin' out on de gal'ry smokin', wid his heels on de banisters." When he heard the hoofs of a horse galloping fast on the clay road toward him, Meaher may have had a feeling it was what he had been expecting for the past few days. When they finally came in sight, the horse was foaming and the messenger was panting at the end of a forty-mile race.[3] Timothy put down his pipe and rushed down the stairs. The horseman whispered, "The niggers have come. The niggers are here." Meaher gave orders to Noah to saddle up his horse and then he was gone, not to be seen again for more than a week. As he knew he would need his services, he had secured beforehand the help of James, the young pilot who had been sold from Charleston and had been in Burns's service since he was a boy.[4]

They went looking for James W. Hollingsworth, a prominent tugboat captain, who on this Sunday morning was worshipping at St. John's. Meaher and James headed for the church. Dennison remained outside while Meaher went in, walked down the pews, and called on the captain to follow him to the vestibule. Meaher acknowledged several years later that he had not told Hollingsworth what was in the ship he wanted him to tug.[5] Before getting on the tugboat, the *Billy Jones*, Timothy asked his brother Burns, who knew all the details of the operation, to fire up his steamboat the *Czar*, and wait for him below the mouth of Spanish River. To put the final touch on his elaborate scheme, he instructed the crew of his *Roger B. Taney* to leave Mobile at the usual time, but to wait until he came aboard to serve supper. Hollingsworth, James, and Timothy boarded the *Billy Jones*, and they sped to the Mississippi Sound where they met the *Clotilda*. Meaher climbed aboard the slave ship, yet in his own account, Foster did not mention the arrival of his old associate and friend. He simply stated that he "took on board five men and $8,000." Besides Meaher with the money, James, and Hollingsworth, there must have been two men working on the tugboat. The crew got busy harnessing the *Clotilda* to the *Billy Jones*. Locked up for a second day, the shipmates were lying in apprehension at the new turn of events. They had been told to be quiet. They were aware that the coast was near—they had caught sight of it—and they had also understood what the branch brought by the crew meant, and the ship had been immobile for hours. They knew they had arrived. It meant they were getting off the boat. It also meant they were about to know what was going to happen to them.

When night fell, and it was safe to go, Hollingsworth started tugging the *Clotilda* toward Mobile. The sudden noise woke up the people in the hold. Everyone was by then thoroughly familiar with all the sounds of a sailing ship, so the new racket was startling. They listened intently to try to connect the sound to something familiar. After some discussion, they concluded it was a swarm of bees, another indication they were nearing the end of the voyage. [6] By Sunday night, the ship had slipped into Spanish River, past the city of Mobile, without incident. Neither the customs nor the port authorities had seen her. The *Clotilda* in tow, the *Billy Jones* made her way up the Mobile River to Twelve-Mile Island, a large, desolate place in the middle of the river. What the Africans went through next has not been recorded. Their first time on deck in view of the land must have felt good after more than forty days of water and waves and nothing but the sky. They must have been overwhelmed by the moment, the scene, the smells, the strangeness of it all; and they must have felt apprehensive, not knowing what was to happen next, but also relieved. Perhaps like Baquaqua, they did not care that they were slaves in a foreign land. Perhaps all that mattered was that they were breathing fresh air again that smelled of land and life.[7]

BUT THE REPRIEVE FROM THE SHIP was not going to last. They did not even get on land. The *Clotilda* and the *Czar* were brought close together and a plank was thrown between them. As the Africans got off one ship, they walked up to another to be locked up again. How did the transfer go? No testimony has been left, but it is interesting to note how the people of the *Wanderer* reacted when they faced the same situation on the Alabama River.

> For some time the Africans could not be induced to go on board the boat, and seemed much frightened at the smoke, &c. Doubtless they had a perfect horror of traveling on the water again, after having so recently endured a long and crowded sea voyage. The manner in which they were finally induced to go on is worthy of notice. The mate tried every means to get them on board, but to no effect. Finally he concerted a plan with a big, black Alabama negro. He tried to get him on board, but he absolutely refused, when the mate laid him down on the gangway-plank, and hit him four or five substantial licks with his ponderous leather strap, when the said Alabama negro got up, yelling awfully, and went straight on board, beckoning to the Africans to follow. And they did follow, to the amusement, and amid the cheers of the crowd.[8]

Possibly persuaded in that manner, the group climbed down into the bowels of the *Czar*, a ship that had no sail and did not look anything like the one they had just left. It was a steamship, powered by an engine fed by a furnace, and it is possible that some thought it was the end, the place where they would all be burned, and their bones gathered and crushed to make gunpowder. Youngsters, like Abile, might have thought they were indeed going to be cooked and eaten. Others must have believed it was the beginning of one more ghastly voyage.

They did not see what happened next, but if they had, they probably would have rejoiced. Captain Foster climbed aboard the now empty *Clotilda*, where he had spent sixteen weeks. He had one more thing to do. His ship was not going to get a new life after all. He knew—and Meaher did too—that they might have been spotted, so they had decided to destroy the evidence, the telling signs of a slaving voyage: the partitions, the platforms, the empty casks of food and water, the big pots, the tubs, the blood, the vomit, the spit, the mucus, the urine, and the feces that soiled the planks, the awful smell that always floated around slave ships. The *Clotilda* sailed into Bayou Canot, north-west of Twelve-Mile Island, and put down anchor. Seven cords of lightwood were placed in strategic locations. Foster lighted them up, walked down the plank, and took a last look at his fine ship. The infamous *Clotilda* went up in smoke. A man was posted near the burning vessel to make sure pieces of the wreckage did not float down the river, a definite sign that something shady had been going on. But it was a futile exercise because her hull remained visible at low tide for three quarters of a century, as if to remind everyone of the Africans' ordeal. Foster was not happy with having to destroy the ship. He believed it was worth more than the people he was going to receive as payment for his four months' work.[9]

With the captives, the crew of the *Clotilda*, and Timothy Meaher on board, Burns ordered his men to fire up the *Czar* with the bacon sides he had loaded to make believe the ship was on a regular delivery trip. She sped up the Tombigbee and reached one of the brothers' friends, John Dabney, the Virginian who had established a successful plantation a few years earlier. Less than a week before, the census-taker had come up to count his "property" for the 1860 Slave Schedules.[10] He had found forty-seven people. Once the official had left, Dabney did not expect any inquisitive visitors.

The Africans had been on the boat for only a few hours before landing once again. And this time, there was no other ship in sight. They left the *Czar* and walked inland to a small clearing among the canebrakes. James and a few trusted men were now in charge.[11] According to Cudjo, he and his companions had received some clothes—Noah called them rags, pieces of corn sacks, and skins—on their way to the canebrakes. Three months before, they would have thrown the scraps away in disgust. But they were so welcome that seventy years later they became the major incident in Cudjo's recollection of the events that unfurled that night, their first in Alabama. The rags were a little privacy restored, a bit of dignity recovered. Over the years, the question of clothes and nudity came up repeatedly in conversations with the Africans, evidence that they had felt intensely humiliated by their forced nakedness. James had a different remembrance; he thought they got the clothes on the last day of their stay at Dabney's.[12]

Once the group had landed, the *Czar* hurried downriver. Back at Twelve-Mile Island, the crew of the *Clotilda* mutinied for the very last time. The men, who by then had done everything they had been asked to do, wanted their money. But Meaher had another plan. When the *Czar* reached the *Roger B. Taney* a few miles away, on her regular trip to Montgomery, he and the *Clotilda* crew got aboard the packet in great secrecy. The passengers heard some noise, people whispering, climbing the stairs; but they did not see anyone. At 9:30 P.M., Timothy Meaher, looking and acting his usual self, entered the dining room. He apologized for the sick cook who had delayed supper, and took his place at the captain's table. Dinner could be served. Some passengers asked where he had been earlier, and what about the people who had just boarded the ship but were nowhere in sight? Why didn't they come to supper? Meaher was evasive and nonchalant, and soon enough the questions stopped. Somewhere far from the diners' eyes and ears, the sailors were fed, given some whiskey and cards, told to keep quiet, and locked up for the rest of the trip. To make sure they would not spill their story in some drunken fit in a sailors' bar as soon as they reached Montgomery, they were put on a mail-train going North. When they finally got their pay, they realized they had been had. They got only what Foster had agreed to give them when they first left Mobile, a grand total of $8,000. There were no double wages. Like other sailors who had been duped into a slaving trip, they got the $600 to $700 that was the normal pay on such expeditions. Foster had never intended to keep the pledge he had made in Cape Verde. As his wife stressed, he always said, "promises were like pie-crust—made to be broken."[13]

MEANWHILE, THE AFRICANS were trying to survive their first days in America. The place where they had been dumped was a wild landscape of soaring bamboos, swamps full of mosquitoes and snakes, and tortuous channels. It was a watery maze, a perfect place to elude detection, and the worst place to be for traumatized, angry people who needed care and answers. As was true for other Africans who had gone through the Middle Passage, they probably had skin infections, lice and fleas, diarrhea, constipation, and dysentery, and they suffered from general weakness and exhaustion.[14] James and his companions' task was to keep their charges out of sight of the federal authorities. Accordingly, each day, they had them move from one part of the swamp to another. They had explained to them, through signs, that they were not allowed to talk loudly, but only to whisper. There was a risk that someone on the river might hear people talk in a strange tongue. The first days were long and empty, because there was nothing to do, or see, nothing even remotely familiar. Swarms of mosquitoes made their lives even more miserable. They slept on the ground without anything to protect them from the elements. Fortunately, it did not rain at all. July 1860 has remained the driest July on record in Alabama. Then one day they were put aboard yet another steamer. According to James they had stayed in the swamps eleven days.[15]

They had no idea where they would end up or how long this trip would be. But the boat only took them on a short voyage upriver to The Bend in Clarke County at the confluence of the Alabama and the Tombigbee, where they landed at Burns's plantation. No one in the group knew what to expect or how long they would remain there, but once they settled down, they finally came up with one explanation for this latest relocation. They believed they had been moved from the first swamp because the mosquitoes were eating them badly.[16] It had not occurred to them that Timothy Meaher had no interest in their well-being, other than making sure they would not die on him, which would mean the loss of a potential $700—$14,000 in today's money—per person. Even in their dejected state, they continued to feel they were men and women whose welfare and wishes mattered to others, not slaves who could only endure and keep quiet. But life at Burns Meaher's was barely a notch above survival on the *Clotilda*. At night, they slept under a wagon shed, and before dawn, they were led to the swamps where they had to stay until dark. They lived and were treated, literally, like animals: "Understanding no word and knowing not what was expected of them, they were made to know the driver's wishes by shooing sound—such as would drive chickens or geese."[17] The memory of these horrendous days still filled them with grief fifty years later.

Several miles away, Mobile had been abuzz for days, excited as much at the Africans' arrival as at their disappearance. Despite Meaher's precautions, the secret landing was all over town. The captain may have thought he had outwitted everybody, but all and sundry had heard of the *Clotilda* and knew what her cargo consisted of. On the eleventh, the Macon *Daily Telegraph* informed its readers that "The schooner Clotilda, with 124 Africans on board, arrived in Mobile Bay to-day, and a steamboat immediately took the negroes up the river."[18] The next day, the *Circular* of Brooklyn, New York, relayed the information, and a Louisiana newspaper, the *Delta*, published a piece on the "secret landing."

A few days ago, within about twenty-four hours of the successful landing of a gang of negroes, in Mobile Bay, twenty-three remarkably fine fellows, field hands, were placed on board of the Mobile steamer for this city, and having safely arrived, are to be sold on Friday, at the St. Charles Hotel, by Julian Neville. There is much discussion and inquiry as to the character of these negroes, whether they are of the recent, or whether they are a portion of the one hundred and ninety for whom graves were dug at Key West, but who, unreasonably enough, preferred rather the comfortable quarters of our river plantations to such narrow accommodations as Uncle Sam proposed to furnish them. One of the lot, a boy of seventeen, weighs one hundred and seventy, and is over six feet high. It is supposed he is of the Bozale tribe, and that his father was a renowned warrior of that warlike race.

The landing of a cargo of Africans right under the nose of Judge Campbell, the most ferocious of all the foes of the traffic, is certainly a very audacious act. The time, too, selected for the landing adds to the gravity of the offense. The Judge's recent ponderous charge to the Grand Jury, and eloquent exhibition of the horrors of the middle passage, had just been delivered, and orders had just been given to the United States Marshal to pursue all offenders under the statute. Judge Jones's decision, that it was no violation of the Act of Congress to buy negroes which had been imported, has been set aside. And yet, in face of all this peril and responsibility, some daring adventurer succeeds in landing a gang of good hands in time for the picking season, which will be a valuable addition to our utterly inadequate force of agricultural laborers. "Can such things be?"[19]

What a strange story. Nobody who came on the *Clotilda* was ever sent to New Orleans, and when they were said to have been sold, the Africans were still suffering in Dabney's canebrakes. But as the journalist insinuated, these twenty-three people may also have been some survivors from the bark *Wildfire* that had landed in Key West on April 30, towed by the steamer *Mohawk* of the African Squadron, with 510 Africans from the Congo. Or maybe he had mixed things up with an episode that had happened a year earlier when John McClusky, a slave trader in Mobile, had housed twenty-three Africans from the *Wanderer* on their way to Louisiana.[20] No one among the purported Africans was a "Bozale," because the word did not apply to an ethnicity. Or everyone was, since the term was used by the Spaniards to designate a person born in Africa, as opposed to a Creole. The *Delta* story was not credible because it collapsed bits and pieces of various actual landings into one, and it can be counted as part of the argument for the *Clotilda* being a hoax. Nevertheless, it was partially true. There had indeed been a landing a few days before in Mobile.

On July 14, the Mobile *Register* was already rejoicing and, as customary, made a reference to the Africans' stroke of luck. "Whoever conducted the affair has our congratulations on his or their success, as the case may be, whether the Africans came from the Gold Coast *via* Key West, or whether they made a straight-out trip by the shortest route from their native land. We take it that the trade is, to all intents and purposes, opened—why not? Why should not those who are in want of negro labor import it at a low cost, when they are civilizing and Christianizing a set of barbarians by the same course which redounds to their interest?" Then the story went all the way to New York, where *Harpers' Weekly* disseminated it to the rest of the country on the twenty-first. "A telegraphic dispatch from New Orleans announces the arrival and landing of a cargo of 124 Africans at Mobile on Monday. They were immediately taken up the Alabama River on board a steamboat, and no doubt by this time are judiciously distributed among the planters. They were landed from the schooner

Clotilde." The *San Antonio Ledger and Texan* published a news item on the same day about the schooner's arrival on the ninth with 103 Africans on board; and the *Weekly San Joaquin Republican* of Stockton, California, informed its readers of the landing on the twenty-eighth.[21]

THE AFRICANS HAD BEEN IN MOBILE for less than two weeks, and already their presence was well known, as was the name of the ship, and therefore who had transported them illegally. The revenue officers at the Customs House and the officials at the U.S. District Court could not ignore what was going on. In addition, the *Clotilda* had not been announced and had not registered with the customs, therefore escaping taxes on the "cargo." Timothy Meaher was arrested and accused of having illegally imported Negroes. The captain stated under oath that he had made each regular trip on the *Roger B. Taney*, which was true. He was released on bond, but closely watched.

Meaher rode back home to Telegraph Road to his worried wife. He could not stop laughing as he recounted his adventure. Noah was listening:

> "I's sho' had er race wid dem niggers. I put them off de ship in de middle ob de night and put em on er steamboat to bring 'em up de ribber, but de Yanks wuz on my track. Dey wuz guardin' de ribber, so I hatter run up in One Mile crick. De nex' day dey 'rested me on 'spicion but dey couldn't prove nothin'. Den dey watch me purty close. I hatter git my partner ter hep me, and we is ben oner stiddy chase for six days." Den he throw back his head an' laugh, "We's done fooled 'em now," he says; "dey is chasin' niggers de yother side er Montgomery, while de whole passel ob 'em is dumped in a cane-brake about er mile from here."[22]

He could have a good laugh because he knew that the people who were after him were not going to be severe. A. J. Requier, the U. S. Attorney for the Southern District of Alabama, who would soon double as a Confederate poet, was no threat. Judge William G. Jones was such a friend that Meaher had given his name to one of his steamers. Everybody knew that when it came to importers of Africans, Judge Jones was as lenient as he possibly could be. Two years earlier, he had rendered a momentous decision alluded to in the *Delta*'s article: buying newly introduced Africans, he had asserted, was not a violation of the law of 1818 that imposed a fine of $1,000 "to anyone who had held, purchased or sold a Negro from abroad." He had done it again a few months before the *Clotilda* had returned from Ouidah. He had presided, in Mobile, over the case of Horatio N. Gould, indicted for introducing into the state about thirty Africans from the *Wanderer* in violation of the same act. Judge Jones had ruled that when the said Negro was no longer with the importer, only the law of the state he was in applied, not the law of the United States. "Whatever laws Congress may enact against the original importer of African slaves, they cannot be made to apply to the purchaser, who acquired the property within the limits and by the laws of the individual State."[23] Judge Jones was not going to create problems. Still, prosecution had to go on. The federal authorities were advised that Africans had been introduced fraudulently.

ON JULY 18, THE U.S. ATTORNEY GENERAL in Washington, D.C., received a letter "relative to the recent importation of negroes in Alabama." It was followed by one dated July 23, reporting "the arrival of the schooner *Clotilde* with African slaves on board." The next day, another correspondence was dispatched "relative to the schooner *Clotilde* and the Africans introduced by her." Finally, on the twenty-eighth, a "writ of habeus corpus was issued for the seizure of the negroes imported into Alabama."[24] On July 27, the U.S. attorney for the Southern District of Alabama informed Judge Jones that according to an affidavit by Marshal Cade M. Godbold, on

> the 7th day of July, 1860, one hundred & three negroes, whose manner & description are to your informant unknown, were imported or brought to the United States, from a foreign kingdom, place, or country, with intent to hold, sell, or dispose of such negroes, as slaves, or to hold them to service or labour. That John M. Dabney, of the county of Clarke, State of Alabama holds a large number of said negroes, to wit, ten men, ten women, ten boys & ten girls. . . . Wherefore the said attorney prays for process for the seizure of said negroes, & against the said John M. Dabney.[25]

The same day, the judge ordered the marshal to seize and take possession of the "Negroes" and to give Dabney notice to appear and answer questions. Two days later, his clerk filed a summons to the marshal ordering him to inform Dabney to appear in court in November. Similar information was opened also on July 27 against Burns Meaher; he was accused of holding "twenty five men, & twenty five women, twenty five boys, & twenty five girls."[26] There was confusion about numbers, who held how many, and where the shipmates were, but the overall picture was accurate.

The authorities' next move was to try and find the Africans, following the judge's orders. According to Timothy Meaher, the marshal chartered the *Eclipse* to sail along the bayous and into the canebrake to search for them. The plan was secret, of course, but "a friend" alerted Meaher, who came up with a new strategy. On the afternoon of the covert operation, the *Roger B. Taney* went upriver to transfer the Africans from Dabney's to Burns Meaher's plantation. Henry Romeyn and Samuel H. M. Byers gave a more colorful version of the event, but did not offer any hint to their sources. Meaher, they claimed, sent alcohol aboard the *Eclipse*. The crew got so drunk that fresh and sober sailors had to be rounded up and brought to the searching vessel. In the meantime, the Africans were secured away.[27] What Meaher recounted fits neatly with what the shipmates reported about their abrupt removal from Dabney's, but they were mistaken about the mosquitoes; the *Eclipse*'s investigation was the real reason for their transfer. They were coming close to being discovered.

In the swamps, dressed in rags, the companions were more dejected than ever. Granted, their time on the *Clotilda* had been worse than their stay in the swamps, where they were on firm ground, had something to cover parts of their bodies, and were not locked up in crowded quarters. But they were desperate nonetheless, as they confided many years later. One can only speculate about what they were thinking, but one thing is sure: what some of them had heard growing up had not materialized: they had not been eaten, but they had not been put to work either. The wasting of days doing nothing must have felt like an incredibly cruel twist of fate. They had been torn from their families and lands, had spent six awful weeks on the sea, had been humiliated, and were starving for no apparent reason. "In this strange land, among strange faces and an unknown tongue," the shipmates later confided "they almost grieved themselves to death."[28] As depressed as they were, they could hardly imagine that their dire situation was going to take an even more tragic turn.

Timothy Meaher was eager to settle his affairs. Once he felt safe enough, he alerted his friends that the sale was imminent. According to Romeyn, a number of men who had placed orders for some Africans months before had gotten cold feet after their arrival had become known, and they were no longer willing to buy them.[29] However, some men did come. James piloted the potential buyers to the spot where the sale was going to take place. The day must have started like all the others. Cudjo, Pollee, Zuma, and their companions had been led from the shed to the marsh and told, through signs, shooing sounds, and clicking tongues, to sit down and be quiet. It was another dreary, sultry day, but it soon turned out to be anything but ordinary as white men made their way through the tall grass. In a scene reminiscent of the *barracoon* in Ouidah, the shipmates, who could only know and fear what was coming next, were exhibited for the customers. They were separated into two rows, men and boys on one side, women and girls on the other. In the middle stood the white men, gawking at them.[30] But there were no interpreters to ask about the people's ages and diseases, no broker or owner to guarantee, in writing, the good health of the people on display. The buyers had to make sure on their own that they were buying useful, healthy people even though after close to sixty catastrophic days they looked sick, shabby, skinny, and dirty. Everyone had to be inspected. How it was done is not known, but according to what the survivors told Roche, the buyers looked at their teeth.[31] It was probably an understatement, a dignified way of glossing over humiliation because the scrutiny must have been as thorough, if not more so, than at an ordinary auction in town. What was the Africans' response to the inspection? Silvia King, whose slave ship landed at New Orleans, recalled how it was done and how some of her companion reacted: "We was all chained and dey strips all our clothes off and de folks what gwine buy us comes round and feels us all over. Iffen any de niggers don't want to take dere clothes off, de man gits a long, black whip and cuts dem up hard."[32]

As the inspection progressed, each buyer made his selection, and the people he had chosen were put aside. When ready to leave the swamp, the new owner made himself understood by tracing a circle with his hand toward his group and then pointing his fingers to his breast. Sixty-seven years later, Cudjo remembered the sale as the worst heartbreak he and his companions had been through since leaving Ouidah, and he was so overcome with emotion that he stopped talking for the day. Their grief was unbearable. They cried for their relatives, they cried at being separated from their shipmates, who had become a second family, and they sang a parting song. Some of its words were *lona se wu* or "no danger on the road."[33] Heartbroken, the companions were wishing one another a safe journey, wherever they were taken.

The sale to different men meant that the community that had protected and comforted its kinless members was no more. For many, it would mean a permanent loss of contact with anyone from their homeland. Very few Africans were ever deported from the Bight of Benin to the United States. Only some 7,000 are known to have been part of the transatlantic slave trade to this country.[34] So the chances they would meet compatriots were exceedingly slim. The largest group, sixteen males and sixteen females, became Timothy Meaher's property. Burns had taken ten "couples" and Foster either five (according to Cudjo) or eight (said his widow) "couples." James Meaher is said to have received eight people, among them Cudjo.[35] From seventy to more than eighty people had been divided between four men. Thomas Buford became the owner of Oluale, Jaba, and probably four or five others.

In the end, perhaps fewer than two dozen people were sold to slave dealers, and their departure from Mobile was not exactly secret. The *Mercury* reported in its July 23 edition:

> Some negroes who never learned to talk English, went up the Railroad the other day. They didn't get aboard at Mobile, but somewhere in the piney woods country. It is not necessary to mention the particular place. There were twenty-five of them, apparently all of the pure, unadulterated African stock. Their destination is unknown. They may have been bound for Entreprise [Coffee County], to supply a demand which existed in that market some while ago for full blooded African slaves, as per advertisement of sundry gentlemen up there, offering to buy such at a certain price. They were in charge of one who knows how to buy and sell Negroes.[36]

A heartrending incident occurred on their way out of the city. A circus was coming along the same side road, and the slave drivers ordered the Africans to hide behind the bushes to avoid detection. As the caravan passed, an elephant trumpeted. For the very first time since they had left Ouidah, the deportees were connecting with something they could identify and relate to. Some screamed with delight, *ajanaku! ajanaku! ile! ile!* (elephant! elephant! home! home! in Yoruba and Fon).[37] But the elephant was the first and last sign from Africa they would see and hear.

TO FIND OUT WHERE THEY WENT after they left Burns Meaher's place and who they were is not an easy task. About ninety Africans born between 1830 and 1850 can be located in Alabama, through records ranging from 1870 to 1920. But not all had arrived on the *Clotilda*: some came on the *Wanderer* and others landed between 1840 and 1857, like Martha Porter of Montgomery County, Abbie Royal of Dallas, and Jake Vangue of Russell.[38] However, some clues can be found in Cudjo's remark that some people were sold in Bogue Chitto.[39] There was indeed a cluster of three Africans in Prairie Bluff, Wilcox County, twenty-five miles from Bogue Chitto: Mary Haywood and Ovay Hunt (born in 1846) and Lucy Hunt (born in 1845, no relation to Ovay) may have arrived on the *Clotilda*.[40] It may also have been the case for Crecy Dansly (born in 1840), Aquila Clanton (born in 1847), and Ossie Hunt (born in 1850), all of Boiling Springs, also twenty-five miles from Bogue Chitto.[41] Dinah and William Seay of Montgomery could have been part of the group too.[42] A woman Zora Neale Hurston met in 1928 had arrived on the *Clotilda* and she lived on the Tombigbee, about 200 miles from Mobile.[43] She may have been Allie Beren—born about 1840—whose home in 1920 was Marengo, Jefferson County.[44] The other Africans alive in the 1920s and enumerated in the census were located far from the Tombigbee. What is apparent is that the group that got sold outside of Mobile was broken up into small units, with the largest probably no more than three or four people.

After the sale, Kanko and her companions—now Burns's property—were led to the available cabins on his plantation. Before this arrival, Burns had nineteen workers. He owned seven men and three women between the ages of fourteen and forty, and nine children ranging from one to fourteen. Only ten people were full hands, and three children were just old enough to help. The twenty Africans were needed and would soon be worked accordingly. The thirty-two men, women, and children Timothy Meaher had chosen for himself were moved to Grub Swamp, about three miles north of his Mobile plantation.[45] Because the U.S. marshal was still looking for the *Clotilda*'s people, Meaher did not want them on Telegraph Road yet. Nor did his brother James, who lived close by.

James's manpower was aging. Nine men were over forty, four of them sixty. There were only two children, one ten years old and the other twelve. The addition of the young men and women from the *Clotilda* was good business. When William Foster, slaveless until his trip, had complained that the people—including Abile—he received in payment for his trip were worth less than his scuttled ship, he was right from a purely financial standpoint, but if slavery had not come to an end less than five years later, he would have benefited handsomely from their labor and that of their children and grandchildren.

Once his group had settled in yet another swamp, Timothy told Noah to bring them something to eat. He and other men got hot meat and hoecakes (thin slices of cornmeal). When he saw the Africans, Noah was stunned: "Dey wuz wanderin' around lak crazy pussons—skeered at ebberyting: half naked."[46] They had reason to be afraid. They still did not know what was going to happen to them, and they might have thought the men were going to buy them in lots and separate them once again. Noah and his companions were enslaved, but the shipmates had no way of knowing it. Where they came from, people who looked like them also bought and sold captives. The meat and the hoecakes were useless. The food made them sick, and they did not eat. Noah remained with them in the swamp for four days, trying to feed them.

On the fifth day Meaher sent word that it was safe for them to move to Telegraph Road, or more exactly, it was now safe for *him* to have them there. They started their fourth transfer and finally reached Meaher's estate. Still half naked in their rags, with their country marks, tattoos, filed teeth, skinny bodies, and sick looks, they were a spectacle for everyone on the plantation. They must have felt unbearably humiliated at being gawked at by strangers, people with clothes, children who probably laughed. Their salvation could only come from a closed door. As evident in the Slave Schedules, the rule was to have at least five or six people share a cabin, so they were likely divided into four or five groups and led to their new homes. For more than three months they had lived in the bush, in a *barracoon*, on a ship, and in the swamps; and it must have felt good to finally have a roof, walls, and a bed. Grimy and miserable as they were, that night at least, the old slave cabins must have looked just fine.

Mary Meaher had given instructions to her seamstresses to make clothes for the newcomers. When they were ready, she called Noah, who remembered: "heer is enough shirts an' pants fer de men, an' enough dresses an' petticoasts fer de wimmen; take 'em to de quarters an' make dem heathen dress lak folks." Prior to their deportation, the Nupe, the Hausa, and the Dendi men had sported large blue or red robes richly embroidered on the front, over a collarless shirt in the same fabric and loose, baggy pants. The women had worn the same type of gown with a different opening at the neck over a wraparound skirt. Yoruba men dressed in baggy trousers, a sleeveless shirt, and a robe that went down to the knees; and women wore a wrap-around from above the breasts down to the ankles, which was kept in place with two narrower strips of cloth around the waist.[47] Discussions certainly went on in the cabins as to how to handle the white people's clothes. The men had seen how the sailors were dressed up close on the *Clotilda*, but for the women, things were a bit more complicated. There was nothing like petticoats and dresses in their usual wardrobe and only days before, on the plantation, they had had their first glimpse of European-dressed females. In the end, they did what they had to do and got dressed. When they ventured outside, they were expected: "Ole Miss seen 'em comin an' all de hands come out to see dat sight."[48]

Noah may have exaggerated what happened next, but in its general outline, his description of the first dressing up of newly arrived Africans in European clothes seems quite plausible and must have been repeated time and again on the plantations of the Americas. Noah's recollection of the episode made him laugh to tears, more than thirty years later.

> I'll 'clar fo' de Lawd, I didn't thunk dat close could get but on in de ongodly ways dat dose Affikins foun'. Dey had 'em on inside out, hind side befo', upside down, tail end fo' most, an' ebbery way dey could but de right way. De wimmen had dey dresses tied around 'em by de sleeves, an' dey skirts trailin' in de san' befo' an' behind. Some had de petticoats tied round de neck, an' one arm stuck out the placket hole. Udders had 'em on outside dey dresses, an' udders didn't have 'em on at all.

From the description, it seems that the women had actually not tried to dress as Americans, but rather to use the garments as they would have *pagnes*, wrapping them around their bodies. More than their ignorance, their efforts were revealing their attachment to their own dress. If Africans had wanted to dress like Europeans, they could have; they had had quite a few models on the African coast to inspire them. During the four centuries of the transatlantic slave trade, Europeans had exchanged millions of yards of textiles for captives, but African tailors and seamstresses did not turn them into Western trousers, shirts, and dresses. In fact, the white man's garb had often elicited laughter in Africa. The tight pants, in particular, were deemed indecent. What the men at Meaher's did with their trousers was even worse, according to Noah, than what the women had put their dresses through. "De fool creeters, ebbery one er dem, had stuck dey legs in de sleeves of de shirts, de cuffs buttoned round dey shins, an' de tail tied up round dey waises, an' hangin' down, floppin' in de breeze. Hit-hit war sho ridic' lous." It certainly was, but on the other hand, the "shirt pants" they had fashioned resembled the African pants, wide in the seat. So, unbeknownst to those who laughed at them, the Africans had not failed at emulating them but had tried to replicate their own dress traditions. First-generation Africans in the Americas never ceased, when they had the opportunity, to sport their own types of clothes. Some West African Muslims, for example, continued to wear the skullcaps, turbans, and baggy pants of their former lives as clerics or teachers. Their dress told their real story that of Muslim scholars, not the cane cutters or cotton pickers they had become.[49]

The clothes designed for the enslaved were ugly, rough, and meant to reinforce their low social position. However, it is doubtful that upon arrival Africans would have noticed. Whether refined or degrading, they simply did not like to wear European clothes. As Charley Barber, the son of an African deported to South Carolina, had observed, "Pappy care nothin' 'bout clothes."[50]

John Brown, the grandson of an African woman—who was sold to a planter in Talladega County, Alabama—remarked: "For a long time the natives didn't like the clothes and try to shake them off." He believed, repeating what he had heard, that it was because "Over there [in Africa] all the natives dressed naked."[51] He was wrong about the reason, but not about the fact that the Africans did not like the clothes they were forced to wear in the West. On Timothy Meaher's plantation, the clothes episode and the arrival in rags that preceded it led to the same kind of misunderstanding: the Americans believed the Africans had always lived naked, and the latter were indignant at the accusations.[52]

A stone's throw away, Cudjo and the men, women, and children who had become James Meaher's property were struggling too. The worst part for them was their accommodations. Their housing arrangements were hardly better than in the canebrake. James's house was built high above ground and the space between his floor and the brick-covered earth was where he had decided the Africans would live.[53] During their years of enslavement, whatever the weather, they slept under the house, exposed to the elements, in a place that other people reserved for their dogs or their poultry.

As THE AFRICANS WERE SETTLING DOWN in their new quarters among strangers, two events in the illegal slave trade saga unfolded on the same day, just one month after their arrival. On August 7, A. J. Requier, the U.S. attorney for the Southern District of Alabama, informed Judge Jones that "William Foster, master or commander of the Schooner Clotilda . . . wholly failed to report the arrival of the said schooner Clotilda to the Collector of the said port within the time prescribed by law."[54] Moreover, he had not provided information to be inserted in a manifest made under oath. For his infractions, he was fined $1,000. There was no word of the "one hundred and three negroes." The court was after Foster not because he was a pirate, but because he had not paid his dues on his cargo. What the cargo consisted of was not the issue. Naturally, the *Clotilda* was no longer there to tell the story of what exactly was transported in her holds; so the only charge that could stick was a minor one. According to the various indictments handed out, no one had transported the Africans to Mobile. They had just appeared and then vanished as miraculously as they had emerged.

That same day, a story that could have been the *Clotilda*'s, Foster's, and the Africans' started to unfurl. Thousands of miles from Mobile, Nathaniel Gordon, who like the Meahers was from Maine, began to load his 122-feet ship, the *Erie*, anchored on the Congo River, with 897 people destined for Cuba. He had promised his sailors "$1 per head of Negro" landing in Havana.[55] After leaving port the next day, the *Erie* was seized by the U.S. steamer *Mohican*. What the crew discovered on board were hundreds of people "so crowded when on the main deck that one could scarcely put his foot down without stepping on them. The stench from the hold was fearful, and the filth and dirt upon their persons indescribably offensive . . . running sores and coetaneous diseases of the most painful as well as contagious character infected the entire load."[56] It was international policy not to let the Africans found on slave ships go back where they had come from, even when the ship was seized in the harbor where they had just boarded, but to send them to Liberia or Sierra Leone, where control of the slave trade was supposedly more efficient. The Congolese of the *Erie* were dumped in Liberia fourteen days later, after thirty had died of dysentery and fevers. The ship then sailed to New York.

On October 3, Gordon and the mates were charged with piracy. It was not as serious as it seemed. Even the district attorney for the Southern District of New York thought he knew the outcome, "if they are tried and found not guilty, (which is highly probable) of piracy, or if they are found guilty, such an outside pressure would be brought to bear upon the President as would compel him to pardon him. In either case he would go scot-free."[57] With a president like James Buchanan little pressure would have been necessary. The pirate believed he had nothing to fear, and he refused to plead guilty to a lesser charge.

The Mobilians had their own rendezvous with the law. Judge William G. Jones had issued orders to have Burns Meaher and John M. Dabney appear at the next regular term of his court, the second Monday of December. For reasons that have remained obscure, the U.S. marshal only notified them on December 17, and he did so verbally. Then three days later, he informed the court, "The within named negroes [are] not found in my district." Since the Africans could not be found, no crime could be proved. On January 10, 1861, on motion of the U.S. attorney, *The United States vs. Burns Meaher*, and *The United States vs. John Dabney* were dismissed. Foster had been handed down his summons on October 28. Probably because there was money to be collected, and his case was easy to prove since it did not involve "unfound Negroes," an order was given on January 10 that *The United States vs. William Foster* be continued.[58] The very next day, Alabama broke away from the Union. The court and everybody else had other priorities. In the spring of 1861, Foster's case was thrown out of court. Timothy Meaher also had his day in court several months after his release on bail. He was cocky, confident that his bluff would not be called. He repeated the same story: he had made all the trips on his packet. His cooks and some of his passengers obligingly confirmed. The famous dinner, tardy but undeniable, was once again brought up. Judge Jones cleared him of all charges.

The story of the *Clotilda* had been all over the newspapers and its protagonists had become so famous that when William Foster wed his lodger's daughter, Adalaide Vanderslice, on September 6, 1860, they did it in Montgomery and decided to spend their honeymoon at Talladega Springs to avoid the curious. But Foster's fame had preceded him, and he was recognized everywhere they went.[59] He and Meaher had become heroes. The *Clotilda* was their glory.

Still, Timothy continued to deny sarcastically that he had played any role in the infamous incident, and a cleaned-up version that apparently nobody believed was served to those who asked. The story went that a number of Mobile men had pooled money to bring a boatload of Africans. They had paid a certain sum for the boat, and another for the cargo. Unfortunately for them, when the ship arrived, the collector at the port heard of it but, conveniently, the authorities were out of town, so the ship went upriver and disappeared. However, the story went, all was not lost. Timothy Meaher just happened to be in the vicinity of the ship full of Africans with his brother's steamer, the *Czar*. Soon after, he began to buy new land, and he had "fine Negroes," and he became rich, and finally, he was able to build the prize of his steamships, the *Southern Republic*. The planters grew suspicious, the tale went on, and asked him for their share of the Africans. Meaher said he had no idea what they were talking about, and if they wanted redress, then they could go to court. Of course, the men were not going to claim they had just brought in contraband and risk being hanged, so they kept quiet. But Meaher, out of the goodness of his heart, "gave them a few old niggers, and kept the rest of the cargo." The hero of the tall tale used to leer as he listened to it.[60]

Abile, Zuma, Kanko, Ossa, and their companions were enslaved, despairing, and out of sight. Even though their arrival was well-known and their owners had been prosecuted, there was little reason why this episode would have ended differently than the others. The more than four hundred Africans of the *Wanderer* had been seen on southern roads, trains, and ships; even the president had mentioned them in his message to Congress, but still they had remained enslaved. The fate of a small group of Africans was not going to matter more. Besides, James Buchanan had already said a year earlier that the international slave trade was completely under control. Because it had been a hot-button issue throughout his presidency, he had had to take some repressive measures. He had centralized enforcement of the act against piracy through the Department of the Interior and had increased the congressional appropriations to the navy, in charge of pursuing and seizing slavers. Nonetheless, Africans had landed on the American shores during his tenure; and in the previous three years, numerous articles all over the country had been devoted to the slave trade.

To gain firsthand knowledge, Buchanan had finally decided to send a secret agent to the South in September 1859. Benjamin F. Slocumb was charged to tour the area "with a view to obtaining correct information, in respect to the extent of importation of negroes direct from Africa." After a two-month journey through North Carolina, Georgia, Florida, Alabama, Mississippi, Louisiana, Texas, and Tennessee, he sent a fourteen-page report to Jacob Thompson, the secretary of the Interior. Everywhere he had gone, Slocumb stressed, he had heard rumors of recently arrived Africans, but "gentlemen of intelligence" had promptly refuted them. The Africans people talked about were in fact, he concluded, those of the *Wanderer*. "I am convinced," he wrote, "that if any negroes have been landed on our Southern coast since the landing of the Wanderer, there has been at most but *one* cargo, and it requires the exercise of a large credulity to believe that even *one* has been landed." In sum, he stated, Southerners were hostile to the reopening of the African slave trade, and all the sightings were attributable to the *Wanderer* "or else they were mere fabrications, manufactured and circulated for political effect, or to fill a column in a sensation[list] newspaper."[61] His report was embraced by the Buchanan administration. It confirmed the official version: the slave trade had stopped when the *Wanderer* had sailed into Jekyll Island, Georgia, and this irrefutable case of slave-smuggling was nothing more than an aberration.

When time came to reflect on the events of 1860, the president stuck to this line. On December 3, less than five months after the *Clotilda* had sailed in, he told Congress in his State of the Union Address, "It is with great satisfaction I communicate the fact that since the date of my last annual message not a single slave has been imported into the United States in violation of the laws prohibiting the African slave trade. This statement is founded upon a thorough examination and investigation of the subject. Indeed, the spirit which prevailed some time since among a portion of our fellow-citizens in favor of this trade seems to have entirely subsided."[62]

He was right about the subsiding of the revival sentiment, but he was wrong about the end of "importation" a year earlier. To the White House and Congress, Cudjo, Zuma, Oluale, Gumpa, Pollee, Adissa, Abile, Shamba, Kanko, Abache, and their one hundred companions did not exist.

CHAPTER FIVE

Slavery

T HEIR VERY EXISTENCE DISREGARDED by President James Buchanan, the men, women, and children of the *Clotilda* were hardly more acknowledged by their owners. They were not people with life stories, families, and personalities, but generic "slaves" who were expected to shed their identity and respond only to their assigned status, starting with new names. When they had first arrived and did not know what was going to happen, the shipmates had decided to be cautious. They thought it prudent not to disclose anything about themselves to hostile strangers. But their names said who they were: who they were named after, how they were born (feet first, for example), if they came after twins, if they were twins, if their mother died at birth, what people they belonged to, what religion they followed, or the day they were born, which meant something too.[1] In their homelands when people said their name, an important part of their identity was revealed. To be on the safe side, during their early days in Mobile, they did not call one another by their real names: they invented new ones, or used other people's names.[2] It was a precaution that made sense, in case someone was listening and was bent on doing something harmful with the information. Although no other instance has come to light, it is quite possible, and actually probable, that other Africans deported to the Americas did the same. It was a logical safety measure that others most likely took.

Then, when they were ready to use their real names again, their owners imposed new ones on them. To rename a person was not a simple matter of identification, but it was a symbolic severance from the past, from an identity other than that of a slave. Designed to annihilate people's own sense of self, culture, kinship, ethnic origin, and religion, it was an act that asserted the owners' total authority, including in the most intimate domain. Name-giving was the realm of the family. By naming the enslaved, the owners plainly established their dominion over them. Their substituting for the parents made painfully clear that the family had no value; children were not relatives but only individuals who depended entirely on the slaveholder and could be disposed of, without the consent or even knowledge of their parents. Enslaved parents did not passively accept this control and often gave nicknames, personal names, or "basket names" to their children. The practice was widespread among Africans on the Sea Islands.[3]

In nineteenth-century America, naming was increasingly done by enslaved parents themselves, but for the Africans, for obvious reasons, the imposition of a name by the owner continued to be the rule. In typical manner, the names the Africans received were in some cases the short versions of formal names. Kanko became Lottie; Omolabi was now Katie, and Abile was renamed Celia. Oluale answered to Charlie; Abache turned into Clara; Gumpa was Peter. A young boy, twelve, was called Bully by Timothy Meaher because he was stocky. With the exception of the latter, those were decent names, nothing like Jupiter, Napoleon, or Hercules, grandiose designations meant to make fun of their bearers. But it is quite apparent that not everyone got renamed. Augustine Meaher, Timothy's son, listed thirteen Africans in 1890 and used American names for some and "African" names for others. This would indicate that he had known them from the start under these names. It is probable that he would have used American names for all, if indeed they all had been renamed, and would not have bothered to inquire about or report their original names. The men and women whose African names he gave were Ausy (Ossa), Polee, Zuma, Jabez, and Cudjoe.[4] Did they insist on keeping them, not responding to whatever they were called? It is quite possible, as examples exist of other Africans who either refused to answer to their new names, or pretended to forget them.[5] To keep one's name was a defiant act, a refusal to surrender part of one's identity. But as owners' control and other factors influencing name-giving or retaining were dissimilar from one plantation to the next, or within one state during one period to the next, comparisons or generalizations cannot be made as to the profile of a Quashe as opposed to a Cupid. For example, African names were much more common in French and Spanish Louisiana than anywhere else.[6] In the colonial period in the Carolinas from 15 to 20 percent of the enslaved had kept African names.[7] Based on that kind of evidence, it would be senseless to assign a higher level of cultural resistance to the Africans there than, say, in New York or Florida.

In general, African names that were short and easy to pronounce had a better probability of surviving. It was not by chance that the (Akan) name (which also became a surname) that was still used by hundreds in the nineteenth century was Cuffee (Kofi), which sounded just like coffee, and not Abubakar. Even some people who had no Akan ancestry bore the name. Paul Cuffee, the famous seaman and abolitionist, was one of them. His father, Saïd Kufa, a Muslim, was renamed Sam Cuffee—by analogy with his real name—by his friend McKinnon Paige.[8] Thus, somebody named Arzuma stood a better chance of keeping her name. Not only was it short, but it was also similar to an English name, a pattern that has been verified with other surviving African names that sounded like European names.[9] Arzuma or Zuma was a West African Muslim name, but the latter also existed in the United States, although it was very rare: the 1870 census only recorded thirteen women who were going by that name. All but two were white, and four—the largest concentration—were born in Alabama. African Muslim Zuma could keep the name her parents had given her not only because it was short and easy, but also because a few white Christian women shared it. The "short and easy" criterion for retention was evident in Mobile, where some of the Africans who did not keep their original names went by Ojo Facha and Ogubiyi.

Cudjo's naming was peculiar and did not belong to the common patterns. His owner, James, had tried to say his name, Kossola, but when he could not get it right, Cudjo asked him, "Well, I yo' property?" Upon Meaher's affirmative answer, he continued, "You call me Cudjo."[10] So Kossola named himself, but why did he choose Cudjo? To the Ewe of Togo and the Fon of Benin, among others, Kodjo is the name given to boys born on Monday. Like other Ewe day-names it is well known in Banté because the Isha's migrations took them from modern Nigeria to Pechi Togo and back east to Benin. Even today, some Isha still carry Ewe first names. It is thus not surprising that Kossola would have offered Kodjo as a short, easy alternative to his real first name. The story also illustrates how at that time, but not before, Cudjo considered himself someone's property.

AFTER SEVERAL DAYS ON THE PLANTATIONS, during which their owners hoped they would start to adapt to their new condition, the shipmates were as inconsolable as ever. The Meahers decided they should start working and instructed their American companions to show them how. Far from being depressed by this tangible expression of their exploitation, they were elated. For the first time since they had arrived, something positive had happened. They had spent countless days confined on the *Clotilda* or moved from one place to the other with nothing to do but worry. Work broke the monotony; but some had another reason to be pleased. They no longer had to wonder why they had been brought there in the first place: they were going to work in the fields and it was reassuring, considering the alternatives. The young farmers, who used to till the soil with their hoes, were surprised at one particular agricultural technique. "We astonish to see the mule behind the plow to pull." They were also taken aback at the amount of work it took to grow anything, compared to how things grew in their homelands. They were good at raising cotton, corn, cane, beans, pumpkins, peas, and other vegetables, and once free, they would put their skills to great use. They could also ably perform different tasks that did not require machines, which was understandable since they had not grown up using them.[11]

They had been glad to start working, but they soon reconsidered when they realized that work as a slave in America was terribly demanding, relentless, and brutal. It was hard, they complained, because they had never been used to work that much and in that way.[12] The amount of work was an issue as was, for some, the type of work. Whatever they had learned to do in their previous life was of no use in Alabama and of no interest to their owners. Scholars have focused with good reason on the transfer of technology from Africa to the Americas, but the slave trade was nonetheless an immense waste in African skills, especially in the nineteenth century. In the seventeenth and eighteenth centuries, when the colonists—ignorant of tropical crops—needed workers versed in rice or indigo culture, they knew where to go in West Africa to find them. When they needed cattle herders, they brought in the Fulani from the Senegambian savannas, the men who introduced open grazing to North America.[13] But as time went by, the people born in America acquired the necessary competence, and the Africans' expertise was no longer crucial. They could be used at any task. And as had been true all along, the jewelers, the embroiderers, and the weavers—male occupations in West Africa—whose talents were completely irrelevant in the Western slave world, raised hogs, rolled tobacco, or pressed cane. The fishermen and the potters picked cotton, the long-distance traders planted rice, the herders and the market women cut cane, and the farmers worked on steamships. As for the judges in customary or Islamic law, the notables, or the Qur'anic teachers, they were, tellingly, nothing more than "hands."

BECAUSE THE MEAHERS' BUSINESSES were diversified, not everyone worked on the plantations growing cotton or corn, or in the Big House cleaning, sweeping, washing, ironing, and sewing. Like several other African men, Cudjo, the young farmer who had never seen the ocean before his enforced trip to America, was assigned to work on a steamer. The river world into which he was thrust was the territory of rough, hard men who drank, boasted, and fought. It was a long way from the quiet, predictable life of rural West Africa. On Southern rivers, steamboats always had white crews, and twenty to thirty-five enslaved deckhands. These stevedores, rollodores (those who rolled the bales down the "slideways" to the stevedores), roustabouts, stockers, firemen, cooks, stewards, and domestics were either owned by the captain or were hired hands whose salaries of about $40 were paid directly to their owners. These men were the lifelines of the Alabama cotton kingdom. They were the ones moving the white gold that produced huge amounts of money for the state, for men like the Meaher brothers, and for Northern industrialists. In 1860, the stevedores and the rollodores had loaded and unloaded 540,000 bales. They had mightily contributed to the $45 million that cotton had brought the South that year.[14]

As the shipmates soon discovered, many were their tasks. About 285 landings dotted the Alabama River's 403 miles between Mobile and Montgomery; some just a few planks next to a plantation, others real warehouses—sometimes a hundred feet long and a few stories high—from which the cotton bales were loaded onto the steamers. At the landings on their route, the firemen walked up the levees and carried back to the boat several logs up to five feet long. They could bring forty cords of wood at a single landing, and after this grueling task, they had to feed the engine in unbearable heat, and later haul away the ashes and clean the boilers. Like all deck hands, when they were not lugging logs, the Africans carried hooks to better take hold of the bales that the men on the shore slid down long steep planes that reached the edge of the water. At night, when it was pitch black, they worked to the light of pine-torches that other men carried high above their heads, and they ran and hurried through, just like in daylight, if they did not want to be whipped.[15] When the steamer was full, the cotton reached up to the second deck, a solid wall of bales one upon the other, extending all around the boat. There was no railing in the part of the ship where the men worked: the lower deck was open so that the bales could be loaded easily. They had to be careful; a missed step and they would tumble into the water. Besides the cotton, they also had to load and unload dry goods, molasses, cottonseeds, hogs, and mules. The overseer, whip in hand, screamed at them to hurry up and lashed those who did not run fast enough for his taste or did not take on a heavy enough load.[16]

Their workday was punctuated by the bell alerting them of yet another landing and another loading. On top of the loud bells, the steam pianos or calliopes belched out tunes like *Irish Washerwoman* and *Bold Soldier Boy*. On Timothy's *Southern Republic*, where some Africans worked, the calliope, appropriately, played *Dixie*. Every deckhand had heard the joke that was the delight of the steamboat captains: when the first calliope played on the Alabama River, "the negroes thought the world was coming to an end and commenced to run, and some say they are running yet."[17] The men slept when they could, mostly on the floor or the rough fabric that covered the cotton bales. But just above their heads, in the confined perimeter of the ship, a good life was going on. The upper decks had beautiful cabins, bars, a dance floor, a band, and gaming tables. There were soft white sheets, and good food. The laborers and the travelers lived in parallel universes, each one examining the other. One observer noted about the deckhands, "Placed in positions the most favorable to witness the pleasures enjoyed by others, the tendency is only to augment their own wretchedness."[18]

Work on the steamers was not only grueling, but it could also be lethal. Several ships had been destroyed by fire. In 1850, the *Orline St. John* had completely burned. The captain was Timothy Meaher, and his first mate was Burns. They wanted to reach Montgomery on time for their passengers to meet the train, and Timothy had told his men to fire up the engine. But they had also loaded large quantities of lightwood, and the heat of the furnace made the resin bleed. The ship was a matchbox. Soon she was in flames. Thirty-nine people died, including all the women and children on board. Abram, a black deckhand, had rescued nine passengers. The ship was insured for $16,000, which came in handy and was invested in the brothers' shipbuilding business. It was said that to the bottom of the river went gold from California—$250,000 worth, according to some; $15,000 plus gold dust, according to others—and rumor had it that someone, perhaps Timothy Meaher, brought in Caribbean divers a few months later. The treasure was recovered, it was believed, and it is possible that Meaher used his passengers' property to expand his fortune.[19]

Since the story of the *Clotilda* had been all over town and far beyond, Meaher's passengers were often curious about the men who worked on his ships and looked like they had come from a faraway place. The captain had a ready routine. He feigned indignation:

"Wall now! You think them niggers I've aboard came from Africa! I'll show you. Jist come up here, Bully!"

"What's your name, sir?"

"My name Bully."

"Where were you born?"

"Me born Sout Karliner, sar!"

"There, you see he wasn't taken from Africa. I've a lot of these black South Caroliny niggers aboard, haven't I, Bully?"

"Yas, sar."

"Are you happy, Bully?"

"Yas, sar."

"Show how you're happy."

The boy rubbed his stomach and said,

"Yummy! Yummy! Plenty belly full."

"That's what I call a real happy feelosophical chap. I guess you've got a lot in your country can't pat *their* stomachs and say 'yummy, yummy, plenty belly full!'"

"Where did he get those marks on his face?"

"Oh, them? Wall, it's a way them nigger women has of marking their children to know them; isn't it, Bully?"

"Yas, sar! Me 'spose so!"

"And on his chest?"

"Wall, r'ally I do b'l 'eve them's marks agin the smallpox."

"Why are his teeth filed?"

"Ah, there now! You'd never have guessed it; Bully done that himself, for the greater ease of biting his vittels."[20]

This ugly episode on the *Southern Republic* that debased Bully, "a boy of some twelve years of age, stout, fat, nearly naked," and perhaps from the Atakora, given his filed teeth, took place in May 1861, less than a year after he and his companions had arrived in Mobile, and it was undoubtedly repeated during the four years left of his captivity. The thorough humiliation of the young boy, the mockery of his appearance—starting with his nickname—and of his people's customs, as well as his forced participation in his own degradation are revealing of the psychological torment enslaved people had to endure. Scholarship on slavery has insisted, with good reason, on the physical violence intrinsic to the institution, the beatings, the whippings, the rapes, the brandings, the mutilations, and the killings. But the viciousness of the slaveholders was also expressed in other ways. Physical and mental humiliation was used as a means of psychological control. The mortification of being auctioned off, half-naked, body poked; the shame of having to undress in front of everyone before a whipping as if the lashing were not enough—there were countless ways in which men, women, and children were debased on a daily basis. Sallie Crane of Arkansas recalled, "We was cussed for so many bitches and sons of bitches and bloody bitches, and blood of bitches. We never heard our names scarcely at all."[21] Humiliation was an integral part of the process of enslavement to try to kill off any sense of self-worth in its victims. It left many people emotionally scarred.

IT CAN BE ARGUED THAT AFRICANS were better armed than many of their American-born companions, including their own children, to resist the onslaught. They had grown up not knowing racism; their appearance, culture, and education had been objects of pride, not shame. As a close observer stated, even though enslaved, the Africans "are proud, arrogant and disdainful, and they have such a good opinion of themselves that they think they are as good as or better than the masters they serve."[22] Men and women who thought highly of themselves and little of the whites, despite their circumstances, were probably less likely to be crippled by humiliation. Rather than being ashamed, they might have been exceedingly angry. Remarks by Charles Ball, who was born in the United States and had an African grandfather, would support that view:

> The native Africans are revengeful, and unforgiving in their tempers, easily provoked, and cruel in their designs. . . . They feel indignant at the servitude that is imposed upon them and only want power to inflict the most cruel retribution upon their oppressors, but they desire only the means of subsistence, and temporary gratification in this country, during their abode here.[23]

Sir William Howard Russell, the London *Times* war correspondent who related the "South Carolina" incident on the *Southern Republic*, noted that Bully was half-naked, and this was certainly more than a figure of speech. Granted it was hot, and firemen and roustabouts ran and sweated, but whether they were hired from other owners or worked for their own boss, it was public knowledge that black men on the steamships were badly clothed.[24] In addition, it was not unusual for adolescents everywhere in the slave states to be left half or completely naked. Mattie Curtis of North Carolina recalled, "I went as naked as yo' han' till I was fourteen years old. I wus naked like dat when my nature come to me."[25] There again, nakedness that was supposed to have the Africans' favor was deliberately or through negligence and contempt imposed on black people by the same slaveholders who presented themselves as the ones charged with "civilizing" them.

Once Meaher had had his fun with Bully, he acknowledged that many of his men had indeed come from Africa and explained it in political terms: "We're obleeged to let 'em in some times to keep up the balance agin the niggers you run into Canaydy [Canada]." He then went on about how miserable they had been in their native land and how happy they were now. To drive the point home, a dance was organized on the lower deck, amid wood fagots, barrels, and cotton bales. The men were forced to perform for an audience of sneering passengers. Meaher concluded, "Yes, sir, jist look at them, how they're enjoying it; they're the happiest people on the face of the airth."[26] Black men also danced on the riverboats for themselves, without being forced, but white passengers often watched, did not understand what they were seeing, and made or published disparaging comments. That night, for example, Russell wrote in his diary,

> There was a fiddler, and also a banjo-player, who played uncouth music to the clumsiest of dances, which it would be insulting to compare to the worst Irish jig; and the men with immense gravity and great effusion of *sudor*, shuffled and cut and heeled and buckled to each other with an overwhelming solemnity, till the rum-bottle warmed them up to the lighter graces of the dance, when they became quite overpowering.[27]

Another traveler on the Alabama River, the English educator and feminist Barbara Bodichon, confided similar thoughts to her own diary: "Last night the negro sailors danced while one played on the violin. It was the drollest sight in the world. They enjoyed it so intensely and moved with such extraordinary agility—so fast and then so slow, now all on their heels then all on their toes."[28]

What Meaher, Russell, Bodichon, and their fellow captains and passengers thought they were witnessing were happy, clumsy fellows having fun. But Russell's surprised remark that the men were grave and solemn, and Bodichon's that they were intense, should have given them a hint. The Africans expressed their lives, their pleasure just as much as their misery. Dancing has never been just entertainment in Africa, where people accompany every event, including the most dreadful, with dance and music. Dance is life, and like life, it is joy and pain. What the passengers observed on the steamboats were Africans and African Americans who had regained possession of their bodies. They used them to express themselves openly, something they were forbidden to do in any other manner and circumstance; and they externalized their feelings, including anger, contempt, and derision for the spectators in ways that were not decipherable by outsiders. Dancing was serious business, contrary to what the onlookers believed; it signified independence, a flaunting of the rules of slavery. As they danced, they could poke fun at the audience, for example, with exaggerated, stiff "white moves."

Roustabouts and firemen, rollodores and stevedores also sang constantly. "A silent slave," noted Frederick Douglass, "is not liked by masters or over-seers," and men and women were expected to sing as they worked. But the slavers' coercion, designed to locate the workers, keep them lively, and make them seem happy, was not in contradiction with African customs. Because sing-ing in Africa is not linked to happiness—as witnessed on the slave ships—it could fit any mood the workers/singers were in, a crucial element lost on white society. "The remark is not unfrequently made, that slaves are the most con-tented and happy laborers in the world," Douglass remarked, but, he corrected, "The songs of the slave represent the sorrows, rather than the joys, of his heart; and he is relieved by them, only as an aching heart is relieved by its tears."[29] In step with Douglass, Martin Robison Delany, the Harvard-educated physician, army major, abolitionist, and Black Nationalist (whose grandparents were Yoruba and Mandinka), noted that the black river men sang their pain, "Fas-tened by the unyielding links of the iron cable of despotism, reconciling them-selves to a lifelong misery, they are seemingly contented by soothing their sorrows with songs and sentiments of apparently cheerful but in reality wailing lamentations."[30]

FAR FROM THE STEAMBOATS and their danger, the other *Clotilda* Africans had settled into the dreadful routine of bondage as field hands. And Cudjo pointed out, the women too worked in the fields.[31] As nineteenth-century evidence has shown, women did not routinely participate in agricultural work in Yoruba societies. In the 1850s, the missionary Thomas Bowen noted, "It is worthy of particular remark that women never cultivate the soil as they do in guinea." William Clarke, who also observed Yoruba communities in the 1850s, com-mented, "So strong is the aversion of the native mind to this kind of female servitude that I have yet to see the first instance of a woman engaged hoe in hand, in cultivating the soil."[32] Even though there were exceptions, the general trend was for women to be involved in trade, not agriculture. British authori-ties attributed this particularly to the fear of kidnapping by slavers.[33] However, this danger was also present in the rest of West and Central Africa, where women still went to the fields, armed and in groups. According to Robin Law, Yoruba women did cultivate at one time, but withdrew from the fields with the development of palm oil in the nineteenth century.[34] Their skills in the pro-duction, transport, and trade of the product were considered more useful. What-ever the cause, the situation has hardly changed, and today it is still less frequent for Yoruba women to be seen in the fields than for women of other cultures. Thus, to the Yoruba women in Mobile—and elsewhere in the Americas—work in the fields was an anomaly. But not only to them: Dendi women did not cultivate either, nor did the Nupe and the Igala. Like the Yoruba, their main occupations consisted in processing agricultural products and selling them. The women in Atakora participated in some agricultural activities, but their main occupations were fetching water and wood, pounding and hulling cereals, cooking, and in the dry season, fishing and making decorative objects and pottery.[35] Thus, as Cudjo's remark implied, the assignment of the girls and women to the fields could only come as a shock to all. Not only were the women ignorant of the work they were required to perform, but their skills as artisans and traders had no value at all in their new world.

Kanko did not follow her companions to the fields. She was sent to Burns's Big House to help the domestics cook, clean, and garden.[36] Perhaps she was awed the first time she passed the back door. But Africans had the reputation of not being impressed with slaveholders' worldly goods. As Charles Ball had noticed, they "generally place[d] little, or even no value, upon the fine houses and superb furniture of their masters."[37] Burns Meaher's interior may have looked rich and commanding to himself and his peers, but to Africans it likely was just another silly sight, like men in tight pants and women's tiny waists.

In addition to the workload itself, domestic work was stressful: the risk of making a mistake, of breaking something, of missing a spot, and being harshly punished for it was always present. The pressure of working under the boss's nose was often unbearable, as Lewis Clarke, a former domestic, explained: "There were four house-slaves in this family, including myself, and though we had not, in all respects, so hard work as the field hands, yet in many things our condition was much worse. We were constantly exposed to the whims and passions of every member of the family; from the least to the greatest their anger was wreaked upon us." Some people, runaways or WPA interviewees, thought that fieldwork was indeed preferable because it got them or their parents out from under the sometimes sadistic scrutiny of their owners and allowed some free time once the task was done, in contrast to domestic labor that never ended.[38] For African women, like Kanko, who had no experience of the kind of work required in an American mansion and were used to spending their days outside—preparing food, cooking, washing dishes, and ironing are outdoor activities in Africa—there is reason to believe that being sent to the Big House was more of a hardship than working in the fields. Not only was the work incessant, closely supervised, and confined, but it was also isolating. Restricted to the house, they were kept away from their companions. This seclusion, decried by some native-born, was likely to have been a particularly heavy burden on the Africans.

Contrary to Kanko, the people who had been sent to the fields had little contact with the Meahers, but they had to endure their overseers and drivers, especially on Burns's and Timothy's plantations. The brothers were brutal enslavers, who from the shipmates' general accord, worked their people hard and had no problem with the overseers knocking them down and beating them up. But as two incidents revealed, the Africans did not take rough treatment well. One day, as everyone was working in the fields, Burns's overseer tried to whip an African woman. Perhaps she had not understood what was expected of her, or maybe she had been slow, not deferent enough, or she had taken a break when she should not have. As was his prerogative, and indeed his job, the man walked up to her, wielding his lash. Suddenly, tools fell down, words flew, and shipmates ran. They jumped on him, grabbed his whip, and lashed him. That was his last attempt, according to the shipmates, at whipping an African woman.[39]

It sounds like a great story of resistance, or a self-serving invention. However, the Africans themselves are not the only source of information on their collective acts of resistance, and the people at Burns's were not the only ones involved in defiance. Noah, who lived and worked with the group that belonged to Timothy, asserted that they too did not accept brutality from anyone, and everybody knew it. "Dey wuz powerful easy critters," he said, "didn't lak no roughnes' an' shoutin', an' I tel you—dey wouldn't stand a lick fum white or black."[40] If what happened in Burns's fields had shown the limits of the overseer's power over the Africans, things were not going any smoother at Timothy's Big House. Mary Meaher had taken a fancy to one of the girls. She was pretty, and had a beautiful smile with shiny teeth. Mary wanted her to be a domestic and had asked the hired cook, Polly, to start her training. On that memorable day, Polly was showing the girl how to sweep and dust, but it did not go quite as she had anticipated. She grew impatient at the girl's clumsiness and slapped her over the head. The girl put her hand to her face and, according to Noah, looked like she had gone crazy. Polly, taken aback, proceeded toward the door when the girl started to yell:

> Nebber in all my life I hear er soun' lak dat gal made. Hit sounded lak de bawl uv er calf, only mo' screechin'—somethin' lak de squall uv er wild cat in the darknes'. . . . Hit ain't soun' so awful lond; but ebbery Affikin on dat plantation heered it, an' dey come er runnin'. Fum de cotton-fields, de crick, de cane-fields, an' way down to de rice fields at de foot of de hill dey come— totin' rakes, an' spades, an' sticks, an' callin' out a cuyus little soun' what sounded ez ungodly as de screech of de gal herself. When Polly seen 'em comin', she tear up stairs to ole Miss' room, howlin' an' cryin' to de Lawd to pertect her fum de heatherns. An' here come de Affikins atter her, beatin' on de do' an' lookin' so terrible dat I sho' thought dey wuz gwine to kill eve'body.[41]

Mary Meaher finally opened the door and acted "sweet and proud," and Noah tried to defuse the situation by reasoning with the group, even though they did not understand one another. The cook left her job and never came back, "an' nobody didn't touch one er dem Affikins no more."

It is interesting to note what Noah had witnessed and reported with some surprise: the fact that even though the girl's scream was not particularly loud, every African, even down the hill in the rice fields, had heard it. It was of course not possible, but someone had indeed heard the scream, and the signal of distress had been relayed by means of other shouts throughout the fields. People in Benin and other areas of West Africa communicate this way over distances with special screams or codes that pinpoint the nature of the danger or can signal that a person is the victim of an unspecified threat and that everyone must immediately come to the rescue.

Another episode that showed how the shipmates were willing to stand up to authority and were unafraid of the consequences involved one man, Sakarago, who had had a quarrel with a white man. He told him, "you killee me, me no care, me tellee Fositer."[42] These incidents and their consequences, or lack thereof, are quite intriguing. In the first one, a white man had been whipped. In the second, slaves had stormed through a mansion, where they should never have gone in the first place, and beat menacingly on a white woman's bedroom door with tools that could turn into weapons. In the third, a black man had defied a white man, to his face, and told him he was going to denounce him. In these cases, according to all evidence, they were not punished. At the time in Mobile, most blacks convicted of assaulting whites received twenty-five lashes for two days.[43] During the war, people resisted more openly. Some refused to get whipped, or made threats, but it is evident that the events in question took place not long after the Africans' arrival, when they hardly or did not speak English at all and new tasks were being assigned to them.[44] Could it be that they benefited from some indulgence because of their ignorance of the system? It seems doubtful. This kind of attitude would normally have been nipped in the bud so that it would not surface again.

What may help explain this unusual outcome to the flagrant flaunting of slavery's most basic conventions is a combination of specific factors. The Africans presented a strong, unified front and clearly showed their determination to use violence to defend themselves. More often on the plantations, individuals resisted, even to the point of killing overseers or owners, but, short of a revolt, people as a group generally did not overtly challenge authority, especially with violence. The "largely non-collective pattern of resistance" of the enslaved population that has been observed in the United States may help explain why the response to the Africans' collective action did not meet with the normal brutal result.[45] It represented a novel situation: they formed a large, solid group that could be expected to retaliate in a violent way, since they had not been afraid of attacking the authority in order to protect one of their own in the first place. Moreover, it is probable that their very Africanity played in their favor. To their owners, they were "heathens," savages, most likely cannibals, whose reactions one could not predict and should fear. Finally, it had been noted that in normal circumstances they "went along jis' as peaceful as lambs." They were "powerful easy critters," but if threatened or screamed at they became redoubtable. As Noah pointed out, once this was understood—and given their numbers and unity—it was decided that it was better for everyone to leave them alone. Frederick Douglass, who knew something about whippings and resistance, said succinctly, but expressively, "He is whipped oftenest, who is whipped easiest."[46]

EVEN IF THEIR UNITY COULD SHIELD THEM from the worst abuses, there was no escaping the absolute destitution of their new lives. Living under James's house, Cudjo and his companions, used as they were to temperatures that hardly dropped below seventy-five degrees in the Bight of Benin, were shivering in their beds in the chilly winter nights that reached the lower forties. They never received enough blankets, and suffered much from the cold. They had shoes when they needed them, though, and Cudjo was grateful to James for it. His appreciation, which still surfaced decades after he had become free again, is a testimony to the material hardships that his companions—and other enslaved people—endured. Shoes were one critical standard by which they measured their quality of life and the "decency" of their owner. Partly because of his steady provision of rough, blistering galoshes, Cudjo considered James a "good man," despite the fact that he too made his laborers work very hard. The Africans at Burns's, ferociously exploited, received only one pair of shoes in five years and were still angry at the recollection half a century later. There again, shoes were used as an indicator of how deprived people were and how pitiless owners could be. Burns's harshness was experienced in other ways. In the fields before daybreak, the workers were driven hard all day long, and only got back home at night by guiding themselves by torch lights.[47]

Poor living conditions and overwork were difficult to bear but it is the extreme, previously unimaginable denial of freedom that most deeply afflicted Cudjo, Zuma, Pollee, and their shipmates. "In night time we cry, we say we born and raised to be free people and now we slave," Cudjo said.[48] This feeling of irremediable loss was so agonizing that it made grown men cry, something that Africans—for whom self-control and concealment of inner feelings learned during initiation are paramount—are generally quite reluctant to do. The death of freedom was a most dramatic event for deported Africans. And it was, indeed, an event. Contrary to people who had been enslaved from birth, they had been deprived of their freedom on a specific day. There was a before and an after, and the chain of events could be retraced starting with a traumatic episode.

As can be construed from other Africans' experience and that of the men and women in Mobile, it is apparent that the deportees went through several stages as they confronted their new reality. The first sentiment as they reached the Americas could only be of relief to leave the absolute horror of the slave ship. Enslavement that had not yet begun could only seem secondary. But this reprieve was quickly followed by the heartbreak of separation from shipmates. The relief of being put to work, as expressed by the people in Mobile, cannot be discounted, even if today, knowing what slave labor was like, this notion may seem outrageous. It was a relief from the unknown, the relief—for the youngsters—of working instead of being killed. However, what followed was the demoralizing realization that the work was back-breakingly difficult and never-ending. And to top it all, they were acutely aware that all of their free-doms were gone.

Nothing could have prepared them for the kind of enslavement they were experiencing. Even the minority among them who had already been enslaved before their deportation could not have figured it out. Growing up, the people who lived in societies where bondage existed had seen captives work as porters, soldiers, palace guards, artisans, domestics, concubines, and, mostly, as agri-cultural laborers, who either lived with their owner's family and worked partly for them and partly for themselves, or were settled in slave villages to work as sharecroppers. In African societies that practiced slavery, the selling of captives born in the family was unacceptable, even shameful, and only those who had been bought could be sold. Household captives became artificial kin of lowly stature. There was a social stigma attached to slavery, but not an ethnic or racial one, so that when a slave became free, he or she would be absorbed into the community. The rule was more or less adhered to but in many societies, including in Dahomey, it was disgraceful to remind a freed person of his or her former status. Among the elite slaves, some achieved power and wealth be-cause, as kinless people, they had the rulers' confidence. A few monarchs were the sons of enslaved concubines or former slaves themselves, but the condition of their birth had carried no negative consequences for their future.[49] In Dahomey, the mother of a future king had to be either a commoner or a slave because it was believed that the monarch would thus be more in tune with all strata of society. Women of slave origin could become very wealthy and rise to high positions serving as ministers of state, counselors, commanders, gover-nors of provinces, and trading agents. There is no reason to glamorize African slavery—especially in Dahomey, where captives were the choice victims of human sacrifices—but it is also true that enslaved people in Africa were often treated like European serfs.[50]

But on the other side of the ocean, work was harder, control tighter, pun-ishments cruel, and manumission rare. There was no possibility for high of-fice, children born in the family could be sold away, and the offspring of free men remained enslaved. American bondage and post-manumission status were so rigidly codified that each state had found it necessary to publish and regu-larly update voluminous slave codes that deprived the enslaved of every shred of independence, and the freed from most rights. The Alabama code of 1852 under which the Africans lived devoted fifteen pages and eighty-three sections exclusively to slavery and detailed all the restrictions that constrained the bondpeople's lives. Keeping a dog, for example, meant "twenty stripes on [the] bare back."[51] Unaware as they were of the extent of fundamental and trivial restrictions placed on enslaved Americans, only with time could the Africans even comprehend the extent of their loss of freedom. When Cudjo said he and his friends cried because they were slaves, the concept means more than just being enslaved, it means to be a victim of that particular type of enslavement.

When that consciousness sank in, the emotional upheaval was tremendous and long lasting. Toby Jones of Texas confided about his parents, "They was captured in Africa and brought to this country whilst they was still young folks, and my father was purty hard to realize he was a slave, 'cause he done what he wanted back in Africa." This applied not only to his folks; the other Africans on the plantation where he grew up had the same problem. On Saturdays, they "would talk 'bout when they lived in Africa and done what they wanted." Another of the Africans' grandchildren, Luke D. Dixon, knew how "it was hard on the Africans to be treated like cattle." Ellis Jefson of Arkansas had a "full blood African" father who "still held a wild animal instinct up in Virginia; they couldn't keep him out of the woods. He would spend two or three days back in there." Jake Terriell, born in South Carolina, was the son of two Africans; his father "was de wild man and he so wild Massa Felix have to keep him locked up at night and in chains by day to keep him from runnin' off."[52] In Jefson's and Terriell's mind, their fathers running away was clearly linked to their being Africans: they equated the men's refusal of bondage and longing to get their freedom back with "wildness," the state that Africans were supposed to have lived in prior to their capture.

What they said about the Africans' sense of loss shows that their children and grandchildren understood their predicament, but did the others? One would assume that the Africans' distinction, as articulated by Cudjo and his friends, between their birthright to freedom and the Americans' enslavement that they took for granted would be judged arrogant and hurtful by people who had never been free. Those perceived differences, if they came to be expressed by the Africans when they finally mastered some English, would likely have elicited a hostile reaction from the native-born. They, in turn, had their own preconceptions about Africans. By the time the shipmates had arrived, few Africans lived on the plantations. However, there were perhaps as many as 10,000 people in the country whose parents (one or both) had been born in Africa, and tens of thousands more whose grandparents had come from the continent. In Alabama, at least a thousand individuals had African parents in the period from 1870 to 1880, but they represented only 0.2 percent of the black population.[53] Moreover, having parents and grandparents who had grown up in Africa did not mean that people knew anything about them as Africans or had any inkling about their cultures, as some of the WPA interviews reveal. Jessie A. Butler of Charleston, South Carolina, thought, "dem heathen didn't have no religion." John Brown said his grandmother was "a savage in Africa—a slave in America." Eliza Evans of Oklahoma believed her great-grandparents ate babies. Chaney Mack said his father—who came from Liberia—had told him "ef dey got too hungry, dey would jest as soon kill each other and eat 'em." Mary Johnson had grown up near a place where "dey brung de Africy people to tame 'em." It was done, she explained, by the whip or the preacher, but "Dey didn' 'low de preacher in de pen by hisse'f, 'cause dey say at times dem preachers don' come back. Some dem wile Africy people done kill 'em and eat 'em."[54]

What some African Americans expressed about the Africans mirrored exactly what the whites were saying, writing, and publishing. From James De Bow to James Buchanan, the message had been hammered home time and again. It had made its way to the quarters. Even some children and grandchildren of Africans believed it. According to Tony Cox, "If we hadn't been brung over an' made slaves, us an' us chillun dat is being educated an' civilized would be naked savages back in Africa, now."[55] What's more, they stated that their own African relatives had told them about nakedness, cannibalism, and paganism. Africans had no reason to think and proclaim that they were savages, pagans, and cannibals. On the contrary, evidence shows that they thought highly of themselves, their cultures, and their homelands. But the Africans' progeny and others had some concrete basis to believe the propaganda. Africans did arrive naked and were sometimes paraded in that state in the streets, as John Brown's grandmother had been. Mary Johnson described them upon arrival as having "hair all over 'em, jis' like a dog, and wo' big hammer rings in dey noses. Dey didn' wo' no clothes." Thus, what the native-born saw or thought they saw of the Africans did seem to confirm what they were told. Still, most were probably not duped and those who wanted to find out did. Ella, from South Carolina, learned from her grandmother that in her homeland the "gals puts on aperns an' shawls roun' dey shoulders an' over dey breasts."[56]

THE SOCIAL ORDER OF THE PLANTATIONS may also have played a role in the Africans' cool reception. Referring to the stratification among the enslaved population, Rosa Starke of South Carolina stated that there were only two classes of white folk, "buckra [white] slave owners and poor whites folks dat didn't own no slaves," but she detailed six classes of enslaved laborers: two ranks of house slaves with butlers, nurses, and chambermaids at the top, and carpenters, carriage drivers, and barbers below them. Artisans came in third, people working with the animals were fourth, millers and cotton gin feeders were fifth, and the "common field niggers" were last.[57] Most Africans who arrived during the illegal slave trade were employed as laborers in the cotton fields of the Gulf States— although at least two of the *Clotilda*'s women worked as domestics—and were thus, one could argue, looked down upon by their American companions. But the vast majority of native-born themselves, more than 75 percent, were field hands, and the formation of social classes was only possible on large estates. Wherever the Africans arrived, in Mobile or Matagorda, they were surrounded by the "common field niggers" and worked side by side with them. The latter could have viewed them as the lower echelon of the labor force, but not as another social "class."

On Timothy Meaher's plantation, the "American niggers," as they called themselves, had been observing their new neighbors carefully. "Dey wuzn't lak us 'Merican niggers at all. Dey wuz mo' blacker an' straighter an' bigger dan us; an' somehow dey seem mo' fiercer, although dey never did fool wid us nor squabble 'mongst deyselves," Noah said. William Davis, whose father came from the Congo, made a point of confiding that he "walk straighter'n anybody I ever seen."[58] The Americans were good observers: Africans do walk very straight, one reason being they carry loads on their heads and keep that posture even when they do not transport anything. The straightness of posture is often interpreted in the West as self-confidence, which can also be perceived as arrogance and potential menace. The Americans may have construed the Africans' straightness for attempts at intimidation. The fierceness Noah and his companions noticed also seemed to have been accurate. Cudjo, the most photographed of the group by far, and certainly the most affable, often had a smile. But photographs of Zuma, Abache, Pollee, and Oluale taken when they were in their seventies and eighties do reveal a certain hardness; there is no hint of a smile, but a frown or a cold impassibility. It is easy to understand why outsiders would have found them fierce-looking, especially when they were strong and young, straight and big, and part of a group.

Noah stressed that they never bothered anyone, but intense as they looked and unafraid as they were to demand to be treated decently, they were mocked by some of their American neighbors, and their attempts at fraternizing were not entirely successful. "We want to talk wid de odder colored folkses," Cudjo stressed, "but dey doan know what we say. Some makee fun at us."[59] Certainly the scarifications, the filed teeth, and the initial clothes-fitting incident could elicit scorn on some people's part, as could awkward attempts at speaking English. The language barrier meant that, even if they wanted to communicate, their efforts could be derided. But at some point, they spoke English well enough to be understood, if not very well. Nevertheless, they did not find a receptive audience. Asked if they shared anything about their life in Africa, Noah acknowledged, "I don't think dat ennybody eber axed 'em erbout it." This lack of curiosity and interest on the part of their neighbors must have been disappointing. Life "before" was freedom, family, friends, good clothes, and familiar surroundings. Talking about it could only take them back to the best times in their lives. Sharing their memories was one way other deported Africans had been able to cope.

ALTHOUGH REBUFFED AT TIMES, the Africans in Mobile still found ways of communicating some of their memories. Every now and then they would bring flowers and berries from the woods and tell their neighbors that they had the same ones back home.[60] These attempts at connecting, and the attachment to their land they reveal, had little impact on some of their native-born companions. There may have been some significant reasons for this peculiar situation. After the language barrier had been removed, there remained the difficulty for outsiders to approach people who had formed a close-knit community. But besides those general grounds for estrangement, there might have been others. Perhaps their companions did not want to hear about how magnificent it was to grow up free, about family glories that went back ten generations, about travels and choices, palm oil stews and pineapples, when all they knew were auction sales, whippings, and toiling for the Meaher brothers. Perhaps some thought they were lying, that Africa was only dangerous beasts, witchcraft, and eating one another. The fact that Cudjo and his friends thought and probably said that servitude was hard on them because they had not been raised as slaves could only exasperate their companions. Still, on other plantations, Africans were able to tell their stories and be listened to, which suggests that there must have been something different about those in Mobile, or more likely about their situation.

To begin with, they had no clue about the plantation rules their companions had established long before they arrived. They did not know how the community, fed by the stream of people sold down the river from the Upper South, had taken shape and was holding itself together. The men and women from back East had had to recreate a world, a community made of depressed strangers torn away from their families, and disheartened workers. The rice growers and the tobacco rollers had had to forget their skills. They now had to fell down forests, break new grounds, plant cotton, and build farms and grand houses. Because cotton production did not require artisans, the coopers, machinists, carpenters, carriage makers, and sawyers had been relegated to fieldhands working with plows and hoes.[61] Their fall from the higher echelons of the social ladder was traumatic and ultimately deprived the community of numerous skills. The migrants also had had to learn to live together, take new spouses, and construct links to people they had never seen before but with whom they had to share rooms. The shipmates did not know that the Virginian and the Carolinian, who had just arrived, the freshly auctioned, and the displaced children had gone through a routine to become part of the group. Like Charles Ball, they had had to do favors to be accepted into a new family, such as working in their garden or giving their "new relatives" some of the money they got from selling their own produce.[62]

Pollee, Zuma, Omolabi, and the others had not come one by one through a sale here and an auction there; they had arrived as a group, a community already formed. They did not have to do favors, and be humble, generous, or ready to lend a hand to be accepted by a family. They were a family; and at Burns's they came in a number equal to the men and women who were already there. On James's plantation, they represented at least a third of the people in the quarters; and their proportion was the same on Thomas Buford's estate. As they had shown to Polly the cook at Timothy's and the overseer at Burns's, they formed a block, ready to fight anyone—white or black—to protect and defend themselves. This disposition could not have gone over well with their native-born neighbors, who certainly saw a difference between themselves and the slaveholders and may have appreciated that the Africans showed solidarity with them as well. There were bullies, traitors, egoists, tyrants, and just plain bad people among the enslaved, as among any group, but loyalty was highly valued. There were "thieves" to protect, runaways to hide, conspiracies to keep secret, the sick and the weak to shield and help. The former slaves' interviews reveal a particular harshness for the men deemed disloyal par excellence: the black drivers.[63] When the Africans showed they would not "stand a lick fum white or black," their stance may have been interpreted as a rejection of their American neighbors, a sign that they could not be trusted, that their loyalty was only geared toward their own group.

In addition, the newcomers could appear as a social threat. The enslaved population in the Deep South had negotiated a regime that they did not want to see crumble. They had used the shortage of workers that had stimulated the domestic and the illegal slave trades to their advantage. As planters demanded more work from them, they resisted gang labor when they could for the better-liked task work that gave them some free time once their job had been done. They often obtained payment for their work on Sundays and in the evening. On some plantations, gardens and chicken coops that had also been part of the labor negotiations provided them with food; cash from the sale of their surplus enabled them to buy things not provided by their owners.[64] When a large labor force, like the *Clotilda* Africans were, unaware of their companions' delicate bargaining, came into the picture, there must have been concern that they would accept any work regime and therefore jeopardize the status quo. And since they did not understand English, there was no possibility of explaining anything to them. It can be argued that the Africans would have been accepted more easily had they arrived individually; but, as large groups of foreigners, they represented a potential menace.

SLAVE NARRATIVES AND FORMER SLAVES' interviews do not expose any animosity toward Africans, but rather, in many cases, ignorance and misconceptions fed by white society rehashed without the benefit of other sources of information. Of course, the very limited number of informants—less than 5 percent of the WPA interviewees mention Africans at all—cannot accurately reflect the views of millions of others, but on the other hand, few of these millions had ever seen a man or a woman born in Africa. Therefore, the testimonies of the small number of people who in the mid-1800s were connected one way or another with Africans should not be dismissed. These testimonies do not reveal shame either at being the child or the grandchild of an African. Dozens of formerly enslaved men and women interviewed in the 1930s eagerly talked about their African parents, grandparents, or great-grandparents and, when they had nothing specific to say about them, they just said they had come from Africa. Some, in a sign that they were not embarrassed by the "savage" connotation they carried, mentioned their scarifications or filed teeth.[65] Others boasted that their parents and themselves were "full blooded." Dora Jerman was defiant: "All my folks is most all full-blooded African. I don't believe in races mixing up." Al Rosboro of South Carolina wanted to keep his lineage "unadulterated" too: "Wid not a drop of blood in me but de pure African, I sets out to find a mate of de pure breed."[66]

But relations between Africans and African Americans in the mid-1800s were no longer what they had been in the eighteenth century, when people with long roots in the United States were either a minority or a slim majority. When Africans and their children formed an overwhelming proportion of the black population, African values, standards, religions, and modes of doing and thinking, although adapted and for some transformed, were preponderant, even if they were for some time "African" in name only, being more precisely Kongo, Igbo, or Akan, as well as strongly shaped by Islam among the Senegambians.[67] By 1810, though, Africans formed only 20 percent of the black population, and by 1860, probably 0.2 percent based on the postbellum censuses. Those arriving during the illegal slave trade had entered a world that was quite foreign to them. Nevertheless, within the black community they would have immediately recognized some elements as familiar: gestures, body language, the way one laughed and clapped at the same time or sucked teeth, music, dance, portage, fictive kinship, and respect for the elders. However, fundamentals—to Africans— like language, lineage, age groups, caste (when relevant), and religion, were no longer there. To ordinary mid-nineteenth-century Africans who had just arrived, a number of Africanisms, or African retentions in the United States would probably have seemed inconsequential, barely noticeable, diluted as many were by then. For example, we understand today that nineteenth-century parents who named their child Monday were following—consciously or not—say, the Akan day-naming practice; but Monday did not mean anything to the Asante newcomer, who could not recognize the name as the equivalent of Kodjo.

By the same token, African Americans could find the Africans alien in trivial as well as important ways. By then the native-born population had been in the country for several generations. If in 1860 50,000 or so individuals had parents and grandparents born in Africa, and thus familiarity with a few Africans, they only represented about 1 percent of the black population of 4.5 million. Tellingly, of the close to 2,000 formerly enslaved men and women interviewed by the WPA (out of 2,358) whose filiations are known only 1 percent said they had an African father, and 0.6 percent an African mother.[68] And there were known Africans, and unfamiliar Africans. The grandparents and parents had been in the country for decades, and all grandparents and most parents had lived in America longer than they had in their homelands. They had absorbed at least a little or, for some, a significant amount of "New World African" culture, especially those who lived isolated from other African-born.

In contrast, those who arrived in the mid-1800s were fresh carriers of foreign manners, languages, behaviors, traditions, and religions. The people of the *Clotilda* and those who preceded them in the last decade of the illegal slave trade were in many ways culturally different from anybody else, including the "old Africans" in their eighties and nineties. The "new Africans" were scattered mostly around the Gulf States and thinly spread over Black Belt plantations. Few clusters existed. There was a group of more than a dozen *Wanderer* survivors in Edgefield, South Carolina, and vicinity. More than thirty Africans born between 1810 and 1835 lived in Lower Caney and surrounding area in Matagorda County, Texas, and over one hundred people born in the same period could be found in three locations in Brazoria County, also in Texas.[69] But besides these last two large groups, the late arrivals did not appear to have formed a critical mass that could maintain a cohesive community elsewhere in the country. They mostly had to fend for themselves as individuals, or part of small entities. That the particular situation in Mobile, where a large cluster of young people arrived quite late in an already settled environment, led to some tensions with part of the native-born population is not surprising.

How the Africans perceived themselves and their neighbors evidently played a major role in the groups' relations. Coming from societies where everyone is black, Africans do not attach the same importance to color, let alone "race," as do Americans, black and white. Actually, in many African cultures the words used for "white people" have no color connotation. Among the Hausa, for example, one expression for "whites" is *anasara*, which means Christians (people from Nazareth); the Temne of Sierra Leone and some populations in Angola use *opoto* (for Portuguese, the first Europeans to land in West and Central Africa). The Yoruba refer to whites as *oyinbo* and the Fon as *yovo*, which in both cases mean a "white" individual who can be European, Asian, Arab, or a light-skinned foreign black. Among the Baatonu, Dendi, and Hausa *bature* (strangers coming from what is called in modern terms "the West") is the term of choice when people are not using *anasara*. What this shows is that Africans from the time of first contact have often identified whites based on place of origin, religion, foreignness, or behavior; when color was a criteria, whiteness did not have the same meaning as it did in the West. Thus, when they arrived in Mobile, the Africans encountered not "blacks" they could readily identify with, but people who on a cultural and religious level—which to them would likely have been quite important—seemed different, unfamiliar.

At some point they certainly understood that their neighbors' ancestors once came from Africa too, but what conclusions they drew from this fact is not known. In that regard, it is worth noting that African Americans who migrated to Liberia in the nineteenth century and did assert an African ancestry did not identify with the Vai, the Mandinka, or the Kru on the basis of color. They maintained a separate identity as "Americo-Liberians," and subjugated the local populations they perceived as being entirely different from themselves. In the case of nineteenth-century African Americans finding themselves among Africans in Liberia, as in the case of at least some if not most Africans living among African Americans, common African ancestry and color were deemed less significant than cultural differences that at this stage had become more accentuated than a century earlier.

Moreover, the racial world of the Africans in the West was not the same as the Americans'. They could not have understood or even perceived the linkage of color and servitude, which was the foundation of the inflexible American system, because they saw enslaved "whites" working in the fields and being just as poorly treated as blacks. Even though they realized that the overwhelming majority of bondpeople were black, they could not help noticing that color could not be the only criterion for enslavement. It is important to understand that to Africans "mulattos," let alone quadroons or octoroons, are not black. They are not mixed or half black, but simply white and today throughout Africa, children routinely call light-skinned men and women *toubab, yovo, mundele, bature*, or *oyinbo* to their face. One can argue that Africans during slavery would have changed their mode of identification to fit the American reality and quickly identified light-skinned people as black, but it is by no means certain. Similarly, a North American living in, say, Benin or Nigeria for decades will not perceive a light-skinned individual as being white just because the rest of the population does.

Thus, in Mobile and elsewhere in the Americas, Africans had a reading of the human environment that was more complex than that of the native born. They saw black and white free men and women, and black and white slaves. And as much as African Americans had created their own culture, different in numerous ways from the predominant Euro-American one, to Africans they would likely appear as men and women whose language, dress, religion, birth, wedding and funeral customs, absence of initiation, family relations, and some mannerisms would be, in their view, more similar to that of the whites than to their own.

As for self-identification in relation with the outside world, the shipmates settled on Africans. It was what people called them and they in turn determined to adopt the identifier, acknowledging their commonalities and the differences they perceived between themselves as a group and the others. It was a new layer of encompassing identity added to the various ones they had come with, one they took on and stuck to with pride even as the larger community did not see it as a badge of honor.

It goes without saying that these differences in perceptions and modes of identification did not mean that both communities were at odds, but they revealed distinctions that in certain circumstances triggered tensions. A gauge of the degree of interaction and integration between Africans and African Americans at the time is intermarriage. And intermarriage there was, including among the people of the *Clotilda* and their American neighbors. But a finer look at the numbers reveals a notable trend. The analysis of a sample of one hundred people of recent African descent living in Alabama in the 1880s shows that fifty-two were the offspring of African couples, while forty-eight had one African parent and one African American.[70] The slight majority of intra-African marriages is significant because the number of Africans was low to begin with, which means that they had fewer opportunities to form couples and so indicates that they actively looked for African spouses.

AMONG THOSE IN MOBILE "endogamy" became the rule too. In the strict sense of the word, there was no endogamy, since people came from various social origins and ethnicities; but in America they formed a specific group. And evidently, as was true throughout the Americas, they had no interdiction against marrying shipmates.[71] But if these intramarriages were the rule, they also had their exceptions.

On June 12, 1861, in Bigbee, Washington County, less than a year after she had arrived, Kanko was married to James, the man who had taken care of her and her companions on the day of their arrival and in the canebrakes at Dabney's.[72] The demographics of Burns Meaher's plantation were conducive to the union. Out of nineteen people, only eight were twenty and over and only three of them were women. One, thirty-five, was probably James's aunt Amy. The other two were twenty and twenty-one, likely married and mothers of some or all of the four children aged one to five enslaved by Meaher. One girl, fourteen, may also have been married.

James was in his early twenties and single. There was nobody available to him on the plantation. The arrival of ten African females bolstered his chances—and that of the other men—at finding a spouse. Why the wedding took place in Bigbee is not known. And what kind of a wedding was it? According to her descendants, Kanko knew exactly why she was married. She was young and not yet used to the plantation world, but they said she understood what was expected of her: increase the size of Burns Meaher's property. From the fragments of information passed on to her children, it is possible to reconstruct what the affair might have been like. A description that matches the Dennison family's story can be found in a former slave's recollection:

> When a girl became a woman, she was required to go to a man and become a mother. There was generally a form of marriage. The master read a paper to them telling them they were man an' wife. Some were married by the master laying down a broom and the two slaves, man and woman, would jump over it. The master would then tell them they were man and wife, and they could

go to bed together. . . . A slave girl was expected to have children as soon as she became a woman. Some of them had children at the age of twelve and thirteen years old.[73]

Mable Dennison, Kanko's granddaughter, stated, "feeling the ceremony to be a fake, she considered the marriage ceremony to be null and void. She would have nothing physically to do with her husband; for she had no faith in the method used in putting them together."[74] Kanko had already seen enough to know that her children would work as soon as they could walk. Their upkeep would be cheap: one pint of cornmeal a week served in a big trough in which a dozen of them would dip their hand, while fighting off the dogs, the geese, and the hogs. They would handsomely pay for themselves. Plus, if money was short, they could be sold by the pound for a few hundred dollars.

But reality was not as clear-cut as Kanko's descendants believed. It is quite possible that Burns had paired her and James for his own benefit, but there is no question that the two got along quite well. Whatever had led to their wedding, their living together must have been a big step for both. A marriage in Africa has always been much less an individual decision than a community affair. Getting married without the knowledge, let alone the consent, of her relatives, and their protection in case of problems must have been hard for Kanko. Marrying a foreigner, someone who did not share her language, her education, her culture, brought trepidations. As for James, it was a big step too. He had seen Kanko in the worst conditions possible, naked, dirty, and sick. Like everyone else, and perhaps even more because he had been dealing directly with the Africans, he had heard the stories of cannibalism and savagery, and that could not have been an incentive to marry one of them.

Moreover, James was not an ordinary man. As a boat pilot, he held a high position in the social order. Kanko worked in the house, not the fields, so she too was on an echelon higher than the "field niggers," including those who were born in the country. Perhaps in James's eyes it counted for something. If the 8 percent of WPA interviewees who mentioned their marital and social status are any indication, among people who lived on the same plantation, 82 percent of the skilled men married house or skilled servants.[75] The proportion was high, and the obvious explanation is the existence of a sharp class-consciousness among skilled people. However, the preference for intramarriage needs not be necessarily and systematically associated with contempt for the field hands. The choice, in some cases, may have stemmed from a legitimate attempt at forming families whose children, trained to be skilled like their parents, would avoid fieldwork. And there was another force at play: owner's interference. Rosa Starke of South Carolina, who was very conscious of stratifications among the enslaved, pointed out that intermarriage between a house woman and a "common field-hand nigger" was not acceptable because "[d]at offend de white folks, 'specially de young misses, who liked de business of match makin' and matin' of de young slaves."[76] The meddling of the owners (which had force of law), and their active involvement in the preservation of the social order has been overlooked in favor of the old cliché of the domestics' contempt for the field hands.

Whatever James and Kanko feared, or hoped, their wedding took place. Not long thereafter, they welcomed their first child, Willie, into the world. Like Kanko, another young woman, Shamba, is likely to have wed an African American. In 1863, she gave birth to a daughter, Jeanne, whose father was probably Hayes, the man she later married. He was ten years her senior, and like Noah had trekked from North Carolina in the coffle of a speculator.

If the Meaher brothers had had breeding in mind, they were not successful, as few Africans had children before emancipation. In 1863, Zuma and her husband had a boy, George. Gumpa, the Fon, and his shipmate Josephina had a son too, Leroy. He may have been the special child Noah had noticed.[77] The baby boy had been tattooed on his chest with a picture of a snake biting its tail. Unbeknownst to Noah, the rainbow snake, Dan Ayidohwèdo, is a sacred symbol for the Fon and it can be seen, for example, on the bas-reliefs of the palaces of Ghezo and Glèlè in Abomey. In Fon cosmology, the snake biting its tail represents the continuity of the kingdom of Dahomey, and the rainbow with its abundance of colors is the symbol of the abundance of riches that the snake can bring.[78] No better symbol of the parents' faith in their culture and hope for the future could be found. What they expressed was that their son, although born in America, was a Fon, his allegiance was to Dahomey, and his religion was Vodun. This tattoo represents a unique, tangible expression in the United States of enslaved African parents' decision to maintain and pass on the essence of their history, culture, and religion. Interestingly, they did not choose to give their son a distinctive family tattoo, or one that would mark him as an adept of a particular Vodun; they selected the symbol that transcended family and religion, that of the permanence of Dahomey, the guarantor of Fon culture. Inscribed on the boy's chest, the strength, riches, and continuity of the kingdom lived on, symbolically, in Alabama.

GUMPA AND HIS SHIPMATES maintained other cultural traditions, including in their leisure time. They gathered in the evening, and their neighbors heard them laugh, talk, and sing into the night. Cudjo was a natural storyteller, famous for his parables. He knew many folktales, including some whose central character was Ajapa the tortoise, the Yoruba trickster.[79] On Sundays, the only rest day, the day when the deckhands came back to the plantations, they made music and danced. But some people laughed at them and called them savages. Even worse, they refused to talk with them.[80] Not talking to others, strangers in general, let alone close neighbors, is akin to an affront in African cultures, in which communicating is a primary proof of humanity, a sign of righteousness, where people who do not talk much are often regarded as harboring evil thoughts. In societies where the community is far more valued than the individual, verbalization is the primordial link that holds people together, and refusal to communicate is not only perceived as disrespectful, it is also unsettling in the deeper sense of the word. So perhaps more than the mockery, it may have been some of the Americans' refusal to talk to them that affected the group.

But somebody was eager to chat. His name was Free George; he too had been enslaved but his wife, a cook who worked for a Creole, was free and she had saved money to pay for his freedom. Free George was troubled by the Africans' dancing. He told them they should stop; it was not good to dance on Sundays and he explained why. From then on, they stopped dancing on the Lord's Day.[81] Free George's religious zeal had put an end to a cultural and social expression that had marked every moment of their lives, something they had maintained in the middle of their tribulations. But contrary to what he may have thought, the Africans were far from being "heathens" in need of salvation, and his efforts notwithstanding, they kept their various faiths for several years.

When Zuma and other Muslims in the group arrived in Alabama, they had coreligionists in the country. About 22 percent of the Africans deported to the United States whose origins are known came from Senegambia, an area where Islam had flourished since the early eleventh century.[82] In the Americas, from Peru to Trinidad, from Belize to Brazil and Saint Domingue, Muslims—some of them literate in Arabic—were a dynamic, active community of men (mostly) and women who strove to maintain their religion, kept their faith, prayed as they could, fasted during Ramadan whenever possible, and gave charity, thus respecting four out of the five Pillars of Islam. Some continued to adhere to the Islamic dress and dietary codes, and managed to keep their names and give Muslim names to their children. They also, when and where possible, operated Qur'anic schools, smuggled paper from Africa, and got a hold of Qur'ans or wrote them themselves since they knew the Holy Book by rote.[83]

Even isolated as they were, there was no reason why the Muslims of Mobile would not have maintained their faith and continued to pray. The only necessity of prayer is a rug or a piece of fabric, water for ablutions, or a stone if water is not available. Like other Muslims did, they could have rearranged their five daily prayers into more convenient sets at night. Africans did not let go of their beliefs when they arrived in the Americas, but the rites of their various faiths were sometimes difficult to preserve. Still, those in Mobile did continue to practice several. Some were highly visible and have been recorded.

One rite shocked their American neighbors on Timothy Meaher's plantation. "When a chile wuz fust born, de mother she pick it up an' run lak mad down to de crick, an' chunk it in." According to Noah, if the baby fought back, the mother would fetch it and "think er mighty heap er it; but if it sinks right off, she turns away an' leave it, an' say it no good."[84] What Noah described can be related to two different customs practiced in Benin. One, no longer extant, consisted in throwing abnormal babies into the water. They were said to be deities belonging to the water, where they had to return. Whether they fought back or not was not at issue; they were left to drown. Another tradition, still practiced, is linked to masculinity. Mothers plunge their sons in a creek or river to ascertain their virility: according to the movement—or lack of it—of the penis in the water, they claim they can assess if the boy will be able to procreate. If it appears that it will not, the child is given a treatment. Both customs belong to the Yoruba and Adja-Fon cultural areas, but are not found in Borgu and Atakora.[85] It is not clear which one some Africans practiced in Mobile. Perhaps it was both, although there is little chance that Meaher would have tolerated infanticide—the destruction of his property—carried on in plain sight.

Another custom that elicited people's attention was the Africans' way of conducting funerals. Noah left a very detailed depiction:

> When one er dey folks dies, de whole passel er 'em turn out to dig de grave. Dey always took de top er some hill, an' dey dug an' dug, until de hole wuz 'most 'bout fifteen feet deep, an' when hit is finish, dey fill it 'bout way up wid big slices er tree bark. Dey lak oak bark the bes' but dey hatter take some pine bark ter fill up. Dey puts oak bark all 'roun' de corpus, an' ties it with strips er saplin' bark until hit is all kyvered up an' den dey carries it to de grave, held high up in de air. When dey lay it in, dey put mo' bark on top, slice atter slice, until hit's level—an' den dey piles on de dirt in han'fuls, ontil dey has er roun' flat moun'.[86]

This type of funeral is known in only one region in the Bight of Benin, the Atakora, and is common to all groups. First, the grave is dug by young men, very often on a hill—as in Mobile—to protect it from flooding. As Noah observed, the hole, a kind of chimney, is deep because the corpse is lowered in an upright position. It is not known how the people in Mobile prepared the corpse, but as a rule it is coated with shea butter before being covered with long rushes secured with liana. In place of rushes and liana, the people in Mobile used bark and strips of sapling bark. The next phase of the funeral consists in carrying the body in a kind of stretcher placed on two men's heads. It appears that in Mobile, for practical reasons, the people did without the stretcher, but they still carried the body above their heads. What they did do like back home was to cover the grave with dirt so as to create a mound.[87]

Although the people of Atakora in the group stuck as faithfully as they could to their traditions, they also introduced some innovations born from their particular circumstances. To begin with, the type of funeral they organized was and still is reserved for people over sixty. Evidently, nobody among them had reached that age, the oldest being in their late twenties. However, in societies based on age groups, one person is always the elder of another; and what happened in this regard on the plantation is highly significant because it reveals the mechanism with which the Africans were able to retain certain traditions. What they did—which is likely to have happened in other parts of the African Diaspora—was a sort of age transfer, with the oldest people being acknowledged as the "ancients." The funerals show that the shipmates maintained the fundamental structures of their communities by sliding the building block, the age group, forward. In other words, they did not eliminate certain rituals because the people they were geared to did not exist among them; they simply shifted the attributes and prerogatives of the elders to the eldest among them, thus assuring the continuity of their culture.

Noah mentioned that "the whole passel" was there, which would indicate that women were present too. In burials performed in Atakora only a few women are allowed to accompany the dead but they cannot walk up to the grave. The possible presence of females at the funerals in Mobile would represent a major departure from tradition—their exclusion is still very much in force today in Benin—and could be interpreted as the desire to pull the whole group together. Another departure from tradition is the fact that, as seen by Noah, the mourners cried. When a youngster dies among the people of Atakora, women are allowed to show some emotion, but men do not cry. Moreover, when an elder passes away, nobody is sad, and thanks are given to God for his or her long life. Crying during an "elder's" funeral in Mobile can be interpreted as the group acknowledging that this person was not a real elder but someone who had not lived long enough, an individual whose life had been cut short and who had passed away far from his family. There was indeed nothing to celebrate, no thanks to give to God.

The fact that Noah described an Atakora funeral as the way the Africans buried their dead could mean that only people from this region died on Meaher's plantation; but he may also have remembered or focused on this particular type of burial because of its strangeness to Westerners. Ironically, even though the ceremony may have looked weird, it was closer to the Euro-American type than others. The people of Atakora, like the Americans, were buried in graveyards but the Yoruba are interned in their home or under the stoop located at the entrance of the family compound.[88] So, if there were Yoruba funerals in Mobile they might have looked "normal" to outsiders, whereas to the Yoruba themselves, they would have been a great departure from tradition.

The Africans also kept a custom that Noah observed with surprise:

Dem Affikins t'ought er mighty heap ob de new moon. . . . At ebbery blessed new moon, dey all go out in de woods, an' git de leaves ob de bay tree, an' make crowns for deyselves. An' at night, when the little young moon is jes' tremblin' on de pine tree tops, dey digs a hole, an' all lays down an' whispers somethin' in it; den dey each puts one leaf in de hole an' kyvers it up, an all jumps an' dances on top er it.[89]

On the new moon, all groups in Atakora carry on certain rituals. It is an important moment because since they use a lunar calendar, the observation of the moon determines the dates of upcoming rites. But it is also the occasion for people to ask the moon to rid them of their problems and to provide them with blessings.[90] The whisperings witnessed by Noah were actually the pleas they addressed to the new moon. It is easy to understand why the custom continued in Mobile, where troubles were many, and miracles were needed.

The preservation of some rituals—others, less visible, were certainly kept too—leads to the issue of transmission from the "elders" to the youngsters since half the group was under fifteen and thus not fully initiated. In such circumstances, those who knew something would teach the younger age group. A man or woman of eighteen or nineteen already possessed a significant part of knowledge and had a duty to transmit it. The physical component of initiation, the rigorous and sometimes dangerous tests, would have been difficult to conduct on the plantation; but the part that dealt with knowledge, customs, and codes could easily be passed on.

LESS THAN A YEAR BEFORE THE AFRICANS ARRIVED in Mobile, John Brown had led his raid on the Federal Arsenal at Harpers Ferry. In the months that followed, the apprehensive South had toughened its laws governing black people, enslaved and free, and enforced more rigorously those already in the books. In Georgia, owners could no longer free their slaves by will or deed after their death. Louisiana and Texas had passed laws that facilitated the re-enslavement of free men and women. In Arkansas, free people had to leave the state by the end of 1859 or choose an owner, and be re-enslaved if they elected to stay. On January 25, 1860, Alabama had taken the drastic step of prohibiting manumission. There was no longer hope for the enslaved; nothing they did to ingratiate themselves to their owners, no amount of allegiance could ever free them. All the small paths to freedom were closed shut. In February, another law made it easy for free people to surrender their freedom and "become a slave of some white person of good moral character and standing." Some did re-enslave themselves because they did not want to leave the state and their families behind.[91] And, of course, the Civil War was looming.

In November 1860, Abraham Lincoln was elected president. Alabama withdrew from the Union in January 1861, and on the twenty-eighth, the state convention adopted a resolution that opposed reopening the international slave trade. In February, Jefferson Davis became the president of the Confederacy organized in Montgomery; and the coup de grace to the revival was given on March 11, 1861, with the adoption of the Constitution of the Confederate States of America. It stipulated in its article I, section IX, "The importation of negroes of the African race from any foreign country other than the slaveholding States or territories of the United States of America, is hereby forbidden." The

Africans had arrived during what turned out to be crucial times in the country's history, but when the war started in April, they hardly noticed it. They saw white folks leaving the plantations and going to Mobile, but could not figure out why until someone told them that the people in the North were making war to free them. However, as nothing happened—they only heard some gunshots—the shipmates concluded that the war was being fought over something else.[92]

But as fighting progressed, news traveled. Seven hundred black men from the Black Belt, who had been forced to accompany their owners to the battle-front in 1861 to dig ditches and split wood for the Third Alabama Regiment in Virginia, shared information when they were sent back home in 1863, as food became scarce in the barracks, their owners were killed, they were needed back home, or they had been sold to other planters.[93] Domestics listened and informed the people in the quarters. Code words were used to spread news discreetly: "If a slave coming back from town greeted a fellow servant with the declaration, "Good-mornin', Sam, yo' look mighty greasy this mornin'," that meant that he had picked up some fresh information about the prospects of freedom which would be divulged later on." "Grease" was the code word for freedom. "Nigger news," as it was called, was sometimes obtained from the Yankees themselves. Bondpeople were so well informed, occasionally so unable or unwilling to hide it, that a journalist observed, "the spirits of the colored citizens rise and fall with the ebb and flow of the tide of blue devils, and when they are glad as larks, the whites are depressed and go about the streets like mourners."[94]

Since there was no invasion or any major battle in the area, life went on almost as before in the Africans' quarters, except that there was as much hard labor to do, and much less to eat. The blockade of the Southern ports meant that few supplies reached the city. The cultivation of cotton had been limited so that foodstuff could be grown instead, but it was not enough. Meat was scarce, salt was in short supply. A woman in Tensaw, not far from Mobile, was sold for a sack of salt.[95] On the Meahers' plantations, like everywhere else, the women made coffee out of burnt rice—others used okra, wheat, or corn—and put molasses in it instead of sugar, and everybody hated it. The situation became so dire that James Meaher sent word to kill some hogs. "He say de hogs dey his and we his, and he doan wantee no dead folks."[96] One piece of property was feeding another.

Still busy on the river, the Meahers were not Confederate soldiers. They did not have to be, since an October 1862 law stipulated that one white man was exempted from the draft on each plantation with twenty or more slaves. Their expertise at exerting labor from their workers in this time of need was more desirable than their skills, or lack thereof, on the battlefield. The "twenty-nigger law," as they called it, did not sit well with the poor whites. Unable to get an exemption or pay $1,500 to $3,000 for a substitute, they had to fight.[97] Although Timothy Meaher did not sport a uniform, he was a Southern patriot, and he did his part for the Confederacy. Since the fall of New Orleans in April 1862, Alabama's only port city had become the most important harbor in the Gulf of Mexico, and in May, the first Union ships sailed into Mobile to prevent the Confederates from trading with the rest of the world. The Confederate government had been buying the cotton shipped to Mobile and selling it overseas to fill its coffers. To counter the Union Navy, the blockade-runners got into action. With his appropriately named *Gray Jacket* and his *Red Gauntlet*, Timothy Meaher was one of the celebrities, and according to those in the know, the most enterprising.[98] On dark, rainy, and stormy nights, after a perilous game of hide and seek at Swash Channel, east of Fort Morgan, the ships—painted grey, their steam blowing off under water and loaded with cotton that had trickled from upriver—sailed straight to Cuba. If any of the Africans made the runs, they could see that Havana was a far cry from Mobile. The city was literally flooded with their compatriots, who arrived continually, mostly aboard American ships. As the men from Mobile rolled the cotton bales down to the quays, the Africans and Afro-Cubans from Havana brought in weapons, ammunition, barrels of food, liquor, and cloth imported from Europe. The blockade-runners and their enslaved men made more than two hundred trips, and many were successful, but as the war dragged on, the Federal authorities caught up with them. Still, it had been a highly profitable business. Between May 1862 and April 1863, more than $1.8 million worth of cotton had been smuggled out, but only $208,000 worth of goods had been downloaded in Mobile—including a lot of liquor—forcing the Confederate government to take measures to better control blockade-running.[99] Timothy Meaher played a dangerous game with much brio, but he was not always lucky. In February 1862, a ship he and William Foster had an interest in, the *Gipsy*, was seized in the Mississippi Sound. She had a hundred and three bales of cotton on board and was preparing to leave for Cuba. The schooner was destroyed.[100]

JUST A FEW DAYS BEFORE THE *GIPSY* incident and three weeks before the adoption of the Constitution of the Confederacy that would put an end to dreams of its revival, the last episode of the illegal slave trade played out in New York City. Tenaciously prosecuted by Republican district attorney Delafield Smith, Nathaniel Gordon was found guilty of piracy after two trials. On February 4, 1862, President Lincoln had refused to commute his death sentence to life in prison but had given him two weeks to prepare "for the awful change which awaits him."[101] On the fourteenth, Chief Justice Roger B. Taney of the U.S. Supreme Court denied the slaver's appeal. A week later, Gordon went into convulsions. He had tried to kill himself by ingesting strychnine that had apparently been smuggled into a cigar. He begged the physicians to let him die, but they revived him with a stomach pump and a glass of brandy. That night, thoroughly drunk, the slaver staggered to the gallows. A guard allegedly told him to die like a man. In the midst of his drunken stupor, he managed to articulate some platitude, "Well, a man can't die but once; I'm not afraid and I did nothing wrong." He was hung in the yard of the Tombs.[102] Nathaniel Gordon, unrepentant, was the only person ever executed in the United States for slave trading illegally. In Mobile, William Foster must have thanked his luck and the ghost of the *Clotilda*. If not for her speed, he could easily have been the one dangling from a noose.

As the war was dragging on, a group of Confederates showed up at Timothy Meaher's plantation. They needed men to work on the fortifications.[103] Actually, putting enslaved men to work on the defenses at Mobile had started as early as January 1861, and many had been killed or injured. After an act was passed on October 31, 1862, allowing the impressment of enslaved men between the ages of eighteen and forty-five, Governor John G. Shorter issued an order for the recruitment of six hundred men drawn from six counties. Mobilians, who feared an attack, clamored for thousands. The planters, however, especially those in the interior who were not directly threatened, were not inclined to part with their free labor. To lose their men, and pay for their shoes, their blankets, and their clothes too, was much more than they were willing to accept. Many balked, and refused to part with their laborers; so in June 1863, the state started to confiscate their "property," impressing the men—when they could find them—into service for two months.[104]

For a minority of men, working in Mobile had some advantages, such as leaving the closed world of the plantation, escaping the owner, the overseer, and the driver, and learning skills. But to most, impressment only meant separation from family and appalling conditions, even by slavery standards. Tines Kendricks, impressed in Georgia, who stated that "slavery time was tough, Boss. You just don't know how tough it was," had this to say about impressments: "Dat was de worst times dis here nigger ever seen an' de way dem white men drive us niggers, it was something awful. De strap, it was goin' from 'fore day till 'way after night. De niggers, heaps of 'em just fall in dey tracks give out an' them white men layin' de strap on dey backs without ceastin'."[105] Desertions were widespread. F. S. Blount, the chief impressment agent of the Confederacy for Alabama, Mississippi, and East Louisiana, complained in June 1864 that in Alabama, "of One Hundred and fifteen negroes at work on the road, all but forty five ran off." Most of the forty-three men impressed to repair the telegraph lines between Selma and Rome ran away several times and "within an hour all but fifteen [of their replacements] had run off again." Blount's solution to try to prevent "this stampeding of negroes" was to send them as far away as possible so that their chances at running away successfully would very much decrease.[106] Some of the planters' worst fears had materialized. In the camps, "the Negroes had opportunities to learn the best methods of running

away; discussing among themselves, as they did the issues of the war, they returned to the plantation with new and dangerous ideas which they imparted
to the other slaves, thus complicating the problem of control and discipline
at home."[107]

The men impressed in Mobile were lodged near Choctaw Point swamps in
Hitchcock's Cotton Press. It was a nasty, overcrowded place, full of mosquitoes. The clothing and the food were as bad as the housing. They went on
bread and molasses for days. Then they received cornmeal, but it was too little.
By the end of the year, they were getting daily rations of three-quarters of a
pound of beef, which was considered much too low even by the men in charge,
and cornmeal was no longer on the menu. Brutalized and whipped, they also
suffered from typhoid, pneumonia, fevers, and measles. So many were sick or
died that in some companies, work could hardly be done.[108] Still, white
Mobilians found a way to assure everyone the men were doing just fine. "It is
quite refreshing to observe how contented and cheerful they are," wrote a Mobile
newspaper: "A good many of the whites observing this pleasant spectacle have
wished that they were 'citizens of African descent,' with a humane master to
stand between them and harm and responsibility."[109]

It is estimated that about 4,500 enslaved men worked on the earthworks in
Mobile in 1864.[110] Their situation was so dire that for the first time in their lives,
they saw their owners concerned about their welfare. Slaveholders who had worked
them half to death, whipped them, underfed them, and sent them down the river
without proper clothes or shoes were now complaining that their property was
being mistreated in Mobile. Enslaved and free black men and, in the last year of
the war, black Union prisoners of war, did most of the grueling work for the
defense of Mobile. The African men from Timothy Meaher's plantation and
their companions had been through a punishing experience.

Meanwhile, their owner had run into new problems with the Union Navy.
On December 31, 1863, after "a long chase in a gale and very heavy cross sea,"
Lieutenant-Commander W. P. McCann of the U.S.S. *Kennebec* had captured
Meaher's *Gray Jacket*. She was bound for Cuba with a cargo of cotton, rosin,
and turpentine. Meaher was sent to New Orleans on the seized ship.[111] He had
lost his cargo—half of the cotton belonged to the Confederacy—and his ship
was put up for sale.

The presence of the Union Navy in Mobile Bay had another consequence
many miles away. At Burns's plantation, something momentous was in the
making. According to his children, James had made up his mind to flee to
Mobile and go to the Yankees.[112] The army had seized Fort Morgan and Fort
Gaines in August 1864 and had control of the bay. If he could make it to the
fort, he was free. Kanko, his aunt Amy, and a few others were in on the plan. It
was a bold move, a very risky affair. The Southern states had tightened their
patrol laws, cancelled exemptions from duty, and imposed fines on the recalci-
trant. The number of runaways had been growing as the war dragged on.

Andrew, one of the men who worked for JM & T Meaher, had escaped in April 1863. He had been captured and was held in jail, awaiting the brothers' claim on him and his punishment.[113] Some owners had taken to locking up their workers at night. In 1864, an Alabama law required that boys from sixteen to seventeen, and men between the ages of forty-five and sixty, enroll in the militias and patrol their communities.[114]

The patrollers were more numerous and more vicious than ever, but James was prepared. The group probably left on a Saturday night because there was no work the next day, so they would not be missed for hours. They got on a boat and gliding silently, they started their journey down the river. But one man who had been in the plot was not there. He had gone to his boss and told him everything, likely hoping for a reward. Burns jumped on his horse to inform his neighbors and gather a posse. The men galloped along the river, but the runaways had already left the Tombigbee and reached the point where the Mobile River separates into two branches around Twelve-Mile Island, and there was no path for the horses to go on. The chase had to be called off, but not before another posse was formed south of the first. On the boat, James, Kanko, Amy, and the others could certainly see the men on shore, their rifles pointing at them. Fort Morgan was too far. The boat was stopped, white men got on board, whips and rifles in hand. The runaways had failed, but they would not have to wait too long to be free.

On April 1, 1865, the Union started its assault on the Mobile defenses. Spanish Fort fell on the eighth, and 16,000 soldiers attacked Fort Blakeley. On the tenth—one day after Robert E. Lee had surrendered at Appomattox—a gray, cloudy day, alarm bells started to ring early in the morning. They were calling the Confederate troops to prepare the evacuation of the city. All available steamers and drays were requisitioned. Timothy Meaher's pride and joy, the *Southern Republic*, was laden with naval supplies.[115] As the soldiers left the city the local defense troops threw their ammunition into the river, broke their tools, burned the gun carriages and everything else they could not take with them. Then, according to the Confederate version of the events, "followed a night of horror in which drunken negroes held the city and roamed the streets, throwing bricks and rocks through the windows of the shuttered and barricaded streets."[116] The next morning, Tuesday the twelfth, another foggy day, Major Dabney Maury and his 4,500 troops planted torpedoes in the harbor to slow the Federal fleet, as they started their retreat toward Meridian. At 11 A.M. the soldiers left. The Federal troops entered the city singing *John Brown's Body* and *The Star-Spangled Banner*.[117] To some local whites, the realization that the town had fallen only sank in when they heard the abhorrent tunes. On that day, Mary Waring wrote in her diary that the "hated Yanks" "marched in to the tune of 'Yankee Doodle.'" It was a dreadful wake-up call. "When I heard *that* and the cheering of the men, I began to realize what *had* and was taking place, as before *that*, I had been so much excited that I had hardly had time for thought."[118]

Cudjo and his colleagues were at their post, ready to leave for Montgomery, but the Meahers were nowhere to be seen. Timothy was on the *Southern Republic* going upriver, struggling to salvage some of the Confederacy's weapons and equipment. His *Red Gauntlet* of blockade-running fame was following the naval squadron up the Tombigbee, where torpedoes were hastily placed near its junction with the Alabama River to preclude Union ships from chasing them.[119] The Africans and the rest of the crew were waiting, trying to make sense of the commotion, when they spotted a group of Union soldiers eating mulberries from a tree. The men asked them what was going on. The soldiers told them to leave, that they were free. They wanted to know where they were supposed to go. "Wherever you want," was the response. Of this memorable event, Cudjo said, "I sho' appreciate dey free me."[120] It was an understatement.

THE DAY FREEDOM CAME, there was singing,

> Abe Lincoln freed the nigger
> With the gun and the trigger;
> And I ain't going to get whipped any more.
> I got my ticket,
> Leaving the thicket,
> And I'm a-heading for the Golden Shore![121]

There was dancing: "my mother in law dropped her hoe and danced up to the turn road and danced right up into Old Master's parlor. She went so fast a bird coulda sot on her dress tail. . . . That night she sent and got all the neighbors, and they danced all night long."[122] And there was leaving. When she heard she was free, "mother came at once to the quarters, and when she found me she pulled the end out of a corn sack, stuck holes on the sides, put a cord through the top, pulled out the end, put it on me, put on the only dress she had, and made it back to the old home." There was all kind of rejoicing: "folks left home, out in the streets, crying, praying, singing, shouting, yelling, and knocking down everything. Some shot off big guns."[123]

After the euphoria, some people were bitter at what that kind of freedom meant. Elbert Head, who had been enslaved in Georgia, Tennessee, and Alabama, had mixed feelings: "I felt great joy that we were free, but it made me feel sad to think that there was a whole nation of us set free and none with homes." Rhody Holsell of Missouri also expressed ambiguity. She was happy when freedom came: "Me and another little old woman done some shoutin' and hollerin' when we heard 'bout freedom. We tore up some corn in de field. De old missus was right there on de fence but wouldn't dare touch us den." But with time to reflect, she became resentful, "When dey turned me loose I was naked, barefoot, and din't have nothin' to start out on. They turned us loose without a thing and we had to kinda pick ourselves up."[124]

After the shipmates heard the news, they grabbed their rags, their shoes, and their hats, put everything in a bundle, and rushed out of the ship. They were jubilant but yet, they too might have had a nagging thought. They had been torn away from family and home, gone through a ghastly voyage, lived a wretched life, just to be turned loose with nothing but their clothes on after a few years. It must have all seemed a cruel, useless waste. They were free but they had been robbed of far more than five years of their lives.

Still, it was an extraordinary day, and the shipmates had their own idea about celebrating the freedom they had regained. They were going to do something "African."[125] Some men went to the woods with an axe, and they came back with a piece of trunk. They carved it, fixed a skin to it, and lighted a fire to stretch it. They had a drum, and when freedom came, the drum took them back home.

CHAPTER SIX

Freedom

*T*HE ROADS HEADING SOUTH to Mobile were crowded, packed with people with baskets on their heads; barefoot children in tattered shirttails, with bundles tied to their backs; women with babies on their hips; families pushing rickety and wobbly old carts, sleeping in ditches, cooking, eating, resting on the side of the road. Four million people had been freed, more than 10 percent of them in Alabama, and they were on the move. Some were gone the minute they heard the news; they gathered children and clothes, and they were gone. "Most of the niggers took what all they have on their heads and walked off," freedman Lindly Hardley recalled.[1] The first restriction that servitude had imposed on its victims was immobility. Their world was circumscribed to the house, the farm, or the plantation, and venturing outside of these limits was not permitted without written permission. So, to feel really free, men, women, and children had to walk away, leave the fields and the quarters, travel wherever they pleased—far away or just up the road—without asking for a pass.[2]

Among those who had left, many had urgent matters to attend to. They were looking for their sons, their wives, their parents, their daughters, trying to piece small hints together—a year of sale, a plantation or a slaveholder's name, a speculator's route. Roads were full of Virginians and Carolinians, having been uprooted by the domestic slave trade, walking from Texas, Mississippi, and Alabama back to their kinfolks. Paths were choked with long-ago runaways, getting down South from Cincinnati or Philadelphia, hoping to find lost relatives. Tens of thousands of others were returning after having been smuggled as "refugees" to safe states. "Nigger running," as it was called, had sent 125,000 people to the Lone Star State alone for safekeeping as the Union Army marched through the South. Reuniting scattered families was the first priority and all means were used. When walking was not possible, letter campaigns were employed instead. "Quiring letters," written by teachers or priests, were sent to black newspapers and churches. They were read at services, and if no one there had any information, the letter was then dispatched to another church. Those who could wrote to the Freedmen's Bureau and other federal agencies to try to get information on the whereabouts of their loved ones.[3] But no amount of questioning, no hundreds of miles walked in battered shoes would ever get the Africans closer to their own families. The Americans had hope (which ended up being shattered in most cases), but Africans could only feel grief when they thought about family reunions that would not be waiting at the end of the road.

Still, those who had spent their years of bondage on Burns Meaher's plantation had reunification in mind. They had decided not only to leave but also to go back to their own "family." It is more than likely that some of the men in Mobile and in Clarke County had been in contact with each other as they worked for the Meaher brothers on the rivers. News of births and deaths must have been exchanged, and shipmates must have been kept abreast of new developments. About fifty people in Mobile were eager to see them, so Kanko and her companions put their clothes in pieces of fabric, tied together at the four ends, and set their packs on their heads; with another piece of cloth the women fastened their babies to their backs.

Wearing their five-year-old shoes, they started walking. But one man, James, was missing from the company. Kanko's husband, free for the first time in his life, did exactly what he had wanted to do for a long time. He left his wife, one month pregnant, and went straight to the Yankees. When he had first tried to reach the Union Army at Fort Morgan, on Meaher's boat, it had been quite a failure; but this time the Confederates were the losers. James enrolled in the army on April 19, five days after Lincoln's assassination. He enlisted for three years in Company K of the Forty-Seventh Infantry regiment of the Colored Troops.[4] After having marched from Pensacola, Florida, its men were among the soldiers who had captured Fort Blakeley on April 9, occupied Mobile on the twelfth, and they were making their way to Montgomery. As they passed through Clarke County, James joined them. Now, armed with a sword and a gun and in his blue uniform, he was the proud representative of a triumphant army. He marched on north as his wife and her friends walked south.

In many ways, the Africans probably had it easier than most people. There was no need to ask around where their old friends might be, or to walk for weeks to Virginia or Maryland. They knew exactly where to find them. But what about their shipmates scattered all over the Black Belt, who had left Burns's swamps without knowing as much as the name of the city of Mobile or that of the Meahers? Did they try to locate their former companions? There is no definitive evidence that any of them made it back to Mobile. Of course, the elephant episode that Cudjo and his companions recounted to Emma Langdon Roche could only have been reported by those who had experienced it. It does not mean, however, that they had necessarily moved to Mobile after the war. The people in Plateau were in contact into the 1910s with two shipmates who had been part of the group and lived upriver, and they could have been the source of the story.[5]

The roads leading to Selma, Montgomery, and Mobile had never been trampled by so many feet in such a short time. Like the *Clotilda* Africans from Burns's plantation, throngs of black people were moving to the urban centers. Between 1860 and 1870, the black presence in Montgomery, Huntsville, and Selma grew by over 57 percent. Almost six thousand African Americans made their way to Mobile, an increase of more than 62 percent, while in the same period the city lost 13 percent of its white population.[6] The men and women of the up country plantations who had never been to town found Mobile dazzling. They were so impressed that even in the 1940s, the expression "like walking up Dauphin Street" was widespread in the Black Belt when someone wanted to express perfection: "A good horse runs like walking up Dauphin Street."[7] Field hands, artisans, domestics, skilled workers from nearby or faraway, what were the freedmen looking for in the cities? For one, not to be free, but to *feel* free. To people who had never known it, freedom had to be concrete, they wanted to touch it, as Felix Haywood, a freedman himself, expressively put it: "They seemed to want to get closer to freedom, so they'd know what it was— like it was a place or a city."[8]

Not to be overlooked was the all-important presence of the Bureau of Refugees, Freedmen and Abandoned Lands, established on March 3, 1865. With offices in the Southern states that needed to be "reconstructed," its mission was to handle matters relating to refugees—black and white—and freed people. It was to ensure that former slaves were effectively freed; hand out rations of bacon and corn, clothes and fuel; supervise labor contracts; act as court; establish schools; and administer land abandoned by or confiscated from the Confederates. In Alabama, it had opened stations at Montgomery, Mobile, Selma, Demopolis, Greenville, Tuscaloosa, Talladega, and Huntsville, and they all experienced an influx of freed men and women in search of food, protection, or redress. But the "exodus"—actually nine out of ten African Americans remained in the rural zones but moved within them—did not sit well with the former slave owners, whether they were at the departure point or the receiving end. Planters and farmers wanted their manpower to stay put. In the cities, even some Freedmen's Bureau officials, whose job it was to help the newcomers, were not sympathetic. "Mobile is thronged to a fearful excess," wrote one, "their manner of living there is destructive to their morals and life. These noisome tenements are overcrowded with these miserable people."[9] As for General Oliver Otis Howard, the commissioner of the Freedmen's Bureau, who gave his name to Howard University, he described the migration in disgusted terms: "They drifted into nooks and corners like *debris* into sloughs and eddies; and were soon to be found in varied ill conditioned masses, all the way from Maryland to Mexico and from the Gulf to the Ohio River. An awful calamitous breaking up of a thoroughly organized society; dark desolation lay in its wake."[10] With derision and contempt, whites called the neighborhoods where the freedpeople had gathered "Little Liberias."[11]

Abhorrence of black freedom combined with the shortage of labor had led many planters and farmers to try to keep their manpower by brutal force. Captain D. W. Whittle of the Alabama Freedmen's Bureau wrote, "there has got to be a constant pressure brought to bear upon the former slave-holders to make them deal fairly with the negroes . . . they were very well as slaves, but in any other relation they hate them, and will place every possible obstacle in the way of their elevation." These euphemistically named "obstacles" to elevation used all over the South turned out to be aggressive intimidation, vicious assaults, and murders. "When my race first got dey freedom an' begin to leave dey mars'," remembered Tines Kendricks, "a heap of de mars got ragin' mad an' just tore up truck. Dey say dey gwine kill every nigger dey find. Some of them did dat very thing, Boss, sure enough. I'se tellin' you de truth. Dey shot niggers down by de hundreds. Dey jus' wasn't gwine let 'em enjoy dey freedom."[12]

Southerners, who had gloated for years that they only knew happy and faithful "darkies" loyal to their masters, now denounced blacks as sassy and dangerous savages.[13] Throughout the region embittered planters who had just lost their investments in black bodies, defeated soldiers, resentful overseers, and slave catchers now out of a job, were eager to put the "niggers" back in their place. Violence rapidly reached alarming proportions. In Alabama, "The colored people will be murdered and driven to untimely graves if the government does not keep provost guards at the county seats and the cities," warned a *New York Times* correspondent on June 12, 1865. Former slaveholders, he continued, "amuse themselves by cutting off the ears, noses or lips of their former slaves. . . . At Montgomery five men came in one day with ears cut off and in an almost nude state."[14] He may have sounded alarmist, but on July 29, three months after freedom came, the Freedmen's Bureau in Mobile issued a report detailing the murders by hanging, burning, drowning, or shooting of seventeen men and four women in Clarke, Choctaw, Washington, and Marengo Counties. It relayed the words of a preacher, who said that one of the roads "stunk with dead bodies of servants who fled their masters." The bureau report stressed that the cases had been verified by numerous witnesses, and that "this [was] only a few of the murders" committed.[15] Patrols with "Negro dogs" and spies disguised as Yankees kept guard on the roads and rivers and created a state of terror to keep laborers on the plantations.

In the summer, rumors of freedmen being sold as slaves overseas began to circulate. According to Wager Swayne, assistant commissioner of the Freedmen's Bureau in Alabama, "parties in Clarke County and perhaps in others, some of them wearing our uniform are engaged in collecting parties of freemen under contracts to go with them to work near the coast, but that when there, they are shipped off to Cuba and Brazil and sold as slaves."[16] Former slaveholders, he stated, were paid $50 to $100 for each freedman they secured and sent to Mobile. The governor, Swayne continued, was incredulous at first but believed that it was "in all probability true." Finally, in May 1866, the bureau commissioned a report "relative to the Slave Trade between ports in the Southern States and the Island of Cuba."[17]

Besides physical abuse, torture, and killings, other, more commonplace means of keeping freedpeople in their place were used. As an official of the Freedmen's Bureau in Alabama reported, there was " a very strong disposition on the part of many to oppress and wrong the freedmen[,] cheating them out of their earnings by various devices and extorting money and valuables by threats of violence, false accusations, onerous lawsuits eventuating in loss of time, excessive fines, hard and inhuman treatment."[18]

Many employers were convinced they had to use force because their former chattel would only work when threatened with the lash.[19] The freedmen, however, had their own ideas about who was lazy. "We used to support ourselves and our masters too when we were slaves," said an Alabamian, "and I reckon we can take care of ourselves now."[20] But on April 19, the day James enrolled in the army, officers in Mobile issued a field order telling workers to stay on their plantations as long as their employers were willing to recognize their rights and pay them. And if people had had any fancy about what freedom was going to hold for them, Wager Swayne had a warning: "hope for nothing, but go to work and behave yourselves."[21] Moreover, while freedmen were moving around looking for better contracts and conditions, or hoping to be their own bosses on their own land, former owners also organized themselves, even though their efforts were less successful than they had envisioned. One Alabama planter gloated, "The nigger is going to be made a serf, sure as you live. Planters will have an understanding among themselves: 'You won't hire my niggers and I won't hire yours.' Then what's left to them? They're attached to the soil, and we're as much their masters as ever."[22] The army, eager to restore or maintain "order," especially in the early months, "came to the assistance of the Planters," Howard stressed, and sent soldiers to punish the freedmen denounced as unruly by their employers. But some bureau agents themselves were as willing as the soldiers to help former slaveholders enforce discipline. As one planter was happy to report, "They had a mighty good man there—let you whip a nigger if you liked."[23] In Mobile the situation was not as dire, but employed men and women were often harassed by "gangs of idle rebel soldiers and other dissolute rowdies [who] insult, rob, and assault the helpless freedmen with impunity" while the police "decidedly hostile to color" made "false imprisonment" and the court exercised "criminal partiality." Those the army found without a job were arrested and put to work cleaning the streets.[24]

When they regained their freedom, the Africans in Mobile left their former owners.[25] They did not want to work for the people who had enslaved them. So they were out of a job, and out of the quarters. For a while they stayed in a section house in town and wondered where they were going to go next. They had walked away, but not for long. Like others were doing, some returned to their former bosses, but they stayed clear of their old jobs. It was their way of making a break with the past, of moving as far away as possible from slavery, which for them had been the rivers and the fields. Cudjo, once a farmer, then a deckhand, started his third career as a shingle maker. He also learned to make bricks. Pollee found work as a lumber stacker. Charlie too worked at the Meahers' mill. Others were employed in lumber mills elsewhere and in the railroad yards. They were considered unskilled, yet they were skilled in a way. Work as a field hand was unskilled, as was that of a deckhand; but the making of shingles, especially for someone who had grown up without seeing one, was a step up. To the American freedmen the wage labor they performed for the first time was the sign of definite progress; it differentiated a free person from a slave. But it may not have looked exactly that way to the Africans. Of course, they would have seen it as an improvement over laboring for nothing, but to people who had been free before and had grown up in caste societies, working for a salary was not a dignified occupation. Free people worked for themselves, and anything short of that was regarded as almost akin to slavery. The offer of wage labor in many nineteenth-century West African societies, including among the Yoruba, was often resented as an insult.[26] It is therefore likely that far from considering their wages as emblematic of their freedom, as their neighbors did, the Africans in Mobile saw them as a symbol of their lack of independence. They were paid a dollar a day for ten hours of work, and, according to one of Pollee's great-granddaughters, the Meahers had demanded that they work an extra hour daily for free.[27] In this way, the brothers were reaffirming their power.

THE AFRICANS HAD EMBARKED on a third life, after freedom at home and enslavement in America. Among the innovations that emancipation brought was for the first time the possibility for freed men and women to openly take on new names. Most wanted to keep their family heritage, and they retained the first names that reflected family ties.[28] However, for people born in Africa, it was a whole different story: they had been renamed, and the stripping of their previous identity marker had been done by their former owners. They had every reason, it would seem, to want to shed these names. Moreover, in Mobile, the Africans of the *Clotilda* had been in the country for only a few years, so they had responded to, say, Celia or Katie for a far shorter time than they had been called Abile and Omolabi.

Nevertheless, Kanko, who had been named Lottie by either Burns or Helen Meaher, continued to be known by that name on all of the official documents that marked her life, from the census to her death certificate. Gumpa, who had become Peter, or African Peter, chose to give this new name to the authorities after emancipation. Omolabi continued to be known as Kate or Katie; Abache as Clara; and Oluale as Charlie. Abile remained Celia. They could have adopted American names of their own choosing, but it would have been irrelevant. What difference would it make to be called Sarah instead of Lottie? American names did not mean anything to them; they did not convey any significance. But why didn't the shipmates retake possession of their previous names? The personal reasons at the root of their individual decisions remain unclear, but it turned out that they were doing exactly the same as Africans elsewhere in the country, who continued to be known as Victoria, George, Robert, or Amy. The Congolese who had arrived on the *Wanderer* had adopted American names after freedom too, like Tom Johnson, Uster Williams, Ward Lee, and Katie Noble.[29] Only 1 percent of the Africans recorded in the 1870 census had African first names. The percentage was the same in the 1880 census, in which no more than a dozen people had gone back to their original first names. It is also possible that some had kept them during slavery.[30]

The Africans' decision to keep their American names may have been no more than a matter of convenience, a way of avoiding confusion. Perhaps it was also a means of fitting in, of avoiding unwanted attention. Almost everybody around them was keeping the same first name. Besides, people in their fifties and beyond had spent more time in the United States than in their homelands and had answered to Frank longer than to Ibrahima or Chinwendu. In Mobile, the elderly Africans, men and women in their seventies and eighties, had American full names: Stephen Hobert, Charles Gier, Victoria Tobe. Not to be dismissed also is the possibility that some Africans may have kept their American names because they "had religion." They were no longer "heathens," and they had Christian names to prove it. But Lottie, Clara, Peter, and the others had none of these reasons. They had been in the country only a few years, and they were not Christians. It is difficult to assess what motivated them, especially in light of what some of their companions did. Cudjo, Jaba, Pollee, Ossa, Zuma, Adissa, and Shamba hung on to "African" names and kept on repeating them patiently to clerks and census takers, who wrote down for posterity whatever they heard: Cudjoe, Kudjoe, Cujo, Cugo, Cager; Zuma, Zimmer, Zoma; Chamba, Chamble, Seamba; Polee, Pollee, Pollyon, Poe L.; Orsa, Osia.[31] In their view, perhaps, taking on another name felt akin to betraying family and roots, besides being a denial of one's true self. But if one follows this line of reasoning, can one then conclude that Peter/Gumpa or Celia/Abile were somehow not (or less) connected to their families, less rooted, less "African," more acculturated? And what is one to make of America, the name first reported by Charlie's wife? Was it a glorification of the land in which she had been enslaved? Whatever her motives for choosing that name, she did not hold it for long. At the next census she gave her name as Maggie and kept it to the end of her life.

One reason why most Africans in Mobile kept their American names may be that it was enough to be Omolabi or Gumpa where it mattered, that is, within the group. They had a private, African life and a public, American one. The public face did not want to be too conspicuous. The Africans had the same names as the Americans, but at the same time, they had their own foreign ones, their rules and values, and their languages. And that distinctiveness could only be preserved if they did not become the object of xenophobia, suspicion, and fear. In this particular context, the American names some kept can be construed as a way to retain some essential Africanness rather than a denial of it.

Once everyone, from Allie to Zuma, had settled on which first name to keep, they were not through yet; they still had to acquire a surname. While some Africans never had family names, many African Americans did. In African societies that use them, they are of the utmost importance: they signify one's ethnic affiliation, ancestry, and status and are a veritable identity marker and source of pride. Similarly, to the Americans, who all their lives had been known by names like Smith's John, Yellow Jane, or Scipio, family names were highly significant and stood for dignity, pride, and lineage. These "titles," as they were called, long hidden, were coming out of the woodwork. An illustration of how names appeared and disappeared from Africa to the South was given by freedman Jacob Stroyer:

> father said that his father's name in Africa was Moncoso, and his mother's Mongomo [a region in Equatorial Guinea]. . . . [F]ather had a surname, Stroyer, which he could not use in public, as the surname Stroyer would be against the law; he was known only by the name of William Singleton, because that was his master's name. So the title Stroyer was forbidden him, and could be used only by his children after the emancipation of the slaves.[32]

The titles were the names used by fathers or grandfathers. They had come from white people first—an owner or neighbor—a borrowing that did not signify particular affection. The value of the title rested in the fact that it established a link to a place, the cradle of the family. By the time it had been transmitted to grandchildren the name had been imbued with a historical and personal identity. With it there was continuity, people knew who their family was, where to go back to if they could after having been sold away. Those names, known within the enslaved community, were fundamental in every sense of the term and were one of the only ways people had to keep track of one another as sales dispersed relatives throughout the South.

The name-choosing process no doubt perplexed some Africans. Yoruba, Hausa, and the people of Atakora, for example, do not use family names as such, so those in Mobile could feel none of the pride and contentment that the Americans did when picking or taking back a title. The shipmates were told that they needed two names: one for the son, one for the father. For Americans, it meant one's first name followed by his or her father's surname. But the custom was foreign to the Yoruba, who traditionally bear the first name of their grandfather, followed by the first name of their father, and then add their first name. Hausa add to their first name the first name of their father. In Atakora all populations use the father's first name, which is followed by the individual's own first name. People do have a surname, though, which is the name of the ancestor recognized as having founded the family; but it is rarely used except to represent the collectivity, i.e., all "the descendants of."[33]

Cudjo's "American" name should have been Oluale Kossola, except that the Americans could not pronounce it. Oluale was thus corrupted into Lewis because of the phonetic resemblance based on the sound "lu." "So dey call me Cudjo Lewis," he explained.[34] Who were "dey"? Chances are they were American friends, most likely the spouses of the Africans who were now part of the community. They had a sensible rationale for picking Lewis for Cudjo and for Oluale, who had become Charlie. Contrary to what their descendants believe, the men were not related, as Cudjo repeatedly stressed he had lost all his family. The reason for their sharing the same last name has to be found elsewhere. It made sense for both Cudjo and Charlie to be called Lewis: Cudjo for a link to his father; Charlie for a reference to his own name, Oluale. Pollee, who had kept his Yoruba first name, settled on Allen, a simple common surname that was favored among the freedmen. Gumpa, or African Peter, picked Lee. He certainly had had a family name before, as the Fon usually do, but he did not keep it. Jaba became Jaba Shade. Allen, Lee, and Shade may have had phonetic links to original names; or they may just have been picked at random. Freed Americans often chose common names like Davis, Jones, or Allen; names of colors; or trades, like Cooper. In Alabama, they favored Brown, Lewis, and Bell, and the pattern the Africans followed was the same.[35]

But some chose names clearly associated with their former lives. John, now seventeen, called himself Auro. It might have been an Edo name from Southern Nigeria that is today spelled Oroh; or Orou (Worou), a name common in Borgu among the Baatonu and the Dendi.[36] Ossa Keeby named himself after the river that had given him the best years of his life. Another John, twenty-five, took African as his last name. Where he came from is not known, but perhaps it does not matter because he recognized that in America he was an African, and he let everybody know he was proud of it. In Montgomery, two African-born families who may have been part of the *Clotilda* group took the name Africa. William and Bettie Africa were born around 1830, and they were thus within the right age range for the group. In another household, a Sarah Africa born about 1825 was too old but she was living with another Sarah Africa born on the continent in 1840.[37]

Those were exceptions, though. As they chose American patronyms, the Africans in Mobile were unwittingly following the same pattern as most other Africans throughout the country. Only a few had turned their ethnic or geographical origin into a name, like Tom Ebo (Igbo), Lindor Limba, Richard

Bobo, Salomon Pollard (Pular or Fulani), Athanase Congo, Jack Congo, Alexander Congo, John Congo, and Charles Senegal.[38] But most of these men lived in Louisiana, where it was common during the French and Spanish periods to add the ethnic origin of an enslaved person to his or her name. No more than a handful, like Henry Colamataka, John Kaloda, Jefferson Ondoo, Sophie Cashee, John Baboo, and Omar Amberee, had taken their surnames back.[39]

As far as can be ascertained through censuses and city directories, not one of the Meahers' former bondpeople—African or native-born—called themselves Meaher. There again, they were part of a much larger trend, since few freedmen and -women took on the names of their immediate past owners. But there might have been one exception. When Omolabi/Katie got married to Richard Cooper in 1872, their marriage license recorded her as Katie Meaher. The name was then crossed out and replaced with Thomas. Katie was a widow, and Thomas might have been her first husband's name, while her "maiden name" would have been Meaher. Another possibility is that she had taken the name Thomas before she got married the first time and Meaher had been erroneously inserted by the clerk who knew she had been enslaved by Timothy or James Meaher.[40]

Abache's case is worthy of note. Clara, as she was known, named herself Aunspaugh.[41] It was not a common patronym to pick. There was only one Aunspaugh couple in Mobile. The husband, John, was a clerk on a steamship, and it is thus quite possible that he had hired Abache/Clara from her owner, one of the Meahers or Foster, perhaps as a domestic for his wife. Rather than take a name at random, Abache deliberately appropriated the name of a specific white family she had been associated with. Unknowingly, she too was representative of a tendency among some freed people to adopt the name of a past owner, hirer, or neighbor, rather than that of the person who had owned them when freedom came. Perhaps the best explanation of the freedpeople's reason for this rejection was given by a young boy on St. Helena Island, South Carolina: "That's my old rebel master's title. Him's nothing to me now. I don't belong to he no longer, an' I don't see no use in being called for him."[42]

Among the minority of freed men and women who appropriated the name of the man who owned them at emancipation was a group of Africans with a peculiar story. Brought during the illegal slave trade—they were born between 1810 and 1830—they had been the property of John Duncan, a former Alabama ship captain who had taken them to his new plantation in Upper Caney, Matagorda County, Texas, sometime in the 1840s. At emancipation, the twenty-one Africans named themselves Duncan. Some could interpret their decision as evidence of their rejection of their African past, combined with a disconcerting dependency on or misplaced loyalty to their former owner. But more than half also took on first names linked to Africa, such as Batta, Byaa, Cladda, Coley, Dada, Frimaka, Fymaka, Ishtaka, Kiffee, Malaka, Mayfaa, and Parto.[43] What this example shows is that, with Africans' names and surnames in the United

States in general, complexity was the norm. It would be reductive to attribute labels—such as "assimilated" or "in search of assimilation" because they selected an American name, or "African-centered" because they retained an African name—to people based on the choices they made after emancipation. Their reasons were complicated. There was no "either/or" in their decisions, but a mix of expediency, acknowledgment of American realities, and attachment to their family and cultural identities that, depending on the weight given to each element based on their various circumstances, translated into Ishtaka Duncan, Cudjo (not Kossola) Lewis, Sarah Africa, or Rose Allen.

Sometimes taking a name was a process that involved a fair amount of change, as James's story exemplifies. As he walked up to the soldiers who were registering new recruits, on that nineteenth day of April, he was asked his name. Perhaps he hesitated to reveal his real one, or he had not yet chosen one. The soldier may have asked him then the name of his last owner, as officials did when freedmen and -women did not come up with a ready answer. The man wrote down James Mayers, a derivation of Meaher. In 1870, even though he said that his parents were James and Clara Dennison, and his aunt Amy gave her name as Dennison to the census taker, James was recorded as Jordan.[44] There were a handful of white Jordans in Hill Grove, Clarke County, where he was from and a few—black and white—Jordans in Mobile's fifth ward, where he had settled. Was there a connection there? Although he must have had a good reason for taking this name, we have no indication what it was. That same year he was listed as James Dennison in the city directory. He remained Mayers or Mayors for the army, but Jordan did not come up again.

After settling on a first and last name, some people still had another step to go through in the process. The women who had taken surnames of their own had to change them once they got married. It was a strange custom to the Africans because where they came from, wives did not take their husbands' surnames. Since a name in Africa is an indicator of lineage, ethnicity, and caste, when applicable, it would make no sense for a married woman to appropriate her husband's. It is still rare today for a wife to do so other than for practical reasons, and she is generally still called in daily life by her own last name. It is more than likely that after emancipation their shipmates continued to call the women by their own surnames rather than by their husbands', whether they were Africans or Americans.

In the following years, as they gave birth to and named a new generation, the African parents gave their children an "African" name as a reminder of their origins and an American one for convenience.[45] But Cudjo and his wife would not precisely follow the rule. Two of their children had in fact only Yoruba names. Although Cudjo shared them with Zora Neale Hurston, who transcribed them as closely as she could, he did not tell her their meaning. The Lewises' eldest—born on July 4, 1867—was Aleck, whose Yoruba name was Yah-jimmy, or more exactly, Iyadjemi. It means "I suffered too much," and indicates that Abile had a difficult pregnancy and/or delivery. James, born on December 15, 1870, was Ahnonotoe. Pollee Dahoo, or "Pollee the elder," was known as Pollee or Pollyon. He did not have an American name. David was called Ah-tenny-Ah, which is Adeniah, or prince, in Yoruba. The fifth boy was Cudjo, and his second name was Fish-ee-ton, or Feïchitan, which signifies "born during troubles."[46] The Lewises' only girl was Celia and Es-bew-O-see, or as it is spelled today, Ebeossi. A Yoruba will say to someone he/she has offended, "es-bew, es-bew" or "I apologize." If the person does not accept it, he/she will respond "es-bew-osee, es-bew-osee," "no apology accepted."[47] Evidently, the Lewises' two youngest children were born in difficult times. The circumstances that led to the selection of their names are not known but they signaled trouble within the African community or with the outside world.

One of Pollee's children, Eva, was named Joko, which in the long version is Bamijoko. The name, which means "stay with me," is given to Yoruba girls born after several other babies have died.[48] Unfortunately, no other African names are known for the second generation, but when they gave American names to their children, the parents continued to follow the tradition widespread in West Africa of honoring friends. Celia and Cudjo called their third child Pollee, in honor of Pollee Allen; Peter and Josephine Lee had a Celia; Lillie Nichol was the mother of Maggie, named for Charlie Lewis's wife; Anthony Thomas had a little Charlie who got his name from Charlie Lewis and a Lillie named after Lillie Nichol. But Cudjo and Abile/Celia also adopted a very American custom when they called one of their sons Cudjo, and their only daughter, Celia. In their homeland, nobody would have ever thought of doing such a peculiar thing. Parents can name their children for their own parents or grandparents, but it is unheard of to name a child for oneself. It can happen that a child has the same name as his father or mother, but only because he or she was born in the same circumstances, such as feet first or after twins. The Lewises' innovation is startling from an African perspective and indicates their readiness to adopt certain foreign customs even for a very personal act.

WHEN THEY HAD REGAINED THEIR FREEDOM, most Africans were between fifteen and thirty, and they had marriage and families in mind. But what they had prepared for their whole life would not match up with what they ultimately experienced, as Cudjo and Abile's case exemplifies. Abile had been too young when deported to have gone through the last stages of initiation and, according to tradition, she—like Cudjo—was therefore not yet ready to be married. That was one psychological obstacle to overcome, and there were others. Marriage in Africa is nothing short of obligatory. It is vital and intrinsically linked to adulthood. The Western figures of the bachelor and the "old maid" have no equivalent. Among the Yoruba and the other peoples represented in Mobile, it was first and foremost an alliance of two families, not the union of two individuals. Back home, Cudjo's father and uncles, as a delegation, would have brought presents to Abile's parents, and the young man would have provided services to his future in-laws, all actions that would have shown his value as a man, the respect his family had for Abile and her kin, and by extension, Abile and her family's worth. A large part of what made a man a valuable husband and a woman a valuable wife in the eyes of the community and in their own was how they fulfilled their respective responsibilities to their in-laws. Absent that fundamental element, marriage in Mobile was reduced to its simplest expression. As families did not exist, engagement and marriage were simply individual acts that lacked the social significance they had held in Banté, Borgu, or Dahomey.

Contrary to everything he had learned and Abile had expected, Cudjo proposed on his own. He told the young woman he had no one else and wanted to marry her. Abile had a question before she would commit herself: could he take care of her? Cudjo responded that he would work for her and would not beat her.[49] This last remark is interesting. Beating one's wife, whether in Africa or America, was a husband's prerogative that did not elicit much thought or comment on the men's part. But perhaps because she had been surrounded by violence and brutal beatings for several years, he understood or knew that Abile might be sensitive to the issue. In addition, even though the group acted as a family, she did not have a father and brothers to whom she could return—as is customary in Africa—if the marriage did not work. Yoruba women have traditionally enjoyed significant legal rights in their fathers' houses, including financial assistance and protection for themselves and their children in case of marital strife.[50] This absence of a safeguard would have worried Abile. Cudjo's assurances were enough and, although they did not marry, they started living together.

THE AFRICAN FAMILIES IN MOBILE were growing, and they needed to make plans for the future. They were a community and had acted collectively in the worst circumstances, so they called a meeting to decide as a group what their next move would be. The agenda was clear: they wanted to go back home. They were preparing to live every deported African's dream. There can be no doubt that each of the ten million men, women, and children who survived the Middle Passage to the Americas had desperately wanted to go back home. The return to Africa is a recurrent theme in the cultures of the African Diaspora, expressed in folktales, funeral practices, and songs. Tales of enslaved Africans flying away, leaving for their homeland, can be found all over the hemisphere.[51] Whether the myth of the Flying Africans is a substitute for death, suicide, maronnage, conjure, or resistance, the crucial point is that home is the object of the desire. The tales express a deep, desperate longing for home that can push one to suicide. They can also convey the happiness that a welcome (natural) death brings because it frees the body and allows the spirit to go back home. And home to Africans means, above all, family. What the tales signify is a return to the family, even in death, because the dead become the ancestors still living among the living.

Far from the myths and the legends, to the Africans in Mobile returning home was a plan, not a dream. The promise of a better life in the United States than the one they had endured so far held no appeal because, in their view, freedom did not mean to be free, it meant to be home. Gumpa's presence was likely a factor in assessing the feasibility of the project. Coming from Ouidah, he knew that the return from overseas deportation was possible; and being close to the royal family, he could not have ignored, for example, that Prince Fruku, who had spent twenty-four years in Brazil, had been redeemed by relatives and once back home had tried to gain access to the throne.[52] And of course, he had seen the large and successful communities of deported Africans returned from Brazil and Cuba that had settled in his town as well as Porto-Novo, Agoué, and Lagos in the 1830s.[53] So the people in Mobile knew there were precedents, and they were also likely aware that the former exiles, whether Fon or Yoruba, elite or commoners, had done well.

Once the decision had been made, how to reach the goal was the point of a passionate discussion, during which the shipmates vented their bitterness at the injustice of their condition. They were free again, but without home, country, or family.[54] Their particular circumstances were a source of frustration, but they could also be a source of hope. Unlike most Africans, they knew who was directly responsible for their ordeal: they had been living and working for the slave captain, and the sponsors and organizers of the voyage, from their first days in Mobile. Given that the Meahers and Foster had brought them and benefited from their free labor for several years, they thought those white men should be the ones sending them back. They believed reparations, in the form of repatriation, were justified. Of course there was talk of compensation floating all around town, but its only expression was about land transfer to freed men. Their circumstances, however, were different: they had had land before their deportation and they wanted to get back to it. They toyed with the idea of asking their former owners but concluded there was nothing to expect from them, so they never asked.[55] The only solution left, they believed, was to go back home through their own efforts.

Apparently, they were not aware that they could make the trip for free. The controversial American Colonization Society (ACS), eager to rid the country of free blacks, had already sent almost 12,000 of them—2 percent of the free population—to Liberia between 1820 and 1866.[56] Throughout the nineteenth century various plans had emerged to send African Americans to Africa, the Caribbean, and Central and South America. Just two years before Cudjo and his friends embarked on their quest to return home, Abraham Lincoln had been involved in emigration schemes to settle freed Virginians in Haiti.[57]

Faithful to its mission, the ACS continued to agitate after emancipation—albeit with dwindling funds—and paid the passage of another 4,000 people, although many more wanted to emigrate. African Americans were thus making their way to Liberia at the time the shipmates were trying to leave, and the prospect of living in an independent black country had proved attractive to several native-born families in Mobile. Disheartened by the violence and the bleak prospects they faced, they had asked Major James Gillette, sub-assistant commissioner of the Freedmen's Bureau, to help them leave the country. On December 26, 1867, he took their case to William Coppinger, secretary of the ACS:

> A number [of colored families] requested me to write in their behalf some the most industrious of this city who have become discouraged at the future troubles threatening the peace of this community, and the probable withdrawal of government protection.
>
> A committee representing a dozen families just left the office and there are many more awaiting the result of their application. I am free to say that I do not encourage any to emigrate who have a fair subsistence secured them where they are. But I agree with the idea of transplanting a family which does not thrive where it is.[58]

Two months later, the ACS agreed to pay for their transportation, support them for six months, and give ten acres to each adult and thirty to each family. The applicants were instructed to go to Savannah—their transportation there was paid by the Freedmen's Bureau—to await the *Golconda*, the ACS ship. They were part of a group of 451 people from several states that left in May 1868.[59]

If families in Mobile had been able to get free transportation, what prevented the Africans from asking the bureau for the same advantages? At least one man from the Congo who had arrived on the *Wanderer* had already emigrated. He had left on May 21, 1867, along with 2 other Africans and 297 African Americans.[60] It is true that for the Africans in Mobile the goal was not to settle in another foreign country, which was quite a ways from their homelands, but as Gumpa knew, many Yoruba and some Hausa freed from the slave ships and sent to Sierra Leone had made the trip back to Ouidah, Porto-Novo, and Lagos, where they were known as Saro. Once in Monrovia, the shipmates could find a boat and sail down the coast to their respective homes as other returned Africans had done. The reason they passed over the exceptional ACS opportunity was that they did not know about it. They were isolated, did not speak English well, and were unfamiliar with anything American. Still, they did go to Mobile, the women in particular who sold their produce, and there were American spouses among them who could have been better informed.

But perhaps it was not them, not entirely, but their Alabama location. In its first forty-four years, the ACS had sent 11,909 individuals to Liberia, including 346 migrants from Barbados; but of all the Southern states, in terms of emigrants, Alabama was second to last, before Texas.[61] Alabamians represented less than 1 percent of the 15,945 African Americans relocated by the ACS. So it is not surprising that Africans just a few years in the country, living in Alabama, would not be cognizant of the opportunities the society offered. What they knew is that the trip would be expensive, and with a dollar a day at the mills, they would have to deprive themselves of everything but the bare minimum. The budget of a man in Talladega sheds some light on what they faced. He too was paid one dollar a day, "By de time I pays ten dollars a month rent fo' my house, an' fifteen cents a poun' for beef or fresh po'k, or thirty cents fo' bacon, an' den buys my clo'es, I doesn't hab much leff. I's done tried it, an' I knows brack man cant stan' dat."[62]

Determined to succeed, the men told the women, "Now we want to go home and it takes a lot of money. You must help us save. You see fine clothes— you must not crave them." They replied, "*You* see fine clothes and new hats— now you don't crave them either. We will work together."[63] Viewed by the men as little more than "helpers" who needed to control their impulses, the women had firmly established themselves as equal partners. Without trying to retroactively label the community a bastion of early feminism, it is worth noting that this episode, which portrays the men as naïve and condescending, and the women as witty and self-confident, was recounted by the men, who were not ashamed at having been rebuffed by the women.

Every morning at dawn, the men walked to the lumber mills, the powder mills, and the railroad yards with only a piece of bread and molasses. They worked all day and walked back home to another slice of bread. The women tended the gardens of their rented cabins. They grew greens, peas, sweet potatoes, and corn. After work, the men gathered oak tree boughs, cut them into strips, and soaked them in hot water to make them pliable. They weaved the strips; and once the oak had dried, they had large, solid baskets that could carry several pounds of vegetables and fruits. Some were used by the women to carry their crops to Mobile on their heads, the others they sold. Three times a week— Tuesdays, Thursdays, and Saturdays—they sold their produce door to door.[64] No African woman worked for the whites and they were proud of that.

In fact, many black women, native or foreign, could no longer be found cooking, cleaning, or nursing in white homes, or hoeing and picking in the fields. Once free, those who could had eagerly looked for and created other avenues of work. Like Zuma, Abache, and Omolabi, they grew and sold their produce, or became independent laundresses or seamstresses. Slavery for females had not only been hard labor, but also much too often involved physical and sexual abuse, and it had left them little time for their own family. In addition, men were more than willing to take on.the role of breadwinners, and they too wished for the women to stay home and take care of their husbands and children.[65] There was a definite pride in having a "home wife," a wife who was "keeping house," as it demonstrated a new kind of worth for the men. It was different than the kind of worth they fetched on the auction block, as a man pointedly stressed, when asked how much he was worth: "I's free. Ain't wuf nuffin."[66] Besides shielding the women from abusive employers—and even though home wives actually *worked* at home, from home, and in the fields at picking time—black men wanted to be able to fill most of the economic needs of the household. During slavery they had had no say about their wives' and children's occupations, work conditions, or schedules, since their owners were the authority. And although most of the heavy work was reserved for men, in the fields, both sexes worked side by side. With emancipation, the kind of equality from the abject bottom that had characterized the workplace—particularly the cotton field—was replaced by a gendered division of labor based on complementarities.[67] The removal of women from under the supervision of whites had been common during the early years of Reconstruction, although its extent was sometimes exaggerated by white Southerners eager to show how freedom had wrecked the economy. Some estimates put the decline in women's participation in the labor force at one-third to one-half.[68] In Alabama, the proportion of home wives varied greatly from one city ward to another and from one county to the next, but a study of the occupations of women in Mobile Ward 2 in 1870 mirrors the most widespread estimates: about 32 percent were "at home."[69] The new state of affairs was denounced by the planters and derided by Southern whites as a ludicrous attempt by freedwomen at playing ladies. Even those who did stay on the job sometimes had demands of their own. "I could not get my colored servant woman to milk my cow when it rained," a distraught farmer lamented; "she would not do it; she thought that thing was 'played out,' and that I must go and milk the cow myself."[70]

FREEDOM HAD BROUGHT OTHER CHANGES to the black family. From largely matrifocal, as fathers often resided on another farm or plantation, it had become patrifocal and more patriarchal, in great part for protection in violent times. It was a poor man's patriarchy, one function of which was the defense of wives and daughters against racism and sexual exploitation. In households where women and girls still worked outside, the men were the negotiators, the relay between the family and white bosses, the public interlocutors in the social, economic, and political spheres. The reinforced patriarchy and stricter gender division of labor that freedom had brought to the larger African American community could only have the Africans' approval. They came from patrilineal and patrifocal societies that also had rigorously defined what kind of occupations males and females could engage in. Yoruba, Dendi, and Nupe women did not do agricultural work, except for the cultivation of personal gardens, but they worked outside the home as market traders, food vendors, and in the various crafts that their castes dictated. In Mobile, even the youngest African girls were accustomed to that type of work, as they had grown up helping their mothers. So, contrary to what was the norm for the formerly enslaved population, full-time self-employment was not unknown to the Africans; in fact, it was a return to long-standing traditions.[71] Thus the exit from the fields and the shift to self-employment were only logical and would likely have happened irrespective of what was going on around them. Still, they had had to adjust to new crops, new techniques, and, more important, a new clientele that was a far cry from the men and women who frequented the markets in Banté or Borgu. In the beginning at least, they certainly had to endure and get over the offensive scrutiny, the gawking, the indiscreet questions that their scarifications, filed teeth, and foreign ways elicited. They were ultimately quite successful at what they did, since they remained their own bosses all their lives.

THE MONTHS THAT FOLLOWED EMANCIPATION, although marred by violence, were also hopeful times. Freed people talked of the lots they were going to receive once the plantations were divided and public land opened to homestead. There were 850,000 vacant acres—very few in Alabama—either confiscated from or abandoned by the Confederates, and understanding that their true emancipation rested on the autonomy that land would give them, freedmen demanded them. "Gib us our own land and we take care ourselves, but widout land, de ole masses can hire us or starve us, as dey please."[72] It was, after all, their land, as many forcefully stated: "We has a right to the land where we are located. For why? I tell you. Our wives, our children, our husbands, has been sold over and over again to purchase the lands we now locates upon; for that reason we have a divine right to the land. . . . And den didn't we clear the land, and raise de crops ob corn, ob cotton, ob tobacco, ob rice, ob sugar, ob everything."[73] The land redistribution, they believed, was going to happen on January 1, 1866, and be announced by the Freedmen's Bureau. They in fact had a good source to back them up: the act of Congress creating the Freedmen's Bureau had clearly stated in Chapter XC, section 4:

> the commissioner, under the direction of the President, shall have authority to set apart, for the use of loyal refugees and freedmen, such tracts of land within the insurrectionary states as shall have been abandoned, or to which the United States shall have acquired title by confiscation or sale, or otherwise, and to every male citizen, whether refugee or freedman, as aforesaid, there shall be assigned not more than forty acres of such land, and the person to whom it was so assigned shall be protected in the use and enjoyment of the land for the term of three years. . . . At the end of said term, or at any time during said term, the occupants of any parcels so assigned may purchase the land.[74]

Although the text said that the forty acres would be free for only three years, many thought they would be theirs forever. And there was another obstacle: on May 29, President Andrew Johnson's Amnesty Proclamation that granted official pardon to all Confederates—except fourteen categories—stated that "all rights in property, except as to slaves" would go back to the former rebels who swore allegiance to the Constitution and the Union. By August, Johnson had given orders to the bureau to give the land it had under control back to the former Confederates.

Parallel and connected to the land rumor among blacks was another spreading among whites since the summer: the Christmas insurrection. Throughout the South, whites had seen and heard evidence of a wide conspiracy to "murder the white race [and] the old slave owners, to get their land and houses." There was horrified talk of Saint Domingue, and of the Morant Bay rebellion in Jamaica, as the scare spread to close to seventy counties and parishes in eleven states.[75] In September 1865, delegates to the Alabama constitutional convention asked provisional Governor Lewis E. Parsons to give them authority to form militias to protect the whites. On November 22, a Convention of Colored People from eleven counties gathered in Mobile and affirmed their commitment to "peace, friendship and goodwill towards our white fellow-citizens," but warned they wanted just wages and would "relinquish none of the rights of our common manhood." They also felt compelled to emphasize, "That the assertion made in certain quarters, that there is a plot among our people to rise in insurrection, is utterly without foundation, inconsistent with our history as a people, and the farthest from our desires or possible intentions."[76]

The main conspirators, according to white Southerners, were the black soldiers who incited the freedmen, provided them with weapons, and would take part in the massacres.[77] The obsession with black soldiers, the symbol of Southern defeat and black freedom, had turned into paranoia. At the end of the war, because white men had been enrolled for longer than African Americans, a great number were mustered out, and the proportion of black soldiers thus vastly increased. From 11 percent of an army of one million, blacks were now more than 36 percent of the 227,000 men still active in the fall of 1865.[78] As many as 35,500 were stationed in the Gulf—by and large in Louisiana—and most of the rest were concentrated in Tennessee, Kentucky, and Texas. Since all black regiments formed in the North had been disbanded, those that remained in operation were made up of Southerners, like James Dennison, who had joined as the Union was sweeping through their states. They were part of an army of occupation in areas where they had recently been enslaved. "Our citizens, who had been accustomed to meet and treat the Negroes only as respectful servants, were mortified, pained, and shocked to encounter them . . . wearing Federal uniforms, and bearing bright muskets and gleaming bayonets," explained a Louisiana newspaper.[79] The very presence of victorious and armed black men was perceived as the utmost offense, a wicked Northern way of thoroughly humiliating the South. Whitelaw Reid, the war correspondent of the Cincinnati *Gazette* who visited Mobile in June 1865, related, "One had to mingle with them to find out how sore they were at the degradation of being guarded by these runaway slaves of theirs. . . . To be conquered by the Yankees was humiliating, but to have their own negroes armed and set over them they felt to be cruel and wanton insult."[80] Whites accused the *smoked Yankees*, as they called them, of being arrogant, of lacking due respect, and of having a deplorable influence on the freedmen—who saw these soldiers as liberators and protectors against violence and abuses—inducing them to refuse contracts and encouraging them to flock to the garrisons where they became "lazy and impudent." Ordinary people, former slave owners, and officials complained bitterly about the soldiers, and violent incidents with the police and militias, as well as with white soldiers, were frequent. On October 30, 1865, at the peak of the Christmas scare, J. Madison Wells, the provisional governor of Louisiana, in step with other colleagues, wrote to Andrew Johnson to ask him to remove the Colored Troops from his state. James and his fellow soldiers were, according to Wells, a "baleful presence."[81]

Still hoping in December that the land was going to be carved up, some freedmen had refused to sign work contracts. White schemers were going around selling red, white, and blue pegs at $4 a set, assuring black buyers that if they put those made-in-Washington stakes anywhere, forty acres were theirs.[82] As tension escalated, the Freedmen's Bureau warned that there would not be any land distribution, that workers had to enter into contracts, and that any insurrection would lead to their destruction. January 1 came and went. There was no declaration about freedmen getting forty acres. No officials were knocking at Big House doors to evict the planters. The red, white, and blue pegs were worthless. There had never been any black plot, but the rumor, as one bureau official emphasized, was "a pretext so that the whites may disarm the colored population and thus control and manage them without danger of resistance."[83] Rather than the fruit of a black conspiracy, the expected Christmas Insurrection turned out to be a successful effort by white Southerners to discredit emancipation and the bureau, hasten the demise of the black troops, and disarm and reclaim control of the freed population.

It had a direct impact on one of the Africans' families. On January 5, 1866, private James Mayers, identified on his soldier's card as James Mayors, was discharged from the army at Baton Rouge, Louisiana.[84] He had entered a private and was leaving a private. That day, the 1,520-men Fourty-Seventh Regiment, United States Colored Infantry, created in 1864 in Mississippi from the Eighth Louisiana Infantry, African Descent, mustered out after having seen service in Mississippi, Louisiana, Alabama, Arkansas, Florida, and Texas. By January 1866, when James was discharged, half the black troops were let go. In October, fewer than 13,000 men were still enrolled and a year later there were none. Some soldiers had actively sought to be discharged and had been retained against their will, but others did not expect to be mustered out so quickly before having taken advantage of what military life could offer them.

It was only nine months since James had enthusiastically enrolled in Company K for three years, but his dreams of a proud military career had quickly evaporated when he was sent to tend stock in the mosquito-infested bayous near Alexandria, two hundred miles from New Orleans. He had developed rheumatism and malaria in October, and had been sick with diarrhea after living in the swamps and drinking their contaminated waters. Instead of being sent to a hospital, he had been treated in the marshes by the Red River.[85] He then had been dispatched with his company to Texas, where he was on duty on the Rio Grande and at various points in the state. His regiment had lost one officer and thirty enlisted men, killed by the enemy. Three officers and 398 men had succumbed to disease.[86]

What had James expected to find and learn in the army that had pushed him to leave a pregnant wife and a son nine months earlier? Probably like many freedmen he had been enticed by the steady pay, the prestige of being a representative of the government, and the possibility of learning to read and write.[87] Soldiers, like the rest of the newly freed population, were eager to learn what had been forbidden to them, and they were also conscious that literacy could improve their lot. Joseph T. Wilson, a Louisiana Native Guard who later fought with the Fifty-fourth Massachusetts Infantry, noted that the illiterate black soldiers "became daily more and more impressed, through their military associations, and by contact with things that required knowledge, with the necessity of having an education. Each soldier felt that but for his illiteracy he might be a sergeant, company clerk, or quartermaster, and not a few, that if educated, they might be lieutenants and captains."[88]

Few literacy programs were in place, but in most regiments, officers appointed the chaplains as teachers, encouraged literate former slaves to teach, and in some cases schools were established at camps. As did men in other regiments, the soldiers of the First Alabama Regiment of Colored Infantry (Fifty-fifth U.S. Colored Troops) pooled their resources to pay Northern teachers 50 cents to one dollar a month each to teach them how to read and write.[89] By the end of the war, it is estimated that "20,000 colored soldiers could read intelligently."[90] After his short tour of service, James could read, but he still could not write. His story of disillusionment was the same as that of many of his peers. Sick and disenchanted, he made his way back to Alabama with his pay and $100 in bounty. He had expected more. Thousands of black men had been discharged without back pay or bounty. They took their grievances to their senators, the War Department, and the Freedmen's Bureau, and like them, James would fight for decades to get his due.[91]

Back in Mobile, the ex-soldier returned to work on a steamboat. His son, Jerry, was almost two months old. But it would prove a short-lived reunion; by April, the baby was dead. The last time James had seen Kanko and her companions, their goal was to get to Mobile and be reunited with their shipmates. This time, the common objective was to go back home. It was a big change in plans. What did he and the other Americans who had married into the group think about the return project? One can only conjecture as to their state of mind. Questions, self-interrogations, apprehensions, and doubts must have abounded. To the men and women who had been uprooted by the domestic slave trade and had lost track of their families, emigration might have seemed less problematic than to those who were born in Alabama and had relatives around. But still, Dahomey, Atakora, and the rest of the places where their husbands or wives came from were unknown, unheard-of territory. Africa beyond Liberia had been associated with savagery and cannibalism, but they had also heard another point of view. The portrait of their homelands the Africans used to paint was highly positive. To the Americans who had just been told they would never get free land, its abundance in West Africa must have sounded appealing. And there was something else that must have been quite alluring: there were no white men in the rural areas their spouses came from, no violence and humiliation based on the color of one's skin.

The situation James had found in Mobile was not good. Hard work and privations had not been enough; the shipmates were dirt poor, and they had started to realize that they were not going to make it. Still, there were avenues opened to them—besides the ACS-sponsored Liberia trips—that they did not take. They could have started an *esusu*, pooling their resources as Africans routinely do and have been doing for generations. A rotating fund, the *esusu* (in Yoruba) gives at agreed-upon intervals all the money gathered by the members to one participant. The difficulty for the Africans in Mobile, though, was obvious: their group could only decrease and there would not be enough members left to pay for the voyage of perhaps half the families. But there was still a way. Once the first beneficiaries of the *esusu* had reached their homelands, the families of those still in Alabama could have helped; and if they did not have the means, other *esusu* in their hometowns could have been launched.

The idea of financial assistance coming from Africa was not completely unheard of. One well-known case concerns Ibrahima abd-al Rahman, a son of the former *Almamy* (Muslim ruler) of Futa Djalon in Guinea, who had been enslaved in Mississippi for thirty-nine years before sailing for Liberia in 1829. Once in Monrovia, he had informed his family in Futa that he needed money to free his children still enslaved in Natchez. They sent a caravan with $6,000 to $7,000 in gold.[92] Some well-connected men, in Africa, had paid for the release of their relatives overseas; among them was King Naimbanna of Sierra Leone, who had obtained the freedom of a family member deported to Jamaica.[93] John Corrente, a headman at Annamabu (Ghana), had seen one of his sons, William Ansah Sessarakoo, shipped to Barbados in the late 1710s. The Royal African Company promised him that he would be recovered, and another of Corrente's sons sailed to the island to retrieve the captive, who was finally redeemed.[94] King Agaja of Dahomey requested and obtained the return, from Maryland, of Captain Tom, also known as Adomo Tomo.[95] Two brothers of King Adandozan were returned from Demerara (in modern Guyana) to Dahomey in 1803, probably through payment to their owners.[96] More obscure people were also successful at locating and freeing their loved ones. In 1751 Rio de Janeiro, an Angolan woman, Lucrécia de André, was freed after her brother in Luanda sent 110 mil-reis to her owner. After twenty years he had been able to locate her, save the money, and find ship captains willing to transmit the funds overseas.[97] Another quite intriguing instance can be found in the United States. In 1936, Shade Richards revealed that his father, Alfred, an African, had almost been freed by Shade's grandfather. He had come from Africa "to buy his son and take him home."[98] The casual manner in which the event was recorded suggests that Richards—and the interviewer—did not consider it an amazing accomplishment. It goes without saying that the redemption in America of family members by Africans was an extraordinary occurrence, but it may have happened a few times. For a family in Africa to have found out the whereabouts of their son enslaved on a plantation near Zebulon in Pike County, Georgia, was a stunning success. It obviously took them time, since Alfred already had eleven children when his father arrived. It also took organization and money to pay for passage from the African coast to Georgia, travel up country to Pike, and still have enough money left to buy the freedom of a son whose loss his family never accepted. Sadly, father and son got sick and died in Georgia, an undoubtedly immense blow to their hopeful relatives in Africa who probably never knew what really happened and had lost two loved ones to America. What Ibrahima, Lucrécia, and Richards's redemption stories evidence is that, in some cases, help in monetary form could be found in Africa when connections were established. It is not far-fetched to imagine that a few Africans from Mobile who sailed back home could have gotten aid from their companions' families and neighbors to assist in the later repatriation efforts of those who had remained in Alabama.

In light of the shipmates' failure it is worth looking at attempts by other deported Africans to return home. During the nineteenth century hundreds of men and women were involved in repatriation schemes from Brazil, Cuba, Jamaica, Trinidad, and the United States on an individual or collective basis. In Trinidad, a very active Muslim association had tried for years to send its members back home.[99] After the unsuccessful Malê (Muslim) uprising in Bahia in January 1835, scores of free Africans had gone back to their homelands in the Bight of Benin. Two hundred had been deported to Ouidah in November, and hundreds of others had paid their own way.

But the Africans in Mobile lived in an entirely different situation. The free Muslims of Trinidad were not poor; some had slaves and they were farmers or peddlers and many had been free for decades. They had organized an efficient association that had been functioning for several years, buying the freedom of other Muslims as they arrived from Africa. Like their coreligionists in Trinidad, the Bahian Africans had an extensive experience of resourceful organization, and many had been free for a long time. In contrast, the Africans in Mobile had just been emancipated, were working for low wages, and they were a tiny minority that lacked the efficient networks other Africans had developed in places where they were numerous. In Trinidad, the Muslim association was ultimately not successful either and the vast majority of its members stayed on the island, their money tied in assets they could not sell, and their pleas for repatriation rebuffed, but a few traveled by themselves and reached their homelands. Did some people in Mobile also leave on their own when it became obvious that the group was not going to make it? There is no record of individual departures either in the Africans' interviews or in their children's reminiscences, and if some had indeed left, such a success would have been known and heralded.

The shipmates talked so much about wanting to leave that there is no reason to doubt the genuine efforts they put into trying to reach their objective. A newspaper article, published in 1870, already stressed that they begged to be sent back home, and another mentioned that they were "very eager to be sent back to their native country, that they may meet their families again and be useful to their people."[100] Still, in light of their achievements in other endeavors, their lack of success in that undertaking, the most important, raises questions. From individual efforts, to the ACS, to a kind of rotating emigration scheme, they had a few options. But the only one they pursued was a collective return. They may have been so far from saving even a fraction of what was needed for their passage that the whole enterprise would have seemed unattainable in a foreseeable future.

In point of fact their failure at emigrating was part of a wider pattern. The overwhelming majority of freed people born in Africa did not make it home. Most were too old to even envision a return. Elderly people were too fragile to withstand a two-month voyage in the rough conditions that were still prevalent. As an indication, only about 2 percent of the immigrants to Liberia were sixty and over, but this very age group represented more than 60 percent of the Africans living in the United States after emancipation.[101] These men and women would not only have been challenged by age, but they also had children and grandchildren they would have had to leave behind precisely at the time when they needed them most to take care of them in their old age. In addition, with only remote possibilities of finding relatives still alive, the prospects of abandoning their offspring for the unknown could not have been appealing. An alternative would have been to take the whole family back, which meant gathering enough funds to emigrate as a group, a difficult enterprise. Practically, a return migration could only concern the able-bodied with few children. Based on the 1870 census, at least 365 individuals, or 21 percent of the African-born population, were under forty-five at emancipation and could have been candidates for return. For some, however, especially those who had been deported as children, the difficulty of even knowing where exactly to return to was an obstacle. Although many people could locate where they came from, especially those from large urban areas, others had little more than names of small towns or villages difficult to even situate in a specific country. The name of the port of embarkation was a necessary clue that helped position a locality, but even Cudjo, who knew the geography of the area, had stressed after sixty-four years in Mobile that he did not know exactly where his home was.[102] The reasons why the Africans in the United States who wanted to leave did not are varied, but perhaps they were impeded mainly because they lacked the funds, and because the necessary information and infrastructure to facilitate or simply make possible their voyage was not in place. Even in Brazil, where returns numbered in the thousands, the largest part of the African population could not afford to emigrate. As representatives of Brazilian and Cuban returnees interviewed in Lagos in 1890 asserted, "Poverty [was] the only obstacle that prevents those who want to come back to Africa."[103]

Although they failed at executing their plan, the shipmates did not give up their dream. If they were going to stay in Alabama, it had to be on their own terms.

CHAPTER SEVEN

African Town

O NCE THEY REALIZED THAT EMIGRATION was not in the foresee-able future and that a second generation was growing up in America, the Africans put together another plan. The first priority, they determined, was to give a formal structure to the community. From the days in the *barracoon*, on the *Clotilda*, and in the canebrakes, they had made their decisions as best they could, probably by consensus. But since they were going to stay in Mobile they decided they needed a leader. There was no pretending from anyone to be a former chief or king. When someone from a royal family lived on a plantation, everyone knew it; there were pointed questions, and no one could fake it. Like examples throughout the Americas show, if there had been royals among them, they would have been served, helped, and treated with respect and deference, irrespective of their enslaved status.[1] Because no one was from royal ancestry, no one could become the king of Mobile's African community. They were ordinary people—not slaves, as they had pointedly reminded themselves and others—and royalty evidently still held too much meaning for them to "demean" it by proclaiming one of them a king. In addition, they had been told that royalty did not exist in America. It may have been a factor in their decision, but if so, a minor one. It was already more than enough that their own traditions prevented them from usurping a title. Over the years, though, a myth about how the settlement was governed developed among outsiders. In the old days, the story went, "most of them looked up to one woman, said to have been the wife of a chief, as a kind of queen or head-woman."[2] The queen version made the settlement appear more exotic, more primitive, more interesting in a paternalistic kind of way, but it was inaccurate.

Far from being a king, Gumpa was a nobleman, the only one among them, so they chose him. He had lived through a dramatic turn of events, fallen from a place at the court to the very bottom, but because he had been close to the top once, he climbed back to it in Mobile. The social conformism of his companions plainly manifested itself in this selection, but interestingly, so did their open-mindedness. Gumpa's noble birth trumped the fact that he had been from Dahomey, the source of the tragedy that had destroyed their lives. They did not hold any grudge against him. Gumpa, they knew, had nothing to do with that.[3] In all probability, he had supported the kingdom's raids and numerous wars of conquest. That he had become a victim of the slave trade initiated by his king had not changed his faith in Dahomey, as the serpent tattooed on his son's breast attested. But his companions were sophisticated enough to reject collective culpability. They also dismissed ethnicity as a factor in the choice of a leader. They were mostly Yoruba being led, as a result of their own choice, by a Fon.

THE NEXT STEP IN THE BUILDING of the community was to acquire land, which would mark their independence vis-à-vis the surroundings and would give them the possibility of re-creating home. Part of the area most of them had lived in belonged to the Meahers, down from Three Mile Creek up to Chickasaw Bogue. People called it Meaher's hummock. It was wild and secluded. Three Mile Creek separated it from Mobile, and one had to take a boat or walk several miles west to the end of the creek before making it to the city. The red clay hills of the north gave way to gentle slopes in Plateau and Magazine Point and turned into flat land at the creek. It was swampy and woody: pines, bays, magnolias, cypresses, beeches, junipers, oaks, and gums grew in abundance. The woods teemed with rabbits, possums, coons, deer, hog bears, ducks, and turtles, and the Africans, methodically, explored every inch of the area, noting the animals, the plants, and the trees that could help them survive.

To discuss the new matter, Gumpa called an assembly. Land tenure had not been an issue to any of them before their deportation. The concept of buying land was foreign to Africans. Free land distribution on the other hand would have seemed natural. But when they came around to the idea of settling in Mobile the issue was moot. The Confederates had recovered their land and freedpeople either had none or had had to buy. Still, at the meeting presided over by their new leader, the shipmates decided that reparations were still in order. It had been their conviction all along, since they had elected to emigrate. They had not asked for assistance then, but their failure at emigrating had evidently persuaded them that they needed to ask for it now. They concluded that since the Meahers had brought them, and worked them hard for no pay, they should give them land.[4] They certainly believed they stood a better chance with the land issue. Repatriation had meant that the Meahers would have had to pay for the passage of several dozen people, but reparations in the form of land did not entail any disbursement of money. As people for whom land was traditionally free, they did not grasp the economic, political, social, and even racial value that it had acquired in the United States.

Cudjo was chosen as the best spokesman to address Meaher.[5] It would be the most important and arguably the most dangerous talk of his life. The future of hundreds of people—born and unborn—depended on him. He had to be firm and, most important, he had to be persuasive, find the right parables, and the right moment. It came one day not long after the meeting, as he was cutting timber for the brothers' mill. He saw Timothy walk toward him. Meaher sat on the tree trunk Cudjo had just felled, took out his pocketknife, and started whittling a stick. Cudjo fell his ax a few times, and stopped. It was his moment. The community's desire for land, and his responsibility, were so great, he almost cried. Meaher, who had not heard the sound of the ax, looked up. He was struck by the young man's grief.

> "Kazoola, what makes you so sad'?"
> "I grieve for my home."
> "But you've got a good home."
> "Captain Tim, how big is Mobile?"
> "I don't know, I've never been to the four corners."
> "If you give Kazoola all Mobile, that railroad, and the banks of Mobile Kazoola does not want them for this is not home."
> . . .
> "Captain Tim, you brought us from our country where we had land and home. You made us slaves. Now we are free, without country, land, or home. Why don't you give us a piece of this land and let us build for ourselves an African Town?"[6]

Cudjo, relaying the group's analysis of the situation, had based their claim on two grounds: compensation was due not only because of the free labor they had provided when enslaved, but also because they had been uprooted from family and land. They thought they had a good case, doubtless better than the people who had not been deported, because they had actually *lost* their own land and homes. They had been doubly robbed, and the man at the origin of this twofold spoliation had continued to exploit some of them. From Ouidah to Mobile, the culprit had been the same. The shipmates' was a unique situation in which there had been a continuum of culpability; and reparations were thus even easier to conceptualize and demand. By presenting the request in such terms, Cudjo had taken considerable risks. He knew Timothy was more ruthless than his brothers, yet he had not minced his words.

In the two versions of the event that have surfaced, Cudjo did not implicate Foster and the other Meahers, only Timothy. By then, he probably knew the genesis of the *Clotilda* voyage and he had put the responsibility for the group's predicament squarely on Timothy's shoulders: as the instigator of the venture, he was the main offender and it was time for him to pay back. Telling a white man he had wronged blacks was risky. Asking for reparations was more than audacious. It was gravely impudent. Black men had been killed for less than that. Cudjo, on the front line, and his companions had stood their ground valiantly, just like they had done when enslaved.

Timothy Meaher was incensed. He jumped up from the tree trunk and screamed in Cudjo's face, calling him a fool, claiming he had taken good care of them when they were his slaves and that he did not owe them anything. "You do not belong to me now!" he concluded.[7] His scathing retort was predictable in its form and in its style, but he was certainly sincere when he responded angrily that he had taken good care of them, which in his mind meant they were even. It was the rarest of enslavers who believed he had not been good to his victims and that their free labor was a fair compensation for his care.

The failed meeting must have left Cudjo revolted, perhaps guilt-ridden at not having lived up to the group's expectations. This encounter is not dated but it must have taken place in the early mid-1860s. According to Eva Jones, a daughter of Pollee and Rose Allen, the Africans created their settlement in 1868.[8] Cudjo mentioned that he built a house only after he took a wife. Their first child, Aleck, was born in July 1867, which would suggest they started living together in 1866. Oral tradition thus establishes two possible dates for the formation of the settlement: 1866—the most probable—and 1868. It is confirmed by another source, an 1870 newspaper article that stated, "Since the war these people have gathered into a little community."[9] The shipmates did not own the land; they rented it and built what were probably no more than shacks, unless they had found ex-slave cabins there. But regardless of housing, they were a recognized community.

After Meaher's refusal, their hope for reparations gone, the shipmates faced another round of hungry stomachs and ragged clothes, but they were as determined to settle in the country on their own terms as they had been eager to leave it. All energies and resources were now directed toward achieving their new goal. The men came back from the mills and the railroad yards exhausted, but still wove baskets at night. The women grew all the vegetables that could fill their small patches. Not only had Meaher emphatically said no to free land, but he made it clear that if they wanted his land, they would have to pay it in full. Whatever he asked them for, they gave him, and he did not make any concession.[10] But Timothy was not the only seller. What appears to be the first documented sale took place in 1870, and it does not involve the Meahers.

Some of Thomas Buford's former bondpeople were the buyers, and they purchased land he once owned. Buford had died in 1866 and part of his eighty-two-acre property had been bought by Hiram M. and Ella E. Posey (brother and sister) from Washington County, and one S. Hooks. On April 5, 1870, they sold seven acres to Jaba and Polly Shade, Charlie and Maggie Lewis, Lucy Wilson, and Horace and Matilda Ely. The women's names appear on the deed separately from their husbands', which indicates that they were equal partners in the purchase. The deed states that the group had previously been living on the land. They paid, collectively, $200 (about $1,430 today) for seven acres.[11]

The place, which became known as Lewis Quarters and was located two miles west of the other Africans' settlement, was woodsy and bordered by the Mobile and Ohio railroad track and Three Mile Creek. Buford laid right by it, his grave enclosed by a brick wall.

The Elys were not Africans, but African Americans born in the state, of Alabamian parents. They had probably been enslaved by Buford at the same time as the Lewises and Shades, and their participation in the birth of the settlement illustrates how relations between the Africans and the native born were far from being one-dimensional.[12] Besides the original buyers, two other Africans settled at Lewis Quarters: Anthony Thomas and his Alabama-born wife Ellen, and Lillie and Alabamian Maxwell Nichol. From the start the small neighborhood was thus not only mixed, but Africans represented only about 60 percent of the community.

On September 30, 1872, Cudjo purchased almost two acres for $100 from Colonel Lorenzo Madison Wilson and his wife, Augusta. A very wealthy self-made man, Wilson was president of Springhill Railroad and vice-president of the Mobile and Northern Railroad. His wife was the most famous female Southern author of her time and a staunch Confederate.[13] A few weeks after Cudjo's deal, on October 21, Pollee bought two acres, for which he paid $200. The sellers this time were James M. and Sarah E. Meaher, and Timothy and Mary C. Meaher. Ossa Keeby acquired two acres from the brothers and their wives for $150 on the twenty-eighth.[14]

Saving money and buying the land had been challenging, but they had done it as a community. As the people at Lewis Quarters had done, some shipmates in Plateau had pooled their resources together, bought the land collectively, and then divided it among the participants. It was an unusual arrangement that was African in its spirit and its application. Generally, whether among the Yoruba, the people of Atakora, the Hausa, the Nupe, or the Dendi, land is held by patrilineages and distributed according to need. Unclaimed land belongs to the man who cleared it and in that case too, it is free. So the Africans in Mobile followed the rule they knew: their collective land was apportioned to each family. The next step was to build houses, and they did it cooperatively. Again, the building of dwellings for one another followed African customs. In rural areas, when a young man gets married, he enlists his friends and they work together to erect his house. In Cudjo's town, a man about to build his house had a cow and palm wine at the ready to offer those who came to help. The African tradition of collectivism was certainly a major part of the reason why the shipmates were able to acquire land and housing early, in contrast to many of their neighbors, who continued to rent from the Meahers.[15]

Their lodgings were simple rectangular wood cabins with brick chimneys, similar to that of Cudjo and Abile's, which had two rooms opening on a gallery that extended across the front length, and two smaller rooms at the rear. Cudjo had cut the logs himself and the log cabin "had mortar made out of sand and lime that was put in the cracks . . . no wind or nothing could go in."[16] In the design and the material, it was very different from the round adobe houses with thatch-roofs they had grown up in and that they had the know-how and the red clay necessary to reproduce. Like their friends from Atakora, Borgu, and Kebbi, they had to get used to this architectural novelty, and they never tried to re-create their original dwellings.[17] They were too pragmatic to cling to customs that would have made them stand out more than they already did, but they likely longed for their cool adobe homes in the hot Alabama summers. To demarcate his property, Cudjo put up a fence with eight gates.[18] It was a highly symbolic gesture that had nothing to do with protection as had been the case in his home-town, but served as a daily reminder of his lost community, family, friends, and youth.

The Africans called their settlement African Town, as an acknowledgement of who they were and wanted to remain, and where they wanted to be. But it was also an acknowledgment of their failure. Because they had not been able to return, the next best thing was to "makee de Affica where dey fetch us."[19] It was an African Town for another reason: various people who had become Africans had created it. They were Africans internally and externally. Internally because they had used their Africanity as a cement transcending cultural differences, externally because, to outsiders, they were all the same, Africans, with the nega-tive connotations the term often implied. Their town was unique; it was the first time that a group of Africans—besides the maroons who had hid their camps in swamps and woods since the seventeenth century—had built their very own town on their own land in the United States. It was not the first black settlement, though. Several had been created earlier by white philanthropists for freed people and fugitives, including in Canada. Lovejoy, Illinois—named after abolitionist Elijah P. Lovejoy and which according to oral tradition was founded as a freedom village in the 1820s by free blacks and runaways—can certainly qualify as the first black town in the United States. However, as early as 1837 it had become a biracial town, governed by a white minority who bap-tized the settlement Brooklyn, the name it still bears. Long after Brooklyn, what are considered the oldest "real" black towns in the country, Kendleton and Broad House, were founded in Texas in 1869, some years after the ship-mates' settlement.[20]

African Town had the attributes of a black town, such as at least 90 to 95 percent black inhabitants, black founders, and black control.[21] It had been wished for, planned, and built by a black community without outside help or interest, with the clear objective of establishing itself as an enclave governed according to its own rules—and it was 100 percent black. But African Town differed from all the other black settlements because it was a black town on the surface and an ethnic one at its core. It was not conceived of as a settlement for "blacks," but for Africans. So, as much as it qualifies as a black town, African Town also qualifies as an ethnic one, perhaps the second in the country. As an enclave of foreign nonwhites it was, in a way, similar to those that would grow in the twentieth and twenty-first centuries, but it was also different. Whereas the modern ethnic enclaves—and their precursor, San Francisco's "Little Canton," founded in the late 1840s—continued to have direct links with the home country, African Town was completely cut off from West Africa from the start. In contrast to ethnic enclaves that grew from natural increase and the arrival of immigrants who continuously reinforced their cultural and linguistic specificities, it could not expect to maintain its initial African character. The African communities that did succeed in preserving much of their heritage even as they were cut off from new arrivals, such as the Boni, Saramaka, and Djuka of French Guiana and Surinam, or the Maroons of Jamaica or Colombia, were also large and isolated. African Town was small and completely surrounded by the larger society. Its residents worked and interacted on a daily basis with Americans. For its very survival it was necessary that the town not be "too foreign." As a black ethnic town growing without "homeland input," but with the contribution of some native-born, African Town was a unique entity.

Black towns were safe havens from racism, but African Town was a refuge from Americans. The Africans had little contact with whites, except on the job. Their neighborhood was isolated, and the only whites with a constant presence were the Meahers and Foster, with whom social contact was not even a remote possibility. The Africans' neighbors were by and large the same people they had known since slavery days, and with freedom, relations with some of them had not markedly improved. Actually, the distance had increased in geographical and other terms. On the Meahers' plantations, both groups lived side by side, but once the Africans decided to create their own settlement, they introduced an unequivocal degree of separation, even if some—and later many—men and women born in the country were living with and among them. To establish and name an African Town was not only an act of self-affirmation that reflected its founders' attachment to their cultures and modes of living; it was also an act of self-segregation. They could picture it as the only way they had to preserve their way of life and protect their community from some people's scorn. African Americans could easily interpret it as rejection, hostility, and disdain. Already in 1870, just as the Africans were buying land, they were perceived as separatists by white outsiders who saw the shipmates' wish for autonomy from their own prejudiced perspective: "Since the war, these people have gathered into a little community, retaining their language, and keeping themselves separate from the inferior blacks about them."[22] The very creation of African Town was an assertion that the Africans did not want to be part of any American community, be it African American. Yet, they were not cut off from their neighbors since they welcomed Americans as spouses, and, at Lewis Quarters, as founders. For their part, the men and women who chose to join the settlement were affirming very concretely the numerous commonalities that linked both groups.

AFRICAN TOWN, AFFIKY TOWN, Affika Town, Little Africa, Africa Town, the Africans' town, whatever name it went by, the settlement was growing and its people were thriving, given the circumstances. The women especially were doing well, maybe not in terms of the amount of money they made, but in terms of the kind of work they did. Now that their families owned some land around the houses—the plots were about two acres—the women could grow more vegetables and fruits. They cultivated all sorts of greens, peas, blackberries, corn, peanuts, and potatoes, and grew fig and pecan trees. They sold their produce house-to-house in Mobile. In later years Zuma—with the help of her son George—and Allie launched another type of business. They cooked peas and rice, cornbread, stew, fish, and chicken, and with the pots in big baskets on their heads, they walked to the lumber mills where the African men worked and Americans, black and white, bought their food.[23] The African women's work was not different from their American colleagues', but the kind of independence it brought them quite likely was. For an African woman, working for cash generally means total control of her finances. African wives do not have to participate monetarily to the household, and they seldom do. The husband must provide housing, food, and clothes, even if his wife works, and even if her income is larger than his. When Zuma and her female companions were growing up—and this remains the case today—a woman's earnings were hers to spend any way she saw fit. The market women, the artisans, and the farmers controlled their own economic activities and kept whatever they made for themselves, without interference from their husbands, who were not even supposed to know the amount of the women's income. Their earnings were usually devoted to taxes (for the markets), tolls, *esusu*, reinvestment in their business, funerals, participation in ceremonies—baptisms and weddings—dress, and whatever their husbands did not provide for their children. Given the fact that they had positioned themselves as equal partners with the men when it had come to repatriation efforts, it is possible that the women of African Town did share the family's expenses, but this is by no means certain, or determined by their new environment. Even today many African immigrants to the West continue to adhere to the custom. Among African Americans, it was, on the contrary, the participation of women in paying the household expenses that gave them a degree of autonomy. What model—African or African American—the African women married to Americans adopted is a matter of conjecture.

At the Dennisons', the situation was innovative. Kanko and James worked together and their income was thus produced in tandem. But she was clearly in charge of the couple's money. Throughout her life, Kanko was the one buying small and big items, from hay to furniture, from feed for the animals to lawyer's fees, and bulk grocery. She was getting receipts in her name, occasionally asking for credit, and paying by installments. Sometimes she spent what today would amount to hundreds of dollars at a time.[24] She was acting very much like an African woman in that she was in control of the money, but unlike what happened in a traditional family, that money was not hers only, it was the couple's.

Freedom had not granted the same kind of self-reliance to the men. Pollee was a lumber stacker at Blackshear Lumber Mill; Cudjo made bricks and shingles for the Meahers, and later so did his son Aleck; Ossa Keeby worked as a carpenter. Within a few years, some men had become skilled workers, but others were laborers, like the vast majority of freedmen. Unlike their wives, whose skills had translated into independent jobs, the men used theirs as a complement to their regular work. Within their families and community, they turned into cabinet makers, sculptors, and successful gardeners and farmers. Charlie was known as the man who could fix anything. Keeby, as could be expected, fished. Most men could make walking sticks and chains from wood and cane, and pirogues to go fishing, the African way, from a single tree.[25] But those were tangential activities. Work in the mills and the railroad yards brought them steady pay that was probably superior to what they could have gotten as independent workers.

In truth it would have been difficult for the African men to establish themselves as artisans. The skilled workers and craftsmen who could live from their expertise—they were about 20 percent of black laborers in the South—had already been employed in the same capacities during slavery, and they had a lot of difficulty finding work. Some occupations were reserved to whites, and in many cases authorities demanded licensing fees only from blacks.[26] The Africans, who while growing up had not learned a trade valued in America, could not expect to be self-employed. They did not have the marketable skills that would have brought them a white clientele (and other freed people were like themselves, too poor to buy their service) whose business could sustain their families. As their parcels of land were not large enough—at least in the early years—they could not become bona fide farmers either. However, as a group, the Africans were faring better than the vast majority of freed people. They owned houses and land and were either self-employed or worked in semiskilled jobs. They had not gone back to the cotton row as day laborers or sharecroppers. In the world of poor former slaves, and with the added handicap of being foreigners, their transition from slavery had been, within these limits, a success.

TRANSITION AT HOME FROM AN AFRICAN family structure to an American one was a more delicate issue. The Africans had been trained to fit into what Westerners call an "extended" family. In the Yoruba family, for example, Cudjo or Pollee had several mothers: their biological one as well as her sisters, cousins, co-wives, and the elder brothers' wives living in the household before the children's birth. Grandfathers were their parents' fathers but also the men's brothers and cousins. Their siblings (including from different wives) and cousins were their brothers and sisters. Zuma, as a Nupe woman, had grown up in a compound with her father, his wives, their young children, their married sons, their daughters-in-law, and their grandchildren.[27] In Alabama a type of extended family still existed, but not among the Africans. Many of their neighbors born in the state did indeed live in multigenerational households. By contrast, the Africans' families in Mobile were nuclear. They had no elders to give them advice, transmit knowledge, or teach skills to their children; everybody in the settlement was about the same age. In addition, the new topography of black life after emancipation had reinforced their isolation. As soon as they could, freed men and women had fled the lack of privacy of the quarters, where everyone had to share rooms, for small cabins spread over the land. Three generations sometimes still lived together, but they were no longer cheek to jowl with their neighbors. If the quarters could, to some extent, be compared to an African village where relatives and neighbors lived in close proximity, the organization of the post-emancipation black social space followed Western standards. The Africans in Mobile had adopted this new geography for their town, with single-family houses on individual lots. The familiar landscape of the family compound and the cultivated field away from the village or town could not be replicated, not only for lack of relatives but also for lack of land.

In the economic sphere—and only this one—the women's lives had not changed dramatically from what they would have been had they not been deported: they worked for themselves, not for wages. Moreover, they were employed in the traditional African female occupations: cooking, gardening, or raising poultry. But in the intimate sphere of the family, their previous experience had little value. In their nuclear households, they had to learn to do everything by themselves. If after freedom, African American women had turned to their extended families—including the in-laws they had not known during slavery—Africans could only rely on one another. The only help they could get was from their female friends who were faced with the same issues and time constraints. Learning how to manage a household by themselves was certainly a daunting task, just as overwhelming as the experience of a Western woman who abruptly finds herself living with a dozen in-laws and their relatives. Abile, Omolabi, and Kanko's lives as sisters, daughters, aunts, co-wives, and daughters-in-law—a major part of a woman's existence in Africa—had been obliterated; in the American familial sphere they could only be mothers and wives. Even if from a Western standpoint the fact that each woman was now the sole mistress of her own household could seem "progressive" and empowering, this development was likely not embraced by the Africans. Not only would it have been intimidating and lonely, but the very essence of their womanliness, as defined by their cultures, would have been diminished.

As for their husbands, they now found themselves the heads of families, a position they would not have held had they lived in Banté, Dahomey, or Borgu.

Even married, Fon, Yoruba, Hausa, and Dendi men were not the final author-ity, because the family head was the patriarch, the eldest of the paternal line. In Mobile, only the couples from Atakora would have been in known territory, as husbands become the head of the family cell, with control and manage-ment powers.[28] Most couples in African Town did not have the particular skills required to run a nuclear family. Therefore the role of the community and its unity were all the more crucial: parents needed all the help, knowledge, skills, and memories they could get from their companions in order to raise their children as African as feasible in an unfamiliar environment and family structure.

As it grew with intramarriages, exogamous unions—which brought their own sets of cultural and educational issues—and children, the community thought it needed not only a chief, but also a controlling body. Outsiders were convinced that the Africans never quarreled, that they all got along famously, and always acted as one. This notion had started during slavery, when Noah and his companions noticed that they never squabbled.[29] Decades later, Roche concurred, they were "very considerate of each other, and their intercourse is marked by kindness, charity, and harmony."[30] Given the rules of etiquette among West Africans, it is not surprising that strangers would have found them par-ticularly kind and deferential to one another. In age-class societies, protocol is quite important and marks of reverence and respect are prominent. Yoruba men, for example, prostrate themselves before "superiors" (in age or status), while two men of equal standing "stoop to the ground as they meet and shake hands all the while saluting each other."[31] Women drop on one leg and place one arm across their breast. Among the Nupe, men of equal rank greet each other by bowing low while women get down on one knee. And in all African societies, greetings are long, elaborate, and detailed, as each party enquires about the other's previous night's sleep and about the health of each member of the family. As the American missionary William H. Clarke noted in the late 1850s, "these salutations, prostrations and genuflections are continued all day, however often the parties may meet."[32]

The appearance of utmost harmony and cohesion the Africans projected was certainly genuine—even though it did not mean there were no quarrels—but it was also calculated to position them as a group whose protection rested in numbers and unity, and it had worked to their advantage. It had been disad-vantageous too, as it contributed to their alienation from some of their neigh-bors. But appearances notwithstanding, they had their share of disagreements and of people who would not follow the rules. In the early years it is more than likely that some youngsters did not know how to behave as expected. Perhaps the "misbehaving" had really begun in the *barracoon* at Ouidah. Their families had raised the children swept away by the transatlantic slave trade for a few years, but when the slavers struck, their kin had disappeared from their lives, leaving them traumatized, confused, tormented by depression, full of questions that could not be answered. When they were growing up at home, things had been easy: they had been told exactly what to do. They had learned they were not individuals first, but members of the family who had to follow very strict rules according to their age, gender, and position. But once they found themselves on their own, they were no longer defined as a son, a daughter, or a nephew: they were just individuals, and they had to figure out what it meant.

IN AFRICAN TOWN, the children of the *Clotilda* were now teenagers who had had an immensely traumatic youth and needed guidance and control, as did anybody who set their mind on doing something of which the others did not approve. The community, reproducing a traditional African pattern of local justice, decided that what they needed were judges. At the meeting they called to choose them, Jaba the doctor and Ossa Keeby were selected.[33] Significantly for Africans, both men were among the oldest in the group. As they had already shown when naming Gumpa as their leader, the shipmates' primary criteria were not ethnicity, place of origin, or religious identity, but rather age and competence.

The next step was to make laws that everyone had to adhere to. Those that have come to light were simple: do not steal, do not get drunk, and do not hurt anybody. The rules were designed to keep harmony within the community and to avoid any appearance of impropriety that would damage the town in the eyes of outsiders. From then on when a problem arose, the shipmates sent word around and met at night. African Town was known for what people thought were secret meetings during which the residents practiced "barbaric rites."[34] The sort of court they had created, different than and outside of the official structures, was unknown to their neighbors, and it is not surprising that they found the nightly comings and goings suspicious. But the Africans were just being pragmatic; they did not have anything to hide, they simply all worked during the day. At the meetings, just as they would have done in West Africa, the offenders or accused stood in front of the community. Both sides of the story were heard, each one examined carefully. The guilty party was reprimanded and sent back home with a warning to "go and keep the peace." If the dispute or the condemned behavior continued, everybody was summoned once again and, in front of the assembly, the culprit was whipped. The judges handled the lash, but they were not above the law. Everybody observed them, and if they did something deemed unacceptable, they were reprimanded too. People told them, "We saw you do this thing. It is not right. How do you expect us to do right if you do not show us the way?"[35] Although Jaba and Ossa commanded absolute obedience, the fact that they too could be reprimanded indicates that the town had built a democratic system of checks and balances that was essential for its unity and cohesion.

AFRICAN TOWN REGROUPED the overwhelming majority of the Africans, but not everyone who had arrived on the *Clotilda* chose to settle there. Kanko lived in downtown Mobile, and Adissa had moved to Mauvilla. They were married to Americans and had in all probability followed their husbands—as expected in America and in their homelands—when the men had found an opportunity elsewhere. It is also possible that these men did not want to live in African Town, where they would have been a minority, quasi-strangers in their own country, governed by rules they may not have liked.

In Mobile, the Dennisons had worked hard for several years, and finally, in 1870, they bought a place at the corner of Royal and Delaware Streets. They did not own just a little house with a garden. It was a farm in the city, and they rented adjacent land, where they raised hogs, cows, chickens, and horses. They grew foodstuff for the animals and the family; fed the cattle and the fine pigs (whose reputation for good meat had spread all around), and washed them; milked the cows; chopped wood; repaired the fences; and kept the dairy farm, the chicken coops, the barn, the grazing land, the horses' stalls, and the pig-pens clean.[36] James, the river man, the pilot who could navigate the bayous and the rivers blindfolded, had become a first-class farmer. According to his son and grandchildren, he studied the stars, the elements, the temperature, the cycles of the insects, and crop rotation, and was constantly researching, analyzing, and patiently observing, his inseparable pipe stuck between his lips. He even had a patch where he grew medicinal plants. Perhaps he had asked advice of Jaba or Kanko, who was also versed in herbal remedies. His family stressed that James was a generous man who always made sure he had extra crops for the needy and even the birds; he was modest and kind, but could have a temper. When he was provoked, they said, he sometimes lost control. Kanko was not to be treaded on either. She was short and thin and did not look like she could beat anybody up, her family recalled, but she was strong and unafraid. One day, a constable came to the farm to discuss some matters. Kanko did not like what he said and the way he said it. According to her descendants, she picked him up and threw him out.[37] Even in her old age, when she was over eighty, she continued breeding and raising her famous hogs, and she was known to "work as a man."[38] If the Dennisons' professional life was a success, their family life was not happy. They had lost their first child, Jerry, and one day, when he was only thirteen, their son William had left home for reasons un-known. His parents did not hear from him until he briefly came back from New Orleans where he had settled, almost thirty years later, to introduce his twenty-one-year-old son. And their only daughter, Equilla, died of tetanus at thirteen in May 1891.[39]

As their business grew, James and Kanko opened a bank account. They chose the Freedman's Savings and Trust Company, incorporated at the same time as the Freedmen's Bureau was created.[40] With the bank, stated one of its founders, "pauperism can be brought to a close; the freedmen made self-supporting and

prosperous, paying for their educational and Christian institutions, and helping to bear the burdens of government by *inducing habits of savings* in what they
earn."[41] Other Africans may have used the Freedman's Bank services, but their
names do not appear among a list of 1,700 depositors in Mobile. Because the
Dennisons' name does not come up either, it cannot be stated with certainty if
other shipmates were clients or not.[42] James and Kanko were given a booklet
with a poem on the back: "'Tis little by little the bee fills her cell; . . . Step by
step we walk miles, and we sew stitch by stitch; Word by word we read books,
cent by cent we grow rich." A table informed them that by placing ten cents a
day at 6 percent, the interest would amount to $36.99 the first year and $489.31
after ten. It was not easy to save ten cents, when wages were a dollar or less a
day, but the prospect of a bank devoted to helping freed people—Frederick
Douglass called them "untutored Africans"—achieve dreams of ownership of
house, land, cattle, or hogs was enticing. In its first month, the Mobile branch
received $4,809 in small sums. By March 1870, its 3,260 depositors had put
down close to $540,000, an average of $165 per person. At least $50,000 had
been used to buy land and another $15,000 bought seeds and agricultural ani-
mals and equipment.[43]

But problems emerged in the early 1870s. Along with the economic panic
of 1873 that plunged the country into the worst depression it had known to
date, mismanagement, corruption, and fraud brought the bank to its knees. As
the depositors were rushing to the tellers to take their money out, a public
relations plan was hastily hatched in Washington. The bank needed credibility. Who better than Frederick Douglass could restore confidence? In March
1874, in his own words, "Frederick, the slave boy, running about . . . with only
a tow linen shirt to cover him, [became] Frederick, President of a bank count-
ing its assets by millions."[44] After having lent the bank $10,000, he discovered
how badly managed his institution was: it had missing money, dishonest agents,
cooked books, and huge deficits. The trustees had so little confidence that they
either had not invested a penny or had taken their assets out. Three months
after he had been appointed, Douglass asked Congress to close down the bank,
as the situation was beyond repair. By the end of June 1874, the Freedman's
Bank had shut its doors for good. It came as a terrible blow to the freedmen
and -women who had had faith in it and believed that the government had guar-
anteed their deposits. During its nine years of existence, seventy thousand people
had opened accounts and deposited a total of more than $55 million nation-
wide. The bank owed them more than $3 million. In Mobile, $95,000 evaporated.[45] What happened to the Dennisons' money is not known. Only half of
the tens of thousands of depositors nationwide received three dollars for every
five they had entrusted to the bank. Some got nothing, and it would take others decades to be partially reimbursed. But money was not the only thing they
lost. Trust in the government and the banking system plummeted. Black people
had done the right thing; they had worked hard, been thrifty, saved up their

money to buy land, a house, mules, hogs, or cattle. They thought their dreams were within reach, and they felt betrayed and abused by the banking system and the government, a sentiment that their descendants would carry on for generations. Douglass was mortified by the experience, humiliated to have been part of a failure that had deprived his "confiding people" of their hard-earned money and dreams.

ON JULY 28, 1868, AFRICAN AMERICANS had become citizens of the United States when the Fourteenth Amendment to the Constitution was ratified, but the Africans were not included. They were still foreigners and if they wanted their citizenship, they had to acquire it. So, on October 24, Tony and Archie Thomas, Charlie Lewis, Gumpa, Pollee, Ossa, Cudjo, and John Reed decided it was time to do just that. They went to court and were ushered into a room full of Germans, English, Irish, Italians, Austrians, and Canadians. A clerk asked their names, their ages, and how long they had been in America. Cudjo, Pollee, and Ossa said they were twenty-one, or perhaps the clerk just thought they looked like they were twenty-one. They were, in reality, in their late twenties. Tony Thomas was recorded as being twenty-eight, and Archie twenty-five. Charlie was thirty. John Reed had not come on the *Clotilda*; he was sixty-five and had arrived when he was only five, just as the international slave trade was coming to an official close. The men of the *Clotilda* told the clerk they had been in the country ten years, when in reality they had arrived just eight years earlier. It must have been an honest mistake because they had no good reason to lie. There were men in the room that day who had arrived a year earlier and were still going to become Americans. After all the mistakes on ages and dates had been duly reported, Cudjo, Ossa, Pollee, Charlie, the Thomases, and John Reed declared "under oath to be *bona fide* their intention to become citizens of the United States."[46]

Soon, all the African men had become Americans, if not in spirit at least in status. Like many other immigrants, they did not acquire a new citizenship simply because of a particular love for their adopted country or to become culturally American, but to be protected and obtain rights denied foreigners. Besides, the concept of citizenship was foreign to the Africans. They had never been citizens of any place. They had been part of the Isha, the Yoruba, or Fon, and some had belonged to a particular kingdom. But to be a citizen of one country was meaningless in pre-colonial Africa. To the African men in Mobile, becoming American citizens did not mean renouncing who they had been and were. They continued to identify as Africans in their dealings with the outside world. But how did this declaring U.S. citizenship fit into their dreams of return? Did it mean that they were in America for good, that they had definitively renounced to go back home when they entered the courtroom and, hands on their hearts, declared their allegiance to the flag? As people to whom the very notion of citizenship could not mean much, the Africans did not view this move as the ultimate rupture with the past and an exclusion of future homecoming. But being Americans gave them rights. It turned out they would not have many as long as they lived, but at least during Reconstruction, they would enjoy a few.

Unbeknownst to them, at the time they were becoming citizens, their former enslavers had to go through similar motions. On October 22, just two days before Ossa, Pollee, Cudjo, and the others became Americans, William Foster, still a Nova Scotian, did too.[47] He had not felt the need to do so during the twenty-five years he had already spent in the country, but Reconstruction was as good an incentive as any for white Southern foreigners to make sure they would have their say in the future political life of the region and the country. As for the Meahers, who had previously belonged to the Confederacy, they too needed to take an oath to be reintegrated into the Union. On September 14, three days after James, Timothy swore allegiance to the United States.[48] Before that day, just like the Africans, the brothers did not have the right to vote. Timothy had not taken the oath in 1865—James had—and he had not asked for a presidential pardon.[49] Timothy was a holdout, fitting well with his personality.

The three Meahers had lost an investment in human beings that today would be valued at almost a million dollars, but they were far from ruined. Like most of their class, they were doing fine. Some planters had lost their land, portions of which had been bought by smaller farmers or wealthy merchants; others had turned to new industries rather than continue working in cotton. A few plantations had passed into the hands of men who had not been slaveholders before, but the large plantocracy persisted through the war and Reconstruction.[50] With their land, their lumber mill, their shipyard, and their boats, the Meahers still had significant worth. James's postwar real estate holdings were valued at $10,000 ($200,000 in today's dollars), although his personal wealth was a piteous $200. Timothy was worth $10,000 in real estate and another $10,000 in personal property. In the area, only William Turner, who owned a sawmill, was wealthier; his net worth was double that of Meaher.[51]

Wisely, after the war, Timothy had dropped the word *Southern* from his largest steamer, which continued to do business between Mobile and Montgomery as the *Republic*. He had been less lucky with his *Red Gauntlet*, the legendary blockade-runner. After escaping from Mobile Bay following the capture of Fort Morgan, the steamer reappeared a few months later, only to be seized by the U.S. Navy.[52] The captain remained a few more years on the rivers, and in 1870, he decided to retire. He did not have to stop working, but he did because he was infuriated at what emancipation had done to the ex-slaves. In the words of the Mobile *Daily Register*, "Freedom ha[d] worked great changes in the negro, bringing out all his inherent savage qualities." Meaher certainly shared that opinion. "I quit the river," he said, "when the colored citizens demanded cabin passage."[53] His contempt of blacks had finally gotten the best of him. He hated their freedom with such a passion that, rather than accepting them as regular passengers on his ships and giving them the amenities that their money could buy, he decided to give up his successful business. And he was eager to let everyone know it. Once again, he revealed himself as an active racist who loathed blacks, not just a Southern swashbuckler as he has been presented.

In African Town, the late 1860s were particularly significant. Christianity descended upon the community. During slavery, the Catholic Meaher brothers had shown no interest in making conversions. They were of the school that believed religion, in convincing the enslaved that everyone was equal before God, could only bring problems. Those who believed, on the contrary, that Christianity, if wisely used, was a tremendous enabler for slavery had forced their bondpeople to sit in the segregated balconies of their churches, or held special services for them on Sunday afternoons with tailored-made sermons. "Obey your massa and missy, don't steal chicken and eggs and meat, but nary a word 'bout havin' a soul to save" is how one freedman remembered them.[54] Jenny Proctor, enslaved in Alabama, recalled that the white preacher said: "Now I takes my text, which is, nigger obey your master and your mistress, 'cause what you git from dem here in dis world am all you ev'r goin' to git, 'cause you jes' like de hogs and de other animals, when you dies you ain't no more, after you been throwed in dat hole."[55] Black pastors did hardly better than whites, pressured as they were to preach obedience and servility. But some took risks and taught instead a gospel of freedom. They did it in secret, because since 1833, black priests in Alabama could preach only if five white slaveholders were present.

Once free again, the Africans had not been touched by divine grace of the Christian kind. They had stopped dancing on Sundays, though, and when they had built a drum and danced again it had been such a triumphant day that even Free George, the evangelist, would have forgiven them. After freedom, he had been a fixture in the community. He was always there, he helped, and he did not make fun of anyone. Cudjo believed he was the best friend the Africans had.[56] He also had the same agenda as before. After several years of trying, he finally convinced them that Christianity was their salvation. The general ambiance helped: with missionaries everywhere, and black churches opening up, conversions and baptisms were going on at a furious pace.

Free George must have been a Methodist, because the first church the Africans attended was a Methodist church in Toulminville, a few miles south of their town.[57] The well-organized African Methodist Episcopal Church and the African Methodist Episcopal Zion Church had been among the very first on the ground in Alabama and the South as soon as the war was over. With emancipation, there were four million souls to put—in the religious activists' words—on the righteous path to honesty, thrift, discipline, moderation, conjugal faithfulness, and piousness. Local black preachers and black and white Northerners from various denominations were competing for the heavenly reward of converting the freedmen. The black Methodists descended south with priests, deacons, elders, teachers, and money. And they immediately set out to train a local clergy and open up churches that attracted most of their coreligionists who had been attending service in the segregated facilities of their white brethren. Seven years after emancipation, the AME Church and the AME Zion Church, once prohibited in Alabama, had a combined membership of about 25,000. They were doing far better than the Colored Methodist Episcopal Church—sponsored and supervised by the Southern whites—that attracted the "good Negroes" and smelled too much of slavery days to be a force among freed people. Five years after emancipation, only 750 black Methodist Mobilians out of more than 10,700 were still members of the Southern Methodist Church.[58]

Another Northern church that came to evangelize the freedmen was the Congregational Church, which had hardly any followers in the state before the war. It did not make much headway afterwards, even though the Congregationalist American Missionary Association worked closely with the Freedmen's Bureau and opened schools. But James Dennison, for one, was convinced, and he converted. He became a member of the First Congregational Church on South Scott and Palmetto Streets in downtown Mobile. He used to make a grand appearance every Sunday, elegantly dressed, with his long braids and his wide hat, riding Fannie, his finest horse. More than ten years after the end of the war, Dennison was one of only six hundred Congregationalists in the entire state.[59]

None of James's African friends had followed him along that path, not even his wife. After having frequented the Methodist Church, they turned to Baptism, like half a million people who by 1870 belonged to the Negro Baptist Church. The Baptists had always had more local autonomy than the Methodists, and here and there, little black Baptist churches led by a local clergy had started to spring up and flourish. Revival meetings were frequent and attracted throngs of people. The Alabama Baptist Convention had not approved, and right after the war, it had passed a resolution that tried to keep "our late slaves" in the fold: "while we recognize their right to withdraw from our churches and form organizations of their own, we nevertheless believe that their highest good will be subserved by their retaining their present relation to those who know them, who love them, and who will labor for the promotion of their welfare."[60] Despite these dubious early claims, by 1867 most white congregants had become active champions of separation. It had quickly dawned on them that in the Tennessee Valley and the Black Belt, blacks outnumbered them by such a margin that whites were a minority in church. Of course, during slavery, there had always been more blacks in the balconies—not seen, not heard—than whites in the aisles, but they were enslaved and they knew their place. And when it became too uncomfortable, the whites abandoned the building, built another church, and gave the old one to the blacks, still retaining control over what was done and said there. But with free men and women, it could become much worse than uncomfortable. Blacks could in theory sit cheek by jowl in the same pews with the whites, bring in African American preachers, have communion not after the whites but at the same time, be baptized in the same water, and control the church. It was judged more advantageous to persuade them to establish their own institutions. But the freed people did not need encouragement. To mark their religious freedom they had deserted the white churches.

Once interested in Baptism, the Africans went to the Stone Street Baptist Church, considered the black "mother church" in Alabama. It had been founded in 1806 by Richard Fields, a freed preacher, under the name African Church. When they joined, Rev. Benjamin Franklin Burke, a fifty-year-old Virginian minister, officiated.[61] Despite its long and distinguished history, the church was criticized by some for its mixed record on education and for not being active in missionary work. Reverend Burke, however, was quite successful with the Africans. According to Cudjo, one day in 1869, he asked him where he wanted to go when he died. Cudjo pointed to the sky and said, "I want to go yonder." He then converted.[62] And so did his companions.

Nothing is known about the interrogations, dilemmas, and soul-searching that led up to their decision. But what is well known is how rare and difficult it is for Muslims to convert. Apostasy is considered a heinous crime in Islam for which the punishment can be, in conservative societies, death. The Muslims in African Town had nothing to fear in that regard; in their respective societies they would have been ostracized, perhaps driven out of town, but not killed. Nevertheless, rejection by the family, which is akin to social death, can be reason enough for an African Muslim not to convert. As perhaps could be expected, Zuma's religious status is ambiguous. She had a reputation. Some said she was a "witch doctor," with all the negative connotations the expression conveyed; others believed she had healing abilities, and was a kind of spiritual advisor.[63] Henry C. Williams, Sr., who grew up close to Cudjo and has a good knowledge of the early-twentieth-century story of the group, was told that she never went to church. Emma Langdon Roche mentioned, "She has been seen to make a cross and spit in the middle of it."[64] According to Roche, her companions did not seem to understand her motive. Two contradictory explanations can be given for her action. In Western cultures, spitting is associated with disgust, contempt, even hate. Within this context, it is logically understood that Zuma despised Christianity and concretely expressed her contempt by spitting on its most sacred symbol. On the other hand, spitting in Islam is an expression of piety. This kind of spitting, however, does not involve the heavy discharge of saliva, but the light, repeated emission of spittle. People spit on their open hands after a prayer, and a religious leader will spit on them after prayer because spittle to which Qur'anic words have been added is considered a source of goodness and even a cure. According to one Hadith (a saying attributed to the Prophet Muhammad), "Aisha [his wife] said that the Prophet told a sick man, 'In the name of Allah, the earth of our ground and the saliva of some of us cure our sick, by God's Grace'."[65] In addition, the Prophet is said to have spit on his hands before going to bed and wiped his face and rubbed his body. Thus, it is possible that Zuma, a Christian with a Muslim past, spat on the cross as a pious gesture. Still, one may argue that after more than forty years as a Christian, she would have learned that spitting on the cross was not acceptable among her coreligionists. It is something Free George would likely have told her from the start.

The religion of a shipmate, who died at work, is unclear too. He was said to have requested that clean clothes, shoes, a pipe, and tobacco be placed in his coffin for his journey to what a witness called the "spirit land."[66] Questions can also be raised as to the extent or depth of Pollee's conversion. He did, after all, keep the earrings that signaled him as an *orisa* devotee and former *ile orisa* initiate. And had Gumpa renounced Vodun? According to Henry C. Williams, Sr., Cudjo said that he went to church and sat down, but left before the reverend started his sermon.[67] If that were the case, it would indicate that Gumpa, as the leader of the town, made a point of being present at the social gathering, but left when the religious part started because he had not converted. Yet, like Keeby's son, one of Gumpa's grandsons became a reverend.

The shipmates had land and houses; they had, for the most part, become Christians; and they were American citizens. They seemed, if not integrated into the wider society, at the very least adapted to life in America. Had the plan of return to Africa definitively become just a dream? One Sunday in 1870, their resolve was put to the test. They had gone to church in Mobile as usual, but that day the preacher was A. D. Phillips, who had just come back from twelve years in Yorubaland. As was his habit, he said the Lord's Prayer in Yoruba. When he was through, the Africans started to shout. They walked up to him after the service and told him they wanted to go back home "that they may meet with their families again, and make known some of the advantages of civilization and the riches of the Gospel."[68] Following their meeting with Phillips, who informed them of its existence, twenty-six sent the ACS a petition to go to Liberia. African Town was ready to pack up, leave, and disappear. The dream was still a plan.

Two years passed, and the shipmates did not hear from the ACS. In the meantime, interest in emigration to Africa had picked up in the state. The ACS claimed to have received 550 applications from Alabama in February 1872, and a group of Africans was trying to get back home.[69] They were said to be the people of the *Wanderer*. According to a clergyman, they had formed an association in Birmingham in 1872, and vowed to do everything in their power to emigrate. One, named Peter, married to a shipmate, was so excited when he heard of the ACS that he joked he and his companions would make the reverend king if they could return home. They were, reportedly, from fifty to one hundred between Montgomery, Lowndes, Dallas, Wilcox, Conecuh, and Mobile.[70] The number of *Wanderer* Africans in Alabama was never as high and, perhaps, the group also counted the people of African Town. Another possibility is that, once again, people had the name of the ship wrong, and that the would-be migrants were in fact the *Clotilda* shipmates scattered all over the Black Belt and Mobile.

On May 22, 1873, A. D. Phillips, who had not forgotten the people of African Town, wrote a letter to the ACS stressing their desire to leave.[71] But no African from Alabama, whether they arrived on the *Clotilda* or the *Wanderer*, emigrated with the ACS, and of the hundreds of African Americans who wished to leave the state during and after Reconstruction, only forty-three succeeded in doing so.[72] Henry Russell, from Greenville, who had a group ready, explained some of the obstacles to emigration: "some . . . own a little property, but such is the financial condition of this region, they are not likely to get anything for it; and besides that the whites are so much opposed to the colored people going to Liberia that it is very hard for them to get away at all."[73]

AFTER A DOZEN YEARS IN THE COUNTRY, and valiant attempts at leaving it, the shipmates had their hopes shattered once more. The prospects of a lifetime in America sank in again, and they resolved to step up their efforts to spend it as best they could. Their new religion had become quite important to them, and their next project revolved around it. Besides attending service in Mobile every week, the shipmates, who displayed quite a religious zeal, had held prayer meetings in one another's homes. But the long walks to church and the makeshift sanctuaries in African Town were starting to take a toll. They thought it would be better to go to church nearby, but they did not want to worship with the Americans who lived in the vicinity because they made fun of them and called them ignorant savages.[74] Relations with some of their neighbors were still not good. They were no longer a threat, but the stigma of being African had remained. So, as the freedmen were establishing their churches independently from the whites, the Africans decided to build their own place where they would be at ease among themselves, and not be the objects of ridicule. Once again, they set themselves apart from the rest of the community.

They started to gather money and material, and continued to attend the Stone Street Baptist Church, where several were baptized by pastor Burke. In their free time, they worked on their church. Finally, in February 1872, the Old Landmark Baptist Church opened its doors on the other side of Cudjo and Abile's fence, facing east toward Africa.[75] The very first church erected in the area, it was a simple white clapboard building with a foyer, four windows in the front and several on the sides, surrounded by trees. Its first pastor was

Elder Henry McCrea, twenty-six, formerly enslaved in Mississippi.[76] After the war, he had become a laborer and, once a preacher, he probably continued to work during the week, because the pastor of a small community of former slaves could not count on much money, vegetables, and chickens and eggs to sustain himself, his wife, and four daughters. Being the reverend of the Africans' church could not do much for him in terms of prestige, but McCrea was young and inexperienced, and he may have seen his tenure at Old Landmark as a stepping-stone. Only nineteen at war's end, he was too young to have been a preacher during slavery. For him and most of his colleagues, the profession was brand new. Their training had been brief, and although most could read and write, many others could only read, or were almost or completely illiterate. McCrea, however, was part of a minority that could neither read nor write. Perhaps he had memorized the passages of the Bible he thought spoke most strongly to his congregation. Or maybe his faith, his eloquence, and his human touch felt better to them than fluent readings of the Gospels. Still, they were aware of their reverend's limitations, and they continued to go to Elder Burke for serious business.

Whites loudly voiced their criticisms of men like McCrea, the preachers they had not formed and trained. They were ignorant, they said, immoral, inept, credulous, and as full of superstition as their flocks. Elders and believers, wrote an Alabama newspaper, were "falling back into their native superstition and idolatry."[77] What really bothered many whites was that the ministers were out of their control. The church had become the cornerstone of the African American community, and it could be subversive. A reverend who preached equality, not just freedom, was a dangerous firebrand. In Mobile, some ministers had been accused of calling the whites "devils and demons" and of inciting a race war. White mobs and the Ku Klux Klan beat up the "uppity" pastors and burned down their churches. In Alabama some Republican ministers were killed.[78] But Elder McCrea was not a rabble-rouser. He was not run out of town, and Old Landmark was not torched. Every Sunday morning, the thirty or so families of African Town, dressed in their good clothes, emerged from the shady paths and the gardens and walked to their white church on the hill. As James Dennison was saddling Fannie to take him to mass at Mobile First Congregationalist Church, Kanko had already made her way to Plateau.

The services in African Town were said to be less lively than those at other black churches.[79] The Africans did not holler, jump, clap, stomp, and shout. They saw the stomping and shouting at Stone Street Baptist Church—which had been vigorously denounced by whites who wanted to close it down in 1840—every time they had attended in the past, but they did not bring it to their church.[80] Perhaps they had been so ridiculed when they danced and sang that they wanted to make a point, or perhaps they thought that since they had to stop dancing in order to honor God it made little sense once they were Christian to hop and skip in church. Their neighbors' services, full of life and energy, were unnerving the whites who had grown used to not seeing or hearing their slaves, quiet in the church galleries, or mute in front of the black preacher flanked by white men on the lookout. Some of these "old plantation preachers" were said to disapprove of the new "religious frenzy," and people complained that the meetings of the "African congregations" were occasions to steal poultry, fruits, and vegetables.[81] Things had changed, indeed. Black folks sang and danced their faith and their love of God and Jesus the way they saw fit. To whites, the services were a circus and the congregants no more than spruced-up pagans not far removed from their heathen past. Dahomey was just around the corner. As one woman fretted, "the negro *en masse*, relapsed promptly into the voodooism of Africa. . . . In some localities, devil-dancing, as imported from Africa centuries ago, still continues."[82] Gumpa, more than anybody else, would have been flabbergasted at the notion that American Protestants could be mistaken for followers of Vodun.

Besides the Sunday service that started at four in the morning and kept them in church almost all day, on and off, the new Christians went to Old Landmark on Wednesday, Friday, and Saturday evenings.[83] Cudjo was devout. He loved listening to passages from the Bible and had even started memorizing them. His new religion had become a major part of his life, but he was not prepared to condemn his old faith. He did not like to be asked about it and sometimes declared that he and the others were already Christians in Africa.[84] He never said anything about his religion before the *Clotilda*, nor did anyone else. "Nothing could be learned regarding the practice or nonpractice of any "fetich" or "voudou rites," noted Romeyn.[85] It was their parents' religions their interlocutors wanted them to dissect and ridicule, and they continuously refused to do so. Abile was as exasperated as her husband when God and Africa came up, and she did not mince her words. One day a white man came to visit. Abile and Cudjo received him well, and they started to talk. They insisted they wanted to go back home. The visitor told them that if they did, they would have to give up their religion. "There was a moment's pause, and then, very solemnly, and with a pitying expression [Abile] said 'White man, yo' no t'ink God in my country same like here?'"[86] The centuries-old American conviction that Africans were "pagans," which justified their enslavement, was repeatedly leveled at the Africans, and they kept on refuting it. As much as they refused to talk about the details of their former religions to those who at least knew they had one, they insisted that they already had a God. Cudjo explained, "he name Alahua [*oluwa* in Yoruba] but po' Affickans we cain read de Bible, so we doan know God got a Son."[87] It was indeed news to them, as it had been for Zuma and the other Muslims, since Islam does not recognize Jesus as the Son of God, but as a prophet. Another way of expressing their belief in one God before their Christian experience was to say they knew somebody had built the sky.[88]

EIGHTEEN-SEVENTY-TWO, the year Old Landmark Baptist Church opened, ushered in the beginning of the end for black rights in the South in general, and Alabama in particular. In May Congress passed a broad Amnesty Act that was to put the Democrats back in power. The law was an ominous sign to the black population. Then they received another blow. The Freedmen's Bureau closed down. Even with all its shortcomings, it had been a protection against abuse. And, importantly, it had run schools that catered to more than 150,000 children throughout the South. The demise of the bureau would augur more difficult times for the freed men and women. A year later in Alabama, two black elected officials, Montgomery County representative L. J. Williams and Dallas County senator Jeremiah Haralson, worked hard to push a civil rights bill through the legislature. Democrats and white Republicans found enough common ground to defeat it.

Then came the state elections of 1874. The Democratic Convention denounced Congress, stating that it had no authority to pass laws on equality, and virulently condemned the civil rights bill being discussed in Washington. As the *Montgomery Advertiser* summed it up, it was "a contest between antagonistic races and for that which is held dearer than life by the white race. If the negro must rule Alabama permanently, whether in person or by proxy, the white man must ultimately leave the state." The Florence *Times Journal* was even more direct: "Nigger or no nigger is the question," it wrote in its September 30 edition.[89] The Democrats had campaigned for months on a "no nigger," white supremacy, and state's rights platform. It was such a success that by the time election came the Republican Party had lost all its white members, except four thousand, to the Democrats.

Freedmen represented 90 percent of the party's members, and they had become disenchanted with the white Radicals and moderates, who kept putting off their demands for equality in order not to lose white northern Alabama, which still voted for Lincoln's party. Black voters wanted better political representation in the Black Belt, equal rights, and mixed schools. When their leaders met in June at an Equal Rights Convention closed to the whites, they demanded equal access to schools, universities, and colleges "in order that the idea of the inferiority of the Negro might be broken up."[90] The Radical state convention, for its part, fearful of alienating white voters, adopted a platform in August that supported political and civil equality but said that in the practical application of these principles they neither "claimed nor desired the social equality of different races or of individuals of the same race."[91]

Given the problems the Republicans faced and their divisions, the Democrats were confident it would be a white man's government once again. They ran on a white supremacy platform, forcefully expressed in the *Mobile Daily Register*, which called on whites to "answer to the roll call of white supremacy over the black monkey mimics of civilization, who arrogate superiority over men whom God made their masters, not in chattel slavery of their persons, but to dominate them in intellect, in morals, in education, in courage, and 'native worth.'"[92] The Democrats wanted to ensure that the "negro party" was soundly defeated so that a two-party system would not be established. The Ku Klux Klan—which claimed 12,000 members in the state—the Knights of the White Camellia, the White Brotherhood, the White League, the Pale Faces, and the Men of Peace set out to do the party's terrorist work. At the least, they intimidated and beat up blacks throughout the state; at worst, they tortured and killed.

Violence was widespread during the 1874 campaign, and so was intimidation. This election was so crucial for the Democrats that, like other white bosses of black men all over the South, Timothy Meaher felt he had to give a speech to the Africans. He obligingly explained the mechanisms and the importance of the vote and told them to give theirs to the Democrats. On November 3, with Timothy Meaher's admonition ringing in their ears, Charlie, Pollee, and Cudjo walked to Whistler. As they approached the polling station, they spotted their boss waiting for them. He had seen them coming down the road, walking one behind the other, like rural Africans do. He had told them what to do, but he must have had a hunch they were not going to obey. Perhaps he had overheard something, or caught a glimpse of defiance in their eyes as they were listening to his speech. Certain they were not going to vote right, he was determined to stop them. In the station, Meaher pointed at the men and said loudly, "See those Africans? Don't let them vote—they are not of this country." Who was going to question Meaher? Charlie, Pollee, and Cudjo were told to get out. They knew voting was not going to be easy; they had certainly heard about the threats, the beatings, and the killings that had been going on before Election Day. But if the Democrats won, life was going to turn even uglier, so the trio took the road again and walked to another station. Meaher was not a fool; he knew what their next move was going to be. For the past fourteen years he had seen them resist; he knew they would not be satisfied until they had given their vote to the Republicans. As soon as they left, he jumped on his horse, and when they got to the polling station, he was already there. Once again, the men were turned away, but they were not going to cave in. They took St. Stephen's Road, where there was another voting station. They were taking risks, openly defying the man who still employed some of them. As soon as they got to the place, they saw him just getting off his horse. Still, they walked to the station. Once more, they heard him say, "Don't let those Africans vote—they have no right—they are not of this country." Meaher had won another round.

The Africans put their hands together, raised their arms to the skies, and prayed to God to let them vote. This time they decided to go as far away as possible. One behind the other, they trekked down to St. Francis Street in Mobile. When they got to the voting station, they looked around and did not see Meaher. They were told that by paying a dollar they could vote. There was a time, not too long before, when one dollar was a full twelve-hour day's pay, but they handed over their money. Cudjo, Pollee, and Charlie cast their ballot for the Republicans and they received a piece of paper proving they had voted. They kept it for decades.[93]

Bullying had not worked, and they had outfoxed their boss and former owner. But most important, they had achieved what they had set out to do several years earlier. Their participation in the American political process was a logical next step after becoming citizens, and on that day in November 1874, they had put their citizenship to work. Their involvement proved that they had a good understanding of the impact that politics had on the survival and progress of their own community and the future of the black population. Although they wanted to remain separate, they knew that whatever happened in the larger society could affect their town and the future of their children.

Even with all their tribulations, the Africans had been lucky. There had been riots in Mobile and Barbour Counties. White mobs armed to the teeth patrolled the streets and gathered at the polls to block all but known Democrats from entering. Neighboring Georgians obligingly came to lend a hand; crossing the Chattahoochee River, they voted wherever they could. The Democrats stuffed the boxes and undercounted the Republican votes. Democrat George S. Houston beat David P. Lewis by more than 13,000 votes and took back power from the Republicans, who had held it since Congressional Reconstruction in May 1867. Fraud, intimidation, and outright terror had been so intense that the U.S. Congress formed a special committee to investigate. Its agents traveled around the state and gathered information on the most blatant offenses. It was serious for the Democrats, as the elections could be voided. The committee published a 1,325-page report the following year, which concluded that although fraud and violence had been widespread, it was in the national interest, in the spirit of reconciliation, to let the results stand.[94] The Democrats had gotten away, in some cases literally, with murder. But the Republicans were equally to blame. As historian Loren Schweninger summed up, they "were in bitter disagreement over the capacity of blacks for citizenship."[95] Their deeply seated prejudices had led them to play with racial divisions, to refuse support to black candidates, and finally to envision a white party coupled with black disenfranchisement. On November 24, as Houston, the "Bald Eagle of the Mountains," took office, Reconstruction in Alabama came to a halt, and with it the hopes and dreams of 600,000 black men and women, and their children.

IN MOBILE, ONE OF THE MAJOR Democratic campaign issues revolved around black children in schools, following an attempt by the Republicans to pass a law on integration. The specter of having black pupils sit on the same benches as their offspring had strongly rallied the white electorate.[96] The education of the freedmen's children had been a very contentious issue for almost a decade. When freedom came there were more than 173,000 black youth in Alabama, ages five to nineteen, whose parents were eager to see in the classroom rather than in the fields.[97] In May 1865, the State Street AME Church opened the very first school for black children, and soon after the Stone Street Baptist Church and the St. Louis Street Colored Baptist Church followed.[98] Other schools were established by the Freedmens' Bureau and benevolent Northern societies throughout the South.[99] In Mobile, the Northwestern Freedmen's Aid Society of Chicago was assigned the job. Within the first year of public education for African Americans, Alabama counted 31 teachers and 3,338 students.

Enslaved people had grown up understanding the value of an education that had been tenaciously, and often violently, refused to them. As John W. Alvord, the Freedmen's Bureau general superintendent of schools, stressed, they had "seen power and influence among white people always coupled with *learning*." Not surprisingly, the first convention of colored people in Alabama, which took place in Mobile in early December 1865, had declared, "we regard the education of our children and youth as vital to the preservation of our liberties."[100] It was exactly what many whites feared. A professor at Richmond College expressed a prevalent sentiment: "The cook, that must read the daily paper, will spoil your beef and your bread; the sable pickaninny, that has to do his grammar and arithmetic, will leave your boots unblackened and your horse uncurried."[101]

Schools and churches that housed classrooms were torched and looted; teachers were beaten, assaulted, threatened with death, kidnapped, and in some cases lynched. In Alabama almost all Bureau agents reported burned schools and threats against teachers. "We are in the midst of a reign of terror," wrote the assistant commissioner.[102] As a Freedmen's Bureau official put it, the objective was to "break up the 'nigger schools,' 'send the damned Yankee nigger teachers back to the North,' and 'keep the niggers in ignorance' as long as possible."[103] During the 1866-67 school year, 175 day and night schools—33 supported in total or in part by the freedpeople themselves—had educated 9,800 pupils, 55 percent of whom were girls. By 1870, there were only 2,100 students left.[104] The first years of public education had been full of promises, but they ended on a heartbreaking note, with countless children back in the fields. Terrorism, the waning of Northern aid, and lack of state funds had condemned the freedmen's schools. But some institutions, built and funded directly by the former slaves, were still in operation.

Freedpeople's thirst for education has been well documented, but what about the Africans in particular? They came from societies where oral tradition was the norm and literacy did not exist. However, some had seen Muslim boys and girls go to Qur'anic school, and others, like Zuma, might have been students. Still, the type of school that existed in America had been unknown to them growing up. Formal education might thus have been of little or no significance to them. Yet, they had become savvy enough to understand that school-based learning was one of the keys to a better life for their children. They wanted for them what other black parents were trying to achieve for the first generation born out of slavery, but they had their own motivations too. They were still called "ignorant savages," and if their children went to school and learned the same things as the Americans, they reasoned, they would not suffer this embarrassment.[105]

As they had done for the houses and the church, the shipmates got together to build a school and asked the county to send them a teacher. They had done it by themselves because, they stressed, they did not want to wait for white people's assistance like other colored people did.[106] The legitimate pride they felt at their achievement could only alienate their neighbors if they touted it as a "better than you" accomplishment. To say that the "colored people" only waited for white handouts was a harsh assessment that, if expressed to their neighbors, must have elicited hostility.

The schoolteacher in African Town was a black woman, as could be expected. There had been a sequence in the origin of the teachers sent to black schools after abolition. The first were the famous Northern schoolmarms full of missionary zeal; the following waves were made up of Southern whites, "rejects from the white institutions," and finally black teachers.[107] The choicest urban schools close to all amenities were reserved to white teachers; the rural one-room shacks scattered along dirt roads were the coloreds' domains.[108] But these educators were in great demand, as black parents consistently expressed a preference for black teachers over whites.[109]

The African children learned reading, writing, and arithmetic, and they also had skills acquired outside of school. They spoke English, but for most, their mother tongues were their parents' languages, and they had been taught something about their families' homelands. An eleven-year-old girl who served as an interpreter between Henry Romeyn and the adults "showed not only a knowledge of African geography, but that of the United States as well."[110] But teaching and learning were not a one-way street. As other youngsters were doing all over the South, some of the children of African Town were also educators, who taught their parents, including Pollee, to read and write.

CHILDREN WERE GROWING UP, families were expanding, but according to the Church they held so dear, most people in African Town were still living in sin. Marriage had been a complicated issue for many freed men and women. The Alabama Constitutional Convention of 1865 recognized slavery-time unions even when people had simply been living together, but whatever the law said, matters were more complex than they seemed. Because local sales and the domestic slave trade had broken apart families, many men and women had been forced to abandon their spouses. The last person they had been living with, who was by now legitimate, was not necessarily the one they wanted to be married to. Many people displaced from the Upper South had remarried in Alabama out of convenience, or been compelled to by their owners, and they wanted a previous marriage, not the last one, to be official. In addition, some men had several wives, and they had to choose one or be considered polygamists. Sometimes the decision was made for them by Bureau officials who appointed as legitimate wife the one who had the most children.[111]

Had they lived in Africa, as Cudjo and his friends could attest to, they would never have had to discard the others. If African religions came up often in conversations with the Africans, polygamy was another subject that outsiders were interested to hear about. Cudjo explained what it was like in great detail, and, in the spirit of the group's infallible defense of their traditions, he supported it.

"My people," he said, "can have three wives and they don't have to support them because, men and women they all work the same, and they have the same rights on property." That, Cudjo would stress, was not the case in America:

> Kazoola has been married about three years. His wife says, "Kazoola, I am growing old—I am tired—I will bring you another wife." Before speaking thus, she has already one in mind—some maid who attracts her and who Kazoola has possibly never seen. The wife goes out and finds the maid—possibly in the market place—and asks, "You know Kazoola?" The maid answers, "I have heard of him." The wife then says, "Kazoola is good—he is kind—I would like you to be his wife." The maid answers, "Come with me to my parents." They go together; questions are exchanged and if these are satisfactory, the parents say, "We give our girl into your keeping—she is ours no more—be good to her."[112]

Cudjo's polished version, although one-sided, was not inaccurate. Polygamy is sometimes initiated—or at least welcomed—by women because it gives them more freedom and more help, but it is most often the husbands' choice. Contrary to what he said, though, only the Muslims limit the number of wives one man may have to four; among the Yoruba, the Fon, and other non-Islamic societies in the Bight of Benin, no restrictions existed as to how many wives a husband could have. Cudjo did not lie to his interlocutors, but he chose to present only one aspect of polygamy, the one he knew would be more acceptable. And if the Americans were still critical, the Africans had a ready response. To those Christians who were offended, they told them to read the Bible and look up the stories of David, who had twelve wives and several mistresses, and Solomon, who made do with seven hundred wives and three hundred concubines.[113]

His fervent defense of multiple marriages notwithstanding, Cudjo did not have several wives. Legally, he did not even have one. The pact he and Abile had entered into had been, in their eyes, quite legitimate, but they knew it did not amount to anything outside their town. Like Americans did, Abile had taken on Cudjo's surname and so had their children. But in the end, they relented for religious reasons. They had been told at church that they needed a real marriage with a license. It did not make much sense to them for two reasons: they had never heard of a marriage license in Africa, and their feelings for each other had nothing to do with a piece of paper. Cudjo, who was greatly enamored of his wife, said he loved her as much before as after the wedding.[114] It took the devout couple a good many years to follow their priest's instructions. On Monday March 15, 1880, Cudjo and Abile, Pollee and Rose, and Ossa and Annie Keeby put on their best dresses, their pants less mended, their starched shirts, and their hats, and started walking toward Stone Street Baptist Church. They all were going to get married by Elder Benjamin Burke. The "new" couples could have tied the knot in their backyard, at Old Landmark, but perhaps they went to Elder Burke because he had baptized them and they wanted to give a special weight to the ceremony. The triple wedding was a close-knit affair, the reaffirming of solid ties not only between husbands and wives who had already been raising children, but also between friends who had been through much together for twenty years. Just a week before, Burke had married Abache, also known as Clara Aunspaugh, to Samuel Turner. It had taken them a long time too. Their twins, Ed and Susie, were already thirteen. But if their parents had been slow, the second generation had quickly adopted the local customs. Just a month after the Turners, Lucy Lee, one of Gumpa's daughters, got married. At eighteen, she became the wife of Luke Winters, a twenty-three-year-old steamboat man born in Alabama.[115]

The Lewises, the Allens, the Turners, and the Keebys had not rushed to the altar, but Zuma had been even slower. First, she had lost her African husband, though when this happened is not known. According to the census, George, their first child, was born in 1863, and the second, Abe, in 1874. This long interval between the boys suggests several deaths or that Zuma may have remained single for years. In general, African women space the births of their children by at least two years. It is therefore probable that Zuma's first husband died between 1865 and 1867, and that she did not enter into a new relationship until 1873. The man she started to live with was John Levinston, also recorded as Livingston. He had been another victim of the domestic slave trade, sold down the river from Richmond, Virginia. As logical in terms of birth spacing, after their first child Abe (for Lincoln?) was born in 1874; their next one, Martin, followed in 1876; the twins, John and Mary Jane, completed the family in 1879. It was not until June 16, 1887, however, that John and Zuma got married. John, who could not write, made his mark on the marriage license. Because they had been living together for several years, Zuma gave her surname as Livingston. Whether she was a Christian or not is a matter of conjecture, but what is not is that she did marry at Old Landmark Baptist Church, her union blessed by Elder Henry McCrea.[116] She had gone against the tenets of her religion: she had either converted or she had ignored the prohibition made to Muslim women to marry non-Muslims. For all intents and purposes, she knew she could only be, in the eyes of her family and coreligionists, a bad Muslim at best, an apostate at worst.

As their first thirty years in America came to a close, to many the Africans in Mobile appeared primitive, "uncivilized." Booker T. Washington touted them as the lowest echelon on the African American ladder of progress:

> I can perhaps best suggest the progress which the negro has made if I recall the fact that there are still living at Mobile, Ala., remnants of the African tribe who were brought over on the last slave ships, and that among those people and their descendents there are numbers who still speak the African dialect and retain a vivid memory of the life in the African bush. . . . [E]xceptional men [such as Paul Laurence Dunbar] and the people of the African colonies at Mobile [who] still cling to the memories and traditions of their savage life in Africa, and may be said to represent the limits, the boundaries, of negro progress during the last half century.[117]

But even if they looked to everybody else as if they had just stepped off the *Clotilda*, the shipmates had spent more time in Alabama than in West Africa. The children deported from Ouidah had actually grown up and become adults in the United States. They lived in houses similar to other wood cabins in the region, dressed like their neighbors, worked the same jobs, sent their children to school, spoke English when needed, and were American citizens. Most, if not all, had also abandoned their religions for Christianity.

Still, they continued to identify as Africans and to live insular lives in the settlement they had proudly named African Town. A map of Mobile, drawn in 1889, called it "African colony."[118] Their languages; their modes of verbal and nonverbal communication; the manner in which they perceived the others; their understandings of hierarchy, age and gender relations, and family structure; their cultural practices that valued community over individuality; their conception of lineage and ethnicity; and their longing for their homelands were among the most significant elements that set them apart. As was the indelible mark of the ordeal they had been through. None of them had recovered from the shock of their capture, their separation from their families, and the Middle Passage. When reminded of these experiences, they were overwhelmed. Cudjo's agony was so intense that he was inarticulate.[119]

Their next thirty years would bring their share of new tragedies and successes, and the coming of age of generations that had never seen West Africa and for whom home was America and an African town in Alabama.

CHAPTER EIGHT

Between Two Worlds

A S THE LAST DECADE of the nineteenth century opened, King Glèlè died after a reign of more than forty years. Wherever they were, in Mobile, Havana, or Rio, the people he had sold away would have rejoiced had they known. Some of the deportees to Brazil had been freed only a year before in 1888. The men and women of African Town who had been taken from his *barracoon* in Ouidah were now in their forties and fifties, parents and grandparents of two generations who had never feared the king and the soldiers of Dahomey. To these young men and women, the most concrete expression of their parents' ordeal was the face of an old white man down the road.

After retiring from the river because the Negroes had become uppity, Timothy Meaher spent his time running the Bay City Lumber Company and the Mobile Steam Brick Works with his brothers and his sons, James and Augustine. They were still powerful and, as years went by, the family became even wealthier. But the brothers were getting old. Burns, the youngest, was the first to die, in 1880. James followed in February 1885. At seventy-four, he was hailed as one of the oldest steamboat men in the state. One of his pallbearers was none other than William Foster. About a year later Timothy developed paralysis and became housebound.[1] On March 3, 1892, the Catholic priest of St. Francis Xavier Church near Three Mile Creek was summoned to his side. The father gave him the last sacraments, and the captain passed away. It was a peaceful death of old age, at eighty. Timothy Meaher's passing made the news not only in Mobile, but as far away as New York. The *Daily Register* gave him a hefty obituary, calling him "a venerable steamboat man . . . one of the best and most successful steamboatmen, who plied the rivers in the palmiest days of the business."[2] The notice dedicated twelve lines to his days as a captain, and fifty-nine to "the famous event with which his name was identified."

Meaher was, first and foremost, the man of the *Clotilda*, or the *Clotilde*, as the newspaper called the ship. It was the arrival of the "160 slaves" in "the spring of 1861," their hiding in the canebrake, the "disposal of the cargo," the captain's trial, and the "African Colony" that were the highlights of Meaher's life. In a dispatch from Mobile, the *New York Times* saluted the death of the "Last of the Slave Traders." Adding its own copious mistakes and prejudices to the story, the *Times* informed its readers,

> Timothy Meaher, who died to-day, was noted as the importer of the last cargo of slaves brought to the United states. This was in the Spring of 1861. He chartered the schooner Clotilde, which brought 160 negroes and managed to spirit them into a cane brake 100 miles up stream. . . . The thirty negroes that fell to his share he settled in a suburb of this city. They have never associated with other negroes, are but partially civilized, still use their native language, and are ruled by a Queen of their own choosing.[3]

It would have been interesting to know what the "partially civilized" thought about Meaher's death. It is only after his funeral that the *Register* published a piece that did not mention his slaver past. Interestingly enough, there was nothing on his heyday as a blockade-runner either, only glowing comments on the captain's fine family, his sensational successes, the wonderful boats he had built and commanded, and the 1.7 million bales of cotton *he* had landed.[4] On Friday, March 4, the last slaver's funeral took place in front of a large crowd. He went off in great pomp and ceremony. The Yankee who had become an exemplary Southerner, the negrophobe who had taken so much pleasure at humiliating the Africans, was buried in the Catholic cemetery in Toulminville in the white and wealthy section among the Italians, the Irish, and the Spaniards, far from the black Catholics' area to the south.

MEAHER'S RESTING PLACE was a reflection of the city. Mobile was as segregated as its burial grounds. Jim Crow would not be legalized until 1901, but a rigid de facto separation had been a fact of life since emancipation, and by the turn of the century half the city's black population was concentrated in just one ward. The city was more racially divided than Charleston, Atlanta, or Nashville.[5] Throughout the South, tensions were high. Whites, unsettled by economic insecurity, political turmoil, and racial and social frustrations, living in fear of a large black population, and realizing that the federal government and the Republican Party would not meddle with their racial agenda, turned their feelings of powerlessness and their rage against blacks. As race relations deteriorated even further, whites made lynching black men their preferred weapon of political, economic, and cultural terror, control, and subjection. Whereas 534 had been executed by mobs nationwide between 1882 and 1889, 1,217 African Americans (overwhelmingly men) were lynched between 1890 and 1900. And during those ten years, which reached the highest recorded number of lynchings in the nation's history, Alabama had the abject distinction of being the leading state. Between 1889 and 1900, Alabamian mobs killed 173 people, including 146 black men and 8 black women.[6] Although Mobile County was spared during that particular decade, the prospect of violence and violation was always present in African Americans' minds.

THE RACIAL DIVIDE WAS PROBABLY not a pressing issue for the Africans, since they had elected from the start to self-segregate. Their town now had all the institutions they needed to live in semi-autonomy. After building the church and the school, they had pooled their resources again to establish a graveyard. "Old Plateau Cemetery" had opened in 1876, south of the Lewises' land. Cudjo said that death had come with the shipmates on the *Clotilda*, and after thirty-three years, it found his door.[7] In the summer of 1893, Celia, his youngest child and only daughter, got sick. A physician came from Mobile to examine her and he prescribed several medicines that Cudjo purchased in town. Nonetheless, Celia's health continued to deteriorate. On August 5, at age fifteen, she died. Her parents held a Christian funeral with open coffin, and everybody sang:

> Shall we meet beyond the river
> Where the surges cease to roll?
> Where in all the bright forever
> Sorrow ne'er shall press the soul?

Cudjo did not sing; he knew the words, but that day, they did not mean anything to him. He knew them in his mouth, as he explained, not in his heart. He needed to say goodbye to his daughter his own way. Not the Christian way, not the American way, but in the manner that was closest to him. To make sure his Ebeossi was sent into the other world properly, he silently sang his own funeral song. Some of his words were *a wa n'lo*. Found in all Yoruba funeral songs, they mean "we are going away."[8]

The concept of a dedicated burial ground was unknown to Yoruba, whose dead are kept close to the living. Celia was thus the first in the lineage to be buried in a graveyard. Because he was used to the deceased being surrounded by their relatives and the walls of their compound, her grave lying alone, something that would not elicit a second thought from an American, did not seem right to Cudjo when he went back to the cemetery to be near his daughter. She looked lonesome to him. So he built a fence around her grave to protect her.[9] It is significant that when a personal tragedy struck, Cudjo—and probably his companions too—drew on the memory of their own culture and religious customs. He had been a Christian—and a pious one at that—for twenty-three years, which was longer than he had been immersed in Yoruba culture and religion. Nevertheless, he looked into his past and his people's traditions for soothing. Like African Town itself, the façade—church, open coffin, graveyard—was definitely Christian American, but the inner self was as definitely Yoruba, and there was no contradiction.

CUT OFF FROM WEST AFRICA for more than thirty years, the Africans could still live on memories, reflexes, and modes of reasoning acquired in their youth, but they had no way of learning anything about the major developments in their homelands. They did not know that Glèlè's son, Kondo, had become king on December 30, 1889, and taken the strong name Gbe-han-zin-aï-djire (Behanzin), "the world holds the egg that the earth desired." From the onset of his reign, the king of Dahomey had faced a formidable enemy, the well-armed French army and its African soldiers. He had allowed the French in Cotonou against payment of a tribute, but Behanzin was determined to stop their encroachment on his lands. Both parties armed themselves in view of the inevitable confrontation, which finally took place in 1892 in a series of battles. Led by the Franco-Senegalese Colonel Alfred-Amédée Dodds, the French army marched on Abomey in 1893. Seven marine companies, 800 legionnaires, 3,450 Senegalese soldiers, an engineering company, the artillery, 200 pirogues, and 5,000 porters followed Ahuan-Li, Dahomey's old war road, up the Weme Valley. For five months in the dry season, the Dahomians fought back, slowing the enemy. But when the foreigners finally reached Cana, rather than have them trample through the streets of the holy city and desecrate the resting place of the kings of Dahomey, Behanzin burned it down. He burned down Abomey, his royal capital, which was captured in November, and fled. But he was betrayed and gave himself up on January 26, 1894, although he did not sign a national surrender. The last traditional African kingdom had fallen.[10] Thousands of miles away, Gumpa the Dahomian and his friends might have never known, isolated as they were. But they did.

About three years after Behanzin's last stand, Captain Henry Romeyn, the former officer of a Colored Infantry regiment during the Civil War, arrived in Mobile. With an interest in colored folks, he inquired about "Little Africa," as he called it, and because he was a man of distinction and renown, his guide was none other than Augustine, Timothy's second son. The best time to meet the Africans, he told Romeyn, was on Sunday because several men worked at making timber in the woods, and they were away most of the week, leaving early and coming back home late.

When they got on the hill, on a hot and humid Sunday afternoon in June, Romeyn discovered the small town in a fifty-acre clearing amid a forest of pine trees. Confederate earthworks built to slow the Union Army's advance were still visible. The thirty or forty wood cabins "scattered irregularly" were, in his opinion, quite comfortable compared to the shacks he had seen around. Meaher told him that the Africans had bought their land from his father but that the "Country Negroes" were still renting theirs from his family. The Africans were indeed part of a small minority: black Alabamians owned about 7,300 urban homes free of mortgage, while they rented more than 64,800.[11] Meaher also stressed that the first-generation Africans and the native-born did not seem to mingle, which would indicate that the second and third generations did. Romeyn was looking for some signs of a difference between the Africans and the "Country Negroes," and he soon found them. Children were running around all over the Africans' place, and they were all dark. There were no mulattos in sight, a good sign he believed, which prompted him to note, "Their morals are said to be better than those of their race, debauched by centuries of slavery," although, he stressed "how much of this may be due to feelings at first entertained against them, as 'barbarians,' is problematical."[12] It was an interesting point of view: African women did not bring mulatto "bastards" into the world, likely because white men did not associate with them due to their perceived barbarity. Like his contemporaries, Romeyn firmly believed in black women's depravity— although as an "open-minded" Yankee he attributed it to slavery—which was responsible for the "mongrelization" of the race.

Some people had left for the day, but there were still a few around. Zuma was there, and so were Cudjo, Gumpa, and several others. As Augustine rode into town and explained why he had come and who the visitor was, they gathered around, children and grandchildren in tow. When Romeyn asked where they were from, several voices responded "Dahomey." He turned to Gumpa, who had been introduced as the headman, and asked him which place he preferred, Mobile or Dahomey? In a split second he had already responded, "Dah-ho-mah. Dah-ho-mah. Dah-ho-mah. Dah-ho-mah." A woman offered her opinion as to why: "In Dah-ho-mah, lan' all free, no buyee any, no payee any tax; go wuk any lan' you want, nobody else wuk." The remark is quite valuable as it shows the issues of interest to the Africans. The difficulty of land acquisition and the burden of taxes in America were obviously a major concern to poor people who had become landowners after great sacrifices. But there was something else that people for whom having to buy land is taken for granted could not have experienced. Even after more than twenty years, the fact that they had had to actually purchase it remained shocking. Romeyn, who could not conceive of any place better than the United States, reminded them that life was not so good in Africa, that after all they had been captured in slave raids. The woman was not impressed with the argument, "Oh no catchee all. It was by bad luck." Given the dearth of comments by Africans about their capture and the slave trade, this is a noteworthy remark. There is, of course, the possibility that she was just on the defensive, trying to rebuff Romeyn' s interpretation. But she may also have been sincere and genuinely blamed her fate on bad luck, just like others attributed it to God's will through the agency of men (and sometimes women) who were foreign to them in terms of culture, religion, or ethnicity. The idea that Africans put the responsibility of their deportation on their own people, let alone their "brothers and sisters" or other "blacks," is widespread but it is anachronistic and does not reflect what they themselves expressed. The deported Africans' biographies and autobiographies reveal that they blamed "infidels," people from other ethnic groups, simply men or women, enemies during a war, slave merchants, or bandits.[13] The woman who responded to Romeyn was thus well in line with what is known of the Africans' view of the factors and people responsible for their ordeal.

After that first exchange, Romeyn had said something stupefying. He talked about "the Dahomey village at the Exposition." He was referring to the 1893 Chicago World's Fair, where a group of Dahomians had been exhibited "in native pursuits." Two years earlier, "Dahomean warriors and amazons" had been exhibited in the Exposition universelle in Paris. They were the survivors of their kings' murderous folly, the French authorities reminded the Parisians, who flocked to take a look at the "savages." A booklet handed out at the gate of the human zoo proclaimed:

> When the king wants to have fun, he orders the victims' martyr. Instead of killing in one stroke, of beheading right and left, the executioners mutilate them, arrange them in a cross, tear them up, and rend them with incredible art and refinement. On the bleeding sores, they put burning coal and ashes and red-hot irons, rejoicing at the sight of the tormented victims' contortions.[14]

For more than a hundred years, "savage Dahomey" had symbolized what Europeans and Americans thought was wrong with Africa and what had been right with the slave trade, which supposedly had saved millions from burning coal and red-hot irons. The human sacrifices held by Ghezo and Glèlè had been widely publicized. In 1859, as agitation for the reopening of the international slave trade grew in the South, numerous articles had been published on "Dahomey's atrocities." The *Southern Intelligencer* had joked about the outcry of some people who deplored the "slaughter of eight hundred darkies" not out of humanity but because of the loss of their potential service.[15] Now that the kingdom was on the verge of colonization—presented as another Western blessing since one of its justifications was the abolition of African slavery—its defeated soldiers could be safely gawked at. Romeyn' s words stunned Gumpa. Dahomians in Chicago? "Who catchee?" From his former vantage point in Ouidah, he had seen Dahomey at its most powerful, and it was hard to imagine it defeated. But, Romeyn insisted, there was no doubt, Dahomey had been crushed by the French. "No! no! no man whip Dah-ho-mah! Got 'em too much men, got 'em too much fight-women. No man whip Dah-ho-mah!"[16]

Incredible as the news was, Gumpa must have been even more shocked if he learned of his last king's fate, which he probably did. Romeyn was a curious intellectual, and the *New York Times* had covered the French campaign since 1892 with more than thirty dispatches and articles. The French had put Behanzin and his entourage on a ship and sent them to the Caribbean, just as his grandfather Ghezo and his father Glèlè had done to so many people. Ironically, Behanzin had never deported anyone to the West, but he had been involved in what amounted to international slave trading. To fight the French and preserve his kingdom's independence, he had bought German rifles, canons, shells, and ammunition and paid in the form of more than seven hundred men sent to work in the German colony of Cameroon.[17] Behanzin arrived in Martinique on March 30, with a small entourage, and was held in a fort on a hill. He was the last man from the Bight of Benin to be forced onto a ship headed for the Americas.

The unexpected news of the downfall of Dahomey certainly gave rise to many interrogations in African Town. Gumpa, for one, must have greatly worried about the fate of his family and friends. The others likely had unanswerable questions too. Now that the French had conquered Dahomey, what about their own homelands? It is possible that the news had an impact—even if only temporary—on their dreams of return. To leave a country where white men ruled cruelly to go back to one's own place now controlled by other whites could not have been appealing.

As THEIR PARENTS GOT WORD for the first time of events at home, the second generation was entering adulthood and the age of marriage in African Town. Some chose spouses outside the shipmate community. But the "outsiders" were also well known, having lived in the vicinity, and each party knew—at least in theory—what they were getting into. Marrying into African Town meant becoming part of a singular, cohesive community, whose second generation adhered to certain foreign rules and traditions.

On October 8, 1891, the elder of the Lewis children, Aleck, twenty-four, married sixteen-year-old Mary Woods.[18] She lived close by and was a second-generation Alabamian whose grandparents had been victims of the domestic slave trade. Martha, her mother, was born in the state in 1850 of a father deported from Virginia, and a mother from South Carolina. Mary's father, Sandy Woods, was a farm laborer. From the time they were young, Mary and her brother William had been helping their mother, a laundress, to make ends meet and raise their two younger sisters. Mary had been too busy working at home to go to school and unlike her husband, she could neither read nor write.[19] Once married, Aleck had not left his parents' house to start a family on his own, a fact Cudjo was proud of. The young man had done what any African son was supposed to do: he had stayed put in the family compound, in a house built by the community.[20] A year after they were married, the young couple had their first child, Zanna. Motley was born in 1895, and he was followed by Emmett in 1897, and Angeline in about 1901. Over the years, Aleck, who had started his professional life making bricks and shingles, had become a grocer.[21] It was a definite step up, making him part of a small minority of black store owners nationwide. In Mobile proper, only ten groceries were owned by African Americans, in the colored section along Davis Avenue.[22]

The family compound also existed at Lewis Quarters, where the children settled on their parents' land. Creating a compound represented the most visible preservation of a fundamental African value, but others were much less detectable, such as the underlying reasons that motivated the choice of a spouse, and who did the choosing. In that regard, one case seems to be revealing of a continued adherence to an African pattern. After more than thirty years in Alabama, Rose, Pollee's wife of twenty-four years, passed away, leaving him with five children. Had he been back home, his mother, his sisters, and his other wives would have continued to take care of them. But in Mobile, there were no female relatives at the ready. Soon thereafter, at fifty-one, Pollee married Lucy, the daughter of Abache and Samuel Turner. If Abache had looked outside the group for a husband, her daughter looked very much within. But did she? She was only twenty-one, and the fact that she married a close friend of her mother, who could easily be her father, has all the appearance of an arranged marriage, the most widespread form of union in Africa. The thirty-year difference could not have been an issue for the community because they were used to seeing men who married much younger women, especially when a husband had several wives.

In short succession, Lucy and Pollee had ten children. Pollee was a good provider for his large family. In the evening, after his twelve-hour shift as a lumber stacker, he spent his time gardening. He cultivated peanuts, corn, potatoes, and fruits. When Lucy sent the children to fetch him for dinner, he used to tell them, "Go tell your mama I can eat by lamplight, but I can't do no planting by lamplight."[23] He also raised chickens, cows, hogs, and horses, and kept beehives. In addition, he sometimes worked as a carpenter.

Like his shipmates, Pollee kept the memory of his homeland alive for his children. His daughter Eva, born in 1894, remembered,

> They say it was good there. Say, like we plant greens here, they didn't have to plant that but once. They plant those things like mustard greens, you could get leaves off them to cook just like these trees here and you didn't have to keep planting them over again. . . . I seen them sit down and shed tears. I see my father and uncle Cudjo weep and shed tears talking about going home. Talk about fruit and such never give out. Bananas, coconuts and everything. They didn't ever give out, those things.[24]

While they were urban dwellers working in industrial jobs, the shipmates were still at heart an agrarian people and they recalled their homeland as farmers do, with reminiscences of plentiful crops and fruits that needed little tending. Pollee often talked about the bananas and oranges that grew all over his homeland but he strenuously refused to eat any in Mobile. Eva believed they made him homesick.[25] Their parents filled the children's imagination with descriptions of a bountiful, almost paradisiacal land, the remembrance of which still made them cry.

HOW MUCH THE CHILDREN KNEW about their parents' homelands and cultures was not uniform. Some, by default, had absorbed more than others. Pollee's children, brought up by two different mothers, are a good example. Eva Jones, who died in 1992, was Pollee's daughter with Lucy, a second-generation woman who had not learned to speak Yoruba from her mother, Abache/Clara Turner. Clara had married an American and the language spoken at home was English. Like many immigrant parents in her situation, she did not teach her language to her children or, if she tried, she did not succeed. The result was that Lucy spoke English with Pollee, and her children never learned Yoruba either, as Eva stressed:

> What we picked of the African talk, we got at home. At the school, they thought it was funny. We talked it some at home. . . . They called it just "African" language. . . . I'm sorry I didn't learn to speak it myself. . . .[T]hey get in there [Pollee's house] and start talking that African, I wouldn't know. That's why we didn't learn, because we'd laugh ourselves. Cause we didn't know what they were saying. They didn't make us talk it. There's only a few things I know to say in African.[26]

By then "African"—Eva thought it was Zulu—had become funny to the children who mimicked their peers at school. At least with Pollee's younger children there was no pride in speaking an African language. Not only did they not speak it, but they did not even know its name or understand that it was one of several languages in their parents' homelands. This linguistic loss could only lead to a cultural loss too. They could not understand what the adults were talking about when together, nor absorb cultural, social, or religious information about the past, including what the shipmates did not want them to hear. They could only learn what was directed specifically at them. The same held true in the Dennison family. None of the children had learned Yoruba from Kanko, and when she and the other shipmates "were speaking about something they did not want the children or grandchildren to hear or understand," her granddaughter Mable stated, "they would speak in their native tongue."[27]

The situation was different with Pollee's other children. "The older children from the first wife also spoke the language," said Eva.[28] They had been raised in a household where Yoruba was the common language of both parents and the dominant one at home. Given the average age of the African women, their youngest children were born in the late 1880s. Those who grew up in a dual-African-parents household still spoke or understood West African languages well into the twentieth century. For example, Joyful Keeby died in 1929; his sister Sylvia in 1945; Julia Allen (Ellis) died in 1946; Joe Lewis, Charlie and Maggie's son, passed away in 1951; and Aaron Keeby in 1955. It is probable that some of the children of the *Wanderer*'s deportees spoke Central African languages well into the 1900s. The fact is that second-generation slave trade Africans still spoke African languages in the United States just a few decades ago, like others did in Cuba and Brazil.

Whether they had one or two parents from overseas, the young men and women of African Town had had to figure out how to navigate their peculiar world. There was no precedent. Neither their parents nor their neighbors, let alone their peers outside town, could give them guidance. They had grown up with fathers and mothers whose backgrounds, rules, and attitudes made them stand out. Because Pollee had fathered her late, Eva Allen was more representative of the third generation than the second, and it seems that the distinctiveness of the community weighed on her and the rest of the children. Their parents, she explained, "would have an African name for us, and my name was Jo-ko. But we didn't recognize those names. We didn't want kids laughing at us for calling us those names. But in the homes we had our names and they'd call me 'Jo-ko,' and they never call me Eva."[29] These names show that the shipmates continued to prefer an African identity for their children; and Eva's comments reveal that even after their families had been in the area for more than forty years, the youngsters were still the butt of jokes among another generation of neighbors because of this very Africanness.

LIKE THEIR PARENTS, THE CHILDREN of African Town formed a cohesive group that was not readily accepted. They were different. Their parents told them so and their peers did too, but each had ideas poles apart as to what being different meant. Information is lacking on the other children, but Cudjo's boys seem to have been at the center of some of the most acute problems that the second generation encountered. Their father complained that the Americans called his children savages, monkeys, and told them Africans killed people to eat them.[30] The Lewis boys' response was to fight, and the parents of their victims constantly complained to Cudjo. They claimed the boys might kill someone. Cudjo always defended his sons since, in his opinion, they only responded to provocations and insults hurled at them because they were Africans. He did not believe they were ever the provocateurs and told the irate parents, "'You see de rattlesnake in de woods? . . . If you both[er] wid him, he bite you. If you know de snake killee you, why you bother wid him? . . . If you leavee my boys alone, dey not bother nobody!'"[31] Only Cudjo's version of the numerous incidents that pitted his sons against the neighborhood boys was recorded, and there is no telling what his sons might have been up to. What is certain is that the issue of violence between them and youngsters from outside the African community went much further than usual boys' fights and continued into their teenage years and their adulthood.

Sometime in 1899, one of these fights escalated, and Cudjo, Jr. killed a neighborhood man, Gilbert Thomas, twenty-six. His father, Brazil, was a shingle maker, like Cudjo, Sr., and they may have been colleagues at the Meaher lumberyard. It is possible that the two young men were brothers-in-law. Cudjo had gotten married on May 4, 1899, to a Louisa Thomas, who may have been Gilbert's sister.[32] The circumstances of the event itself are not clear: official records of the arrest and the trial are no longer extant, and Cudjo, Sr. remained silent about the episode.[33] Only one version has surfaced; it is sketchy and biased because it emanates from Cudjo's lawyers and supporters. According to them, he did not kill Thomas in self-defense, but he had probably been provoked and there were mitigating circumstances.[34] Nothing else could be found about a murder that must have profoundly horrified the Thomases, but also distressed the Lewis family and traumatized African Town. As a black man who had killed another black man, the shipmates knew that Cudjo would likely not face the death penalty, but he might spend many years in prison. One can only speculate about the community's state of mind but, given the Lewises' reputation and the tense relationship between African Town and some people in the surrounding area, there is reason to believe that the Africans may have been wary of reprisals, or at least apprehensive about hardened tensions and reinforced isolation. This was the type of incident that they probably had dreaded all along. As for the neighbors who had warned for years that the Lewis boys might murder someone, they were finally proven right. After four decades of sometimes strained relations, Gilbert Thomas's killing had the potential to pit one community against another.

Cudjo was detained in the county jail among 120 defendants. His offense, manslaughter, was the second most serious, following that of murder. Some of the other inmates were held for larceny or abusive language, but most for vagrancy and gaming on Sunday.[35] On January 17, 1900, prospective jurors for Cudjo's trial were gathered.[36] Sixty-four names were provided by the Probate Court to the City Court from the voting rolls. Fifty were white men, and fourteen were African Americans. A jury of eight whites and four blacks was finally empanelled. While it did not reflect the composition of the city at the time— 44 percent were African Americans—a third of the jurors were black and, in theory, at least, they could wield some power. How deliberations worked practically within the larger framework of black subjugation and intimidation is another matter.

On the twenty-third, the twelve jurors heard the case. They found Cudjo guilty of manslaughter in the first degree and condemned him to prison for five years. As was the law in Alabama, he was also charged the cost of his own prosecution. He never paid, however, because he was insolvent.[37] On Saturday, February 3, Cudjo was brought into court to be sentenced. Asked if he had anything to say as to why the sentence should not be passed upon him, he responded he did not; he was condemned to the state penitentiary and sent to Jefferson County.

CUDJO HAD BECOME ONE of the tens of thousands of convicts handed over between 1865 and 1928 by the state of Alabama to private businesses as part of the infamous convict-leasing system that ferociously exploited and socially and racially subjugated African Americans throughout the South.[38] It was an idea that had started to take a firm hold, for expediency, during the early months of Reconstruction when there was little money to maintain and few infrastructures to house black convicts whose control and punishment during slavery had been mostly the prerogative of the individual slaveholders. The practice had continued during Radical Reconstruction, but it became firmly entrenched when the Democrats regained power. The system had definite financial advantages: states could expand and maintain their prison facilities without imposing additional taxes, always the bane of nineteenth-century Democrats. In Alabama, convict leasing had been used since 1846 but it greatly expanded after emancipation. From then on convict leasing—to the railroad companies, the farms, the mines, and the turpentine industry—became big business. By 1883, it represented 10 percent of Alabama's revenues, bringing in $109,000 in 1890.[39]

Besides its obvious financial reward, the system had immense social advantages for the state. Stringent laws on property and the criminalization of "black behavior" and poverty targeted a population of young black men it was deemed an absolute necessity to control tightly. In 1850 the Alabama state penitentiary at Wetumpka had held 167 white males, 1 white female, and only 4 African Americans.[40] As soon as 1865, that trend reversed and Alabama counted thirty-one black state inmates (males and females) and six whites. The poor, the uneducated, and the illiterate, in particular, became entangled in a vicious racist system that took away their political rights at the same time as it pushed them into another form of forced labor and degradation.

Petty theft by impoverished tenants and sharecroppers, who were routinely robbed of their fair earnings by their employers, became a crime. Section 7506 of the Alabama legal code was amended to make it a felony carrying a punishment of two to five years in prison. Through an amendment to the constitution, breaking and entering not only into a house but also a garden or a smoke house was punishable by from two to twenty years. In addition to new regulations devised to protect white property, severe vagrancy and loitering laws were put in the books. Anyone "leading an idle, immoral, profligate life" could be arrested. What amounted to Black Codes in disguise provided a constant supply of manpower to the state's industries. The discriminatory system sent black men and women to long prison terms for misdemeanors that resulted in fines or reprimands for whites. In 1900-1902, for example, false pretense, bastardy, gaming, betting at cards, nightwalking, public drunkenness, disturbing religious worship, prostitution, selling whiskey to minors, injuring an animal, throwing something into a railroad car, were some of the crimes for which black men and women were spending several months or years in the mines and the farms as leased county convicts.[41]

All through the 1880s and 1890s, black men and women represented over 90 percent of the prison population in Alabama, and about 83 percent thereafter. When Cudjo went to prison in 1900, the state counted 1,577 black prisoners and just 167 whites.[42] The disproportionate number of African Americans in the convict leasing arrangement served to intimidate, scare, control, humiliate, and exploit the black population, to reinforce racial hierarchy, and to entrench white supremacy. According to contemporary black scholars who studied the effect of the system on African Americans in the early 1900s, "it linked crime and slavery indissolubly in their minds as simply forms of the white man's oppression. Punishment, consequently, lost the most effective of its deterrent effects, and the criminal gained pity instead of disdain."[43]

Cudjo's case, however, was different. He had not been sentenced on trumped-up allegations or been convicted of a frivolous charge. If anything, he had been a beneficiary of sorts of a racist legal system that gave little value to the life of an African American victim. Attempted assault of a white man, let alone a woman, would have cost him much more than what he got for killing a black man. When he entered the state penal system, Cudjo was first sent to the central penitentiary at Wetumpka to be examined by a physician. His record shows that, according to someone's aesthetic canons, he had a large nose and thick lips. He also had a scar on the right side of his forehead at the hedge of the hair and one on his left thumb. A dark birthmark could be seen on his left shoulder, and he had good teeth. He was also deemed "intemperate."[44] What that exactly meant is difficult to assess. He may have been generally hotheaded, or he may have been quick-tempered when he felt his dignity was threatened, as his father emphasized, a disposition that prison might have exacerbated.

After his inspection, Cudjo was assigned to a mine. His institution was Prison no. 2 of the Tennessee Coal and Iron Railroad Company (TCI), and he worked at Pratt Mines, the largest coal mining development in the South, which TCI had taken over in 1886. It operated eight mines with free labor and two, Shaft no. 1 and Slope no. 2, with convicts from all over the state in two prisons with accommodations for more than eight hundred. The state convicts were so-called hardened felons, serving time for grand larceny and burglary (mainly), murder, and manslaughter, but also for seduction, miscegenation, felonious adultery, carnal knowledge, obstructing the railroad, and selling mortgaged property.[45]

Once at Pratt, Cudjo was "classified" to determine how much coal he should dig up each day. When they first arrived, the men were classified as fourth class for one month, then as third, second, and first class after three months if they were still fit. The daily task of the first-class man was to extract four tons of pure coal free of rock and slate. The second class had to produce three tons, the third, two, and the fourth class, also called dead head—new arrivals and injured or sick men—"only" one. The mine superintendent, the company physician, and the warden reviewed the classification once a month on a Sunday. At 160 pounds and five feet, five and three-fourth inches, Cudjo was a second class, leased for $10 a month.[46]

Despite how little his wages were, the state was not getting its due. The president of the Board of Inspectors of Convicts, Sydeman B. Trapp, who said he had Governor Joseph F. Johnston's accord, had excused irregularities in the lease agreements. The Joint Committee appointed by the Alabama legislature to look into the convict system denounced what it saw as a collusion between the lessee and officials that robbed the state of its profits. Its 1901 report noted, "It is remarkable that prior to this administration the prices for convicts ran $9.00, $13.50 and $18.50 in the mines and $11.00 on the outside, making a total of $52.00; but for the last four years the prices have been $7.00, $10.00 and $14.00 in the mines and $5.00 on the outside, making $36.00." The committee was as diplomatic as possible—although it clearly denounced the fact that Trapp's personal household was supplied by the prison farm—but the truth of the matter was that the rate of fraud and corruption was almost as high as during the heyday of Reconstruction. Still, with all its corruption, the United States Industrial Commission cited the Alabama convict-leasing system as the most profitable in the country.[47]

The year Cudjo entered the mine, the Board of Inspectors of Convicts had changed the output requirements to take into account the thickness of the coal seam and the use of mechanical equipment. A first class now had to produce eight tons, a second class, six.[48] To men like Cudjo, who had never seen one before, the mine was frightening and oppressive. The thought of having to spend years in the dark burrows where they could not stand up was debilitating. Cudjo's work, which started around 6 A.M., was first to undercut the coal seam, a task done while laying on one's side and swinging a pick for several hours. He then drilled a hole, filled it with blasting powder, and ignited it in order to remove the coal. The next operation after the coal had been carefully sorted from the slate and rocks was to shovel it into a car. The last task of the routine had the miner push the car to the opening of the mine, where it was attached to others pulled by a mule or a locomotive. Since the prisoner's quota was not reached in one operation, he had to start the whole procedure again until he was done. If he failed to meet it, he was certain to be brutally punished. Lying on his belly on the mine floor, his pants off, he was whipped. Cudjo and his companions' daily lives were full of misery:

> Their eyes and lungs were filled with coal dust; they gasped for air because generally ventilation was of the most primitive sort; perspiration made their tattered mining outfits sodden wet and sticky with coal dust. And all the while they were sick with fear—fear of tons of rock falling down upon them, fear of imminent gas or dust explosion, fear of those spying eyes slinking in the dark recesses, the eyes of "check runners," or straw bosses, who goaded them with lethal weapons, and finally the fear of the dungeon, the doghouse, the water hole, the vat, and other medieval punishment meted out regularly to those who failed to pour out their last ounce of energy.[49]

After ten to twelve hours of grueling and dangerous work, the convicts exchanged their filthy day pants and shirt for their grimy night pants and shirt and had to wear them until they literally fell apart. They formed "a mass of filthy and foul-smelling rags covered with vermin."[50] Many convicts were barefoot because asking for new shoes to replace a damaged pair meant a whipping for carelessness.

Pratt, when Cudjo was there, was home to 41 white and 448 black convicts.[51] It goes without saying that the prisons were segregated, and the racial hierarchy was actively promoted, with white convicts acting as trusties (the Alabama spelling), put in charge of supervising and punishing black inmates not only in the prison but in the mines as well. A 1901 report of the joint legislative committee appointed to inquire into the convict system found that there were "too many trusties *de jure* and *de facto*." These inmates, who were given enormous latitude to enforce a vicious discipline and "to drive their hapless charges to work beyond the point of human endurance," were more often than not "hardened killers and bullies . . . convicted man-killers serving life terms."[52] In contrast, many of the black men they brutalized were imprisoned for felonies that would have been misdemeanors, and for misdemeanors that would have been peccadilloes, had they been white. For the prison authorities, one benefit of the trusties is that they whipped the men off the books. Guards were required to obtain the warden's permission to whip convicts, but trusties were not.[53] Whippings were of the most brutal kind. Jack Kytle, a former guard at Red Diamond mine, recalled:

> We useta keep a big barr'l out back of a shed at th' mines, an' when I think back on it now, I know we whooped niggers jes' to have fun. We'd pull their britches off an' strop' em across th' barr'l by their hands an' feet so they couldn't move, an' then we'd lay it on 'em with a leather strop. I've seen niggers with their rumps lookin' like a piece of raw beef. Some of 'em would pass out like a light, but they'd all put up a awful howl, beggin' us to stop.[54]

Kytle's actions were not an aberration; extreme whippings by racist guards and trusties were the norm.[55]

After barbarous punishments such as the shower bath, the crucifix, and the yoke and buck had been abolished in 1891, the "sweatbox" or "doghouse," considered less harmful, had remained. It was "a coffin-like cell with just enough space to accommodate a man standing erect. Generally made of wood or tin, it is completely closed except for a hole two inches in diameter at nose level. When placed under the blistering southern sun the temperature inside becomes unbearable. In a few hours a man's body swells and occasionally bleeds."[56] As sadistic as it was, the box did not have the favors of some guards and trusties. Jack Kytle and his colleagues avoided using it, "Didn't nobody want to put a convict in th' sweat box, or feed him on bread an' water, fer they wasn't no fun in watchin' that."[57]

The mortality rate of the leased convicts was commensurate to the cruelty, the lack of adequate health services, and the exploitation that reigned in the mines. In 1869, 100 convicts out of 225, or over 44 percent, had died. Conditions improved somewhat from 1890 to 1892 when, according to the report of the Inspectors of Convicts, the death rate was 14 percent.[58] In addition to diseases, frequent accidents killed the miners. They were crushed by falling rocks, coal, slate, and collapsing roofs; burned to death by electric shocks; pulverized by gas explosions; and run over by coal cars. Injuries were frequent. Up to 90 percent of the handicapped convicts had been wounded in the mines. Between September 1898 and August 31, 1900—when Cudjo was at Pratt—six men were killed in an accident, twenty-seven had died of tuberculosis, thirteen of pneumonia, and seven of dysentery.[59]

Not surprisingly, when they looked at their odds of surviving after ten or twenty years in the mines, convicts who could took their chance at escape, even though they knew that they could be killed or be harshly punished if caught. From 1898 to 1900, seventy-four men (state and county convicts) had escaped and seventeen had been recaptured. Escape from work at times took the form of self-mutilation. Men used dynamite to blow up their fingers or toes.[60]

While Cudjo was bidding his time at Pratt, his lawyer, Edward M. Robinson, was working diligently on his behalf. Robinson's objective was to get the young man pardoned, or at the very least paroled. Sure that he had a good case, he sought the help of prominent Mobilians. Among them was a man who had known Cudjo's family and everybody in African Town for forty years, and was the first to sign the petition for the young man's pardon. He was Augustine Meaher, the slaver's son, coming to the rescue of the deportee's son. But the most famous Lewis supporter was Jabez J. Parker. He had been Alabama's secretary of state from 1870 to 1872. Parker had worked on Cudjo's defense and attended his trial, although in what capacity exactly is not clear since he was not his lawyer. His presence was not altogether astonishing. He was no stranger to the Africans because in 1893, James Dennison had retained him for "legal services."[61] It is quite possible that he and Kanko had advised the Lewises to ask for his help. Robinson also got the support of Samuel Barnett Browne. A lawyer, he was a Democrat who went on to be elected judge of the Thirteenth Judicial Circuit in Mobile four years later.[62] Both men sent an impassioned letter to Governor Johnston asking for Cudjo's pardon. Their argument was simple: Cudjo was really good and Thomas was awfully bad. Parker did not show the slightest restraint when he wrote about the victim: "A vivid impression was made upon my mind that Gilbert Thomas, the negro he killed, was shown to have been a desperate, dangerous, turbulent and blood-thirsty scoundrel whose taking off was an unspeakable blessing to the community in which he lived. He was a *perambulating arsenal* of homicidal fury and destruction." Robinson, Cudjo's lawyer, was somewhat more circumspect: "Thomas, who was killed, seems to have been a most desperate character, with an unenviable court record, and his taking off was really a riddance to the county."[63]

As for Cudjo, according to Parker and Browne, he was "a peaceable, quiet, well-behaved and industrious man." Robinson concurred. He "was always a peaceful, law-abiding citizen in every respect." The incoming sheriff, John F. Powers, who had known Cudjo for several years, was said to speak highly of him and was "strongly of the opinion that the ends of justice justify his release." Along with the current sheriff, Charles E. McLean, and five deputy sheriffs, all white, he signed a petition for his pardon.[64]

Why would such an impressive deployment of white law enforcers come to the rescue of a black killer from African Town? Robinson explained that Cudjo had been "of great service to the officers of the law in the apprehension of criminals" and Parker stressed he had "been of invaluable service to [Sheriff McLean] and his deputies in ferreting out crime and arresting criminals of his own race." Apparently, Cudjo Lewis, a grocer, had become a kind of police auxiliary. There is more than one way of looking at his involvement with one of the most racist institutions in the South. One was spelled out by Parker: "This of course made him unpopular with the negroes, and caused him to incur the lasting resentment of the fiend Gilbert Thomas whom he was inexorably compelled to kill." As seen by the former secretary of state, other blacks resented Cudjo's association with the white authority and one of them forced him into a deadly confrontation. That racist law enforcement which led to unwarranted (or even reasonable) arrests and dispatch to labor camps was loathed by the black population does not need an explanation. That black informers and collaborators were hated is as evident. Cudjo, the friend of the police, who was "extremely popular with the white people," according to Parker, could be seen by some people in black Mobile as a despicable "race traitor." For whites, of course, he was a "good negro" (in the words of Robinson), someone well worth saving from the misery of Pratt mine no. 2.

But there are other possibilities. As acknowledged by Cudjo, Sr., his sons had always had violent altercations with some young men because of their African origin and their determination at not being bullied and ridiculed because of it. One scenario could be that, as they became older, Cudjo and his brothers took on the role their father had had when growing up as defender and protector of his community. In Banté, Cudjo, Sr. had received military training and been told the secret of the gates, through which he should have led his relatives and neighbors to safety. It is possible that the sons, following in their father's footsteps, saw themselves as protectors of their town, ready to fight men they perceived as threats even if it meant allying with white deputy sheriffs.

There is still a further explanation for Cudjo's involvement with the sheriff's office: the men he helped "ferret out" could indeed have been real criminals feared not only in African Town but in the surrounding area as well. His lawyer, departing from the blunt assertions of Jabez Parker, stated, "There can be no doubt that he has always borne a splendid reputation with both white and colored, and has had the confidence of the community." Some evidence of this can be found in the petition sent to Governor Johnston. It read: "[Cudjo] has always been a man of excellent character, and has stood well with all the people who knew him, white or colored." It was signed by three of the four black jurors and seven of the eight whites. Thus there appears to be some truth to the statement that Cudjo was not only appreciated by whites but also by blacks, in contrast to what Parker stated.

On July 25, Robinson sent a letter to Governor Johnston with accompanying documents: Parker and Browne's letter and the petition signed by thirty-three Mobilians. According to the joint legislative committee on the prisons, his correspondence had little chance of being read. Its members had noticed that because the number of convicts had become so large and "the duties of the Governor's office have so multiplied . . . it is nearly impossible for our Chief Executive to give to the subject of pardons that close and persistent attention that it demands."[65] To counteract the negative effects of this situation on the convicts, it had recommended the creation of a pardoning board.

Joseph Forney Johnston may have been very busy, but he knew a lot about convict leasing, not only because he was the governor, but also because he had been the first president of Sloss Iron and Steel Company in 1887.[66] He got Cudjo's paperwork by the end of July. It did not stay long on his desk. He signed a pardon on August 7, making the young man one of 175 convicts he had pardoned in two years.[67] The speed of the process was astonishing, but his likely motivation was not. Cudjo was one of the safest convicts to pardon. Here was a man who had not committed any felony or misdemeanor against whites, had presumably gotten rid of a black criminal, and was vouched for by law enforcement and prominent whites. If any "Negro" deserved a pardon in 1900 Alabama, it was Cudjo Lewis.

After six months in the hell of Pratt, he was free. Like all liberated prisoners, he must have received a ticket home and a new suit of clothes.[68] His safe and fast return no doubt delighted his community. To those who disliked African Town, and the Lewis sons in particular, Cudjo's release would have been just another proof of their complicity with racist law enforcement.

FOLLOWING HIS NINE MONTHS OF SERVICE in the United States Army, James Dennison had been in a protracted war with the Treasury Department. In September 1882, someone acting on his behalf—James could not write—had contacted John T. Burch, a Washington attorney and general claim agent, who boasted of being a stalwart Republican, to inquire about a bounty. James also filed a declaration for an invalid pension because of the health problems he had suffered during his bout in the Louisiana swamps. For this, he had retained the firm of T. W. Tallmadge of Washington.[69] His claim for a bounty was denied by the Treasury Department in November 1891 on the grounds that he had been paid in full on discharge and had received a $100 bounty. What he wanted, the unaccrued installments of bounty, was refused because "he was not discharged on account of expiration of term of service or wounds received in the line of duty."[70] The department's booklet, *Bounties of Colored Soldiers*, published for the benefit of the Freedmen's Bureau officers, clearly stated that "colored men" who had enrolled for three years, like James, were entitled to $300 in three installments, but if mustered out prior to the expiration of their term of service they could not claim the unaccrued installment.[71]

But Dennison did not let it go. In 1899, he retained the firm of James H. Vermilya, one of many Washington lawyers who specialized in soldiers' claims for pension and bounty. His literature stated quite accurately, "Every Soldier of the late War, 1861 to 1865, WHO SERVED NINETY DAYS or more and was honorably discharged, is entitled to pension under Act of June 27, 1890, if disabled by wound, disease or injury, whether contracted in the service or not." In addition, soldiers, Vermilya went on, had often not received the totality of the bounty they were entitled to and they could now get, depending on when they had enlisted, up to $402. With a new act in effect, James believed he stood a better chance at getting his money, but like many black veterans, he had to struggle hard. Only 75 percent of them were successful at getting pensions, while 92 percent of their white colleagues were. Added to discrimination, the complicated bureaucratic process, the costs, the high illiteracy rate of black troops, the confusion brought about by different names (like Mayers, Mayors, and Dennison), the difficulty of providing birth dates, and the dishonesty of some agents were some of the reasons many claims were rejected.[72]

Regardless of the obstacles, Dennison was determined to get what he believed were his rights as a soldier, so unsurprisingly, he also threw himself into the battle for his rights as a former slave. He and his wife heard of an association that was trying to get pensions for the ex-slaves, and they decided to join the movement. Whether other Africans did the same cannot be ascertained for lack of documents either from their side or from the association's side, since few of its papers are extant.[73] First, the Dennisons set out to get proof of their former status. Burns Meaher had been dead for several years, so they asked someone with access to the letterhead of a shipping company in Mobile, Wright & Co., to give them a certificate. An individual with an unsure hand, and spelling skills to match, wrote them the note: "Lotta Denison, Native of africa, age 62 yrs James Denison of Charleston, south carolisna age 60; Amy Denison also of Charleston sout Carolina age 110 all belong to Burns Meyers in the state of Alabama."[74] Evidence in hand, on March 13, 1900, James, Amy, and Kanko became members of The National Ex-Slave Mutual Relief, Bounty and Pension Association, with headquarters in Nashville, Tennessee. The association sent them certificates emblazoned with an eagle and a motto that said "Love one another." When the clerk was filling out Kanko's certificate, he had written that she had been born, like her husband, in Charleston. But someone crossed out the line and wrote that she was born a slave in Dahomey, Africa, still not accurate.[75] The Dennisons paid a fee of twenty-five cents each and agreed to send ten cents every month to the local chapter of the association. With their money order to Nashville, James, Amy, and Kanko had become part of the first efforts led by black people to get reparations for two and a half centuries of slavery.

The association's immediate goal was to secure passage of the Ex-Slave Bounty and Pension Bill that had been reintroduced in the Senate by Edmund M. Pettus, Democrat of Alabama, on December 11, 1899. That day, the Republican of New Hampshire who was the chairman of the Committee on Pensions had declared, "In my judgment, this is a bill that ought not to and probably will not receive the favorable consideration of the committee. The promoters of the bill are deluding thousands of poor people and are simply trying to keep this agitation alive for their benefit."[76] It did not augur well. Almost everything linked to the bill had been less than auspicious from the start. The movement was not new when the Dennisons joined; it had been brewing and then spreading for twenty years and been mired in controversy from the start.

The idea was the brainchild of Walter Raleigh Vaughan, the son of a former slaveholder from Selma. He had lived a comfortable life thanks to the free labor of his father's enslaved workforce, but he was so interested in their condition that when he was still in his early teens, he claimed, he had asked his father to give them half their Saturday off.[77] After studying business in the East, Vaughan had moved to Nebraska and become the editor of the *Daily Democrat* in Omaha. He had firmly believed in the cause of the Confederacy and in the benefits of bondage for the enslaved. Freedom had wronged them, he proclaimed, because it had robbed them of the good lives they enjoyed before. Therefore "the government should pension [the] ex-slaves if they would right a great wrong. They formerly had good homes, were well fed, were provided with the best medical attention in sickness, and since their freedom, just the reverse has been their position."[78] His first bill was introduced into Congress in 1890 and he formed what he called a "secret association," the Vaughan's Ex-Slave Pension Club, with headquarters in Chicago. Closed to whites—except for himself and his family—it was open to "any colored person of good moral character" who "must believe in a Supreme Being, must pledge eternal loyalty to their Government and devotion to their race." It would also act as a mutual aid society.[79]

Vaughan's attempts at gaining politicians' endorsements were a failure. Republican senator—and future president—Benjamin Harrison of Indiana stressed in 1883 that he had no time to devote to the discussion about the wrongs done to colored people, but, he thought, "some provision in aid of education in the south" would be the most efficient way to resolve the issue.[80] As Vaughan pointed out, education would hardly do anything for the elderly former slaves. Rebuffed right and left, ignored by the black press, he finally got Frederick Douglass on his side. On July 25, 1891, the former president of the

Freedman's Bank sent a vibrant two-page letter of support. At first, Douglass confessed, he had been somewhat "startled by the apparent impracticability of the Bill," but the more he thought about it, the more it made sense. He finally came to the conclusion that:

> The nation, as a nation, has sinned against the Negro. It robbed him of the rewards of his labor during more than two hundred years, and its repentance will not be genuine and complete till, according to the measure of its ability, it shall have made restitution. It can never fully atone for the wrong done to the millions who have lived and died under the galling yoke of bondage, but it can, if it will, do justice and mercy to the living.[81]

Douglass's position ran contrary to that of most black leaders, who believed the pension bill was not only impractical but also contrary to their ideals of self-help "for the race." The few black congressmen were preoccupied with political rights and education for African Americans, and viewed the call for pensions as a distraction that would never result in anything concrete. The black elite and the middle class were critical, but the project had white supporters.[82] Like Vaughan, they believed that the pensions would add wealth to the South and result in greater industrial and business development. It was a claim Vaughan had made in an open letter to the congressional committee reviewing the proposed bill. Noting that the South had not received pensions after the war, which he viewed as having built prosperity in the North, he explained, "The passage of a measure that would place former slaves upon the pension rolls would not only be the performance of a delayed act of justice . . . but it would occasion an expenditure of treasure throughout the entire southern region that would visibly enhance the material prosperity of all classes within that section."[83] In other words, pensioners would spend their money in (mostly) white businesses and give a boost to the Southern economy as a whole. In his newsletter, *U.S. Department News-Eagle*, published in Washington, D.C. to better represent his association as a quasi-federal entity, Vaughan had claimed that the bill "should be more properly called 'A Southern tax-relief bill.'"[84]

As the idea of demanding pensions was taking root among freed men and women, other organizations appeared: the Ex-Slave Petitioners Assembly; the Western Division Association; the Great National Ex-Slave Union; Congressional, Legislative, and Pension Association of U.S.A.; the Ex-Slave Pension Association of Texas; and the Ex-Slave Pension Association of Kansas. Some were legitimate, others were simply fraudulent.[85] Tennesseans Reverend Isaiah H. Dickerson—a former Vaughan agent—and Callie D. House, a washerwoman, founded the most famous, The National Ex-Slave Mutual Relief, Bounty and Pension Association, in 1894. They had stated from its inception that blacks did not need a white man to speak and act for them. Theirs was a colored organization for colored people. When the Dennisons joined, Dickerson himself signed their certificates.[86]

The association had enrolled 34,000 members by April 1899 and would add thousands more in the following years. It lobbied in Washington, held annual meetings, sent pamphlets to its members, acted as a mutual aid society, and had twenty-two agents operating in the South, the Midwest, and New York. The black elite and the black press were as skeptical of the association as they had been toward Vaughan's Secret Clubs.[87] They generally did not cover the issue of pensions and often refused the association's ads. They contended that since it had no chance of reaching its goal, the whole movement was likely a fraud. Because bills would never be passed and money would never be paid, the only logical explanation for the association's efforts, many blacks and whites thought, was that it was simply a scheme to enrich Dickerson and House. In the words of one detractor, the "coons are swallowing it down and are biting freely."[88] Some of its most determined opponents were whites claiming to defend the "ignorant darkeys." The Senate Committee on Pensions speculated that "the ignorant and credulous freedmen and their children . . . the poor and deluded victims of this nefarious scheme" had been duped out of almost $100,000.[89] Alarmed that "their unfortunate brethren"—100,000 of them according to *The New York Times*—were being defrauded by the association's principals, the Post Office, under instruction of the pension commissioner informed its branches in mid-August 1899 that they should not pay any money order made out to the association and should not distribute its pamphlets.[90] This unanimous concern for the alleged victimization of "credulous" former slaves, doubled by swift governmental action, came at a time when African Americans were disenfranchised, legally segregated, and lynched at the rate of one every other day amid general indifference, and this hypocrisy was not lost on them.

No records of the activities and membership of local chapters of the association in Alabama have been found, but its annual convention in Montgomery on October 29 and 30, 1900, indicates that it had a strong enough following there to warrant the expenses and organization of a two-day event. In 1903, an agent was arrested in Mobile, and he stated that he had signed about a hundred people since the state convention. It amounted to only about one a month, but he was not the only one canvassing the state. He had told the new members that those over seventy were to receive a $500 bounty and a pension of $15 a month; those over sixty, like the Dennisons, would get $300 and $12 a month if the law passed.[91]

Even with intense surveillance and probes into its books, the association could not be charged because it had not broken any federal law. Upping the ante, in July 1915, Callie House retained Cornelius Jones, a prominent black lawyer and former Mississippi state representative, to file a suit against the United States in federal court. Jones argued that the Treasury Department owed former slaves $68,073,388.99, representing the sale of cotton hoed, picked, and chopped by enslaved and freed people between 1862 and 1868 and confiscated by the army for tax payments. The suit was dismissed but it had generated renewed interest among African Americans. The defrauders were on the alert too. In a letter dated April 24, 1917, Laurence Dudley of Marianna, Florida, asked the commissioner of pensions if, as he had been told, the 68 million dollars were going to be given to the ex-slaves, because a man from South Florida was asking $2 to submit his application.[92]

The last chapter in the association's difficult twenty-three years of existence opened in February 1916, when the U.S. attorney in Mobile, Alexander R. Pitts, suggested to Attorney General Thomas Gregory that the new language used to reformulate the fraud law could help prosecute Callie House.[93] She was indicted in Nashville of violating the postal laws and of conspiracy to defraud the freedmen. She refused to plead guilty to a lesser charge and went to trial in September 1917. House was found guilty and sentenced to a year in the Missouri State Prison. Released on March 18, 1918, the woman convicted of defrauding the ex-slaves of hundreds of thousands of dollars went back to her mortgaged house in Nashville to continue working as a washerwoman.[94]

House and Dickerson had not done anything vastly different than Vaughan, but their premises and their objectives were poles apart, and so was the treatment they received. Vaughan acted with impunity: he was white, he had some support among Southern Democrats, and his goal was ultimately to benefit them. He was not a threat. At worst, he was viewed as "an eccentric person, probably ill-balanced mentally" but sincere.[95] House and Dickerson, on the other hand, had put together a black organization, controlled by blacks and whose intended beneficiaries would be poor freedmen and -women, not wealthy white Southerners. They were perceived as a threat even though they did not ask for equality, desegregation, or an end to white supremacy. The real danger they represented was expressed in 1899 by the inspector of the Pension Bureau. He had warned that the movement "is setting the negroes wild, robbing them of their money, and making anarchists of them." He predicted that, should the agitation go on, the government "will have some very serious questions to settle in connection with the control of race."[96] By 1900, there were 8.8 million African Americans in the country; a little over 89 percent lived in the South—more than one third of the total Southern population—and almost every one of those over thirty-five had been enslaved. If they united in an all-black movement, independent of the white-controlled political parties, they could become a force to be reckoned with. They were organizing at a time when Jim Crow was becoming law, and they and their children could later make sociopolitical demands that would go well beyond pensions.

There is no doubt that many men and women—those who could least afford it—were defrauded of their money and trust by white and black swindlers, but there was much more to the larger pension movement than broken dreams. It had given rise to or bolstered among African Americans a consciousness of what the country owed the people it had maintained in slavery, and it had organized and given voice to the underprivileged. Like tens of thousands of their contemporaries, the Dennisons had been part of the first large-scale, grassroots black organization of the poor and the first reparations movement that paved the way for later efforts.

LESS THAN A YEAR after James and Kanko joined the Ex-Slave Pension Association, William Foster, seventy-seven, died. He had been in failing health since at least November 1900, when he had made his will, and he passed away on February 9, 1901.[97] The two men responsible for the Africans' landing in Mobile were now dead. They had been survived by dozens of their victims all over the state and by a second and a third generation that numbered in the hundreds. Unfortunately, what the passing of the emblematic figure of the *Clotilda*'s last trip represented to the people in African Town was not recorded.

For a modest immigrant, Foster had done passably well. He had no children and he left his wife Adalaide his furniture, china plate ware, horse carriage and harness, a house, and eight acres. He also willed her one-twelfth of the claim of $373,000 he had, along with Timothy Meaher, on the federal government for the seizure of the *Gipsy*.

But his success has to be put in perspective with that of the people he had brought over. He was a man with the privilege whiteness conferred in the United States; he had built famous ships, and he had made men and women work unpaid for him for close to five years. They, in turn, started with nothing but their rags, had raised large families, built a church and a school, and bought land for their graveyard, all the while working at low-paying jobs; by 1900, almost all owned at least two acres. Ossa and Annie Keeby, in particular, had been quite successful. They had raised nine children, six of whom were still at home. They were farmers who owned several plots of land, and they were doing so well that they had filled five farm schedules for their taxes.[98] All things considered, Foster had been less accomplished in life than many of the people of African Town.

And in death the captain was upstaged by his old associate, Timothy Meaher. Foster's demise did not make it into the *New York Times*, although *he* was the real last slaver. What had Foster felt when he had read Meaher's obituary nine years earlier? Perhaps a pang of jealousy, some resentment at being robbed of the glory of the trip of a century, the historical voyage people were still talking about. The *Prichard Herald*, a small newspaper, was the most loquacious about the death of "Capt. Wm. Foster. Commander of Last American Slave Vessel." "From his residence on Telegraph road, a typical house of the old South," it wrote:

> A third of a century ago the name of Captain Foster was sounded throughout
> the world by reason of an adventure, which if written in detail, would read

like a chapter from a romantic novel. Captain Foster is the courageous com-mander of the Clotilda, a vessel which brought the LAST CARGO OF SLAVES to the United States. The trip was made only after many thrilling scenes, numerous weeks of skillful maneuvering and dangerous exploits but was successfully accomplished just before the South and the North engaged in the bloody war of the century.[99]

Like Meaher, Foster was hailed as a model citizen, a good Southerner, "ro-mantic" and "courageous." In 1901 Alabama there was no shame at having been the last slaver.

CHAPTER NINE

Going Back Home

T HE YEAR 1901 MARKED THE BEGINNING of a new era in Alabama, one that for African Americans looked ominously like Southern whites' idea of "the good old days" of William Foster and Timothy Meaher's fame. On April 23, 70,300 men voted for and 45,500 against a convention to draft a new constitution that, among other reactionary items, would disfranchise the overwhelming majority of blacks and many poor whites.[1] The Democratic Campaign Committee had sent out letters advising party members to ratify the constitution in envelopes marked "White Supremacy, Honest Elections, and the New Constitution One and Inseparable."[2] One of the cynical rationales for black disfranchisement was that the black vote had been so flagrantly manipulated—to maintain white domination—that it was necessary, in order to have fair and honest elections, to simply suppress it. As the convention's president, John B. Knox, summed up, "the negro is not being discriminated against on account of his race, but on account of his intellectual and moral condition."[3] The Mobile *Daily Register* explained that disenfranchisement "was the best thing that could happen for them, not excepting even their emancipation." Liberation, it continued, came only with manhood and intelligence and "the negro has not had any of these conferred upon him." By disenfranchising the masses, the constitution would help intelligent Negro men strive for education and elevation.[4]

African Americans, who had been barred from the convention, reacted by sending petitions to the delegates. The first of four was signed by Booker T. Washington and fourteen members of the black elite. On the one hand, in typical Washingtonian fashion, they argued reverently for justice and political rights, and battled against the proposal that each race pay taxes for its own, separate schools. On the other, in order to rally unconvinced whites, they played upon the worst stereotypes about African Americans. "Let the Negro feel that no matter how intelligent or useful he makes himself, there is no hope of reward held out before him, and there will be danger that he will become a beast, reveling in crime and a body of death about the neck of the state. In a thousand ways, the ignorant, shiftless, criminal Negro will retard the progress of the white race." It may have been a subterfuge to scare the delegates into preserving the black franchise, but it seems to have had a contrary effect by repelling and hardening several attendees, as a correspondent for the New York *Evening Post* noted.[5]

Arguably the most intriguing reaction to the proposed disenfranchisement came from a meeting of African Americans held in May at Camp Hill, Tallapoosa County. They adopted a resolution entitled "What Confronts Us and How to Better Our Condition" that advocated a return to Africa. In paternalistic prose reminiscent of nineteenth-century emigration apologists, the Afro-American Exodus Union asserted that God had first made the Negro a slave so that he "might imbibe the principles of civilization, be freed from ignorance and superstitions, elevated to a higher plane among the races of this earth." God's objective was for this Negro, once redeemed, to go back home to civilize the ignorant, superstitious Africans, and develop the resources of the "Dark Continent and plant a nation thereon." God's sign that it was time to go was the constitutional convention. The union called on every man to liquidate his debt and live frugally, with the help of his wife and daughters, so that there would be enough money to make the trip. Finally, it announced the formation of a committee to work on transportation with Great Britain and Cuba.[6] Nothing came of the plan, which may have been little more than wishful thinking, a warning to whites, or another attempt at defrauding would-be emigrants.[7] But the threat of taking black labor elsewhere had also been brandished by Washington and his co-signers. They had pointed in their petition to emigration agents and exodus associations looking for recruits in the cotton and mining areas.[8] The outcome of a potential black emigration was made clear by a reader who wrote to the Montgomery *Advertiser*, "Those who clamor to take the Negro's place at the ballot box may take his place in the cotton patch."[9]

The election on November 11, 1902, marked an all-time high for fraud. If the results are to be believed in some Black Belt counties, every black man voted, and each voted for his own disenfranchisement. The new Alabama Constitution was ratified 108,613 to 81,734. Its sections 177 to 182 (article 8) established who could and could not vote. Before December 20, 1902, only men who had honorably served in wars from 1812 up could register, as could those whose ancestors had taken part in wars back to the American Revolution, and "All persons who are of good character and who understand the duties and obligations of citizenship under a republican form of government." James Dennison and other black veterans were eligible, but almost all other African Americans were out since it was easy to dismiss them as not being "of good character" or not understanding the duties of citizenship. Some poor whites could qualify thanks to their veteran ancestors and their good character. After January 1, 1903, the restrictions were more severe. In addition to paying a poll tax every year, only men who could read and write any article of the U.S. Constitution in English and had worked most of the preceding year or were physically unable to work could register, as could men who owned forty acres, or held real estate property of at least $300 on which all taxes were paid. Men who had committed miscegenation, adultery, any crime punishable by imprisonment in the penitentiary, or who had been convicted as a vagrant or tramp, were banned from registering and voting. James Dennison could not write, so this time he could not vote. The vast majority of black men were day workers, sharecroppers, and tenant farmers without property; only 73,400 (17 percent) over twenty-one were literate; and countless others had been condemned on trumped-up charges that had sent them to the penitentiary.

In 1900, 181,000 black men could vote. Three years later, the number had been reduced to 2,980. The Alabama constitution had disenfranchised more than 98 percent of the black electorate. Poor whites had lost, too, but not in the same proportions. White voters were reduced from 232,800 to 191,500.[10] For the men of African Town, suffrage was but a memory. The days of standing up to Timothy Meaher at the poll stations were long gone. Neither Cudjo, Oluale, Pollee, nor anyone else who had arrived on the *Clotilda* would ever cast a ballot again.

In the wake of the new constitution, segregation that had existed informally since the 1870s became legalized. One of its first consequences in Mobile was the adoption in October 1902 of a city ordinance on the "separation of the races" that affected, among other services, the city transportation system. Throughout the South, African Americans had responded vigorously to the humiliation of de jure segregation with streetcar boycotts that touched at least twenty-six cities between 1900 and 1906 and lasted from a few weeks to two or three years. On November 1, black Mobilians launched theirs. The movement lasted about two months but did not result in any change.[11]

The new constitution also called for separate schools for black and white children. Poorly funded, many black establishments were so disadvantaged that even in the 1920s, just 59 percent of black children were in school—compared to more than 70 percent of whites—and Alabama was near the bottom of Southern states in that regard, trailed only by Louisiana and Mississippi.[12] But in African Town, the push for education started by the shipmates had spectacular results. In 1946, a book titled *The Alabama Negro*, published "To show the world what 900,000 Negroes have done in Alabama in a short space of 83 years," explained—lyrically and with a few factual mistakes—the genesis of what became the first training school for African Americans in Mobile County: "Since the landing of the slaveship Clotilde, on the Chicksabogue in 1858; since the founding of Plateau, Alabama, by Cudjoe Lewis, one of the twenty slaves brought over on the Clotilde, an educational center has been in the making. From bush arbor to church, from church to modern school buildings a real institution has developed."[13] The shipmates had built a primary school, but the children of

Plateau also needed a high school. Following the Africans' example, the community took matters into its own hands and in the late 1890s, a neighborhood farmer and large landowner, Fred Green, provided a building. In 1910 his son Isaac—who had married Sarah, the daughter of Ossa and Annie Keeby—and Jeff Giles donated three acres each and a new school was built.[14] That year it became part of the Mobile County public school system, under the leadership of I. J. Whitley, a disciple of Booker T. Washington. The school burned down twice, but was rebuilt and expanded each time, and in 1936, the private high school with four grades was accredited by the Southern Association of Colleges and Secondary Schools, the only black school in the county to receive the distinction.[15] Mobile County Training School, right in Plateau, educated many of the Africans' descendants.

Besides the massive disenfranchisement that politically crippled the African American community and rippled through African Town, the streetcar boycott, and Timothy Meaher's house burning down, the year 1902 was a most notable one for the Lewis family and their friends. The first episode in a disastrous cycle started on March 12, when Cudjo went to Mobile with his horse and cart to buy beans to plant. After he had made his purchases, he drove on Government Street near Common Street, where the Louisville and Nashville Railroad Company ran tracks. A slow cart was in the middle of the road, and as he was passing it on the tracks, he saw a train approaching. He screamed at the engineer to stop but the train sped on. It hit the buggy and sent Cudjo rolling on the tracks. He was badly hurt on the left side of his body. Passersby carried him to a doctor's office. Given morphine to alleviate the pain, the old man made his way back home. His horse had run away, and his son David found it the next day. Cudjo was in bed for two weeks with three broken ribs. One of the witnesses of the accident, a white woman, had sent him a gift basket and she later paid a visit, telling him that, from what she had seen, the railroad was wrong. There had been no whistle, no bell, no signal to let people know the train was coming. She then took it upon herself to go to the company to ask for damages, but her request was turned down under the pretext that the accident had happened during daytime. She told Cudjo to get a lawyer.[16]

Cudjo retained Richard H. Clarke, a prominent attorney who lived in the best section of downtown Mobile, the area of big mansions and old money. His fees were well above what anybody in African Town could afford, and Cudjo told him he could not hire him, but he offered him half the settlement.[17] Clarke accepted. On January 14, 1903, *Cudjo Lewis vs. The Louisville and Nashville Railroad Company* went to court. It was an improbable case. Cudjo, the African from Banté and African Town, former slave and poor free man, was going after the L&N, as it was known, one of the most powerful corporations in the South, with a jury that was not exactly of his peers. Once again, he was standing up for his rights.

Judge William Strudwick Anderson started the session by stating that the claim was for $5,000 (more than $105,000 today), a large sum that surprised Cudjo, who had not asked for any specific amount. The railroad's lawyers asserted that the company was not going to give the plaintiff anything, since the accident occurred in daylight and the train was plainly visible. Clarke countered that the train should have used its whistle. He argued that Cudjo had been so badly hurt that he could no longer work. He even asked his client to take off his shirt and show his left side to the jurors. Clarke also held the city of Mobile responsible: the tracks were in the middle of the streets, they were dangerous, and therefore the city had a duty to see to it that the company paid when people got hurt. The case rapidly went to the jury. The last two handwritten pages of a set of six that seem to have come from the judge reminded the jurors that the employees were under no duty to stop the train, and that if they believed all the evidence, and the fact that the plaintiff had time to get off the track, they should find for the defendant.[18] It did not bode well. The judge did not seem impartial and his initial statement about the $5,000 claim appeared to be aimed at discouraging the jurors from giving Cudjo anything. Cudjo was tired and he left, instructing David to stay in court.

The deliberations did not last long. In a stunning verdict for Jim Crow Mobile, the jury found for the plaintiff. It awarded Cudjo $650 (more than $13,000 today) in damages. The defendant was ordered to pay the expenses, $78.80.[19] The jury had inflicted an unexpected defeat on one of the most powerful companies in the South, and sided with a "Negro" who was also an African and a poor man. In contrast to what had happened when young Cudjo had been a defendant, now that blacks had been removed from the voter rolls, his father's jury was most likely all white. In the absence of documentation, there is no informed way to assess the reason for the men's verdict, but it is evident that at least in this case, race and class did not trump other considerations. The ruling had been so swift that Cudjo was still in town, buying provisions at the market. David hurried to tell him the news. The next day Cudjo sent him to Clarke to get the money but he was told it was too soon. He kept on sending David but Clarke continued to urge him to wait.

A few months after Cudjo's accident, another train-related tragedy hit African Town. In early September 1902 Gumpa was struck by a train of the Mobile and Bay Shore Railroad Company. The circumstances of the accident are not known, but it appears that the railroad was negligent. Like Cudjo, Gumpa had started a claim against the company, but he passed away on September 11.[20] The end of Gumpa's life had been heartbreaking, not only because of how he died, but also because he had spent it in what for an African was the worst possible way: alone. Not much is known about his family except that in 1880 he and his wife Josephine had three sons at home—Charles, William, and James—and four daughters—Celia, Clara, Polly and Mary. But by at least 1900, Gumpa was living on his own with two grandchildren, Sidney, nine, and Phene,

eight.[21] He had died intestate and the children were said to be his only family
and heirs. Did his wife and all seven of their children pass away? Were there
desertions or disputes? It is doubtful. Abandoning a parent is reviled in African
cultures; it is so abhorrent that even today the concept of nursing homes and
hospices is shunned. Besides, none of the Lees appear in the censuses from
1900 to 1930, which would suggest that they had indeed passed away, a colos-
sal tragedy for the elderly man that would explain why, at seventy, Gumpa was
raising his grandchildren. He was poor, his personal property was valued at no
more than ten dollars, and he owned two acres with a couple of houses. The
real estate was not worth more than forty dollars. After his death, a friend and
neighbor, Nick Caffey, had taken his grandchildren in, and he continued the
claim against the railroad. On October 2, Caffey took the matter to Judge Price
Williams, Jr. of the Mobile County Probate Court. He wanted letters of administration upon the estate so that he could collect the claim for damages for the
negligent killing of Peter Lee, as Gumpa was officially known, in order to maintain his grandchildren. Caffey asked to be allowed to take eight dollars a month
for each child out of the claim. The judge ordered a compromise. Stressing that
the contention for damages was "wholly speculative" he ordered him to accept
five hundred dollars and to renounce any further action against the railroad.
Caffey was allowed to take sixteen dollars a month for the maintenance and education of Sidney and Phene.[22] Gumpa's life was worth less than Cudjo's injuries.

Gumpa's had been a distressing story of loss and traumas. He had risen
from his downfall in Ouidah and his enslavement to become the leader of a
unique and thriving community, but in the end his luck had turned again. He
had suffered the loss of his entire family and a dreadful demise. Not only were
his grandchildren left without any relatives in America, but Gumpa's death
also cast a serious blow for African Town, which lost its leader of thirty years.

THE SERIES OF MISFORTUNES that had fallen upon the community that year was
not over. Young Cudjo had been out of jail for less than two years when he ran
into serious troubles. After his release from Pratt, he had gone back to work as
a grocer. There is no information as to whether he continued his activities as a
"friend" of the sheriff's department. The deputy sheriffs who had petitioned
for his release were all whites, and it has not been possible to ascertain if there
were any blacks in their ranks in 1900 in Plateau and Magazine Point. However, in 1902, there was one: Samuel Powe, twenty. According to Cudjo, Sr.,
his son and Powe had had words. He believed that if Cudjo had done something wrong, Powe should have arrested him; and if it were personal, he should
have fought him face to face.[23] But the deputy sheriff, Cudjo alleged, afraid to
confront the young man, hid himself in the butcher's wagon. When Cudjo
walked out of the store to talk business with the butcher, Powe emerged and
shot him in the throat.[24]

When Zora Neale Hurston heard the story in 1928, unable to get a more detailed and clear account of the incident from Cudjo, she decided to enquire in the community. She got the distinct impression that people feared the Lewis boys. After many rebuffs, as most neighbors did not want to speak about the incident, she finally found one informant willing to talk. According to him there had been several fights between the Lewis sons and other young men over a long period of time. The Lewises felt cornered and fought desperately. On July 28, one man was shot dead and another was seriously stabbed; people said Cudjo had done both, but then only when attacked. The deputy sheriff, afraid to arrest him, tried for three weeks to catch him off guard, but as he had repeatedly failed, he hid in the butcher's wagon and shot him.[25]

As Cudjo was lying in a pool of blood, neighbors came running to the Lewises' house, yelling to Cudjo and Abile that their son had been hurt. Abile was so distraught, Cudjo said, that her breasts swelled up, and seeing her in agony made him cry. For two days and two nights, Cudjo laid on his bed, his throat making horrible sounds. As Cudjo, Sr. was praying for God to spare him, his son died, leaving him, he confessed, with guilty feelings at not having prayed "right." Young Cudjo's life and death had been an exercise in contradictions. Like all convicts, he had risked his life at Pratt, but he had survived falling rocks, pneumonia, and tuberculosis. His swift pardon had been an unexpected blessing, but had he finished his sentence he might have lived much longer. He had been saved from the mine by white deputy sheriffs, but he was killed by a black one. Fittingly, his Yoruba name was Feïchitan; he was born during disputes, and he died in the middle of one. Sam Powe, who had killed a man, became a reverend. The pastor of Hay Chapel (now First Baptist) in Prichard, he should have asked for pardon but, the elder Cudjo complained, he never did.[26] As a Christian, the father had tried on his own to forgive his son's killer, but since Powe ignored him, he remained bitter.

The truth about Cudjo's killing will probably never be known. If he had indeed shot a man and wounded another, there was no reason why he would not have been arrested, and this time sent to Pratt for a long while. There was no reason for a young, fearful deputy sheriff to try to arrest him on his own if he posed a threat even to law enforcement. If Cudjo had killed again and was a menace to the community, Powe would have received help from his colleagues. Was there even a fatal fight? Or did Powe decide to act alone because he believed that the white men who, two years earlier, had stood up for Cudjo would not arrest him because he was still valuable to them? Was the problem between Cudjo and Powe more personal? Or did Powe act as an executioner, who knew he would not get into trouble, on behalf of some people? What appears through the various incidents involving the Lewis boys does not seem to totally contradict their father's account. In the July episode, the unnamed informant clearly suggested that Cudjo had acted in self-defense after being attacked. The larger community also seems to have backed up this assumption, as people acknowledged that the Lewises were cornered and fought desperately.

Cudjo was profoundly aggrieved by his son's death. He was still hearing the bell toll for Celia, when it tolled again for Feïchitan, his "po' African boy dat doan never see Afficky soil."[27] As he had done when he was mourning his daughter, he let go of his American "layer" and turned to his culture and his home for solace. His son was no longer Cudjo, the public, American persona of the young man, but Feïchitan. It was the private, intimate, African personality of his son that he was conjuring by calling him by his Yoruba name. And, as he acknowledged without any ambiguity the Africanness of his son, even though the young man was born and had grown up in America, he also admitted his own failure to return home. Feïchitan had never seen Africa because his father had not been able to take him there. In the midst of misery, Africa was the refuge.

As they mourned their son, Cudjo and Abile were also besieged with new problems. After the accident, Cudjo could no longer work and he still had not received half of the $650 from the railroad verdict. The L&N had appealed the decision up to the Alabama Supreme Court. The sum was insignificant to the company, and it must have pursued the matter because it could not let Cudjo's victory stand: if a poor African could win, then anyone who laid a claim against L&N could. The case of *Louisville & Nashville Railroad Company v. Lewis* was reviewed on November 21, 1904, and Cudjo, who did not even know of the appeal, had no lawyer. There had been yellow fever in Mobile that year, and Clarke, his lawyer, along with his wife and two daughters, had taken a train to New York to escape the disease, but he died en route.[28] In the courtroom in Montgomery, the train brakeman and the flagman both testified that they had warned Cudjo, had done what they could to prevent the accident, and that he had had plenty of time to get off the track. The Supreme Court reversed the Circuit Court decision and ordered Cudjo to pay the costs of the appeal. He later said he never knew what had become of his money, which means he did not know of the Supreme Court decision and likely never paid the appeal fees.[29]

Since Cudjo could no longer work, the people of African Town created a source of income for him by appointing him the church sexton. Once a week, he took out all the globes of the oil lamps and put them on a small bench. He thoroughly cleaned them of the soot that had accumulated, filled the lamps with oil, and put the globes back on before taking his broom and sweeping the floor. It was also Cudjo's job to ring the bell for service every Wednesday, Friday, and Sunday night, and for baptisms, weddings, and funerals, and to open the door to the congregants, who in 1903 had changed the name of the church to Union Missionary Baptist Church.[30]

As in other black communities, the church was very much at the center of African Town and it served various purposes. One was as a social center. Along with the church, the Africans had built a long shed that accommodated a table for picnics. One of the most memorable was held on January 1, 1900, to celebrate the New Year and the dawn of the twentieth century. Pollee and Lucy's daughter, Eva, who was six at the time, remembered: "Everybody who knew the way out to Plateau came for the free picnic. A half cow was cooked all at once, and everything was free. The deacons spent all night making barbeque. There were two or three hundred pounds of ice in huge pots cooling down a wonderful red drink which was made with fruit and food coloring."[31] On other occasions, they asked people to pay a small sum. Viola Allen, Pollee and Rose's granddaughter, recalled that for $1.20 a whole family, regardless of its size, could eat the huge amounts of food prepared by the town's men and women. "The people in Mobile were thrilled to come to the picnics they gave up there."[32] Why did the Africans open these picnics to all instead of keeping them to themselves? Was it only out of Christian goodness? Mobilians avoided African Town because of its "primitive" reputation.[33] Offering food, inviting anyone who wished to come, was thus a smart way to open up the community to the outside world, a way of making strangers understand that nothing nefarious and barbaric was going on in the town. In a period marked by anti-black violence, it may have been a simple question of survival.

In 1906 and 1907, seventeen African American men had been lynched in the state, three in Mobile County. On October 6, 1906, Richard Robinson and Henry Peters, accused of raping a white girl, were lynched in Prichard, not far from Plateau. Fear of a race riot was widespread. The white leadership dispatched Andrew N. Johnson, former editor of the black newspaper the *Weekly Press* and owner of the most prominent black funeral home in Mobile, to calm the community. Peace prevailed, but the situation had been so explosive that Johnson received death threats and had to leave the city. In 1909, Douglass Robertson was lynched in Mobile and hung opposite a church.[34] Then on February 12, 1910, a mob tried to lynch a man accused of wounding a twelve-year old white girl in Whistler, close to African Town. Someone shot him in the thigh in the melee as he was taken to the Mobile County jail. Another man was also arrested in Whistler for the same incident, and confusion and fear of escalated violence reigned in the neighborhood.[35] Dallas County had the highest number of lynchings—seventeen—between 1889 and 1921, but Mobile was fourth, with twelve men and women put to death by white mobs.[36] A quarter of the killings in the county occurred near African Town, and its residents were likely aware that an unfamiliar, suspicious settlement of "savage Africans," who were landowners and whose men were employed in jobs for which whites could compete, might be a target.

AFTER THEY HAD LOST THEIR TWO YOUNGEST CHILDREN and Aleck had moved out of the house to live down the slope, Cudjo and Abile still had three sons at home: James, Pollee, and David. On Saturday before Easter 1905, David came home hungry. He asked his mother to give him his plate of baked fish, but following African etiquette, she responded that he would not get it before his father did. So David went to the yard, and when he found Cudjo chopping wood, he asked him if he could hurry up. Then he took the axe, finished the job, and brought the wood inside the house. After the meal, he told his parents he was going to get the laundry in Mobile. A while later, his parents heard two men talking and laughing near the fence and thought David had come back with a friend. But the strangers told them that their son was dead in Plateau.[37]

Cudjo and Abile knew he was in Mobile and they were not worried, but the men insisted David had been killed nearby by a train. Cudjo followed them and saw a large crowd near the tracks. As he approached, he discovered a headless body. People kept on saying it was his son but he did not believe them. Then a shipmate pointed at the head on the other side of the track, and told the crowd to pick up David and carry him home. The young man was laid on a window shutter, his head put in a cracker box. When Abile saw him, she screamed and fell down. Cudjo looked at the head, and chased everyone away. He passed his hand under David's shirt and felt the mark on his breast. Abile yelled again and could not stop. Cudjo ran away to the pine grove where he fell down and stayed there until his shipmates came to bring him home. He asked a friend to attach David's head back to his body so that he looked like he was sleeping. The next day the bell tolled for another Lewis child, dead at thirty-one.

Cudjo and his wife were devastated, but their son Pollee was incensed. He wanted to sue the train company. Cudjo, burned by his experience with L&N, told him it was useless. His parents quoted the Bible and talked forgiveness, but Pollee did not care for soothing words. He was bitter, sullen, and refused to listen. He said that when he was a boy the children fought him and called him a savage; when he grew up, they cheated him; his father had been hurt and not compensated, and his two brothers had been killed. And, like his father had done before in his moments of grief, he too invoked Africa. What the Africans had told their children since they were young crystallized in that moment. Cudjo acknowledged, "Poe-lee say in Afficky soil it ain lak in de Americky. He ain been in de Afficky . . . but he hear whut we tellee him and he think dat better dan where he at."[38] Raised with a deep longing for the homeland while living in the cruel Alabama reality, the second generation held on to Africa as the dream, the hope, and the safe haven where one could return in his or her mind when real life was too hard to bear.

That Alabama reality soon caught up with Pollee. One day he told his parents he was going fishing. Someone said he walked toward Three Mile Creek. The young man, thirty-three, was never seen again. Cudjo believed he might have been killed because many people hated him. Once more, his explanation was that Pollee and his brothers did not accept being treated like dogs.[39] And again, Africa became the refuge. Somebody had said that perhaps Pollee was in Africa, and Cudjo wanted to believe it.

Cudjo had been killed in August, Pollee had disappeared shortly thereafter, and before long James, thirty-five, got sick. He had come from work looking bad and his father had told him to stay home. But James went back to work
the next day. In the evening he was so ill that his parents put him to bed and
Abile stayed with him all through the night. Cudjo fetched the doctor. On
November 17, James died holding his father's hand. The coroner's report stated
that he had died of paralysis.[40]

The death of five of her children, three of them in less than four months,
had a profound effect on Abile. As Cudjo recounted it, one night she woke him
up to tell him she had dreamed about their children and they were cold. It was
a November night, and Cudjo recalled how she used to pull up the quilts she
made to the children's chins when they were asleep. The next day she asked
him to go with her to the graveyard to see them. Cudjo, worried that it would
depress her further, went to church to work in an effort to have her forget her
plan. He took his time, sweeping the floor, dusting the pews, cleaning a few
lamps. When he could no longer pretend he had chores to do, he walked out
and saw her down the slope, going from one child's grave to the other, acting
as if she was covering them with quilts.[41] Cudjo said she felt she was going to
die and told him so. She cried because she did not want to leave him alone, but
she had to go and stay with her children.

A week later, on November 14, 1908, Abile was dead. Cudjo believed she
had died of grief and longing to be with her children again. It was a way for him
to cope, to make sense of another tragedy. And perhaps he was right, but the
physician had another explanation. The chronic intestinal nephritis (a major
form of kidney disease) she had suffered from for years had finally killed her.[42]
Cudjo, who would later talk about her in movingly loving terms, was distraught.
She had been his companion of more than forty years; they had raised a strong
family and endured together the terrible pain of seeing it disappear. The next
day, a Sunday, the shipmates gathered at Cudjo's house and Oluale/Charlie
asked him to make a parable. Cudjo bowed his head and lifted it again:

> Suppose Charlee comes to my house and wants to go on to Poleete's. He has
> an umbrella which he leaves in my care. When he comes back he asks for his
> umbrella—must I give it to him or must I keep it? [the shipmates responded]
> "No Kazoola! You cannot keep it—it is not yours!" And Kazoola answered,
> "Neither could I keep Albiné; she was just left in my care."[43]

When the group gathered on another Sunday to lift Cudjo's spirits, he again
made a parable to try to convey his feelings about Abile's departure and how he
understood one's life journey,

> I will make a parable. Kazoola and Albiné have gone to Mobile together.
> They get on the train to go home and sit side by side. The conductor comes
> along and says to Kazoola, "Where are you going to get off?" and Kazoola

replies, "Mount Vernon." The conductor then asks Albiné, "Where are you going to get off?" and she replies "Plateau." Kazoola surprised . . . asks. . . . "Why do you say you are going to get off at Plateau?" She answers, "I must get off." . . . Kazoola stays on—he is alone. But old Kazoola has not reached Mount Vernon yet—he is still journeying on.[44]

Just a week after Abile's death, Cudjo, for the first time, sold some of his land. On November 21, accompanied by Aleck, he put his mark on a deed that transferred a piece of land he had bought for $64.50 in April 1887 from Edward Hauser—an engineer for the L&N Railroad—to Edly W. Cawthon, Sr., the white physician and drugstore owner who had reported Abile's death to the authorities. He sold it for $170 ($3,400 today).[45] To sell land is always a significant decision, and to do so just a few days after a loved one's death is evidence of a pressing need. The fact that he sold it to the physician suggests that he had faced unexpectedly high medical and funeral bills. For people with little revenues a sudden need of cash often translates into the immediate selling of assets, even when the value of these assets is disproportionately higher than the actual need. Whatever money was required after Abile's death was likely less than the value of a piece of land. But Cudjo would need the extra cash almost immediately.

Two weeks after he had helped his father with the sale, Aleck died at age forty-two.[46] Like his brothers, he disappeared unexpectedly. To Cudjo, who was still in shock after Abile's death one month before, the passing of his last child was overwhelming. Within fifteen years, all his children had died. It was the second family he had lost after being separated from his loved ones forty-eight years earlier. He had built a family of his own, only to see it vanish in his old age when, as a patriarch, he was supposed to rest and enjoy the company and help of his descendants. Many years later, he made a parable about his life as an old man without his children: "Once there was a bird beeg and strong. He have a nest of leetle birds who open they mouths, and the beeg bird feed them and they all sing happy. Then the leetle birds grow strong. The old bird get old. And he open his mouth, but the birds have all fly away."[47] He was, in his words, just like when he had arrived—alone. His disastrous series of losses paralleled Gumpa's. Still, there was Mary, Aleck's widow and the mother of Cudjo's four grandchildren. He told her she could stay in the compound and would get the land once he, as he put it, departed to be with Abile and the children.[48]

Motley, one of his grandsons, became his constant companion. The boy's main task was to read him the Bible, the Psalms in particular, which was his favorite book. Cudjo was illiterate but a skill he had acquired in his youth greatly helped him in his religious "readings." As an African, he had trained from a young age to develop his memory, an ability indispensable in oral cultures where long genealogies, historical events, and minute cultural details are transmitted from generation to generation through memorization. Many decades later, he had applied this aptitude to a religion based on the written word. Motley recalled that as he read several chapters, "There would be some words I couldn't pronounce. I would skip that and go on and he'd notice. He would say, 'You're skipping something there.' I'd turn and go back up to the top and go back to those words and when I'd get there again I would say, 'Oh Grandpa, what is that?' And he'd say, 'Why didn't you ask me that at first?'" Cudjo's "remarkable memory" was also noted by Emma Langdon Roche, who commented that "he knew his Scriptures, could repeat many lines, and tell correctly the verse and chapter from which they were taken."[49]

Mary, Cudjo's daughter-in-law, was in her early thirties when she became a widow, and a few years later, she gave birth to a son, Eddie Banks.[50] What happened to the father is not known but soon after, she remarried. Her second husband, Joe, was no stranger to African Town. He had come straight from Lewis Quarters and his entry into the family must have heartened Cudjo. Joe was the eldest child of Charlie and Maggie Lewis, and as such, in the African tradition, he was like a nephew to his parents' friends. Joe had been married to Eugenia Davis, the daughter of Charles and Mary, a laborer and a home wife, both born in Alabama in 1890.[51] A week after delivering their thirteenth child, Eugenia had died on August 17, 1913. According to his descendants, Joe left the oldest daughter in charge of the family.[52] He moved in with Mary, whom he married in December 1915, and they almost simultaneously had a son, Creary.[53] Joe was forty-eight, he worked at the lumber mill, and was now the father of fourteen children. Even though he was an absentee parent—something his descendants are still bitter about—he continued to financially support his offspring at Lewis Quarters.[54] Besides Eddie Banks, he took care of Emmett, Zanna, Motley, and Angeline, who were still in their early teens when he married their mother. Angeline was not home for long; on July 12, 1917, at sixteen, she married Alex West, thirty-five, a laborer at the lumber mill. Within five years, they had Melvin, Bernice, and twins Martha and Mary.[55] After the loss of his children, Cudjo had a sizeable family once again: four grandchildren and at least four great-grandchildren.

AFRICAN TOWN WAS WELCOMING a fourth generation into the world and its founders were reaching the ends of their lives. By 1912, there were only nine survivors left, those known as Clara Turner, Katie Cooper, Shamba Wigfall, Lottie Dennison, Zuma Levinson/Livingston, Charlie Lewis, Pollee Allen, Ossa Keeby, and Cudjo Lewis. When Emma Langdon Roche told the group she was writing a book about their lives, they asked her to use their original names: Abache, Omolabi, Shamba, Kanko, Zuma, Pollee, Oluale, Kossola, and Ossa Keeby. They loved them, they told her, but mostly, they thought that somehow their story could make its way back home, where some people might remember them.[56] It was a gesture that more than anything else spoke eloquently of their attachment to their peoples and their homes, and of their unwavering identity as small-town West Africans even after half a century in the United States. They thought that their given names would be sufficient to identify them, because they had grown up in places where everybody knew everybody, their families, and their lineages. It was also an indication of how much confidence they had in their relatives' love for them, in the strength of the bond that they knew had not been severed by deportation fifty years earlier. Africans in the Americas knew their families and friends missed them, and would do all they could to find them. If a man in Angola could spend twenty years looking for his sister in Brazil and involve two slave ship captains in her release, if a father could locate his son in rural Georgia, then it is also certain that others tried—and failed—to find their loved ones; and their deported relatives kept their faith in them.

Shortly after Roche finished her book, a man who presented himself as an African prince, the Reverend "U Kabe Rega," and was on a mission to organize "evangelistic meetings among his race," planned on "exhibiting" the survivors in order to raise funds for their welfare. Cudjo, or Kogo as he was called, was interviewed by the press on that occasion, and the result was a dubious version of the shipmates' story. King Takko, the story went, and his people lived in the Congo Free State, about two hundred miles from the coast. They were attacked by King Dahomi and brought over on the *Krotiley*. Zuma was 125 years old.[57]

At their weekly meetings on Sundays after church, the old shipmates continued to talk about their previous lives, exchanging memories of home, still dreaming. Ossa Keeby had told Booker T. Washington, "Yes, I goes back to Africa every night, in my dreams." Cudjo dreamed too: he often thought, he confided, that if he had wings he would fly back.[58] On May 18, 1912, Shamba Wigfall was the first of the old survivors to go home. She died of unknown causes, with no physician in attendance. Oluale, the oldest, passed away a few months later, on November 29.[59] He had done well: he had raised three children to adulthood, owned a piece of land that accommodated them and their families, and had been a well-respected chief who got along with everyone. His shipmates were said to have looked upon him as their leader after Gumpa's death, observed his admonitions, and never disobeyed him.[60] Oluale was about seventy-seven, but his death certificate recorded his age as sixty. The strangest part, however, concerned his parents, whose names were said—implausibly for Africans—to be Jim and Mary Lewis. Ossa Keeby probably passed away in 1914.[61]

The next one to depart was not an African, but someone who had been an important part of the community. James Dennison had always been an organized and methodical man who kept all his papers and receipts, so it is no surprise that on March 30, 1914, he had dictated his will and put his X on it.[62] He had appointed his son Napoleon executor and had left everything he owned to his wife and, upon her death, to his son. As could be expected, Kanko, who still took care of most expenses, paid the lawyer who executed the will and other documents. On October 17, 1915, with his affairs in order, James Dennison, about seventy-five, passed away.[63] Reflecting, perhaps, the Dennisons' status and means, Kanko and Napoleon requested the assistance of the famous Johnson-Allen Undertaking Company, founded by journalist and activist A. N. Johnson.

James, the boy from Charleston sold to Alabama, had led a truly unique life. He had been among the minority of skilled bondpeople, a gifted boat pilot, a would-be runaway, a soldier in the Union Army, and finally the owner of a dairy farm at a time when there were only a handful of black-owned businesses of this type in the country. Just as important, he had been part of African American history. He had put his money in the Freedman's Bank, and later had been a member of the important black Southern Mutual Aid Association of Birmingham.[64] He had fought along with thousands of other black veterans for his bounty as a soldier, and been a participant in the first reparations movement. James had also been involved in the Africans' story from the very beginning and had chosen to tie his life to theirs while still maintaining his independence. Even though he never lived in African Town, he was buried in the Africans' graveyard.

After James's death, Kanko continued to keep abreast of developments concerning the ex-soldiers. She renewed James's subscription to *National Tribune*, the newspaper for Civil War Union veterans and, with her son, continued to fight the Pension Bureau. On October 22, Napoleon wrote to the Department of the Interior on behalf of his mother, asking that James's pension be sent to her. The bureau responded that she had to have been his wife prior to June 1890.[65] The Dennisons had been married in 1875, and the case was thus easy to resolve. But in December, they received another letter from the bureau, asking Kanko for a certified copy of James's death certificate and a sworn statement of persons having the requisite knowledge, showing that the Dennisons had lived together without divorce or separation from the date of their marriage to the date of James's death.[66] It was a legitimate request, but one that should have come earlier.

Kanko died on April 16, 1917. Like her husband, she was attended to and buried by Johnson-Allen. The undertaker's statement mentioned that she was born in Dahomey and, strangely, that her father was Joe Joseph and her mother Conco Joseph. Some time later, Napoleon asked the Pension Bureau to reimburse him for the burial fees, for which he was asked to furnish a bill.[67] It was the last act in the Dennisons' fifty-year dealings with the bureau. Father, mother, and son were self-reliant, self-employed hard workers, but they had been very keen on asking for whatever they thought they were entitled to. Sometimes their requests were satisfied, sometimes not, but all along they tried to get whatever rights they had as citizens, even if only second-class ones. In the rabidly racist Alabama of the time, to be self-confident and standing up for one's rights was no small accomplishment.

Kanko had led a life as remarkable as her husband's. From the Freedman's Bank to the Southern Mutual Aid Association, from her struggle with the Pension Bureau to the National Ex-Slave Mutual Relief, Bounty and Pension Association, she had engaged American society perhaps more than any other shipmate. The diminutive woman who had married a foreigner, worked "like a man," handled the family's finances, and told folktales from her Yoruba childhood to her children and grandchildren, had been a strong and quiet force.

After Kanko's death, Cudjo's world got smaller. For several years, on the first and third Sundays of each month, he had taken the segregated trolley to downtown Mobile to visit the Dennisons. For a few hours, sitting on a blue bench on the porch, he talked with Kanko in Yoruba, then had dinner and returned to African Town for night service.[68] With his old companion gone, his circle of friends kept on shrinking. Then Omolabi/Katie Cooper died on October 10, 1919. She had seen a doctor on September 13, but her tuberculosis was too advanced. Her disease was, by far, the leading cause of death among black Mobilians.[69] She was buried at the Prichard cemetery, not in African Town. Emmet, Cudjo's third grandson, died in 1921, at only twenty-four. The details of Zuma's death are unknown, but she passed away in or before 1923, since her husband, John, died a widower that year of senility at the presumed age of 115.[70] He was buried in the Africans' cemetery.

Pollee, the man with the earrings, the *orisa* initiate, the father of fifteen, passed away on August 19, 1922. He had been suffering from severe chill and high temperature, and had seen a physician two days earlier. Pneumonia had infected an entire lobe of his lungs, and he died of lobar pneumonian fever. Pollee left with his dream unrealized. "Even to the day he died," his daughter Eva said, "he talked about going back to his home over there in Africa."[71] His wife, Lucy, declared his death to the registrar. She gave his age as fifty-eight even though he was in his eighties. She also stated he was a sawmill laborer. It is not clear if he was still working or if she referred to his former job. Contrary to what Napoleon Dennison and the Lewises had done for their own parents, rather than invent something, she simply said she did not know his parents' names.

In death Abile, Oluale, Pollee, Kanko, Omolabi, Shamba, and others were the children of parents unknown, or parents who, absurdly, had American names. The family members who made the declarations probably knew the parents' names but did not have them recorded perhaps because they thought the clerks would not bother writing down an "African" name. "Jim and Mary Lewis" and "Joe Joseph," however, open up interrogations. One explanation for these inventions may be that the children or spouse thought it more dignified to make up American names rather than have the mention "unknown" written on the death certificates.

With all the founders but one gone, the formal structure of the town disappeared. The shipmates had decided that a leader and judges were necessary for the cohesion and endurance of the community, but their children and grandchildren did not preserve the organization their parents had respected scrupulously for more than forty years. It had been feasible when African Town counted two dozen families all linked by culture and history, but by the 1920s, it was home to 1,500 people, including many whose African ancestry was much more remote than 1860. It had become the fourth-largest black town in the country after Buxton, Iowa (4,000); Brooklyn, Illinois (3,000); and Boley, Oklahoma (3,000.)[72] Its unique character was largely on the wane. Without its particular governing structure, without the presence of men and women who had grown up in Africa, and without new arrivals from the continent, it could not sustain itself as an "African town." But there were still men and women who had been raised by Africans, spoke languages from the Bight of Benin, and had inherited cultural traits, mannerisms, and modes of thinking that continued to set them apart. By then, though, the families they never knew in West Africa would not have recognized these elements as Isha, Batammariba, or Nupe, but likely as something vaguely familiar. The third and fourth generations made African Town their own, neither distinctly African nor indistinctly African American.

The passing of the founders happened at a time of great change in the United States. African Town had been growing with marriages and births, but it had also seen young people depart. The Great Migration had reached town. Between 1916 and 1930, 1.5 million African Americans had left the South, pushed by the demise of King Cotton, the deteriorating social and political climate, and the violence. In Mobile, the Ku Klux Klan claimed 2,500 members in 1921.[73] One Mobilian, expressing a common sentiment, wrote to the *Chicago Defender:* "There is nothing here for the colored man but a hard time wich these southern crackers gives us. We has not had any work to do in 4 wks. and every thing is high to the colored man." But would-be migrants were not only pushed by the deleterious climate, they were also pulled by the prospect of industrial jobs in the war industries of the North and the Midwest and their own desire to control their lives. Another representative Mobilian conveyed their search for better opportunities: "I am a man that would like to get work in some place where I can elevate my self & family & I think some where in the north is the place for me."[74] By the early 1930s, following the railroad lines, more than 34,300 Alabamians had migrated to Cleveland and Cincinnati, 25,000 to Chicago, and 20,200 to Detroit. The black population had dipped from 908,282 in 1910 to 900,652 ten years later.[75]

In Mobile, African Americans fell from 44 percent in 1910 to 39 percent in 1920. The numbers for African Town are not known, but several families saw some of their members leave. At Lewis Quarters, the first to migrate were two children. Their mother, Martha, Charlie and Maggie Lewis's daughter, had married Henry Lawson, who contrary to what was expected of an African (or an American) son-in-law, had settled among his wife's relatives. He was a day laborer with a reputation as a "sporting man," and the Lewis family was said to have thought he was beneath Martha.[76] She died in 1912 of tuberculosis, leaving him with Lewis, born in 1908, and Bessie, who was born two years later. By 1918, the children had followed their father to Toledo, Ohio. Other people of the third generation left African Town, like Pollee's granddaughter (Eva's daughter), Olivette, who moved to Pittsburgh, another common destination for Alabamian migrants.[77]

By 1922, sixty-two years after his arrival in Mobile, Cudjo Lewis embarked on another unknown and difficult journey. Every one of his shipmates was gone and he was forever cut off from the concrete, human expressions of his past and the collective remembrances that had linked him back to his home. According to Emma Langdon Roche, one of the saddest parts of his life was "that there was no one left in all the world who could speak to him in his native language."[78] But was it true? There were people in their forties who spoke or understood his language, including Joe Lewis. What Cudjo most likely missed were fluent conversations in eloquent Yoruba, discussions about the past, shared memories of long-gone relatives and friends, and conversations about the taste of food, the shape of trees, the smell of fruit. He could talk about his memories, but he had no one with whom to share them.

Moreover, the twenties and thirties ushered in a time of great financial difficulty for people like him, the formerly enslaved men and women who were in their eighties. Most could certainly count on their children to help out, but these children were themselves poor. Over 44 percent worked in agriculture, 76 percent of them on somebody else's land, and almost 23 percent were domestics.[79] Cudjo no longer had children, and his income was whatever he derived from his job as the church sexton. But he also had accumulated some land. His way of dealing with his dwindling resources was to sell his property, bit by bit. In July 1920, accompanied by Joe, he sold a piece of land fifty feet by one hundred feet, east of his house, to Thomas Dawson, forty-one, a fireman at the lumber mill. Cudjo got $100 for the deal. Four months later, he sold Dawson a second plot for $175. Then by January 1922, another piece of Lewis's assets was gone. Cudjo had sold an acre and a quarter to Earl Amos Hill, thirty-three, a laborer at the lumber mill.[80] This time, he got $500. Within two years, Cudjo had received $775, at a time when the average teacher's salary in Alabama was $600 a year. He owned his house and land, but still, he had to take care of basic needs and pay taxes on his property. Evidently, selling his land was an absolute necessity. Four years later, he let go of another plot. He sold it for $108 to Mobile County, presumably for the construction of the Cochrane Bridge, which opened in 1927.[81]

That was the year Cudjo received Zora Neale Hurston's first visit. She got very little from him, and decided to plagiarize Roche's book. Her article, "Cudjo's Own Story of the Last African Slaver," was published in *The Journal of Negro History* in October. A footnote mentioned that she had used records of the Mobile Historical Society and *Voyage of Clotilde*, but no reference was made to *Historic Sketches of the South*, which formed 75 percent of her article. It is possible that *Voyage of Clotilde* was in reality *Historic Sketches*, but it is difficult to figure out how such a mistake in the title could have been made.[82] A month before her article was published, she had met benefactor Charlotte Osgood Mason in New York. Mason funded her research, $200 a month for two years, and in June 1928, Hurston was back in Mobile.[83] This time, besides recording Cudjo's story at length for her manuscript, *Barraccon*, she also took pictures and filmed him with equipment Mason had given her. Cudjo told her someone had taken pictures of him before but had not given him any. He then went inside to change and came back with his best shirt on, but no shoes. He wanted to look as if he were in Africa, he said, because that was where he wanted to be. He then asked to be photographed in the graveyard among his family's tombs.[84] The attire and the request expressed more exactly and poignantly than words the sad reality and heartbreak of his life. His bare feet represented Africa, where he longed to be; his Western clothes were a reminder of where he was; and his family's tombs spoke of his American ordeal, his loneliness, his inability to ever return home, and what linked him now to the Alabama soil. A picture of him in a suit and light colored shirt but with no shoes on has survived.[85] The short silent footage Hurston recorded—forty-three seconds—shows Cudjo in light-colored, much mended pants, dark jacket, white shirt, and hat sitting on the steps of his porch. He then stands up and, looking vigorous for an eighty-seven-year-old man, handles an axe as if splitting logs. Finally, he takes off his hat and stands facing the camera.[86] These few seconds represent the only animated record of an African deported to the United States through the slave trade.

It is not clear if Hurston had paid him for his story, but Mason sent him money between 1930 and 1932. On September 4, 1930, Cudjo dictated a letter thanking her profusely. He told her he had been sick for eight months but his spirits were lifted because "you has don more for me then any one elce in this world since I ben in this country no one has thought enough of me to look out for my well fair as you has the Lord will Bless you for what you has don."[87] The thanks went on for two pages, but the real purpose of the correspondence was on pages three and four. It was a response to a letter she had sent him, and a justification. According to Cudjo, Mason had told him not to let "the white folks read my history." It is accepted that *Barracoon* was finished by April 17, 1931, as Hurston stated, so it seems that what Cudjo had was the *Journal of Negro History* article. Since the piece had been published three years earlier there was no reason to hide it unless Hurston was afraid that the "white folks" in Mobile would discover the truth about it. Ironically, she might have presented her request to Mason as a protection against potential unauthorized copying or plagiarism. It is also possible that she sent Cudjo a first draft of *Barracoon* and in that case, the precautions would have been entirely legitimate, since the manuscript had not been published yet. At any rate, whichever text Cudjo had in his possession, he told Mason, "the young lady [Hurston] told me you said not to there fore I don't let any one see it." The letter concluded with a prayer to see each other, if not face-to-face, at least in heaven. The signature followed.

However, a fourth page was added, probably on another day, as the pencil used is not the same. There, contrary to what he had stated earlier, Cudjo acknowledged, "you may have seen in the papers about my history but this has been over three years since I has let any one take it off to copy from it I only did that so they would help me but there is no one did for me as you has." What seems to have happened is that Mason sent Cudjo a reminder about not show-ing the story, along with money, and he responded by defending himself from having let "white folks" see it. But it then came to his attention that she might see or had already seen an article about him, and he thought it prudent to acknowledge it. The article he referred to may be "Plateau Negro Remembers Capture in Jungle Lands," published by *The Mobile Register* on September 29, 1929. The journalist emphasized that Cudjo was reluctant to talk; he was "re-served and reticent." The reporter boasted of having succeeded in getting in-formation from him because he too had lived in the "jungle," knew how to grind cornmeal with two stones, could "do magic," and had some knowledge of "primitive religions." If Cudjo had showed him Hurston's plagiarized piece, the reporter would have discovered—and likely heralded—the deception be-cause he quoted Roche's book at length and with attribution.

Interestingly, the *Register* article is detailed and contains previously un-published information mentioning Cudjo's six dead children, the train acci-dent, and the trial that ensued, all episodes that did not appear in the *Journal of Negro History* but can be found in *Barracoon*. Cudjo, by his own admission, had been trying to make some money with his story, a legitimate move. He had few resources, it was the Great Depression, and he had no children to help him. Mason was apparently not upset by his confession and kept sending him money, some of which he did not receive. In 1932, she and Hurston decided to inves-tigate. Hurston asked someone to check up on Cudjo and informed the post office in Plateau to be on the lookout for letters to him coming from New York. Mason and her protégé believed his daughter-in-law, Mary, and his grand-daughter, Angeline, had been stealing the money.[88]

In 1931, Cudjo got large local and national exposure. The *Press-Forum Weekly*, the black periodical founded in 1894 by A. N. Johnson under the name *Mobile Weekly Press*, decided to celebrate "the last survivor of the last shipload of slaves brought to this country in the year 1857 [sic]."[89] A few days before the event, the newspaper had advertised the benefit affair by telling its readers, "At times [Cudjo] is joyous; at times he is sad and yet there are times you will behold him in a defiant mood." It would have been quite interesting to know what he reacted defiantly to. Perhaps it was, as had been the case in the past, to uninformed probes into his people's religion and traditions. The high point of the evening would be to hear him talk about "his seventy days on the sea as he made the voyage over . . . [and] the many incidents surrounding his slave days." Admission was fixed at fifteen and twenty-five cents. The newspaper urged readers to come early to get good seats, stressing that there would be "a reserved section for the large number of white citizens who have already made reservation."[90]

On October 21 at 8 P.M., high-class white Mobile came out in force to the Big Zion AMEZ Church in town. The mayor, a senator, members of the Chamber of Commerce, educators, lawyers, and religious leaders joined together, in the *Press-Forum Weekly*'s prose, "to assist in paying honor to a Negro slave." The black paper's tone was remarkably paternalistic: "Never before in the history of the city has such a demonstration been paid to an individual of lowly character. . . . Lonely, humble, seemingly forgotten, yet a city takes time to honor the last survivor of an African tribe (The Tarkars) bought [*sic*] to this country a slave."[91] Tellingly, it was also quite deferential to whites, starting the article with a report on their presence at the church. After a few speeches, including one by Dr. Benjamin F. Baker, principal of Mobile County Training School, and various church anthems, Cudjo talked about his life and sang a song in "his native tongue" that he then translated into English. The proceeds from the door and the donations amounted to $65.72, the equivalent of $800 today. The money, however, was not given to Cudjo. Either he was not judged responsible enough to handle it, or people believed that his family might take advantage of him. It was turned over to the Trust Fund Committee to be deposited in the Cudjoe Lewis Fund, from which he would receive a weekly allowance.

Following the event, author Walter Hart Blumenthal visited him and wrote an article for the New York *Evening Post*. Calling him a "grizzled old darky" who lived in "a ramshackle hut which he calls his home," Blumenthal went on to explain how Cudjo "roamed in the Kongo River basin, about 200 miles from the western coast of Africa." Like most journalists and writers who went to African Town, he had read Roche's book and was more interested in the *Clotilda* and Timothy Meaher than in Cudjo himself, let alone his origin and culture. To Blumenthal he was a Tarkar from Kongo captured by the "savage Dahomeys." To the inevitable question about God, Cudjo responded, "We knew somebody built de sky." Bidding farewell to the New Yorker, he said, "Some of dese days, I tek time to die." Blumenthal's awful piece was reprinted almost completely in the weekly magazine *The Literary Digest* under the equally awful title "America's Last Piece of African 'Black Ivory'." The three-column article gave Cudjo a national exposure and soon enough he was offered a substantial sum of money to appear in a vaudeville show in New York.[92] He refused, even though his finances were still in bad shape. On May 11, 1932, another benefit was held at Franklin Street Baptist Church in Mobile. The addresses were given by Rabbi Moses and John Francis Glennon, a local historian.[93] This time, and strangely enough, no African American dignitaries were invited to speak.

UNTIL THE BEGINNING OF 1935, Cudjo rang the bell of Union Baptist Church every Sunday morning and afternoon, walking the few yards from his log cabin. His house was that of an old man, full of broken tools, the fraying quilts Abile had made for the children, old calendars on the walls, chipped dishes. Visitors had often noted that his clothes were mostly rags; "his trousers," wrote Alabama author James Saxon Childers, "were only patches sewn one overlapping the other."[94] His poverty was enough to account for the state of his pants, but Emma Langdon Roche had a more perceptive explanation. His clothing, always clean, was "a marvelous piece of patchwork," she wrote, remarking that even his old derby was much mended. But, she added, "His patches need elicit no sympathy, for patching is an accomplishment in which he takes keen delight; even in the old days when his Albiné was alive, she would wash his clothes and lay them aside for him to patch during the evenings."[95] It was an odd occupation for a man in the United States, but it was not peculiar for an African. West African men are routinely involved in sewing activities. Muslims do extraordinary embroideries; Fon make appliqué, and "conversely, [Yoruba] males use the needle entirely but never, or at least, very seldom engage in the art of selling," a female activity, reported missionary William H. Clarke in the mid-nineteenth century.[96] Notwithstanding the fact that Cudjo had lived for seventy-five years in a world where sewing—other than as a professional tailor—was strictly a female activity, he had made a decision not to abandon a practice that was male-related in his culture.

Until the end of his life, Cudjo's yearning for his home had remained constant. Childers, who saw him in 1934, stressed how "on and on he talked of his home; and as he talked he was once more a 19-year-old boy, living in that African village, his people around him and a happiness in his heart."[97] This deep, unwavering nostalgia had been steadily expressed by all the shipmates, from their arrival in America until they passed away. The dream of return that had sustained them had not died, but for many years it had been just that, a dream, no longer a plan. Six months before his death, Cudjo could say, lucidly, "Cudjo no want to go back. No fadder, no mudder, no sister, no brudder, no child there to meet Cudjo."[98]

In January 1935, he was visited by another literary celebrity, Tennessee journalist and author Roark Bradford, who had won a Pulitzer Prize and become famous by writing stereotypical books in "Negro dialect" on black Southerners. Once again, Cudjo was asked to recount "the harrowing story of the African manhunt which resulted in his capture and his bondage in America."[99] He had been sick since the beginning of the month and from then on, he spent his days in the darkness of his home, the wood shutters closed tight. Mary brought him food and an elderly man took care of him. On her last visit, Roche found him in a rocking chair by the window, the shutter opened. As she asked him why this change, he went back to Africa once again. He explained that when he was growing up people carried the sick in the sun just before dusk and took them back to bed when it had set.[100] He sang, in Yoruba, a death song that with Charlie and Pollee he had adapted to fit their Christian faith. The English translation was:

> Jesus Christ, Son of God
> Please, Jesus save my soul.
> I want to go to heaven
> When I die
> Jesus Christ, Son of God.[101]

On July 17, a physician was summoned, as his health had deteriorated. On the twenty-fifth, he suffered a cardiac incident, and at 5 P.M. on Friday, July 26, Cudjo, as he used to say, took the time to die. The cause of his death was arteriosclerosis, a hardening of the arteries. A neighbor, Mrs. Singleton, who reported it, told the clerk he was a 105-year-old day laborer, born in Nigeria.[102] Everything was wrong. Once again, but not for the last time, the home he had loved so much was misrepresented.

Cudjo's was a solitary death, the kind he never could have envisioned in his youth. Longevity had been cruel, accompanied with the brevity of his loved ones' lives. It had forced him to witness the demise of everyone he held dear, and to survive with the tragic feeling that he was the only one left of "his kind." He had not been a leader like Gumpa and Oluale, or a wise man like Ossa and Jaba, but he had been just as important. He had been a wordsmith, a storyteller whose imagination and creativity had delighted his companions; the man who could make them laugh or think, to whom they had entrusted their future by sending him to Meaher to convey their hopes. His contribution to his community might have been intangible, but it was essential. He had brought with him the art of the word, so important to Africans, and it had helped them through. He had looked at life with a sensitive eye. Once, when he had seen two corn stalks intertwined and was about to get rid of one, he had stopped, feeling that they had grown together like he and his wife, and pulling one out would hurt the other.[103] Outside his world, he had been just another African whose "broken English" was laughable or picturesque, but in Yoruba, he had been a poet. He had lived through immense tragedies and overcome them with his words, his faith, and his optimism.

On the twenty-ninth Cudjo was laid to rest. The bell he had rung for thirty-three years was tolled by his granddaughter Angeline in the manner he had taught her: brisk for a child's funeral, slow for an adult.[104] Union Missionary

Baptist Church was packed hours before 11 A.M., when the program was sched-
uled to start. Some people had brought boxes and small benches to sit on.[105] It
was a crowd of well-dressed men in light suits and shoes, of women in summer
dresses, some in black velvet, with hats and white gloves. Mary and Angeline,
in the first pew, wore heavy black veils. The third and the fourth generations
had gathered along with neighbors and friends. White Mobile was conspicu-
ously absent, except for five people, ushered into the front pew. To the only
white reporter who covered the service, the whites' absence was a clear sign of
Cudjo's past exploitation. Mobile, he wrote, "had claimed Cudjo while he was
alive and being publicized as 'the country's most historic Negro.' . . . As soon as
Cudjo died he lost his commercial worth." To the whites, he concluded, Cudjo's
was "just another nigger funeral."[106] The service lasted four hours, with ten
preachers officiating. One of the sermons delved into history and politics, "It
ain't shameful to be a colored man. We've got a lot to be proud of. We've
come a long long way, from off in Africa where we were free and owned the
land, to this country where we were slaves before we could be free again."
During the service, the undertakers closed the top of the coffin, and because
Cudjo's head had been somewhat elevated, his face was said to have been mashed
down. Money was collected to pay for the casket. In the graveyard where almost all the shipmates and too many of their children had been buried, the
small crowd threw wildflowers wrapped in newspapers on the coffin, which
had only one floral arrangement.

The *Mobile Register* published a piece on Cudjo's death, dripping with old-
time paternalism. "Upon his arrival here he was sold to a proud plantation
owner, with whom he stayed until he was free. . . . 'Uncle' Cujo often related
with tears in his eyes his parting from 'Marse Tom' and his return to freedom."
That his owner had been James was of little interest, and how much he and his
shipmates had wished for and appreciated their regained freedom was of even
less value to the paper's readers. All the derogatory vocabulary that defined
Africans was in the short piece: jungle, hut, dialect. Dahomey was forgotten,
Cudjo now hailed from Nigeria. The *New York Times* related Cudjo's passing
by summarizing the *Register*'s article, and the Associated Press reported that he
had "roamed the Congo free state, some 200 miles inland. He was a member of
the industrious and peaceful Tarkar tribe."[107]

A year after Cudjo passed away, the remainder of his property was disposed of. Mary presented a claim against the estate for $525 (about $7,300
today) for "nursing, cooking and washing and other personal services . . . rendered for him during his last illness," services provided at his request, she
stressed, and "for which he promised to pay." She calculated that she had helped
him for twenty-five weeks at $21 a week.[108] Few requests could have been more
alien to Yoruba—or African—culture. Cudjo had grown up seeing daughters-
in-law at the beck and call of their husbands' families. Sons' wives were expected to take care of their in-laws, while daughters left the household to do

the same for their own in-laws. The idea of paying Mary, if such was the arrangement, must have been profoundly disturbing to Cudjo and could only have reinforced his sense of isolation and estrangement. A year before his death, he had made a parable for Emma Roche, who had asked him how he was after she had not visited him for a long time. "Suppose you own a little cat and a little dog. In the morning you get up and feed the little cat and give it water, but you forget all about the little dog—how is it that you expect the little dog to live?"[109] This is not to suggest that Mary Lewis had been careless, since Cudjo was addressing Roche, but he undoubtedly felt, justified or not, lonely and somewhat neglected. Finally, in June 1939, the last piece of his property was sold. Mary stated that Cudjo had given the land on which she lived to her deceased husband Aleck, and it was excluded from the transaction. The rest was sold for $1,200 to James Floyd Pate, a white contractor who owned a construction business.[110]

Except for a small plot, everything Cudjo had worked for had passed into strangers' hands. The last survivor was the least able to hold on to his property because he had lived longer than his shipmates, and of course because all his children had passed away, while theirs had been able to preserve the land they had inherited. Maybe Cudjo would not have minded. *His* land was the "African soil," as he called it, and the most important thing he passed on besides his own "history" was his community's story, kept alive by his willingness to talk.

IT IS NOTEWORTHY THAT EVEN THOUGH he had been questioned on his and his friends' origins, their ethnicities were not recorded. Only linguistic, religious, geographical, architectural, and ritual hints can painstakingly lead to deciphering some of their backgrounds. African ethnicities—real, constructed, imaginary— had always been important to slaveholders and dealers, who assigned good or bad qualities to specific peoples, and often made their choice of workers accordingly. But in the nineteenth century, when fewer Africans were living in or entering the United States, this absurd pseudoscience had lost its interest. Nevertheless, in the case of the people in Mobile, there were a few curious enquirers, but all they got were geographic names: Dahomey, Atakora, "Tarkar." The shipmates' main preoccupation partly explains why they chose to focus on location. Ossa, Pollee, Cudjo, and Zuma knew it was their place of origin, not their ethnicity, that could help their relatives locate them, and that was what they were interested in. Given their silence about ethnicity and their choice of leaders that had nothing to do with ethnic origin, it is obvious that this was a non-issue to them. Though heterogeneous in origin, they formed a close-knit community linked by a shared experience as well as by real and perceived distinctions from the "others." At a time when these others were convinced that cannibalistic Africans sold their relatives for two beads and a pouch of tobacco and that Africa was a hideous, heathen place, they proudly affirmed time and again the love of and for their families, the beauty and richness of their land, the religiosity of its peoples, and their desire to go back home.

The teenagers and young adults from Atakora, Banté, Bornu, and Dahomey could have become Americans after spending four times longer in Alabama than in their homelands, but they made a point not to do so. They viewed and called themselves Africans and willfully maintained this identity with all the attendant manners, languages, behaviors, and practices that sustained it. They were not just Africans because they were born in Africa and had lived there a few years, but because they continued to function in significant ways like they had done before their deportation or had seen their people do. They had adapted some practices and adopted others and in that they were typically African, too. The cultural and linguistic borrowing had not started in Alabama but in the Bight of Benin and its hinterland long before they were born, between Fon and Yoruba, Isha and Ewe, Hausa and Songhay.

They lived in Mobile as much on their own terms as they could have, but they were also part of the country's fabric. They had had close encounters with Confederate impressment; the Union Army; the Freedman's Bank; the Baptist Church; the elections of 1874; The National Ex-Slave Mutual Relief, Bounty and Pension Association; a major Southern corporation; the Mobile County court; the Alabama Supreme Court; the convict leasing system; the local, regional, and national press; and already-famous or future celebrated writers. Despite their deliberate insularity, they had been directly involved, much more than many of their contemporaries, in a series of events that had marked their times.

They had also lived an awful experience that very few of their generation had gone through, and none of them ever recovered from the shock of capture, the Middle Passage, and enslavement. When reminded of these moments more than half a century later, they would be overwhelmed.[111] Throughout their ordeal, their deep-rooted sense of family, of belonging to a land and a people far away, yet close and present, had sustained them. The town they created was meant to be temporary, until they were able to return home, but it endured and gave their descendants the same sense of family, of belonging to a place, of being part of a distinctive people.

Ossa, Oluale, Kanko, Abile, Abache, Gumpa, Cudjo, Pollee, Zuma, and the others who resisted with grace, and survived too many hardships, were men and women of stone and of iron.[112] But they were dreamers too, dreaming of Africa in Alabama.

Epilogue

*O*N JANUARY 21, 2002, AT ABOUT 4 P.M., a worker for a telephone company called the police in Daphne, about twenty miles south of Plateau. He said he had been installing lines in a new subdivision when he spotted what looked like the bust of Cudjo Lewis. When the police got to the end of Landing Eagle Drive, a dead-end street near Whispering Pines, they found it, face down in the dirt. It had been pushed down to the bottom of a ditch, six feet below.[1]

News of the discovery brought relief to the congregation at Union Missionary Baptist Church. Aside from being soiled with red dirt, the bust was intact, with only minor scratches on the face and a crack where it had been ripped off its base. The parishioners, funds in hand, were ready to reward the man who had tipped the police, but he wanted to remain anonymous. The story could have ended there, but it was only the beginning.

The bust—like the church, facing east toward Africa—had been erected in 1959 on a pyramid symbolizing African history and culture, made of bricks fashioned long before by the shipmates. It had been personally commissioned and offered by Henry C. Williams, Sr., a local educator, welder, amateur historian, activist, and founder in 1957 of the Progressive League. A grassroots organization that counted some of the shipmates' descendants in its ranks, the league fought hard and alone for years for the recognition and preservation of African Town. In his young days Williams had been a friend of Cudjo.

Forty-three years after its dedication, the bust was found on Williams's property. Some believed he had stolen it to get a reward. He vigorously denied it, but kept it in his workshop, arguing he would not give it back until he received the funds raised for its return. With the money, he said, he would build a more secure and bigger monument.[2] Cudjo's bust remained with him until the first-ever Peace and Unity Walk from Plateau to Prichard, held on Martin Luther King Jr. Day 2003. Councilwoman Earline Martin-Harris of Prichard—the neighboring town, where many African descendants live today—told Williams that in the spirit of reconciliation the statue was going to be rededicated at the church. He brought it back on his pickup truck famous all over town for its life-size iron buffalo attached to the bed in honor of the Buffalo Soldiers. When the church leaders saw him approach, they called the police and, as he tried to put the statue back in place, they had him removed from the property. After placing the bust in a black garbage bag, they left it in the dirt. "We don't want it anymore. We're seeking bids to get our own bust to replace it," said Rev. A. J. Crawford, Sr.[3] Four years later, there is still nothing on top of the brick pyramid.

The dispute is emblematic of the passions that history and memory have aroused in African Town, officially renamed Africatown. The small town, a neighborhood of Mobile since the integration of Plateau and Magazine Point into the city limits in 1948, is now home to about three thousand inhabitants.[4] The interest in preserving and publicizing its past started in the 1950s and was mostly pushed forward by Williams and his Progressive League. Their efforts culminated with the erection of the notorious bust on August 30, 1959. The same year also saw related developments in downtown Mobile, where the Historic Mobile Preservation Society replaced a 1940 plaque dedicated to the "*Clotilde*" at the corner of Royal and St. Louis. It now read, "On This Site Stood One Of The Old Slave Markets. Last cargo of slaves arrived on the Schooner Clotilde in August of 1859." The plaque, besides having the date and the spelling of the ship's name wrong, is misleading, as it suggests that the people of the *Clotilda* were sold at the market.

In Africatown, the quest for a link between the African past and the American present was well ahead of its time. As early as 1961, when few if any African American communities expressed any interest in the continent, Africatown reached out to Africa. Because they thought they had a direct connection to Ghana—it is unclear how this historical fallacy came to be—the town residents invited the Ghanaian ambassador to visit.[5] The significance of Africatown was bolstered in the 1970s in the wake of Alex Haley's *Roots*. In July 1977, a commemoration was organized by the Amoco Foundation and the Association for the Study of Afro-American Life and History, Inc. (ASALH), founded in 1915 by Carter Goodwin Woodson, a Harvard-trained scholar, creator of Negro History Week, and son of enslaved parents. They offered a bronze plaque to be erected in Bienville Square recognizing Cudjo Lewis as the last survivor of the last slave ship.[6] The ceremony was marked by a profound misunderstanding— not unusual for the times—of who the Africans were. Dr. Thomas Knight of Alabama State University and a board member of ASALH had these words about Cudjo: "He arrived as a slave and became a man."[7] A year later, the Alabama Historical Commission asked the Progressive League, which wanted to create a national historic park, to provide information on Africatown for possible inclusion into the Alabama Register of Landmarks and Heritage. An initial survey, funded by the commission for $10,000, included thirty-seven sites, among them the homes and graves of the Africans; three Baptist Churches;

the Mobile County Training School; Foster's shipyard and grave; and the site of Timothy Meaher's home.[8]

The 1980s saw a flurry of activity in and around Africatown. In 1982, Prichard's mayor, John H. Smith, toured Benin and established a twin city agreement between Prichard and Ouidah.[9] The first annual Africatown Folk Festival to celebrate the ancestors and help the living protect the community's history and culture was launched. It was a gamble. An African American journalist who grew up in the area wrote, "blacks in Mobile have been trained to reject anything that attempts to remind them of their Blackness. . . . The sponsors of the Festival knew what they were up against. They realized that not only would the whites in Mobile attempt to ignore this concept, but also some blacks in the city would try to discredit the event."[10] The festival was a success and has been held every year since. In 1984, descendants of the Lewis, Cooper, Allen, and other families founded the Africatown Direct Descendants, Inc. to preserve and promote the site and its heritage, and the first International Conference on Origins took place in Benin. It was followed, two years later, by one in Prichard. In 1987 and 1988, the voyage of the *Clotilda*, including the scuttling, was reenacted as part of the Africatown Folk Festival, and the Catholic archbishop of Cotonou, Isidore de Souza, a descendant of Chacha Francisco de Souza, apologized for the role his ancestors had played in the slave trade.[11]

In 1997 another association was born, the Africatown Community Mobilization Project, Inc., with an office at the foot of the bridge, opposite the graveyard. Its objective is to establish an Africatown historical district and encourage the restoration and development of the site.

In addition to gaining recognition of Africatown, USA, as an official designation, the people and their associations have also succeeded in having the Cochrane Bridge that ends in town renamed Cochrane–Africatown USA Bridge. Ties with Benin have been strengthened, and Beninese diplomats and artists are regular visitors. In February 2004, Simon Pierre Adovèlandé, director of Benin's Agency for Reconciliation and Development, formally apologized for the slave trade on behalf of former president Mathieu Kérékou at a gathering at Union Baptist Church. Only seven descendants were present, and so was Henry C. Williams, Sr., but the young generation was noticeably absent.

The celebration of the African past has been going on for decades in Africatown, much longer than anywhere else in the country, but working for the future is also very much on the agenda. In 2005, the Alabama Benin Trade & Economic Cooperative Forum took place in Montgomery and Tuskegee with the objective of strengthening the economies of Alabama and Benin by using the facilities of the Africa Growth and Opportunity Act. Passed by Congress in 2004, it offers incentives for African countries to open their economies and build free markets. As a result, the Alabama State Constitution was amended to enable the city of Tuskegee to establish a Foreign Trade Zone and Experimental Tax District.

But other projects have not yet been successful. Efforts to create an Africatown, USA National Historic Park have stalled. A first bill was introduced in Congress in February 1983.[12] The idea was opposed from the start by the powerful paper industry, as Scott Paper Co. and International Paper Co. had opened plants adjacent to Africatown—their high walls border several backyards—and wanted to protect their ability to expand. Many in the community, as well as some ecologists, have denounced pollution from the plants as a form of environmental racism they say plagues Africatown. There was talk (that some interpreted as veiled threats) of closing down the mills, where many Africatown residents and descendants worked, if the park plan went ahead. The project had little chance of succeeding, anyway, because the Mobile Historic Development Commission had made it clear that the area could not be an architectural preservation district since the original architecture had long since disappeared, and the National Park Service had stated that it could not identify any site or building of national historical significance in the area. [13]

In 2002, the year of Mobile's tricentennial, the commission in charge of the celebrations envisioned, as a tourist attraction, the recreation of an African Town, complete with a wax museum, trips in "African canoes," arts and crafts demonstrations, fishing, agricultural projects, a play, and a sound and light show.[14] Nothing came of the idea, but efforts for the creation of the park, which will now be located in Prichard, have continued with new bills in 1998 and 2003. As a long-term project, a Sub-Saharan Africa Trade Center is also envisioned.

FROM THE LOCAL TO THE STATE to the international level, the people of Africatown, or others speaking in their name, have thus tried to preserve, promote, and capitalize on their heritage. But more than half a century of dedication, epic fights, and hard work have yet to translate concretely in terms of economic, tourist, and cultural development in Africatown proper, where the associations have to vie for meager funds amid much indifference. Paradoxically, the historical research that should have been the foundation of all other activities has been singularly lacking. Although the National Endowment for the Humanities has given tens of thousands of dollars in grants to outside researchers since at least 1994, no study has been published. As a consequence, approximations and flat-out mistakes that should have been corrected long ago continue to flourish. In May 2003, a bill aimed at requiring the Alabama Historical Commission to provide a current inventory of landmarks in the site eligible for inclusion in the National Register of Historic Places could thus state:

> The history of Africatown, USA originated in Ghana, West Africa, near the present city of Tamale in 1859. The tribes of Africa were engaged in civil

war, and the prevailing tribes sold the members of the conquered tribes into slavery. The village of the Tarkbar tribe near the city of Tamale was raided by Dahomey warriors, and the survivors of the raid were taken to Whydah, now the People's Republic of Benin, and put up for sale. The captured tribesmen were sold for $100 each at Whydah. They were taken to the United States on board the schooner Clotilde, under the command of Maine Capt. William Foster who had been hired by Capt. Timothy Meaher, a wealthy Mobile shipper and shipyard owner who had built the schooner Clotilde in Mobile in 1856.[15]

This is the official version of the story, also found in a piece emanating from the office of former representative Herbert "Sonny" Callahan, created in 2000 for the Local Legacies Project of the Library of Congress.[16] The Africatown Community Mobilization Project uses it on its brochure. In addition to the offensive misuse of "tribe," almost everything in this text is historically inaccurate and unwittingly derogatory. The project's brochure contains further mistakes that come from a 1993 article produced by the Alabama State Council on the Arts.[17]

The unearthing of history, the recording of memory, and the preservation of historic places, documents, artifacts, and photographs are pressing issues. The Africans' houses in Mobile have been torn down or completely remodeled, and none of the original wood cabins is extant; many photographs and objects have been lost or stolen, and several headstones have disappeared. But still intact is Gumpa's brick chimney by the four-lane Bay Bridge Road and the drive that bears his American name, Peter Lee. This visible material memento of the Africans' presence stands a few feet from another marker: a concrete pillar with the name "Meaher" on it. The Meaher family, still rich and powerful, has interests in banking, law, and real estate. In contrast to the people of Africatown, it does have a park, Meaher State Park, on 1,327 acres it donated to the state. The family has been quite discreet about the brothers' story as it pertains to the Africans. None of their family papers have been made available. When the Meahers do speak, they limit themselves to the family's philanthropy. "We donated property there [Africatown] for the churches, the park, the cemetery," stressed Joseph L. Meaher.[18] Another descendant, who requested anonymity, would only say that Timothy was a benefactor of Spring Hill College and was instrumental in the building of the pillars of the Cathedral of the Immaculate Conception in Mobile. Asked in 1998 when the family would speak on the record, he responded, "in twenty years."[19]

As for the *Clotilda* herself, her story did not end when she was engulfed in flames in a remote bayou. What became of the ship is still very much an issue today. In 1890, one of the documents attached to Foster's narrative detailing his voyage stated that he had sold the schooner to speculators for $6,000.[20] But Emma Langdon Roche photographed it in the 1910s, still in the water. Shortly afterwards, when Rev. "U Kabe Rega" visited African Town, he was said by the press to have hoisted the hull.[21] There is no information as to its whereabouts, nor is it absolutely certain that it was indeed a piece of the *Clotilda*. In the 1990s, a retired businessman and historian, Jack Friend, raised money and received a state grant to search for, preserve, and display the ship. According to his research, the hull was made of copper, much more resistant than wood, and his *Clotilda* Project has carried out underwater archeological investigations. Nothing conclusive has been found but investigators believe that parts of the ship could be located if enough money—the estimate is in the millions of dollars—was allocated to the search.[22] In the meantime, an antiques dealer in Georgia has been trying to sell what he advertises as "a piece of the Slave Ship Clothilde" supposedly found in the 1920s and presented to Cudjo. The purported floorboard with a wooden peg has been on display on the Internet for years. Offered at $8,000 in 2002, it reached $29,500 four years later. The dealer sells it with a certificate of authenticity given to him by the director of the defunct Black American Historical Museum, formerly of Harlem, who acknowledges that he cannot in fact authenticate the piece of wood. He got it from an Alabamian living in New York City, who claimed to have bought it from the Lewis estate.[23]

AFRICATOWN TODAY IS HOME to a "mixed" population: men and women related to the founders, others who are not but whose ancestors settled in the area long ago, and still others who have no nineteenth-century roots in the community. Many descendants have left for Prichard, Mobile, Cincinnati, New York, Detroit, California, and even Korea. But Gumpa's family still live on the land he owned. His grandson Sidney Lee, who was nine at his grandfather's death, retained his property. He became the pastor of Liberty Baptist Church and Third Baptist Church.[24] Great-great-grandchildren of Omolabi/Katie Cooper have kept her land, behind the cemetery. Some families have disappeared; others now count hundreds of living descendants. At the first Keeby family reunion held in 1998, two hundred people gathered in Mobile.[25] Charlie and Maggie Lewis have more than two hundred direct descendants, including three dozen great-great-great-great-grandchildren. Some still live at Lewis Quarters. Besides the renovated houses of the founders, an old wood cabin from the 1920s has endured, and in the quarters' small cemetery several Africans, African Americans, and their children are buried. Unfortunately, the Gulf Lumber Company removed their headstones when it built the lumberyard in 1940.[26]

Over the years, Lewis Quarters has lost its economic life, as well as several acres. It was once a flourishing enclave with a brick mill, a food store, a barber and beauty shops, and a sewing center. The women made quilts, the men fixed trucks, and all grew foodstuff.[27] Lorna Woods, a Lewis great-great-grandchild, active in the Africatown Direct Descendants Association, works diligently for the preservation of the town and of Lewis Quarters. With relatives she has done research in her family history and gathered documents that she eagerly shares. In order to educate new generations to the significance of Africatown, she regularly tours schools to present the story of her ancestors and their companions.

A great-great-granddaughter of Pollee Allen and his first wife, Rose, Dr. Dorothy Ford, general secretary of the Friends of Africatown, USA National Committee, was born in 1932 and remembers life in the 1940s, a time when the founders were no longer there but the fourth generation was still the victim of particular prejudice. "We were looked upon as 'those Africans.' Black people were second-class and we were sub-class to second class," she explains. "It put fire under us. At a time when other black people did not know where they came from or did not want to acknowledge their Africanity, we had this sense of belonging, of defiance and pride. We knew who we were." She also recalls the resourcefulness and strong unity of the community.[28] Olivette Howze, a granddaughter of Pollee and his second wife, Lucy, has fond memories of her childhood and her ancestors: "They came here, and they made something. Because of them, we had a deeper culture, a better culture than most."[29]

Helen Richardson Jackson, who grew up in the tight-knit neighborhood on Keeby land in the 1950s, recalled, "Nobody ever missed a meal in Africatown. If you didn't have enough, why, your neighbor gave you some of his. We were all one family. We were taught to call every other African our own age 'cousin.' We knew they were the same as us—and that we were all different from everyone else."[30]

Mable Dennison, Kanko and James's granddaughter, was born in 1921 after they passed away, but she knew Cudjo. Growing up in the thirties, she too recalls that she and the founders' grandchildren were mocked by neighbors and called "old Africans." More than anyone else, Ms. Dennison, who worked after retirement at The Museum of Mobile, has documented her grandparents' story. Every day when she came back from work, she says, she went by their house, where everything had been left intact, and took papers and objects, from pots to musical instruments, furniture to old receipts. With the material she gathered and her siblings' recollections, she wrote two booklets that narrate her grandparents' story and include copies of invaluable documents. In her bedroom, Ms. Dennison still has Kanko's chair, but she acknowledges that most of her grandmother's possessions have been sold, given away, or deteriorated, as has been the case in other Africatown families.[31] Preoccupied with preservation issues, she tried more than twenty-five years ago to draw attention to the fact that artifacts were being destroyed or removed.[32]

Martha West Davis, a former schoolteacher born in 1923, who is Cudjo's great-granddaughter, lives in Mobile, whereas her twin, Mary, migrated to Philadelphia. The family has not retained any property in Africatown, and mobile homes are now aligned on Cudjo's land. On February 20, 2001, the Mobile Alumnae Chapter of the Delta Sigma Theta Sorority erected a tall, white monument on his tomb. Regrettably, half of it is dedicated to listing its sponsors. Only two of the Lewis children's graves can be seen, James's and Aleck's. Abile's headstone is lost, but the tombstones of James, Equilla, and Napoleon Dennison are intact. Several headstones have been displaced; some were used to prop up the caretaker's cabin. Others fell down and have been buried under dirt and grass.

There is a real urgency in preserving Africatown, not only for the people who are heirs to an exceptional part of African, African American, and American history, but also for others. African Americans still face daunting obstacles when reconstructing their past and retracing their families' histories, even with the help of new technologies. Thirty years after the phenomenon unleashed by *Roots*, online genealogical databases and genetic analysis have given anonymous and famous people a new impetus to search for their African ancestry, and increasing numbers put their faith in "ethnic" DNA testing, despite its limitations. [33] Africatown descendants know for sure who their African ancestors were, from where they left, and when they arrived. They are the only ones with an African Town to call their own, and they are eager to share.

John Smith, chairman of Africatown, USA Reconciliation and Development Committee, who is not a descendant, expressed the need to protect their unique heritage as he appealed for recognizing Africatown "as a national homeplace for those of us who cannot find our history, cannot find the records of how we got here, and who our relatives were." [34]

Appendix

The Numbers of the Illegal Slave Trade

HE NUMBER OF AFRICANS INTRODUCED during the illegal slave trade has been a matter of controversy for two hundred years. After 1820, on one side of the debate were the successive presidential administrations defending their repression record; on the other were abolitionists denouncing, and Southerners rejoicing over, what they presented as frequent landings that brought in, they claimed, several thousands Africans every year. Just a year before the *Clotilda* sailed back into Mobile, the New York *Herald* and the *Weekly Tribune* had asserted that sixty to seventy ships each with 250 people on board had arrived within the prior eighteen months.[1] From 15,000 to 17,500 Africans were thus supposed to have entered the country. Early scholars of the transatlantic slave trade also proposed high numbers. W. E. B. Du Bois assessed the post-1808 entries at 250,000; Winfield H. Collins at 270,000; and Lewis Gray at 260,000.[2] Noel Deerr's estimate reached 1,000,000 from 1809 to 1861.[3]

According to modern scholarship, those figures were grossly inflated because the authors did not make the necessary distinction between American involvement in the slave trade, which was considerable but mostly directed toward Brazil and Cuba, and the introduction of Africans into the United States.[4] In other words, dozens of American slave ships did leave the country every year, but most ended their trip in Cuba, or in the Brazilian cities of Bahia and Rio. Historian Philip D. Curtin has proposed what he called "a shot in the dark" range of about 1,000 persons introduced into the United States every year for the period 1811–1860.[5] David Eltis estimates the arrivals between 1801 and 1810 at 156,000; 10,000 from 1811 to 1820; 2,000 from 1821 to 1830; zero between 1831 and 1850; and 300 from 1851 to 1860; or a total of 12,300 after 1810.[6] The numbers for the later decades are manifestly too low. The *Wanderer* and the *Clotilda* alone had more people on board than the 300 listed for 1851–1860.

On the other hand, Gwendolyn Midlo Hall states that the introduction of Africans during the illegal slave trade was massive.[7] She bases her assertion on her study of the mean age of some 6,000 Africans living in Louisiana between 1800 and 1820. Noting that it had decreased in many instances, she concludes that the smuggling was considerable in particular for the Wolof, Kisi, Chamba, Yoruba, Hausa, and Mandongo. Similar research has not been conducted for other states.

Another approximate, and arguably limited, way to tackle the issue is to analyze the censuses. All censuses until 1930—the last published—list black (and white) men and women born in Africa, including during the illegal slave trade. The first census that counted African Americans as people was taken in 1870, ten years after the last slave ship had landed. It should thus paint a passable enough picture of the magnitude of the post-1808 arrivals, particularly in the last decades. The total number of "colored" people born in Africa recorded in 1870 was between 1,690 and 1,984 out of 4,880,009 African Americans.[8] But these figures cannot be entirely trusted because the Census Bureau, by its own admission, had missed more than 500,000 blacks—more than one out of ten— mostly in the South, due to the confusion following the war.[9] A substantial number of the missing could have been born in Africa, if the case of the *Clotilda* Africans is any indication. Only twenty appeared in the census in Mobile out of a possible seventy to eighty.

However, the more reliable 1880 census counts no more than a thousand Africans. Of course, some had died in the previous decade, but it is improbable that thousands of people unreported in 1870 had passed away. Could there have been a conspiracy of silence among Africans to conceal their origin? A possible motivation, it has been suggested, could have been that the Fourteenth Amendment gave rights to persons born or naturalized in the United States, not to illegal immigrants.[10] Yet, by 1870 some of the *Clotilda* Africans had become citizens; they did not have anything to hide, but still, they did not appear in the census. The conspiracy makes little sense for another reason. It would have been impossible for Africans with an accent and/or scarifications or tattoos to fool a census taker, even when their names were Tom Johnson or Mary Brown. Thus their not being recorded likely stems from the fact that they were not visited rather than that they had successfully concealed their origins. This leads to another conspiracy theory: for some reason, the Republican administration of Ulysses S. Grant sought to minimize the illegal slave trade by undercounting the Africans.

Whatever the case may be, there is no doubt that more than two thousand were living in the United States in the 1870s. But if we assume that the average age of a thousand Africans who arrived every year after 1808 was twenty-five and that they all survived and then lived until fifty there should have been about 15,000 of them in 1870 and 5,000 in 1880; many more if the average age at arrival was eighteen and seventy at death. We are far from these numbers, and the undercount would have had to be considerable, as high as 90 percent.

It is difficult to draw a definitive conclusion from the censuses, but if any-thing, these computations would indicate that the illegal slave trade, at least post-1820, was not massive. Evidently this method, like the others, has its lim-its and it is only a combination of information gathered from shipping ac-counts, court records, private papers, censuses, and plantation books that could give us a clearer picture.

The geographical reach of the illegal slave trade, however, has not been disputed and is indeed reflected in the censuses. The Africans born after 1808 are highly concentrated in three Gulf States. Only 41 out of 295 Africans (13 percent) who were born after the end of the legal trade (the number of those who were born up to twenty years before 1808 and might or not have been part of the illegal trade is of course higher) lived in Georgia; 30 out of 191 (15 percent) in South Carolina, and 17 out of 83 (20 percent) in Florida. But 24 percent of the Africans in Louisiana were born after 1808 (55 out of 221), as were at least 37 percent of the Alabamian Africans (85 out of 228, or 50 percent if all the people of the *Clotilda* are counted). Thirty-one percent (27 out of 87) of the Africans living in Mississippi, and 75 percent (207 out of 276) of those in Texas were clearly deported during the illegal slave trade.[11] Actual numbers are doubtless higher, but percentages are not likely to differ greatly.

An Essay on Sources

*I*N THE SPAN OF A HUNDRED AND THIRTY-FIVE YEARS, as they appeared episodically in the press, several versions of the Africans' story, their origins, and even their names were offered. Besides the notice of the arrival of the *Clotilda*, which was published in several newspapers, what seems to be the first article to mention them appeared on December 3, 1870, in *The Christian Union*. It stated that they had come on the *Wanderer*, an obvious mistake. Other articles on the twelfth and nineteenth of the same month repeated the error, but brought interesting information as to the origin and occupation of some of the shipmates.[1] In February 1871, a longer and more detailed piece on the same topic was published in *The African Repository*, the organ of the American Colonization Society.[2] Because its readers were somewhat familiar with West Africa, the monthly provided additional geographical particulars. After Reconstruction, a few articles based on interviews with the survivors appeared in the press. In addition to journalists, the shipmates met and talked with a string of celebrities, including several writers and a Pulitzer Prize winner.

One such personality was Henry Romeyn, a native New Yorker who had been an officer with the Fourteenth U.S. Colored Infantry regiment. After the Civil War, he had gone West to help dispossess Native Americans of their land and was the author of *The Capture of Chief Joseph and the Nez Perce Indians*. Romeyn elicited valuable information on the Africans' origins and their lives, in the early 1890s.[3] But it is without a doubt the 1893 visit of Mary McNeil Scott—the famous Mobile poetess and wife of renowned Japanese art expert Ernest Francisco Fenollosa—or more precisely the detailed observations of her guide, Noah Hart, who had lived on Timothy Meaher's plantation, that provided some of the most rewarding insights into the shipmates' lives during slavery, their relations with African Americans, and how a particular group among them had maintained several traditions.[4] Hart proved to be a superbly reliable eyewitness, and Scott a very dependable reporter. Samuel Hawkins Marshall Byers, poet, writer, diplomat, and composer of *Sherman's March to the*

Sea and of the state song of Iowa, interviewed three Africans, got further information from white Mobilians, and wrote an article for *Harper's Monthly* in 1906.[5]
Booker T. Washington, the Africans' Tuskegee neighbor, visited them but
had nothing much to say, except for some negative comments published in *The
New York Times* in 1909.[6]

Shortly afterwards Emma Langdon Roche produced a most detailed and
lengthy account of their story. She interviewed, photographed, and sketched
them. Her only book, *Historic Sketches of the South*, is based on the reminiscences of the last nine survivors and William Foster's widow, Adalaide.[7] She
continued to visit Cudjo until his death and wrote an article about him right
after he passed away.[8] She was a sympathetic, attentive, and sensitive listener.
Roche is the original source for the supposed ethnicity of the Africans. Since
she understood that they were "Tarkars," this pseudo-ethnicity has been repeated by reporters, scholars, and even the Africans' descendants. Her book
became an obligatory reference for journalists and others, who used it abundantly, but also added a number of inaccuracies and misinterpretations that
passed from one article to the next. In some versions, the Africans had fled the
burning *Clotilda* and lived in the woods and swamps on their own.[9]

The most comprehensive account of the Africans' story was penned by
Zora Neale Hurston, whose plagiarism of Roche's book was discovered only in
1972, twelve years after Hurston's death. On her second trip to Mobile, in
1928, she established a rapport with Cudjo over the course of two months, and
produced *Barracoon*.[10] Her biographer, Robert E. Hemenway, dismissed her
work as a "highly dramatic, semifictionalized narrative . . . [that] makes extensive use of Roche and other anthropological sources . . . it is Hurston's imagi-
native recreation of [Cudjo's] experience."[11] His characterization was uncalled
for, because not having done research on Cudjo and his companions, he was
not in a position to assess the veracity of Hurston's work.

Her narrative is a long interview in the first person, and when she used
sources other than Cudjo, she quoted them. Although they appear as notes in
her handwritten draft, they are absent from the typewritten manuscript.[12] She
also intervened within the narrative to clarify—at least that was her intention—
a few things, but there again she was cautious and used parentheses. She tried
to transcribe Yoruba, a tonal language quite difficult to record, and managed
to get some words right. She may have conflated some of what Cudjo said with
some of what she knew as a scholar, but she made a genuine effort at separating
the two. With few exceptions, the information provided in *Barracoon* is confirmed by other sources. Witnesses, experts in Yoruba cultures, contemporary
newspaper articles, and abundant archival material corroborate the various
events in Cudjo's life as described in *Barracoon*. Far from being fictionalized,
Cudjo's story, as transmitted by Hurston, is as close to veracity as can possibly
be ascertained with the help of other records.

Unable to get the manuscript published, she used parts of the story in her autobiography, *Dust Tracks on the Road*, and in an article she wrote for *The American Mercury*, with problematic results. Not only are there variations between the four versions Hurston produced between 1927 and 1944, but in the last two there are also inventions. In *Barracoon*, Cudjo was captured by men, not a particularly exciting fact, but in *The American Mercury* and *Dust Tracks*, she had him seized by Amazons, most likely because it spiced up the story.[13] In *Barracoon*, Cudjo explained that Glèlè raided his town because its king refused to pay tribute; but in *The American Mercury*, she added an explanation about the king making fun of the death of King Glèlè's father she had read in Richard Burton's book *A Mission to Gelele*.[14] In her 1927 article Cudjo and his companions were "Togo," living fourteen days from the sea and "one sleep away about 200 miles" from Dahomey. She mentioned they were Takkoi from Nigeria in *Barracoon*. In *Dust Tracks*, they were Takkoi living "three sleeps from Dahomey."[15] Worse, she created a guided tour of Ouidah given to William Foster by the prince who oversaw the sale and invented a dinner between the two, during which the prince showed the American a drum made with the skin of a trader who had tried to bypass the Dahomian.[16] The basic story she relayed was fundamentally the same, but Hurston took liberties with what Cudjo told her in 1928.

She was not an impeccably honest scholar, and she proved it again in a dramatic way during the 1928 trip. She discovered another *Clotilda* survivor about two hundred miles north of Mobile, but kept silent about her even though she claimed the woman was older and a better talker than Cudjo.[17] This person's testimony would have proved priceless, since there are no known accounts by deported African women of their experience before, during, and after the Middle Passage. If she was not from the same region as Cudjo, her story prior to capture would have added greatly to our knowledge. The fact that she did not live in an African community in Alabama, contrary to Cudjo, would also have been instructive as to issues of cultural continuity. But she remained anonymous, her life unknown. Hurston wrote to Langston Hughes, "no one will ever know about her but us."

In addition to several articles based on conversations with the protagonists— mostly Cudjo—interviews with some of the Africans' early descendants (children and grandchildren) were published in Southern newspapers in the 1980s and early 1990s. They provide precious information on the first generation's activities, thoughts about their homelands, cultural transmission or lack thereof to their offspring, and the second and third generations' relations with neighbors.

The story behind the voyage of the *Clotilda*, the journey to and from Ouidah, and the arrival of the Africans in Mobile was also reported by the men who organized the expedition. A crucial document in that regard is William Foster's own account of the events. The handwritten twelve-page *Last Slaver to the U.S.*, signed by Foster, gives the date of the voyage as March 4, 1860.[18] However, it was written thirty years after the fact. Foster sent it to a Mr. Donaldson on September 29, 1890. One may wonder what made him write it. The most likely reason can be found in the draft of a letter written by a Mr. Creek of Baldwin County, addressed to the editor of the *Glasgow Weekly Herald*.[19] Creek referred to a short notice published by the newspaper on July 12, 1890, about "The Last Slave-ship," an article that had just appeared in *Scribner's* magazine.[20] In this piece, George Howe, a physician, recounted how in April 1859 he had been sent as a medical student to accompany a group of former slaves from New Orleans on their way to Liberia. Their ship, however, was actually a slaver that had disguised its purpose because the customhouse, suspicious of the captain's intents, had refused to give him the necessary papers. After a stopover in Monrovia, the ship was said to have sailed to the Congo where twelve hundred people between twelve and thirty had been embarked, and then from there to Cuba. When Creek read the piece in the *Herald*, he decided he had to correct the error made by Dr. Howe, based on information he had recently obtained from "Captain Tim Meagher [*sic*] and Captain William Foster." His letter is not complete, but the gist of it is that Howe, who had sailed to Cuba in 1859, was not on the last slave ship, since that distinction belonged to William Foster.

Foster's account surfaced two months after *Scribner's* article, and it is thus quite likely that Howe's claim had prompted some people to urge the *Clotilda*'s captain to write down his own narrative of the true "last slaver." Strictly concerned with the voyage itself, it is corroborated by Cudjo's account; the shipmates' recollections; court documents; and contemporary newspapers articles. It is also consistent with the way affairs were conducted at Ouidah at the very time Foster was there. There is no doubt that the manuscript is authentic. It may have been handwritten by someone else, but the story it tells came from Foster and is easily verified. A letter summarizing it and relating the circumstances that led Timothy Meaher to sponsor the voyage accompanied Foster's narrative. The writer stated he had obtained the particulars from Meaher and Foster, "two gentlemen well and favorably known in Southern Alabama."[21]

Foster was not the only one asked to state the facts and seemingly revel in their glory. The Meahers soon joined in. On November 10, Augustine, Timothy's son, responded to a letter from Donaldson, who had asked for information, giving him the names and some biographical background on fourteen Africans brought on the *Clotilda*.[22] In the space of three months after Howe's article, there was a flurry of epistolary activity concerning the *Clotilda*, her captain, and her passengers, all bent on reestablishing the truth as to who was on the last slave ship. Then Timothy Meaher himself granted a long interview on November 26 to tell his side of the story, which was published on November 30, 1890, in at least two newspapers.[23]

If not for George Howe's bragging, Foster and Meaher may not have felt the need to come forward. Three weeks before *Scribner's* article, the *Clarke*

County Democrat had interviewed Meaher, but no mention was made of the *Clotilda*.[24] Howe had emphasized that almost all the people connected with the trip had died and he therefore did not feel he had violated any confidence.[25] But Foster and Meaher were actually so proud of what they had accomplished that they were doing all they could to make sure everyone knew about it.

Far from being a hoax, the last slave voyage to the United States—and the lives of the people on board—is probably the best-documented story of the American slave trade.

Notes

Introduction

1. "Ceremony Honors Cudjoe Lewis," Mobile *Press Register*, August 30, 1959.
2. W. E. B. Du Bois, *The Suppression of the African Slave-Trade*; Warren S. Howard, *American Slavers and the Federal Law 1837–1862*; Hugh Thomas, *The Slave Trade*; Don E. Fehrenbacher, in *The Slaveholding Republic: An Account of the United States Government's Relations to Slavery*, states that the *Wanderer*'s is the last documented voyage, as does Erik Calonius in the 2006 book *The Wanderer: The Last American Slave Ship and the Conspiracy That Set Its Sails*.
3. Two typescripts and a handwritten version are held in the Alain Locke Collection at the Moorland-Spingarn Research Center of Howard University.
4. Olaudah Equiano, *The interesting narrative of Olaudah Equiano: or Gustavus Vassa, the African / written by himself*. It has been suggested that Equiano was born in South Carolina; see Vincent Carretta, *Equiano, the African: Biography of a Self-Made Man*. For a convincing refutation, see Paul E. Lovejoy, "Autobiography and Memory: Gustavus Vassa, alias Olaudah Equiano, the African." Quobna Ottobah Cugoano, *Thoughts and Sentiments on the Evil of Slavery and Other Writings*; Venture Smith, *A Narrative of the Life and Adventures of Venture a Native of Africa: But Resident above Sixty Years in the United States of America, Related by Himself*.

CHAPTER ONE   Mobile and the Slave Trades

1. Hiram Fuller, *Belle Brittan on a Tour, at Newport, and Here and There*, 112. See also Harriet E. Amos Doss, "Cotton City, 1813–1860," 65–94.
2. Joseph Casimir O'Meagher, *Some Historical Notices of the O'Meaghers of Ikerrin*, 175–6.
3. The Meahers are somewhat difficult to track in the censuses because their name has been spelled in different manners. In the 1830 Maine census, they are listed as Meagher (Whitefield, Lincoln County, 28). In 1840, they are called Meaher (Whitefield, Lincoln County, 10). In 1850, they are again Meagher in Maine (Whitefield, Lincoln County, 313), but Tim and Abby are also recorded in the Alabama census a few months later as Meher (Mobile, Mobile County, 354). Burns is alternatively called Byrnes, or Burnes.
4. Joseph O'Meagher, *Some Historical Notices*, 176–8.

5. Albert Burton Moore, *History of Alabama*, 307.
6. James Silk Buckingham, *The Slave States of America*, 1, 257.
7. Moore, *History of Alabama*, 381.
8. During the nineteenth century, few Europeans settled in the South, but those who did immigrate chose to live in the urban areas. Mobile was particularly attractive and, by 1860, a third of Mobilians were foreign. For a discussion of immigrant workers in the South, see Ira Berlin and Herbert G. Gutman, "Natives and Immigrants, Free Men and Slaves: Urban Workingmen in the Antebellum American South." Compiled from the United States Federal Census, 1850. In 1860, as much as a quarter of Mobile's white population was foreign-born.
9. Weymouth T. Jordan, "Ante-Bellum Mobile: Alabama's Agricultural Emporium," 200; Melton McLaurin and Michael Thomason, *Mobile: The Life and Times of a Great Southern City*, 42, 55.
10. Sir William Howard Russell, *My Diary, North and South*, 185.
11. United States Federal Census 1840, Maine, and Alabama; McLaurin and Thomason, *Mobile*, 42.
12. Oddly, more than twenty years later, another ship also named the *Wanderer* would make headlines all over the country as the last slave ship. "Capt. Tim Meaher's Sketch of His River History"; Harvey H. Jackson, *Rivers of History: Life on the Coosa, Tallapoosa, Cahaba, and Alabama*, 87–97. Remembering his roots, Meaher named the ship after the Maine captain who in 1824 had filled the hold of his brig, *Orion*, with ice from the Kennebec and sold it in Baltimore, launching a lucrative industry for Maine seafarers.
13. O'Meagher, *Some Historical Notices*, 176–8; U.S. Federal Census 1850, Whitefield, Lincoln County, Maine, 313; U.S. Federal Census Alabama, Mobile, 158; Alabama Marriages, 1809–1920 (selected counties) online database, www.ancestry.com. U.S. Federal Census 1870, 1880, Alabama, Mobile County.
14. "The Funeral of Captain Timothy Meaher"; Winfield Scott Downs, ed., *Encyclopedia of American Biography*, 54. According to Joseph Casimir O'Meagher, Miss Waters was Sarah, James's wife; see *Some Historical Notices*, 176.
15. "Capt. Tim Meaher's Sketch."
16. Cited in *De Bow's Review*, 26, 1 (January 1859), 81.
17. Amos Doss, "Cotton City," 80. In 1850, the total number of slaveholders (not including their families) in Alabama was reported at 29,295 for a white population of 426,514. See Hinton Rowan Helper, *The Impending Crisis of the South: How to Meet It*, 146. Half of the citizens of Mobile owned fewer than five people; 16,000 enslaved from 5 to 30 men, women and children; and a few large planters had more than a hundred. Moore, *History of Alabama*, 354.
18. U.S. Federal Census 1860, Alabama, Grove Hill, Clarke County, 37–8.
19. City Tax Books for J. M. & T. Meaher for property listed Square 313 and Square 336 (Orange Grove) 1860 and 1861.
20. U.S. Censuses 1850, 1860, and 1870, Mobile, Alabama. For the recollections of Julia Hemming, one of Dabney's slaves who moved with her mother Mandy Moore and her siblings from Virginia while their father Jordan was sold away, see George P. Rawick, ed., *The American Slave: A Composite Autobiography*, Supplement, Series 1, volume 1, Alabama Narratives, 28.
21. See in particular, Michael Tadman, *Speculators and Slaves: Masters, Traders and Slaves in the Old South*; Walter Johnson, *Soul by Soul: Life Inside the Antebellum Slave Market*; Walter Johnson, ed., *The Chattel Principle: Internal Slave Trade in*

the Americas; Adam Rothman, *Slave Country: American Expansion and the Origins of the Deep South*; Stephen Deyle, *Carry Me Back: The Domestic Slave Trade in American Life*.

22. George W. Featherstonhaugh, *Excursion Through the Slave States*, 152.
23. The percentage of African Americans displaced by the planters' migration within the overall number of deportees from the seaboard region is contested. According to Frederic Bancroft, in *Slave-Trading in the Old South*, they represented 70 percent, 398; Robert W. Fogel and Stanley L. Engerman, in *Time on the Cross: The Economics of American Negro Slavery*, I 47–9 estimate their percentage at 50; while Michael Tadman, *Speculators and Slaves*, refutes their analysis and gives an estimate for planters' migration of 20 to 30 percent; Robert H. Gudmestad, in *A Troublesome Commerce: The Transformation of the Interstate Slave trade* (21–2, 210), states that probably no more than 14 percent of pre-1820 displacement was due to the trade, but that the percentage increased afterward; Steven Deyle, in *Carry Me Back*, 288–9, agrees with Tadman's estimates.
24. James De Bow, "The Non-Slaveholders of the South: Their Interest in the Present Sectional Controversy Identical with That of the Slaveholders," 77.
25. Alfred H. Conrad and John R. Meyer, "The Economics of Slavery in the Ante-Bellum South," 112.
26. For a detailed breakdown by five-year-period, see Evans, "Some Economic," 332.
27. For excerpts of former slaves' testimonies on sales and auctions, see B. A. Botkin, ed., *Lay My Burden Down: A Folk History of Slavery*, 153–62.
28. "Domestic Slave Trade."
29. Peter J. Hamilton, *Mobile of the Five Flags: The Story of the River Basin and the Coast about Mobile From the Earliest Times to the Present*, 284.
30. Rawick, *The American Slave*, Alabama Narratives, vol. I, 350.
31. Mable Dennison, *Biographical Memoirs of James Dennison*.
32. William W. Freehling, *The Reintegration of American History: Slavery and the Civil War*, 181. There were 85,451 whites in Alabama in 1820 and 526,271 on the eve of the Civil War. U. S. Federal Census 1870; Pickett, *History of Alabama*, 749. For percentage rate of population increase by race in the Deep South and the Border States, 1800–1860, see Conrad and Meyer, "The Economics of Slavery," 113.
33. Price list of Betts & Gregory of Richmond. D. M. Pulliam Papers, Perkins Library, Duke University. For prices in Alabama, see Bancroft, *Slave Trading*, 356–62. Moore, *History of Alabama*, 355. For details on the prices of slaves in the nineteenth century, see Lewis C. Gray, *History of Agriculture in the United States to 1860*, 2, 663–7.
34. "The Negro Fever."
35. Article I, Section 9, Clause 1 of the American Constitution reads thus: "The Migration or Importation of such Persons as any of the States now existing shall think proper to admit, shall not be prohibited by the Congress prior to the Year one thousand eight hundred and eight, but a Tax or duty may be imposed on such Importation, not exceeding ten dollars for each Person." Acting on the Constitution, Congress passed the U.S. Slave Trade Act that abolished the "importation" of Africans—63 in favor and 49 against—in February 1807. It was nevertheless a half victory for the South since it stipulated that the people brought to slaveholding states would still be sold and enslaved. The only difference between 1808 and the preceding decades was that the offenders would be fined.
36. John G. Aikin, *A Digest of the Laws of the State of Alabama*, 398.

37. Dr. Kilpatrick, "Early Life in the Southwest: The Bowies."
38. W. E. B. Du Bois, *The Suppression of the African Slave-Trade to the United States, 1638–1870*, 128–9.
39. Dunbar Rowland, ed., *Jefferson Davis, Constitutionalist, His Letters, Papers, and Speeches*, 66–9.
40. William Law Mathieson, *Great Britain and the Slave Trade 1839–1865*, 166–70; Johnson U. J. Asiegbu, *Slavery and the Politics of Liberation, 1787–1861: A Study of Liberated African Emigration and British Anti-Slavery Policy*; Howard Johnson, *After the Crossing: Immigrants and Minorities in Caribbean Creole Society*; Michael Craton, *Islanders in the Stream: A History of the Bahamian People*; Herbert S. Klein, *The Atlantic Slave Trade*, 204–5; Maureen Warner Lewis, *Central Africa in the Caribbean: Transcending Time, Transforming Cultures*; Monica Schuler, *Alas, Alas, Kongo: A Social History of Indentured African American Immigration into Jamaica 1861–1865*.
41. Leonidas W. Spratt, *The Foreign Slave Trade: The Source of Political Power, of Material Progress, of Social Integrity, and of Social Emancipation to the South*, 4.
42. "Southern Convention at Savannah."
43. Quoted in American Anti-Slavery Society, *Annual Report* (1855–1859), 42.
44. See Ronald T. Takaki, *A Pro-Slavery Crusade: The Agitation to Reopen the African Slave Trade*, 27–32.
45. "Report of the Special Committee on the Importation of Free Black Laborers Within the State," *Documents of the First Session of the Fourth Legislature of the State of Louisiana*.
46. John J. Ormond, Arthur P. Bagby, George Goldthwaite, *The Code of Alabama*, 241, 391.
47. James De Bow, "African Labor Association," 233.
48. E. Deloney, "The South Demands More Negro Labor—Address to the People of Louisiana," 493.
49. Anti-Slavery Society, *Annual Report* (1860–61), 13–5; *De Bow's Review*, 24, 6 (June 1858), 601; 27, 2 (August 1859), 234; Edward Alfred Pollard, *A New Southern Policy: The Slave Trade as Meaning Union and Conservatism*.
50. Some revival advocates, like Governor James Hopkins Adams of South Carolina, thoroughly disliked the European newcomers, alien "by birth, training, and education," and feared the Marxist threat: labor rising against capital. De Bow was also an ardent foe of "the crazy, socialistic Germans in Texas" and both believed that if all menial jobs were done by slaves, including the indispensable new ones from Africa, the menace would be removed. See James De Bow, "The Non-Slaveholders," 69. For big planters, see James De Bow, "African Labor," 234; Deloney, "The South Demands More Negro Labor," 494.
51. "The Slave Trade. Mr. Stephens."
52. Barton J. Berstein, "Southern Politics and Attempts to Reopen the African Slave Trade," 32. Manish Sinha, "Judicial Nullification: The South Carolinian Movement to Reopen the African Slave Trade in the 1850s."
53. "The Slave Trade," *The National Era*, April 7, 1859.
54. U.S. Federal Census 1860.
55. *Report of the Minority of the Special Committee of Seven* (Charleston, 1858) cited in Harvey Wish "The Revival," 574; James Johnston Pettigrew, "Protest Against the Renewal of the Slave Trade," *Journal of the House of Representatives of South Carolina for 1854*, in Wish, "The Revival," 571.
56. "The President's Message: The Slave-Trade."

57. "A Great Change Coming Over the South: Disunion and the Slave Trade."
58. Anti-Slavery Society, *Annual Report* (1860–61), 16–7.
59. Charleston *Mercury*, July 14, 1859, cited in Wish, "The Revival," 588.
60. Letter from William H. Woodberry to Mr. Donaldson, Boston October 20, 1890; "Last Cargo of Slaves"; Romeyn, "Little Africa," 14–7; Samuel Hawkins Marshall Byers, "The Last Slave Ship," 742–6; Emma Langdon Roche, in *Historic Sketches* (71), writes that the place where it all started was the wharf in Mobile.
61. On rumors, see "An Error."
62. Anti-Slavery Society, *Annual Report* (1860), 21. Quoted by James Benson Sellers, *Slavery in Alabama*, 193. New York *Herald*, July 10, 1859, August 6, 1859, August 9, 1859; New York *Weekly Tribune*, March 6, 1858, July 23, 1859, August 13, 1859; Richmond *South*, March 5, 1858; Eugene C. Barker, "The African Slave Trade in Texas"; Charleston *Mercury*, May 21, 1859; *Liberator*, September 16, 1859; Anti-Slavery Society, *Annual Report* (1859), 41 (1860), 21–5, and (1859–1861), 23; *Harper's Weekly*, September 3, 1859, July 7, 1860, and July 28; Warren S. Howard, *American Slavers and the Federal Law 1837–1862*, 141–7.
63. "The Slave-Trade in New York," 87. On New York's role in the slave trade in the 1850s, see John Randolph Spears, *The American Slave-Trade: An Account of its Origin, Growth and Suppression*, 225–8; Mathieson, *Great Britain and the Slave Trade*, 161–5; Philip Sheldon Foner, *Business & Slavery: The New York Merchants & the Irrepressible Conflict*; Kenneth Milton Stampp, *The Peculiar Institution: Slavery in the Ante-bellum South*, 271; Peter Duignan and L. H. Gann, *The United States and Africa: A History*, 38–9; Robert Trent Vinson, "The Law as Lawbreaker: The Promotion and Encouragement of the Atlantic Slave Trade by the New York Judiciary System, 1857–1862," 35–58; Graham Russell Hodges, *Root and Branch: African Americans in New York and East Jersey 1613–1863*, 256; Craig Steven Wilder, *A Covenant with Color: Race and Social Power in Brooklyn, 1636–1990*, 53; Don E. Fehrenbacher, *The Slaveholding Republic: An Account of the United States Government's Relations to Slavery*, 199–200. On Betts's judgments concerning the slave trade, see Howard, *American Slavers*, 155–69; Wells, *The Slave Ship Wanderer*, 9–10; Vinson, "The Law as Lawbreaker"; Fehrenbacher, *The Slaveholding Republic*, 196–7. Great Britain had signed an "Equipment Clause" agreement with the Netherlands (1822), France (1833), Spain (1835), and Portugal (1842). The U.S. Navy was instructed to follow the clause only in 1849. These agreements stated that the following equipment designated a ship as a slave ship even in the absence of passengers: gratings for ventilation instead of slide hatches; extra bulkheads and spare planks to increase the carrying capacity; shackles, bolts, and handcuffs; food and water that exceeded the crew's needs; huge cooking pots and mess tubs; and small African-style canoes to transport people from the beach to the ship in a hurry. The Equipment Clause was aimed at preventing crews from throwing Africans overboard when their ships were approached by the British Navy.
64. For the *Wanderer* story, see in particular, Charles J. Montgomery, "Survivors from the Cargo of the Negro Slave Yacht *Wanderer*," 611–23; Wish, "The Revival of the African Slave Trade in the United States, 1856–1860," 569–88; Tom Henderson Wells, *The Slave Ship Wanderer*.
65. "The Newly Imported Africans," quoting a letter to the *New York Daily Times*.
66. *Dallas Gazette* (Cahaba, Alabama), January 7, 1859, cited in Sellers, *Slavery in Alabama*, 153.

67. William Kauffman Scarborough, ed. *The Diary of Edmund Ruffin*, 1, 300.
68. U.S. Federal Census 1860, Mobile Ward 6, 460; 1860 Slave Schedules, Mobile City Ward 6, 1. *U.S. v. Gould*, 25 F. Cas.1375, 8 Am. Law Reg. 525, No. 15, 239 (S.D.Ala.,1860). *U.S. v. John F. Tucker, U.S. v. Randolph L. Mott, U.S. v. William R. Fleming, U.S. v. Henry Dubignon*, cited in Wells, *The Wanderer*, 57–8. Mott was a wealthy planter (U.S. Federal Census 1860, Georgia, Columbus, Muscogee County, 171), Dubignon was a farmer (Georgia, District 26, Glynn, 232), and Fleming, an affluent merchant (Georgia, Savannah District 3, Chatham, 188); Anti-Slavery Society, *Annual Report* (1859), 45–9.
69. Naturalization record. October 22, 1868, page 42; U.S. Federal Census 1860, Mobile, Northern Division, 172.
70. See Robert E. May, *Manifest Destiny's Underworld: Filibustering in Antebellum America*, 2002; Albert Z. Carr, *The World and William Walker*. For the *Susan*, see "The Filibusters Again"; "The Mobile Filibusters."
71. Untitled Contemporary Newspaper Clipping.
72. *Permanent License of Clotilda*, April 19, 1855.
73. Herbert Klein, *The Atlantic Slave Trade*, 133.
74. "A Slave-Trader's Letter-Book," 459.
75. "Last Cargo of Slaves."
76. Byers, "The Last Slave Ship," 744.
77. William Foster, *Last Slaver from U.S. to Africa. A.D. 1860*, 1.
78. Ibid., 1. According to Romeyn, some of the trade goods were cloth, "Little Africa," 14.
79. *New York Daily Tribune*, May 30, 1860, quoted in Howard, *American Slavers*, 129; Anti-Slavery Society, *Annual Report* (1861), 131–3. David Turnbull, *Travels in the West with Notices of Porto Rico, and the Slave trade*, 383. For other schemes, see Howard, *American Slavers*, 22–4.
80. "On Board a Slaver by One of the Trade."
81. Cited in Roche, *Historic Sketches*, 71; Caldwell Delaney, *The Story of Mobile*, 73.
82. Emma Christopher, *Slave Ship Sailors and Their Captive Cargoes, 1730–1807*, 9, 23–33, 138–41, 158–9; "The African Slave-Trade," *The New York Times*, June 28, 1856; "The Brig Gen. Pierce Captured by a Portuguese Man-of-War"; Anti-Slavery Society, *Annual Report* (1860), 26; "On Board a Slaver." Scottish explorer John Duncan, who traveled to Dahomey in 1844, reported a mutiny by American sailors in Ouidah when the owner of their Maine ship sold it to slave traders. They refused to work on what had become a slave ship and were replaced by a Spanish crew that had been left on shore by a British man-of-war after their slave ship had been seized; John Duncan, *Travels in Western Africa in 1845 & 1846*, Bentley, I, 200. Dr. George Howe, the American who sailed on a slave ship to the Congo and Cuba in 1859, reported about sailors discharged in Sierra Leone after their ship had been captured; and in the Congo, his ship took on sailors who had been stranded there for the same reasons. Howe, "The Last Slave-Ship," 121, 122.
83. Handwritten note on crew, written in the first person, probably by William Foster. The Museum of Mobile. George Duncan: U.S. Federal Census 1870, New Bedford Ward 1, Rhode Island, 78.
84. "Capt. WM. Foster Commander of Last American Slave Vessel Buried Yesterday."
85. Roche, *Historic Sketches*, 84.
86. "Last Cargo of Slaves."
87. Roche, *Historic Sketches*, 84–5. A large deposit of gold can interfere with the earth's magnetic field and cause the north tip to rise.

88. Foster, *Last Slaver*, 2.
89. Ibid., 3.
90. "On Board a Slaver."
91. "The African Slave-Trade," *The New York Times*, June 28, 1856.
92. Foster, *Last Slaver*, 3.
93. Roche, *Historic Sketches*, 85.
94. Foster, *Last Slaver*, 4.
95. Carroll Storrs Alden, *George Hamilton Perkins, Commodore, U. S. N.: His Life and Letters*, 87–8. The captain of one of the ships, the *Sultana*, was notorious slaver Francis Bowen, who in April 1860 deported 2,000 Congolese—according to Perkins—on the *Nightingale*. On January 14, 1861, she was seized in Cabinda with 961 people on board—more were expected—who were dispatched to Liberia. The ship was sent to New York but Lieutenant John J. Guthrie of the U.S. Navy helped Bowen to escape to St. Thomas. The *Nightingale* was later used as a supply and store ship by the blockading squadron in the Gulf; see also George Francis Dow, *Slave Ships and Slaving*, 274–6.
96. Foster, *Last Slaver*, 4–5.
97. Howard, *American Slavers*, 18.

CHAPTER TWO   **West African Origins**

1. See John Reid, "Warrior Aristocrats in Crisis: The Political Effects of the Transition from the Slave Trade to Palm Oil Commerce in the Nineteenth Century Kingdom of Dahomey"; Robin Law, "Slave-Raiders and Middlemen, Monopolists and Free-Traders: The Supply of Slaves for the Atlantic Trade in Dahomey c. 1715–1850," 45–68; Elisée Soumonni, "The compatibility of the slave and palm oil trades in Dahomey, 1818–1858," 83.
2. Robin Law, *Ouidah: The Social History of a West African Slaving 'Port' 1727–1892*, 231–2.
3. Soumonni, "The compatibility," 86–9. Between the 1830s and the 1860s, about 39,000 African indentured workers were sent to the British Caribbean, while France transported 18,000 in the 1850s and 1860s. Herbert S. Klein, *The Atlantic Slave Trade*, 204; Reid, "Warrior Aristocrats," 398–9. The French plan was a precursor to the 1858 project of the Louisiana House of Representatives to introduce 2,500 "free" African workers into the state; and also to the African Labor Supply Association created in 1859. "The African Apprentice System," from the Augusta, Georgia, *Constitutionalist*, cited in *The Pittsfield Sun* (Massachusetts), May 20, 1858.
4. Correspondence from Consul Campbell at Lagos to the earl of Clarendon, British Foreign Office, quoted in Reid, "Warrior Aristocrats," 393–4.
5. Paul Hazoumé, *Le pacte de sang au Dahomey*, 110; Edward Geoffrey Parrinder, *Les vicissitudes de l'histoire de Ketu*, 73–5.
6. "Death of a King."
7. After the customs were held, the *New York Times* informed its readers that "the Kingdom of Dahomey showed the sincerity of its affliction by sacrificing, with the utmost unniggardly sacrifice, eight hundred niggers to his honored mannes." April 9, 1859.
8. "The Slave-Trade During the Last Two Years," *Church Missionary Intelligencer*, 154. The information came from a dispatch from Consul-General Crawford at

Havana to Lord John Russell, dated September 30, 1860; Christopher Lloyd, *The Navy and the Slave Trade: The Suppression of African Slave Trade in the Nineteenth Century*, 171.

9. Henry Romeyn, "Little Africa," 16; Mary McNeil Scott, "Affika Town."
10. The Dendi and Baatonu called these populations *kafiri*, "infidels" in Arabic; during colonization the French referred to them all as Somba. Since then, each group has insisted on being called by its specific name.
11. For detailed information on the social, economic, and political landscape of the region, see Roger N'Tia, "Géopolitique de l'Atakora précolonial," 107–24.
12. H. Desanti, *Du Danhomé au Bénin-Niger*, 54–8; Paul Mercier, "Mouvements de population dans les traditions Betâmmaribè"; Paul Mercier, *Tradition, changement, histoire: les "Somba" du Dahomey septentrional*, 159–60; Albert-Marie Maurice, *Atakora Otiau Otammari Osuri Peuples du Nord Benin (1950)*, 151–6.
13. The meaning of Batammariba is "those who build well." Paul Mercier, "L'habitation à étage dans l'Atakora."
14. Romeyn, "Little Africa," 16.
15. A. Le Herissé, *L'ancien royaume du Dahomey: moeurs, religion, histoire*, 56, 291. For a detailed analysis of captive supply, see Robin Law, "Slave-raiders and Middlemen, Monopolists and Free-Traders: The Supply of Slaves for the Atlantic Trade in Dahomey c. 1715–1850"; A. Felix Iroko, "Condamnations pénales et ravitaillement en esclaves de la traite negrière," in *Le Bénin et la route de l'esclave*, ed. Elisée Soumonni et al., 93–5; Edna G. Bay, "Protection, Political Exile, and the Atlantic Slave-Trade: History and Collective Memory in Dahomey." The memory of these sales is still passed on in Benin. Anthropologist Melville Herskovits was told in the 1930s, "You have nearly all the people of this family in your country. They knew too much magic. We sold them because they made too much trouble." Of another family, he heard, "This family has strong men. They are good warriors, but bad enemies. When they troubled our King they were caught and sold. You have their big men in your country," Melville J. Herskovits, *Dahomey: An Ancient West African Kingdom*, 63–4.
16. Letter from Augustine Meaher to G. Donaldson; Roche, *Historic Sketches*, 86; Hurston, *Barracoon*, 68. Maurice Ahanhanzo Glélé, *Le Danxome: du pouvoir aja à la nation fon*, 156–61.
17. "Applications," 39.
18. Letter from Smith to Rev. Gollmer, February 28, 1860, cited in *Church Missionary Intelligencer* 11 (May 1, 1860); Parrinder, *Les vicissitudes*.
19. Romeyn, "Little Africa," 16.
20. Daryll C. Forde, "The Nupe."
21. The proportion was probably lower for men, who tended to marry in their late twenties or early thirties.
22. Romeyn, "Little Africa," 16.
23. Explanation of name: Nalla Raoufou Amidou, January 5, 2006; Dennison, *A Memoir of Lottie Dennison*, 19.
24. Dennison, *A Memoir of Lottie*, 29; John Iliffe, *Honour in African History*, 78.
25. Her birthplace is given as Dahomey on a certificate issued in 1900; Dennison, *A Memoir of Lottie*, 34. Her death certificate also mentions Dahomey. Death Certificate, Lottie Dennison, April 16, 1917.
26. Dennison, *A Memoir of Lottie*, 19.
27. Olaudah Equiano, *The interesting narrative of Olaudah Equiano : or Gustavus Vassa, the African / written by himself*; Philip D. Curtin, "Ayuba Suleiman Diallo of Bondu,"

in *Africa Remembered: Narratives by West Africans From the Era of the Slave Trade*, ed. Philip D. Curtin: 17–59; Ivor Wilks, "Salih Bilali of Massina," ibid., 145–51; H. F. C. Smith et al., "Ali Eisami Gazirmabe of Bornu," ibid.: 199–216; P. C. Lloyd, "Osifekunde of Ijebu," ibid.: 217–88; Quobna Ottobah Cugoano, "Narrative of the Enslavement of Ottobah Cugoana, a Native of Africa; Published by Himself in the Year 1787, in Thomas Fisher, *The Negro's Memorial; or, Abolitionist's Catechism; by an Abolitionist*, 120–7; Samuel Moore, *Biography of Mahommah G. Baquaqua, a Native of Zoogoo in the Interior of Africa*; Nicholas Said, *The Autobiography of Nicolas Said, a native of Bornu*.

28. Byers, "The Last Slave-Ship," 743. Byers gives the name Gossalow; Cozaloo is found in "Religion of the Dahomans," an undated, unsigned manuscript by a contemporary that lists the original names of twenty-six Africans in Mobile.

29. Lt-Col. Med. Tereau and Dr. Huttel, "Monographie du Hollidjé"; Paul Mercier, "Notice sur le peuplement Yoruba au Dahomey-Togo," 36; Geoffrey Parrinder, "Yoruba-Speaking Peoples in Dahomey," 125.

30. Scott, "Affika Town."

31. Andrew Dalby, *Dictionary of Languages: The Definitive Reference to More than 400 Languages*, 572.

32. Robert Cornevin, *Histoire du Dahomey*, 162–3; A. Serpos Tidjani, "Notes sur le mariage au Dahomey," 28–9; John O. Hunwick, *Timbuktu and the Songhay Empire: Al-Sa di's Ta'rikh al-sudan down to 1613 and other Contemporary Documents*, xxxiii; Nassirou Bako-Arifari, "Peuplement et populations dendi du Bénin: approaches anthropo-historiques," 113–46; Paul Marty, *Etudes sur l'islam au Dahomey: le bas Dahomey, le haut Dahomey*, 162–4; Roger N'Tia, "Commerce caravanier et installation des communautés zarma-dendi dans l'Atakora précolonial," 161–4.

33. Letter from Augustine Meaher to Donaldson, "Ausy Keba took his name from an African river." Booker T. Washington, *The Story of the Negro*, 104.

34. Meaher to Kebee, Deed Book 30, 655, October 28, 1872; "Religion of the Dahomans." The Hausa are called Gambari or Kambari in Benin, but they call themselves Hausa in Nigeria. Ossa is also a Yoruba name, meaning "you fled." "Kibby" is a Danish American name. There were no Kibbys in Alabama when Keeby took his name.

35. Dr. Henrich Barth, *Travels and Discoveries in North and Central Africa, 1849–1855*, vol. III, 146.

36. Addie E. Pettaway, *Africatown, U.S.A.: Some aspects of Folklife and Material Culture of an Historic Landscape*, 15.

37. Sidney John Hogben, *An Introduction to the History of the Islamic States of Northern Nigeria*, 132–3, 224–5; David C. Tambo, "The Sokoto Caliphate Slave Trade in the Nineteenth Century," 187–217.

38. Letter from Augustine Meaher to Donaldson mentioning "Jabez—the African doctor"; Henry C. Williams, Sr., September 25, 2002; oral tradition among the descendants in AfricaTown.

39. Scott, "Affika Town."

40. Robert G. Armstrong, "The Igala," 83–4.

41. Romeyn, "Little Africa," 16; Byers; "Last Slave-Ship," 743.

42. Richard F. Burton, *A Mission to Gelele, King of Dahome*, I, 171.

43. Law, *Ouidah*, 138. Robin Law to author, August 14, 2006.

44. Romeyn, "Little Africa," 16; Washington, *The Story*, 104; Roche, *Historic Sketches*, 75–6; Hurston, *Barracoon*, 44–5, 49.

45. Oba Onitako Oyiguin Adedounloye, king of Itakon, January 5, 2006.

46. Round cult houses exist among the Fon, but they are not used as residences.
47. Oba Onitako Oyiguin Adedounloye; see also Paul Mercier, "Notice sur le peuplement Yoruba au Dahomey-Togo," 34.
48. Roche, *Historic Sketches*, 88.
49. Natalie Suzette Robertson, "The African Ancestry of the Founders of Africa Town, Alabama," 61–2; Alain Morel, "Un exemple d'urbanisation en Afrique occidentale: Dassa-Zoumé (Dahomey moyen)."
50. For a detailed discussion of Yoruba as a descriptive category for people in the Bight of Benin since the sixteenth century, see Paul E. Lovejoy, "The Yoruba Factor in the Trans-Atlantic Slave Trade": 40–55. Benjamin Gbaguidi, "Chronique ethnographique-origine des noms de villages—Cercle de Savalou," 74.
51. Roche, *Historic Sketches*, 79; Léon F. Degny, February 9, 2006.
52. Hurston, *Barracoon*, 27–9; Léon F. Degny, April 20, 2006.
53. See description of the building process in Roche, *Historic Sketches*, 76.
54. Léon F. Degny, *Histoire du peuplement de la sous-préfecture de Banté*, 39. See also Jean Fonssagrives, *Notice sur le Dahomey. Publiée à l'occasion de l'Exposition universelle*, 292. Léon F. Degny, February 9, 2006.
55. Degny, *Histoire*, 47. Given the lack of specific details provided by Cudjo and his companions; their American interlocutors' various interpretations, renditions, and distortions; and the changing landscape and nomenclature associated with it in their homeland, where some villages and towns became deserted and died out; it may be incautious to pinpoint with absolute certitude one precise town.
56. Mercier, "Notice," 38–9; Degny, *Histoire du peuplement*, 12–8.
57. For information on Yoruba towns, see Ogunsola John Igue, "Sur l'origine des villes Yoruba."
58. Hurston, *Barracoon*, 22.
59. British Foreign Office correspondence, 1854, 1857, 1859, quoted in Reid, "Warrior Aristocrats," 395–6.
60. Hurston, *Barracoon*, 19. There is an abundant literature on de Souza and his descendants, see in particular, David A. Ross, "The Fist Chacha of Whydah: Francisco Felix de Souza"; David A. Ross, "The Dahomean middleman system, 1727–c. 1818"; Roberto Francisco de Souza, "Contribution à l'histoire de la famille de Souza"; Law, *Ouidah*, 155–88. For tobacco, see Pierre Verger, "Rôle joué par le tabac de Bahia dans la traite des esclaves au Golfe du Bénin."
61. Hurston, *Barracoon*, 18–9, 39–40.
62. Daniel Tchobo, January 13, 2006.
63. Roche, *Historic Sketches*, 124. It is difficult today to draw any useful information from the people's scarifications because the descriptions that exist vary from one observer to the next. For example, Romeyn stated that Zuma had a "huge crescent on her face across the nose, from cheek to cheek" (16), while Roche described her as having "three deep gashes meeting at the bridge of the nose and running diagonally across each cheek" (127.) Roche also affirmed that all the survivors had "two lines between the eyes and three on the cheek" (124). However, a close-up photograph of Cudjo does not show these specific scarifications but one vertical, slightly bent on the right cheek, which is also how he was represented in the bust erected in Mobile, based on Henry C. Williams' recollections.
64. Hurston, *Barracoon*, 40–3; Léon F. Degny, February 9, 2006.
65. Thomas Jefferson Bowen, *Adventures and Missionary Labours in Several Countries in the Interior of Africa from 1849 to 1856*, 138–41.
66. William H. Clarke, *Travels and Explorations in Yorubaland 1854–1858*, 282.

67. Hurston, *Barracoon*, 44, 45.
68. Montserrat Palau Marti, *Société et religion au Bénin (les Sabe-Opara)*, 259–62. For legends concerning the birth of *oro* and its relation to women, see John Parkinson, "The Legend of Oro." For a description of the bull-roarers, see R. Braithwaite Batty, "Notes on the Yoruba Country"; Alfred Burdon Ellis, *The Yoruba-Speaking Peoples of the Slave Coast of Africa, their Religion, Manners, Customs, Laws, Languages*, 110–1.
69. Roche, *Historic Sketches*, 124.
70. For a description of the convents, see Geoffrey Parrinder, *West African Religion: A Study of the Beliefs and Practices of Akan, Ewe, Yoruba, Ibo, and Kindred Peoples*, 78–94; Peter McKenzie, *Hail Orisha! A Phenomenology of a West African Religion in the Mid-Nineteenth Century*,178–85.
71. Parrinder, *West African Religion*, 93.
72. Among the deportees were people with Yoruba, or specifically Isha, names. They were Sakaru (Sacahrahgo in original document), a name originally from the town of Banté; Gohoby (Gocby), "interim chief"; Ahdabi (Ahdabee), "we have arrived here"; Fabumi (Fahboom), "given by the *fa* or oracle"; Alloko (Banté name from N'Koko given to a child whose mother has lost several children); Koloco, "has no field"; Bossah, "if you flee"; Ojo Facha, "born during a rainfall"; Okégbalê (Ockballa), "top of the shrine"; Adjua (Absha), in Mina/Ewe, a language from Togo, the name is given to a girl born on Monday (the Isha who migrated from Togo still use these names). "Religion of the Dahomans," translations by Léon Degny, Cotonou, April 20, 2006. Other names whose origin or meaning have not been found were Cooyaka, Sanalowa, Gockilago, Goobee, Ajemo, Deza or Dezo, Foloroah, Iyouha, Messa, and Lahla.
73. Roche, *Historic Sketches*, 82. Roche spelled the words as she heard them: Tarkbar, Goombardi, Filanee, and Ejasha. The Hausa are known as Kamberi or Kambari in Nigeria. For a detailed analysis of the name and the trade, see Paul E. Lovejoy, "The Kambarin Beriberi: The Formation of a Specialized Group of Hausa Kola Traders in the Nineteenth Century." See also Mahdi Adamu, *The Hausa Factor in West African History*, 4.
74. "West Coast of Africa." Le Herissé, *L'ancien royaume*, 329.
75. "Recent Intelligence." The *Church Missionary Intelligencer* reproduced a February 28 letter from a Mr. Smith to Rev. C. A. Gollmer giving a detailed description of the events. U.K. Parliamentary Papers, Correspondence relating to the Slave Trade, 1 April–31 Dec. 1860, Class B, Inclosure 22 in no. 1: Rev. H. Townsend to Consul Brand, Abeokuta, March 6, 1860. I am thankful to Robin Law for pointing out these sources.
76. U.K. Parliamentary Papers, Correspondence relating to the Slave Trade, 1 April–31 Dec. 1860, Class B, No.2: Consul Brand to Lord J. Russell, Lagos, April 9, 1860. If there were questions as to the possibility that Cudjo and his companions had been captured in Idigni or vicinity, this chronology (added to the absence of hills, round houses, and any town whose name resembled Tarkar, Takkoi, of Tekki) eliminates this eventuality. The convoy that left Idigni was on the road for at least a month, perhaps six weeks, which is much longer than what Cudjo seems to remember for his own journey (Hurston, *Barracoon*, 52–3; Hurston, "The Last Slave Ship," 354). He said he was in the *barracoon* at Ouidah for three weeks after having stayed in Abomey less than a week. It is worth noting that when he mentioned lengths of time—in other significant cases such as the Middle Passage or the time he spent enslaved in Alabama—he largely overestimated them, and it is

therefore possible that he was in Ouidah less than three weeks. Since the *Clotilda* sailed back the last week of May, it means that he would have arrived in the city sometime during the first week, or more than a month after the people captured in Idigni had reached either Abomey or Ouidah.

77. Roche, *Historic Sketches*, 81; Hurston, *Barracoon*, 47. According to oral tradition, the king of Oyo told the Dahomian king, Adandozan, to cultivate. The king replied, "Our ancestors . . . did not cultivate with hoes, but with guns. The kings of Dahomey cultivate only war!" Le Herissé, *L'ancien royaume*, 313.

78. William John Argyle, *The Fon of Dahomey: A History and Ethnography of the Old Kingdom*, 83; Burton, *Dahomey*, I, 15–7, II, 129–31; Bouche, *La côte des esclaves*, 365; Edouard Foà, *Le Dahomey: histoire, géographie, moeurs, coutumes, commerce, industrie, expeditions françaises (1891–1894)*, 260–3; Hazoumé, *Le pacte*, 19–36.

79. Ivor Wilks, "Abu Bakr al-Siddiq of Timbuktu"; J. F. Ade Ajayi, "Samuel Ajayi Crowther of Oyo"; Curtin, "Joseph Wright of the Egba."

80. Hurston, "Cudjo's Own Story," 65.

81. Hurston, *Barracoon*, 50; Iliffe, *Honour*, 67–82.

82. Hurston, *Barracoon*, 51.

83. Ibid., 51–2.

84. Ibid., 55–6.

85. Roche, *Historic Sketches*, 82. Hurston also recounts this version in "The Last Slave-Ship," 354.

86. Hurston, *Barracoon*, 55.

87. Mandirola, Renzo, ed., *Journal de Francesco Borghero, premier missionnaire du Dahomey (1861–1865): Sa vie, son Journal (1860–1864), la Relation de 1863*, 69.

88. Hurston, *Barracoon*, 55. James Saxon Childers, "From Jungle to Slavery and Freedom." This depiction of events—supposedly at Ouidah—confirms the stop in Abomey that did not appear in Roche's narrative. There, the prisoners were still held by the army, and it made sense for them to ask to be returned in exchange for their crops, the premise of the raid. In addition, their relatives' skulls were indeed held in Abomey, not in Ouidah; nor did Dahomian soldiers in the second city detain the captives.

89. William Snelgrave, *A New Account of Some Parts of Guinea, and the Slave-Trade*, 37–8; Forbes, *Dahomey*, I, 17; Herskovits, *Dahomey*, 2, 95–6.

90. Burton, *A Mission*, II, 149–50.

91. Romuald Michozounou, "Le peuplement du plateau d'Abomey des origines à 1889," 212–4, 272.

92. Oral tradition says that taking a stone would bring terrible hardships.

93. Gilles Soglo, "Notes sur la traite de esclaves à Glexwe (Ouidah)," 69; Justin Fakambi, *La Route des Esclaves au Benin (ex-Dahomey) dans une approche regionale*, 20.

94. Law, *Ouidah*, 140.

95. David Eltis, Paul E. Lovejoy, and David Richardson, "Slave-Trading Ports: Towards an Atlantic-Wide Perspective, 1676-1832," 18–21.

96. Law, *Ouidah*, 137.

97. According to the "new oral tradition" of the 1990s, the expression meant "light was not allowed in." The slave merchants, some claim, wanted to recreate for the captives the conditions of the ships' holds. According to other sources, Zomaï was the mulattos and notables' neighborhood with beautiful buildings covered with thatch. It was forbidden to circulate there with an open fire, as a safety precau-

tion, see Bouche, *La côte des esclaves*, 323; "Chronique ethnographique: origine des noms de lieux," 60.

98. Law, *Ouidah*, 138; Hurston, *Barracoon*, 56. Roche, *Historic Sketches*, 82–3.
99. John Duncan, *Travels in Western Africa, in 1845 & 1846*, I, 112. Burton described it as a "dirty clump of ragged mat-huts" (Burton, *A Mission*, I, 20). It is difficult to reconcile this portrayal with a "big white house," but it is important to note that Burton and Cudjo certainly had different ways, based on their respective cultures, of assessing the sizes and styles of dwellings.
100. Ajayi, "Samuel Ajayi Crowther," 310–1; Curtin, "Joseph Wright," 330; Cugoano, *Narrative*, 124.
101. Hurston, *Barracoon*, 56.
102. See Sylviane A. Diouf, "The Last Resort: Redeeming Relatives and Friends," in Diouf, ed., *Fighting the Slave Trade*, 81–100.
103. Hurston, *Dust Tracks*, 212.
104. Hurston, *Barracoon*, 56. Charles Ball, *Fifty Years in Chains*, 184; Hubert Deschamps, ed., *L'Afrique occidentale en 1818 vue par un explorateur francais Gaspard Theodore Mollien*, 60; Equiano, *The Interesting Narrative*, 72.
105. See William D. Piersen, "White Cannibals, Black Martyrs: Fear, Depression, and Religious Faith as Causes of Suicide Among New Slaves"; Robert Harms, *The Diligent: A Voyage Through the Worlds of the Slave Trade*, 299. Roche, *Historic Sketches*, 123. Roche called her Albiné, but Cudjo referred to her as Abila, in Hurston's transcription.
106. Alvise Ca' da Mosto, *Voyages en Afrique noire d'Alvise Ca' da Mosto (1455 et 1456)*, 103; Paul Erdmann Isert, *Letters on West Africa and the Slave Trade: Paul Erdmann Isert's Journey to Guinea and the Caribbean Islands in Columbia*, 175; Jean Baptiste Labat, *Voyage du Chevalier Des Marchais en Guinée*, 2, 145; Curtin, "Joseph Wright," 331.
107. Piersen, "White Cannibals," 148.
108. Equiano, *The Interesting Narrative*, 71–2; *Report from the Select Committee of the House of Lords . . . for the Final Extinction of the African Slave Trade* (London, 1849) quoted in Edgar Conrad, *Children of God's Fire: A Documentary History of Black Slavery in Brazil*, 39; Cugoano, *Narrative*, 124; Curtin, "Joseph Wright," 331; Ajayi, " Samuel Ajayi Cowther," 313.

CHAPTER THREE **Ouidah**

1. Foster, *Last Slaver*, 5. For a description of the entry into Ouidah with a hammock, see Duncan, *Travels*, I, 119.
2. Foster, *Last Slaver*, 6; Law, *Ouidah*, 249; Mandirola, ed., *Journal de Francesco Borghero*, 55; Richard Francis Burton, *A Mission to Gelele*, I, 209.
3. Mandirola, ed., *Journal*, 113; Burton, *A Mission*, I, 53; Law, *Ouidah*, 249–50.
4. Foster, *Last Slaver*, 7. See Parrinder, *West African Religion*, 50–2.
5. Foster, *Last Slaver*, 7.
6. Roche, *Historic Sketches*, 87; Hurston, *Barracoon*, 57; James Saxon Childers, "From Jungle to Slavery and Freedom."
7. William Bosman, *A New and Accurate Description of the Coast of Guinea*, 403; Francis Moore, *Travels in the Inland Parts of Africa*, 75; Thomas Astley, *A New General Collection Of Voyages And Travels*, II, 435, 561, 582, III, 218; Carson I. E. Ritchie, "Deux textes sur le Sénégal (1673–1677)," 313.
8. Samuel Moore, *Biography of Mahommah G. Baquaqua, a Native of Zoogoo in the Interior of Africa*. See also his annotated biography, Paul E. Lovejoy and Robin

Law, eds., *The Biography of Mahommah Gardo Baquaqua: His Passage From Slavery to Freedom in Africa and America.*

9. Curtin, "Ayuba," 40.

10. Baquaqua, *Biography*, 35.

11. Foster, *Last Slaver*, 8.

12. Ibid.

13. John Duncan, *Travels in Western Africa in 1845 & 1846*, I, 201.

14. Hurston, *Barracoon*, 57.

15. Administrateur Gavoy, "Note historique sur Ouidah, 1913," 63. More than ninety cases of attacks from the shore against slave ships or longboats have been recorded; see David Richardson, "Shipboard Revolts, African Authority, and the Transatlantic Slave Trade," in Diouf, ed., *Fighting the Slave Trade*, 199–218.

16. Hurston, *Barracoon*, 57.

17. Foster, *Last Slaver*, 8.

18. According to Cudjo (*Barracoon*, 58 and note 6) the canoe men were Kru and he called them "Many Costs," explaining they had acquired the nickname because only many of them could do the work of a single good laborer. Kru from Liberia were employed as canoe men by the Europeans all along the African Coast. In Ouidah, in the mid-nineteenth century they worked for the British Navy, while men from the Gold Coast were hired by the commercial companies, including for the transportation of captives to the slave ships. Cudjo may have been confused about who the men were, or his testimony may bring new information as to the role of the Kru in 1860 Ouidah.

19. Dennison, *A Memoir of Lottie*, 19–20.

20. Hurston, *Barracoon*, 58.

21. Description by Rev. W. Allen in *Wesleyan Missionary Notices* (September 1847) quoted in William Fox, *A Brief History of the Wesleyan Missions on the West Coast of Africa*, 114.

22. Cugoano, *Narrative*, 124; Baquaqua, *Autobiography*, 42.

23. Baquaqua, *Autobiography*, 42; Curtin, "Joseph Wright," 331; "West Coast of Africa."

24. Roche, *Historic Sketches*, 87.

25. Smith, "Ali Eisami," 213. See also Baquaqua, *Autobiography*, 42; Robert Edgar Conrad, *Children of God's Fire*, 39; Duncan, *Travels*, I, 143; Captain Theophilus Conneau, *A Slaver's Logbook or 20 Years' Residence in Africa*, 82.

26. Hurston, *Barracoon*, 58; Roche, *Historic Sketches*, 87–8.

27. Foster, *Last Slaver*, 8–9.

28. Roche, *Historic Sketches*, 113–4.

29. Hurston, *Barracoon*, 58. The fact that Ossa Keeby was a friend would seem to indicate that he and Cudjo were from the same town; however, they may also have become friends in the *barracoon*.

30. Foster, *Last Slaver*, 9; Dennison, *A Memoir of Lottie*, 20.

31. *Extracts from the evidence delivered before a Select Committee of the House of Commons, in the years 1790 and 1791*, 10.

32. Baquaqua, *Biography*, 43; Conrad, *Children*, 35; Orland Armstrong, *Old Massa's People*, 52.

33. Hurston, *Barracoon*, 59; Roche, *Historic Sketches*, 88.

34. Crowther, *Narrative*, 313; Foster, *Last Slaver*, 10.

35. Roche, *Historic Sketches*, 89–90; Hurston, *Barracoon*, 59; Childers, "From Jungle."

36. Byers, "The Last Slave-Ship," 743.

37. New Haven *Record*, October 12, 1839, quoted in Blassingame, *Slave Testimony*, 199. Conrad, *Children*, 38; Baquaqua, *Biography*, 43. For quantities, see Robert Harms, *The Diligent*, 309.

38. Roche, *Historic Sketches*, 90; Hurston, *Barracoon*, 60.

39. Childers, "From Jungle."

40. David Eltis, Stephen Behrendt, David Richardson, and Herbert Klein, *The Trans-Atlantic Slave Trade: A Database on CD-ROM*. David Eltis, *Economic Growth and the Ending of the Transatlantic Slave Trade*, 125–44; Herbert S. Klein, *The Atlantic Slave Trade*, 130–60.

41. Eltis et al., *The Trans-Atlantic Slave Trade*.

42. See John Newton, *The Journal of a Slave Trader 1750–1754*, 75; Alexander Falconbridge, *An Account of the Slave Trade on the Coast of Africa*, 24; Silas Told, *The Life of Mr. Silas Told*, 20–1; George Francis Dow, *Slave Ships and Slaving*, 174. Cugoano, *Narrative*, 124.

43. *Anti-Slavery Reporter* 4 (February 8, 1843): 22–3.

44. *Extracts*, 9–10. Italics in original text.

45. *Extracts*, 11–2; Armstrong, *Old Massa*, 52. Quoted in Dena J. Epstein, *Sinful Tunes and Spirituals: Black Folk Music to the Civil War*, 9.

46. Epstein, *Sinful Tunes*, 8.

47. Sidney W. Mintz and Richard Price, *The Birth of African-American Culture: An Anthropological Perspective*, 42–4.

48. Revolts or other incidents occurred on at least 10 percent of slave ships, David Richardson, "Shipboard Revolts," 199–218; Roche, *Historic Sketches*, 90.

49. Roche, *Historic Sketches*, 89–90; Foster, *Last Slaver*, 10.

50. Klein, *The Atlantic Slave Trade*, 199.

51. "Last Slave Ship Sunk Here Raised"; Hurston, *Barracoon*, 59; "Celebration for a Former Slave."

52. Romeyn, "Little Africa," 17.

53. "West Coast of Africa." Law, *Ouidah*, 234.

54. Eltis et al., *The Trans-Atlantic Slave Trade*.

55. Roche, *Historic Sketches*, 90.

56. Snelgrave, *A New Account*, 170–1; Wilks, "Abu Bakr," 162. See also Sylviane A. Diouf, *Servants of Allah: African Muslims Enslaved in the Americas*, 142–3; Cugoano, *Narrative*, 125; Baquaqua, *Autobiography*, 44; Hurston, *Barracoon*, 62, 66.

CHAPTER FOUR **Arrival in Mobile**

1. Foster, *Last Slaver*, 10.

2. Ibid., 11–2; Byers, "The Last Slave Ship," 744; Erwin Craighead, *Mobile: Fact and Tradition*, 358.

3. Scott, "Affika Town"; "Last Cargo of Slaves"; Byers, "The Last Slave Ship," 745.

4. Roche, *Historic Sketches*, 94.

5. "Last Cargo of Slaves"; Byers, "The Last Slave Ship," 745; Roche, *Historic Sketches*, 94; Craighead, *Mobile*, 358.

6. Hurston, *Barracoon*, 96.

7. Baquaqua, *Biography*, 44.

8. Marion *Commonwealth*, quoted by Thomas Henderson Wells, *The Slave Ship Wanderer*, 42.

9. Bayou Corne according to Roche, *Historic Sketches*, 97. A detailed map of the area does not show a Bayou Corne, but a Bayou Canot. "Last Cargo of Slaves"; Romeyn,

"Little Africa," 15; Byers, "The Last Slave Ship," 745; Roche, *Historic Sketches*, 96–7; Hurston, *Barracoon*, 60; Craighead, *Mobile*, 358.

10. Slave Schedules 1860, Mobile, Northern Division, 3.
11. "Last Cargo of Slaves;" Romeyn, "Little Africa," 15; Byers, "The Last Slave Ship," 745; Roche, *Historic Sketches*, 98. Romeyn mistakenly wrote, "The Africans were landed in a dense canebrake on a plantation of Gen. Dabney Maury." It was of course John Dabney. General Dabney H. Maury was the Confederate commander of the District of the Gulf in Mobile from 1863 to the end of the war.
12. Hurston, *Barracoon*, 60; Scott, "Affika Town"; Roche, *Historic Sketches*, 98; Hurston, *Barracoon*, 60.
13. Foster, *Last Slaver*, 12; "Last Cargo of Slaves"; Roche, *Historic Sketches*, 85, 97; Romeyn, "Little Africa," 15; Byers, "The Last Slave Ship," 746.
14. "The Africans of the Slave Bark Wildfire."
15. Roche, *Historic Sketches*, 98.
16. Hurston, *Barracoon*, 60.
17. Roche, *Historic Sketches*, 99.
18. "Africans Arrived."
19. "Items of Mention"; New Orleans *Delta*, July 12, 1860, quoted in *Harpers' Weekly*, under the title "More Africans at New Orleans," July 28, 1860.
20. "The Africans of the Slave Bark Wildfire"; Robert Ralph Davis, Jr., "Buchanian Espionage: A Report on Illegal Slave Trading in the South in 1859," 275.
21. Anti-Slavery Society, *Annual Report* (1860–1861), 127–8; "More Africans Landed"; "Very Latest News. Mobile, Ala"; "Arrival of the Pony Express."
22. Scott, "Affika Town."
23. See chapter 1, *U.S. v. Gould*, 25 F. Cas. 1375, 8 Am. Law Reg. 525, No. 15,239 (S.D.Ala., 1860); Anti-Slavery Society, *Annual Report* (1860), 29.
24. These letters were supposed to be held at the National Archives and Records Administration in Washington, D.C. but they cannot be found. According to a senior archivist they were probably never sent to NARA. Alphabetical List of Sender—Attorney General—Register of Letters Received, 1809–1863. Vol. A. LOC 230/01/30/01.
25. *United States vs. John M. Dabney.*
26. Summons 2620.
27. "Last Cargo of Slaves"; Romeyn, "Little Africa," 15; Byers, "The Last Slave Ship," 746. Roche stated that the steamboat that took the Africans to Clarke County was the *Commodore* (*Historic Sketches*, 98).
28. Roche, *Historic Sketches*, 98–9.
29. Romeyn, "Little Africa," 16.
30. Roche, *Historic Sketches*, 99.
31. Ibid., 99.
32. Rawick, *The American Slave*. Texas Narrative, XVI, part 2, 290–1.
33. Hurston, *Barracoon*, 61. Translation by Elisée Soumonni, January 13, 2006.
34. David Eltis et al., *The Trans-Atlantic Slave Trade*. Of those, about 4,99 are estimated to be Yoruba; see David Eltis, "The Diaspora of Yoruba Speakers, 1650–1865: Dimensions and Implications," 30.
35. In the 1890 document "Slavery, Clotilda in 1860," Foster was said to have received fourteen people and some cash. Roche (*Historic Sketches*, 97) stated that he got "ten Africans given him by the Meahers as his booty." According to Hurston's *Barracoon* Cudjo said that Timothy Meaher took thirty-two people, Burns ten couples, Foster eight couples, and James got the rest minus those sold upriver.

36. "In the Original Package"; Anti-Slavery Society, *Annual Report* (1860–61), 127.

37. Roche, *Historic Sketches*, 100.

38. Martha Poster: U.S. Federal Census 1900, Montgomery, Walkers, 30A; Abbie Royal: 1900, Dallas, Selma Ward 5, 18A; Jake Vangue 1900, Russell, Seale, 14A. A cluster of three Africans in Russell County was likely part of the *Wanderer* group. One of them took Sango as a last name, which is a language and ethnic group in the Congo and the Central African Republic. They were Sam and Mary Malance and Jacob Sango, U.S. Federal Census 1870, Russell, Hogg Island, 219.

39. Hurston, *Barracoon*, 60.

40. Mary Haywood: U.S. Federal Census 1870, Wilcox, Prairie Bluff, 249; Ovay Hunt, 253; Lucy Hunt, 266.

41. Crecy Dansly: U.S. Federal Census 1880, Wilcox, Boiling Springs, 487; Aquila Clanton, 485; Ossie Hunt, 485.

42. U.S. Federal Census 1900, Dallas, Montgomery Ward 5, 7B.

43. Carla Kaplan, ed., *Zora Neale Hurston*, 123.

44. U.S. Federal Census 1920, Jefferson, Marengo, 4B. Allie Beren would have been eighty-seven when Hurston visited, the same age as Cudjo. Beren was married to an African born around 1824 who could not have arrived on the *Clotilda*. He was most likely dead in 1927.

45. Scott, "Affika Town."

46. Ibid.

47. Daryll Forde, *The Yoruba-Speaking Peoples of South-Western Nigeria*, 27.

48. Scott, "Affika Town."

49. Sylviane A. Diouf, *Servants of Allah*.

50. Rawick, *The American Slave*, South Carolina Narratives, vol. XIV, part 1, 30.

51. Rawick, *The American Slave*, Oklahoma Narratives, vol. XIII, 24–5.

52. Roche, *Historic Sketches*, 88.

53. Hurston, *Baracoon*, 62.

54. *United States vs. John M. Dabney*, and case no. 2621, *United States vs. William Foster*.

55. "The Slave Trade," *The New York Times*, October 4, 1860; October 24.

56. "The Case of Gordon"; "The Execution of Gordon, the Slave Trader."

57. "The Case of Gordon."

58. *United States vs. John M. Dabney*, and case no. 2621, *United States vs. William Foster*.

59. Necrology of William Foster, *Prichard Herald*, published between February 10 and 17, 1901.

60. Sir William Howard Russell, *My Diary, North and South*, 187–8.

61. For the complete text of the report, see Davis, "Buchanian Espionage."

62. Du Bois, *The Suppression*, 282.

CHAPTER FIVE **Slavery**

1. For significance of Yoruba names, see Rev. Samuel Johnson, *The History of the Yorubas From the Earliest Times to the Beginning of the British Protectorate*, 79–89.

2. Dennison, *A Memoir of Lottie*, 40.

3. Lorenzo Dow Turner, *Africanisms in the Gullah Dialect*.

4. Augustine Meaher to G. Donaldson.

5. John C. Inscoe, "Carolina Slave Names: An Index to Acculturation," 533–4.
6. See Gwendolyn Midlo Hall's website, *Afro-Louisiana History and Genealogy, 1718–1820*. For African names from all over the South, see Newbell Pucket, *Black Names in America: Origins and Usage*.
7. Inscoe, "Carolina Slave Names," 532.
8. Captain Harry Dean, *Umbala: The Adventures of a Negro Sea-Captain in Africa and on the Seven Seas in his Attempts to Found an Ethiopian Empire*, 11.
9. See Joey L. Dillard, *Black English: Its History and Usage in the United States*, 123–35, and Peter H. Wood, *Black Majority: Negroes in Colonial South Carolina from 1670 through the Stono Rebellion*, 181–6.
10. Hurston, *Barracoon*, 18.
11. Roche, *Historic Sketches*, 101; Scott, "Affika Town."
12. Hurston, *Barracoon*, 62.
13. For the role of Africans in American rice cultivation, see Wood, *Black Majority*; Daniel C. Littlefield, *Rice and Slaves: Ethnicity and the Slave Trade in Colonial South Carolina*; Leslie A. Schwalm, *A Hard Fight for We: Women's Transition from Slavery to Freedom in South Carolina*; Judith Ann Carney, *Black Rice: The African Origin of Rice Cultivation in the Americas*; for cattle-raising see John Thornton, *Africa and Africans in the Making of the Atlantic World, 1400–1800*; Robert A. Voeks, *Sacred Leaves of Candomble: African Magic, Medicine, and Religion in Brazil*; for an overview, see Hall, *Slavery*, 66–8.
14. Buckingham, *The Slave States of America*, vol. 1, 264; Moore, *History of Alabama*, 306; Peter J. Hamilton, *Mobile of the Five Flags: The Story of the River Basin and the Coast about Mobile From the Earliest Times to the Present*, 270; John Hebron Moore, *The Emergence of the Cotton Kingdom in the Old Southwest: Mississippi, 1770–1860*, 381.
15. For a description of work on the steamboats, see Charles Lanman, *Adventures in the Wilds of America*, vol. 2, 167–8; Harvey H. Jackson, *Rivers of History: Life on the Coosa, Tallapoosa, Cahaba, and Alabama*; Thomas C. Buchanan, *Black Life on the Mississippi: Slaves, Free Blacks, and the Western Steamboat World*, 52–80; James Silk Buckingham, *The Slave States of America*, vol. 1, 472.
16. Hurston, *Barracoon*, 64.
17. "Capt. Owen Finnegan."
18. Martin Robison Delany, *Blake or The Huts of America*, 100.
19. Jackson, *Rivers of History*, 87–97. More than a hundred years later, a man in Camden found the remains of the *Orline St. John*. He brought back to land pottery, razors, knives, buckles, and chinaware bearing the mark "T. Meaher," but no gold. See also Jack N. Nelms, "Early Days with the Alabama River Steamboats," 17–8.
20. Russell, *My Diary*, 188.
21. Rawick, *The American Slave*. Arkansas Narratives, vol. II, part 2, 52–3.
22. Révérend Père Jean Baptiste Dutertre, *Histoire naturelle des Antilles habitées par les François*, vol. 1, 164.
23. Charles Ball, *Fifty Years in Chains*, 219.
24. Buckingham, *The Slave States of America*, vol. 1, 264.
25. Rawick, *The American Slave*, North Carolina Narratives, vol. XI, part 1, 218. See also Ball, *Fifty Years In Chains*, 108–9; B. A. Botkin, ed., *Lay My Burden Down: A Folk History of Slavery*, 90; Blassingame, *Slave Testimony*, 134, 341, 687.
26. Russell, *My Diary*, 189.
27. Ibid., 189.
28. Barbara Leigh Smith Bodichon, *An American Diary 1857–1858*, 113.

29. Frederick Douglass, *My Bondage and My Freedom*, 97, 99.
30. Delany, *Blake*, 100. This particular chapter was published in *The Anglo-African Magazine* in 1859, less than two years before the episode described by Russell.
31. Hurston, *Barracoon*, 63.
32. Bowen, *Adventures*, 308; Clarke, *Travels*, 260.
33. See Francine Shields, "Palm Oil and Power: Women in an Era of Economic and Social Transition in 19th-century Yorubaland (South Western Nigeria)," 60–1.
34. Robin Law, "'Legitimate' Trade and Gender Relations in Yorubaland and Dahomey," 201.
35. For Nupe, see Forde, "The Nupe," 26–7; for Igala, see Robert G. Armstrong, "The Igala," 84; for Dendi, Marty, *Etudes sur l'islam*, 208. For women from Atakora: Roger N'Tia, April 12, 2006.
36. Dennison, *A Memoir of Lottie*, 31.
37. Ball, *Fifty Years in Chains*, 219.
38. Lewis G. Clarke, *Narrative of the Sufferings of Lewis Clarke*, 17; Rawick, *The American Slave*, Alabama Narratives, vol. I, 329 (Mary Rice); South Carolina Narratives, vol. XIV, part 4, 126 (Mom Jessie Sparrow); Florida Narratives, vol. III, 356 (Claude Augusta Wilson); Mississippi Narratives, vol. IX, 158 (Mollie Williams). For life and work in the Big House, see Blassingame, *The Slave Community*, 154–8; Eugene D. Genovese, *Roll, Jordan, Roll: The World the Slaves Made*, 327–65; Escott, *Slavery Remembered*, 64–5.
39. The incident was recounted by Emma Langdon Roche, Zora Neale Hurston, and Henry Romeyn, who did not specify on which Meaher's plantation it happened. However, we know from Cudjo that only Burns and Timothy had particularly brutal overseers, and since Noah did not mention the episode, it is probable that it did not occur on Timothy's plantation. Romeyn, "Little Africa," 17; Roche, *Historic Sketches*, 101; Hurston, *Barracoon*, 62.
40. Scott, "Affika Town."
41. Ibid.
42. "Religion of the Dahomans."
43. Arthur W. Bergeron, *Confederate Mobile*, 107.
44. For examples of bondpeople's resistance during the war, see Bell Irvin Wiley, *Southern Negroes 1861–1865*, 73–83.
45. Herbert Aptheker, who gives the most exhaustive account of individual acts of resistance, conspiracies, and revolts—real and sometimes presumed—does not provide examples of this type of collective action. Herbert Aptheker, *American Negro Slave Revolts*. For a discussion and comparison of collective/noncollective models of resistance among enslaved and serf populations, see Peter Kolchin, "Reevaluating the Antebellum Slave Community: A Comparative Perspective."
46. Douglass, *My Bondage*, 95.
47. Hurston, *Barracoon*, 62–3; Roche, *Historic Sketches*, 102.
48. Hurston, *Barracoon*, 62.
49. For slavery in Africa, see Suzanne Miers and Igor Kopytoff, eds., *Slavery In Africa: Historic and Anthropological Perspectives*; Paul E. Lovejoy, *Transformations in Slavery: A History of Slavery in Africa*; Peter Haenger and Paul E. Lovejoy, eds., *Slave and Slave Holders on the Gold Coast: Towards an Understanding of Social Bondage in West Africa*; Boubacar Barry, *Senegambia and the Atlantic Slave Trade*; Clément Cakpo Vodouhè, Félix A. Iroko, Yolande Béhanzin-Joseph-Noel et Michel Videgla, *La Traite des Noirs (XVe siècle – XIX siècle)*.

50. Edna G. Bay, "Servitude and Worldly Success in the Palace of Dahomey"; Thornton, *Africa and Africans*, 87–8.

51. John J. Ormond, Arthur P. Bagby, George Goldthwaite, *The Code of Alabama*, 238.

52. Rawick, *The American Slave*, Texas Narratives, vol. XVI, part 2, 249; Arkansas Narratives, vol. II, part 2, 158; Arkansas Narratives, vol. II, part 4, 43–4; Texas Narratives, vol. XVI, part 4, 78.

53. The 1870 U.S. Census counts 1,703 persons who had one or two parents born in Africa, while the more reliable 1880 census counts 8,099. Because many names that appeared in 1870 do not come up ten years later, and also because of undercounting in both censuses, as well as deaths between 1860 and 1880, it is safe to estimate the number of Africans' children to about 10,000 in 1860. If these 10,000 individuals had six children each, and taking into account the fact that children of African parents would also intermarry, reducing the overall number, it is possible that 50,000 people or more had African grandparents. The largest number of Africans' children was found in South Carolina, 1,178; Georgia followed with 1,154; Louisiana, 1,041; Alabama, 945; Texas, 924; Mississippi, 884; Florida, 257; North Carolina, 227; and Virginia, 100. Figures compiled from the 1870 and 1880 Federal Censuses.

54. Rawick, *The American Slave*, South Carolina Narratives, vol. XIV, part 2, 230; Oklahoma Narratives, vol. XIII, 24, 92; James Mellon, ed., *Bullwhip Days: The Slaves Remember*, 50; Rawick, *The American Slave*, South Carolina Narratives, vol. XIV, part 2, 191; North Carolina Narratives, vol. XI, part 1, 33–43; Texas Narratives, vol. XVI, part 2, 219–20.

55. Mellon, *Bullwhip Days*, 50.

56. Rawick, *The American Slave*, Texas Narratives, vol. XVI, part 2, 220; Orland Kay Armstrong, *Old Massa's People*, 46.

57. Rawick, *The American Slave*, South Carolina Narratives, vol. XIV, part 4, 148.

58. Scott, "Affika Town"; Rawick, *The American Slave*, Texas Narratives, vol. XVI, part 1, 290.

59. Hurston, *Barracoon*, 62.

60. Scott, "Affika Town."

61. Michael P. Johnson, "Work, Culture, and the Slave Community: Slave Occupations in the Cotton Belt in 1860."

62. Ball, *Fifty Years in Chains*, 131.

63. Escott, *Slavery Remembered*, 67–8.

64. For a discussion of labor practices in the Deep South, see Ira Berlin, *Generations of Captivity: A History of African-American Slaves*, 159–244.

65. Rawick, *The American Slave*, Texas Narratives, vol. XVI, part 1, 290; part 2, 201.

66. Rawick, *The American Slave*, Arkansas Narratives, vol. II, part 4, 51; South Carolina Narratives, vol. XIV, part 4, 41.

67. Gwendolyn Midlo Hall, *Africans in Colonial Louisiana: The Development of Afro-Creole Culture in the Eighteenth Century* and *Slavery and African Ethnicities in the Americas: Restoring the Links*; Diouf, *Servants of Allah*; Michael A. Gomez, *Exchanging Our Country Marks: The Transformation of African Identities in the Colonial and Antebellum South*; Paul E. Lovejoy and David Trotman, eds., *Trans-Atlantic Dimensions of Ethnicity in the African Diaspora*.

68. Escott, *Slavery Remembered*, 47.

69. Culled from the 1870 U.S. Federal Census.

70. Random sample of one hundred people with at least one African parent, culled from the 1880 U.S. Census for Alabama.

71. The often-repeated notion that "sexual intercourse between shipmates . . . was considered incestuous" has its origin in Orlando Patterson, *The Sociology of Slavery*, 150. Patterson does not give any source for his assertion, but mentions it came from "one observer." Sidney Mintz and Richard Price reiterate it in *The Birth of African-American Culture*, but do not give a source either; they quote Patterson.

72. Dennison, *A Memoir of Lottie*, 30.

73. Rawick, *The American Slave*, North Carolina Narratives, vol. XI, part 2, 434 (Hilliard Yellerday).

74. Dennison, *A Memoir of Lottie*, 29.

75. Escott, *Slavery Remembered*, 61. Field hands intermarried in 66.7 percent of the cases.

76. Rawick, *The American Slave*, South Carolina Narratives, vol. XIV, 4, 148.

77. U.S. Federal Census 1870, Mobile, Beat 3, 315. Scott, "Affika Town."

78. Susan Preston Blier, *African Vodun: Art, Psychology and Power*, 269; and *The Royal Arts of Africa: The Majesty of Form*, 104.

79. Scott, "Affika Town." For tales by Cudjo, see Hurston, *Barraccon*, Appendix; Alain Locke, *The New Negro: An Interpretation*, 245–7; also published in Langston Hughes and Arna Bontemps, eds., *The Book of Negro Folklore*, 20–3. Part of one of Cudjo's tales about the tortoise can be found in Ellis, *The Yoruba-Speaking*, 271–4. It seems that Cudjo's version conflates two stories.

80. Hurston, *Barracoon*, 65.

81. Ibid., 66.

82. Eltis et al., *The Trans-Atlantic Slave Trade*.

83. Diouf, *Servants of Allah*, 49–70. For dress and names, 71–106; literacy, 107–44; cultural legacy, 179–210.

84. Scott, "Affika Town."

85. A. Serpos Tidjani, "Notes sur le mariage au Dahomey," 68. Marie-Josée Menongbe, January 2, 2006.

86. Scott, "Affika Town."

87. Description of the funerals by Roger N'Tia, January 12, 2006; additional information in Dominique Sewane, *Le souffle du mort: La tragédie de la mort chez les Batãmmariba du Togo, Bénin*.

88. Elisha P. Renee, *Population and Progress in a Yoruba Town*, 33–4. Cudjo mentioned that his grandfather had been buried in his house, Hurston, *Barracoon*, second manuscript, 18.

89. Scott, "Affika Town."

90. Roger N'tia, January 12, 2006.

91. Joe Brayton Free, "Petitions to Become a Slave."

92. Hurston, *Barracoon*, 64–5.

93. Walter L. Fleming, *Civil War and Reconstruction in Alabama*, 207; Wiley, *Southern Negroes*, 18.

94. Robert Russa Moton, *What the Negro Thinks*, 10; Montgomery *Weekly Mail*, August 15, 1863, quoting Chattanooga *Confederate*, in Wiley, *Southern Negroes*, 19.

95. Rawick, *The American Slave*, Alabama Narratives, vol. I, 338.

96. Hurston, *Barracoon*, 65.

97. See Bessie Martin, *A Rich Man's War, A Poor Man's Fight: Desertion of Alabama Troops from the Confederate Army*.

98. Caldwell Delaney, *Confederate Mobile: A Pictorial History*, 155. For blockade-running, see also Fleming, *Civil War*, 183–8.
99. Bergeron, *Confederate Mobile*, 121.
100. "Arrival of Gunboat Massachusetts."
101. Don E. Fehrenbacher, *The Slaveholding Republic*, 199; Abraham Lincoln Respite of Execution.
102. "The Execution of Gordon, the Slave Trader."
103. Scott, "Affika Town."
104. For military laborers and impressments, see Fleming, *Civil War*, 205–8; Wiley, *Southern Negroes*, 110–33; Robert D. Reid, "The Negro in Alabama During the Civil War"; Ira Berlin, et al., *The Destruction of Slavery*, 663–818; Bergeron, *Confederate Mobile*; 115–25.
105. Rawick, *The American Slave*, Arkansas Narratives, vol. II, part 4, 182.
106. F. S. Blount to Major P. Ellis, Jr., 23 June 1864, quoted in Berlin et al., *The Destruction*, 738–41.
107. Wiley, *Southern Negroes*, 124–5.
108. Bergeron, *Confederate Mobile*; 115–25.
109. Published in the *Tribune*, quoted in "Wanting to Exchange Places."
110. Fleming, *Civil War*, 206.
111. McCann to Gideon Welles, Secretary of the Navy, Off Mobile Bay, January 2, 1864; Commodore H. K. Thatcher to Commodore H. H. Bell Commander of the Western Gulf Blockading Squadron, New Orleans, off Mobile Bay, January 3, 1864 in *Official records of the Union and Confederate Navies in the War of the Rebellion, Series 1, vol. 20: West Gulf Blockading Squadron (March 15, 1863–December 31, 1863)*, 752–3. Captain Thornton A. Jenkins to Commodore H. H. Bell, Blockade off Mobile, January 13, 1864 in Series I, vol. 21 (January 1, 1864–December 31, 1864), 29; Rear Admiral D. G. Farragut to Commodore James Palmer, West Gulf Blockading Squadron, New Orleans, at sea, March 3, 1864, ibid., Series I, vol. 21, 123–4.
112. Dennison, *A Memoir of Lottie*, 31.
113. Runaway Records. April 13, 1863. Record Book of Runaway Slaves 1 (08/24/1857–03/20/1865), 148.
114. Wiley, *Southern Negroes*, 33–4.
115. Bergeron, *Confederate Mobile*, 190.
116. Delaney, *Remember Mobile*, 210.
117. Bergeron, *Confederate Mobile*, 191.
118. Thad Holt, Jr., ed. *Miss Waring's Journal: 1863 and 1865. Being the Diary of Miss Mary Waring of Mobile*, 15.
119. United States. War Dept., United States. Record and Pension Office, United States. War Records Office., et al. *The War of the Rebellion: A Compilation of the Official Records of the Union and Confederate Armies*, Series 1–vol. 48, Part I, 603; Bergeron, *Confederate Mobile*, 190.
120. Hurston, *Barracoon*, 66.
121. Rawick, *The American Slave*, Texas Narratives, vol. XVI, part 2, 133 (Felix Haywood).
122. Rawick, *The American Slave*, Arkansas Narratives, vol. II, part 3, 164 (Eda Harper).
123. Rawick, *The American Slave*, Arkansas Narratives, vol. II, part 5, 18 (Waters McIntosh), 124 (Patsy Moore).

124. *AME Church Review*, VI (July, 1889), 106, quoted in Blassingame, *The Slave Community*, 501; Rawick, *The American Slave*, Missouri Narratives, vol. X, 191–2.
125. Hurston, *Barracoon*, 67.

CHAPTER SIX **Freedom**

1. Rawick, *The American Slave*, Arkansas Narrative, vol. II, part 3, 127.
2. For freedpeople's migrations, see Peter Kolchin, *First Freedom: The Responses of Alabama's Blacks to Emancipation and Reconstruction*, 4–23; Leon F. Litwack, *Been in the Storm So Long: The Aftermath of Slavery*, 296–301; Michael W. Fitzgerald, *Urban Emancipation: Popular Politics in Reconstruction Mobile, 1860–1890*, 9–48.
3. Elizabeth Kilham, "Sketches in Color," 744; Ira Berlin and Leslie S. Rowland, eds., *Families and Freedom: A Documentary History of the African-American Kinship in the Civil War Era*; Litwack, *Been in the Storm So Long*, 229–34; Dorothy Sterling, ed. *The Trouble They Seen: The Story of Reconstruction in the Words of African Americans*, 214–21.
4. Certificate of Service for James Mayers, September 14, 1889, in Dennison, *Memoirs of James*, 37.
5. Roche, *Historic Sketches*, 100.
6. Litwack, *Been in the Storm*, 310–6; Foner, *Reconstruction*, 81–2; Kolchin, *First Freedom*, 3–29. According to the flawed 1870 census, there were 14,000 African Americans and 18,000 whites in Mobile. The freedpeople's migrations in the early years changed the urban landscape. Southern cities with populations of over four thousand in 1870 had seen their black population increase by 80 percent over the 1860 numbers. In the same time, the white population had grown by only 13 percent. See John Kellogg, "Negro Urban Clusters in the Postbellum South," 312.
7. Delaney, *Remember Mobile*, 213.
8. Rawick, *The American Slave*, Texas Narratives, vol. IV, part 2, 133.
9. Capt. William A. Poillon to Brig. Gen. Wager Swayne, November 1865, Records of the Assistant Commissioners, Alabama (Letters Received) quoted in Litwack, *Been in the Storm*, 314.
10. Oliver O. Howard, *Autobiography of Oliver Otis Howard, Major General, United States Army*, 2, 164.
11. C. W. Tebeau, "Some Aspects of Planter-Freedman Relations, 1865–1880," 133.
12. D. W. Whittle to General Howard, June 8, 1865, quoted in John Carpenter, "Atrocities in the Reconstruction Period," 237. Rawick, *The American Slave*, Arkansas Narratives, vol. II, part 4, 184.
13. For the traditional Southern Democrat view on loyalty, see Walter L. Fleming, *Civil War and Reconstruction in Alabama*, 210–2; see also Tebeau, "Some Aspects," 136–8. For a counterargument, see George H. Hepworth, *The Whip, Hoe, and Sword, or the Gulf-Department in '63*, 142–4; Harvey Wish, "Slave Disloyalty under the Confederacy," 435–50; Wiley, "Southern Negroes," 77–84.
14. "The Gulf States: Political and Social Condition in Alabama."
15. W. A. Poillon, Captain and Assistant Superintendent Freedmen to Brig. Gen. Swayne, July 29, 1865, in Carl Schurz, *Report on the Condition of the South*, 73. See

also Carpenter, "Atrocities in the Reconstruction Period"; Litwack, *Been in the Storm*, 274–82; George C. Rable, *But There Was No Peace: The Role of Violence in the Politics of Reconstruction.*

16. Schurz, *Condition*, 19; Fleming, *Civil War*, 368.
17. Wager Swayne to Colonel George D. Robinson, Superintendent of the District of Mobile, Montgomery, September 18, 1865. J. D. Kinnay to Captain L. J. Whiting, Montgomery, May 22, 1866.
18. S. Moore to George H. Tracy, Eastern Shore, Baldwin, April 17, 1867.
19. Schurz, *Condition*, 16–7; Reid, *A Southern Tour*, 503–4.
20. F. J. Massey to Orlando Brown, May 1, 1866, quoted in Foner, *Reconstruction*, 103.
21. General Field Orders no 28, Headquarters, Army and Division of West Mississippi, Mobile, April 19, 1865, quoted in Kolchin, *First Freedom*, 31. John B. Myers "The Alabama Freedmen and the Economic Adjustments During Presidential Reconstruction, 1865–1867," 260.
22. For employers' collusion, see Jonathan M. Wiener, *Social Origins of the New South: Alabama, 1860–1880;* for a counter argument, see Ralph Shlomotvitz, "'Bound' or 'Free'? Black Labor in Cotton and Sugarcane Farming, 1865–1880." Quote in Loren Schweninger, "James Rapier and the Negro Labor Movement, 1869–1872," 186.
23. John Richard Dennett, *The South As It Is: 1865–186*, 292; see also Kolchin, *First Freedom*, 33; Michael W. Fitzgerald, "Emancipation and Military Pacification: The Freedmen's Bureau and Social Control in Alabama," 54–62.
24. W. A. Poillon to Carl Schurz, September 9, 1865 in Schurz, *Condition*, 72; Henry M. McKiven Jr., "Secession, War, Reconstruction," 114–5. Fitzgerald, "Emancipation," 51–2.
25. Hurston, *Barracoon*, 67.
26. Iliffe, *Honour*, 77.
27. Roche, *Historic Sketches*, 114; Suzette Robertson, "The African Ancestry," 75.
28. Litwack, *Been in the Storm*, 249. For a detailed analysis of freedpeople's names, see Herbert G. Gutman, *The Black Family in Slavery and Freedom 1750–1925*, 230–56; and John C. Inscoe, "Carolina Slave Names: An Index to Acculturation," 527–54.
29. Charles J. Montgomery, "Survivors from the Cargo of the Negro Slave Yacht *Wanderer*," 613.
30. In 1870, the African first names recorded in the census were: Cuffy, Quash, Cuffie, Cuff, Cuffer, Cudgo, all Akan day-names; Kiziahe, Zura, Segnbee, Maylaa, Kiffle, Ishtaka, Malaka, Frimka, Bobolo, Sitka, Sharka. In 1880, some of these names were: Akdar Abdallah, Malackie and Omar Amberee, Yasser Boren, four Muslims; Feby Dago (Guere name common in Côte d'Ivoire), Dembo (probably Demba, Senegambian male name) Dunkins, Abardo and Dofgai Edward, Dimado (Ghana) and Zinga (Angola) Johnson.
31. U.S. Federal Censuses from 1870 to 1930.
32. Stroyer, *My Life in the South*, 15–6. Stroyer went on: "There were two reasons given by the slave holders why they did not allow a slave to use his own name, but rather that of the master. The first was that if he ran away, he would not be so easily detected by using his own name, as if he used that of his master instead. The second was, that to allow him to use his own name would be sharing an honor which was due only to his master, and that would be too much for a negro, said they, who was nothing more than a servant. So it was held as a crime for the slave to be caught using his own name, which would expose him to severe punishment."
33. Roger N'Tia, January 26, 2006.

34. "Plateau Negro." Hurston, *Baracoon*, 73.
35. Compiled from the 1870 U.S. census.
36. Salimata Orou-Yoruba, January 5, 2006.
37. 1870 U.S. Census, Montgomery, Township 16 Range 19, 354. According to the 1870 and 1880 censuses, three Africans (in Louisiana, Connecticut, and Georgia) took the last name African, as did three native-born. Forty people (only four of them females) were given the first name Africa; and two men born in Africa chose that name for themselves. One, in his seventies at emancipation, in a burst of beautiful self-confidence, called himself Africa Smart (U.S. Federal Census 1870, Florida, Franklin County, Yalachicola, 703). It was as arresting a name as Bright Yankee, which is what another African, in South Carolina, called himself (U.S. Federal Census 1870, South Carolina, Richland County, Fourth, 208).
38. U.S. Federal Census 1870: Tom Ebo (Florida, Wakulla, Wakulla, 778); Athanase Congo (Louisiana, Ward 10 Natchitoches, 454); Jack Congo (Louisiana, Pointe Coupee, Police Jury Ward 4, 321); Alexander Congo (Louisiana, St. John the Baptist, Ward 2, 281); John Congo (Louisiana, St. Landry, Ward 1, 3); Lindor Limba (Louisiana, St. Martin, St. Martinsville, 381); Salomon Pollard (Louisiana, Iberville, Ward 1, 268); Richard Bobo (South Carolina, Laurens, Jacks, 74); Charles Senegal (Louisiana, Pointe Coupee, Police Jury Ward 4, 325.)
39. U.S. Federal Census 1870: Henry Colomataka (Louisiana, St Martin, St Martinsville, 382); John Kaloda (Texas, Matagorda, Upper Caney, 498); Jefferson Ondoo (Texas, Burleson, Western District, 204); Sophy Cashee (South Carolina, Orangeburg, Amelia, 144); John E. Baboo (New York, New York, New York Ward 18 District 2, 43); U.S. Federal Census 1880: Omar Amberee (Texas, Matagorda, Precinct 3 & 4, 31).
40. Marriage certificate of Katie Thomas and Richard Cooper, Mobile, June 5, 1872.
41. Marriage certificate of Clara Aunspaugh and Samuel Turner, Mobile, March 8, 1880.
42. Elizabeth Hyde Botume, *First Days Amongst the Contrabands*, 49.
43. U.S. Federal Census, 1870, Matagorda, Upper Caney, Texas, 26–8.
44. U.S. Federal Census 1870, Mobile, Ward 5, 131.
45. Hurston, *Barraccon*, 74.
46. Ibid., 73–4. Translations by Nalla Raoufou Amidou, Kowiou Efidi, and Aroua Adénlé, January 7, 2006.
47. Léon F. Degny, February 9, 2006.
48. Chris McFadyen, "Legacy of a 'peculiar institution.'" Translation by Maria Soumonni, January 4, 2006.
49. Hurston, *Barracoon*, 72.
50. N. A. Fadipe, *The Sociology of the Yoruba*, 87–9; LaRay Denzer, "Yoruba Women: A Historiographical Study," 5.
51. Gay Wilentz, "If You Surrender to the Air: Folk Legends of Flight and Resistance in African American Literature"; Wendy W. Waters, "'One of Dese Mornings, Bright and Fair, Take My Wings and Cleave De Air': The Legend of the Flying Africans and Diasporic Consciousness," 3–29; Lorna McDaniel, *The Big Drum Ritual of Carriacou: Praisesongs in Rememory of Flight*.
52. Archibald Dalzel, *The History of Dahomy, an Inland Kingdom of Africa*, 222–3; Edna G. Bay, "Protection, Political Exile, and the Atlantic Slave-Trade," 54.
53. For Brazilian returnees, see: John Duncan, *Travels in Western Africa in 1845 and 1846*, 1, 185; James Fletcher & D. P. Kidder, *Brazil and the Brazilian*, 136, 607; Elisée Reclus, *Africa*, 316; Ross, "The Career of Domingo Martinez"; Pierre

Verger, "Retour des 'Brésiliens' au Golfe du Bénin au XIX ème siècle"; Pierre Verger, *Flux et reflux de la traite des nègres entre le Golfe de Bénin et Bahia de todos os Santos, du XVIIe au XIX siècle*; Robin Law, "Yoruba Liberated Slaves Who Returned to West Africa"; Robin Law and Kristin Mann, "West Africa in the Atlantic Community: The Case of the Slave Coast"; Silke Strickrodt, "'Afro-Brazilians' of the Western Slave Coast in the Nineteenth Century."

54. Roche, *Historic Sketches*, 114–5; Hurston, *Barracoon*, 68–9.
55. Hurston, ibid., 69.
56. Among the ACS founders were President James Madison, Chief Justice of the Supreme Court John Marshall, Associate Justice Bushrod Washington (a nephew of George), Senator Henry Clay, and Francis Scott Key; not the least because of this filiation, to most black leaders the colonization movement was no more than a scheme by which white Americans hoped to preserve the country for whites and enslaved blacks, with no place for free people of color.
57. Willis D. Boyd, "The Ile a Vache Colonization Venture, 1862–1864"; William Freehling, *The Reintegration*, 138–57.
58. James Gillette to William Coppinger, Mobile, December 26, 1867.
59. The original group from Mobile counted twenty-one adults and thirteen children, but according to a note added in April on the December 26 letter, transportation to Savannah for only twelve adults "and some" children was paid for by the bureau. Some people may have elected to stay or had paid their own fare. William Coppinger to James Gillette, Washington, March 7, 1868; Savannah, May 2, 1868. Among the passengers of the *Golconda* were 283 Georgians, 65 South Carolinians, 42 Mississippians, 9 individuals from Tennessee, and 1 from Washington, D.C. The list was published in *The African Repository*, 58, 3 (March 1872), 79.
60. Article published in the Charleston *Daily News*, May 21, 1867, reproduced as "The Packet-Ship Golconda," 201–2.
61. While 3,733 Virginians, 1,371 North Carolinians, 1,341 Georgians, and 870 Tennesseans had emigrated, only 105 Alabamians had left. Other Gulf States were better represented: Mississippi had 551 emigrants, and Louisiana 309. Texas, with 16 emigrants, was by far the laggard. *The African Repository*, 43, 4 (April 1867), 117.
62. Reid, *A Southern Tour*, 385.
63. Roche, *Historic Sketches*, 114–5; Hurston, *Barracoon*, 67–8.
64. Addie E. Pettaway, *Africatown, U.S.A.*, 12, 17; Hurston, *Barracoon*, 68–9.
65. See Litwack, *Been in the Storm*, 244–6; Foner, *Reconstruction*, 85–7; Catherine Clinton, "Reconstructing Freedwomen"; Jacqueline Jones, *Labor of Love, Labor of Sorrow: Black Women, Work and the Family, From Slavery to the Present*, 44–78; Noralee Frankel, *Break Those Chains At Last: African Americans 1860–1880*.
66. Reid, A *Southern Tour*, 370.
67. In the domestic sphere, though, gender roles had been strictly defined: women cooked, washed, and mended while men fished, hunted, or did the heavy work. Skilled work was also sexually segregated: men were coopers and blacksmiths, for example, and women seamstresses or cooks.
68. Roger L. Ransom and Richard Sutch, *One Kind of Freedom: The Economic Consequences of Emancipation*, 233.
69. Kolchin, *First Freedom*, 68. Numbers declined, however, in the 1870s because of poverty and the depression of 1873, and many women—and children—went back to the fields or whites' houses where they worked for wages; see in particular Foner, *Reconstruction*, 86–7.

70. Litwack, *Been in the Storm*, 245; Walter L. Fleming, *Documentary History of Reconstruction*, 2, 281.

71. Some enslaved men and women were partially self-employed as they grew and sold their own produce independently. They too had acquired skills in that domain, even though most of their time was devoted to working for their owner.

72. Whitelaw Reid, *After the War, a Southern Tour: May 1, 1865 to May 1, 1866*, 59.

73. Quoted in Foner, *Reconstruction*, 105.

74. U.S., *Statutes at Large, Treaties, and Proclamations of the United States of America*, 13, 507–9.

75. Dan T. Carter, "The Anatomy of Fear: The Christmas Day Insurrection Scare of 1865," 347–8, 357. Reid, *A Southern Tour*, 386.

76. *The Nationalist*, December 14, 1865, quoted in Montgomery, "Alabama Freedmen," 247–8.

77. For arming of freedmen, see Schurz, *Report on the Condition*; Reid, *A Southern Tour*, 422; Fleming, *Civil War*, 412.

78. Ira Berlin et al., eds. *The Black Military Experience*, 733.

79. Editorial in a New Orleans newspaper, quoted in Reid, *A Southern Tour*, 422.

80. Reid, *A Southern Tour*, 212.

81. Myrta Lockett Avary, *Dixie After the War: An Exposition of Social Conditions Existing in the South During the Twelve Years Succeeding the Fall of Richmond*, 141; Marvin Fletcher, "The Negro Volunteer in Reconstruction, 1865–66," 126–7. Letter from J. Madison Wells to Andrew Johnson, October 30, 1865, Johnson Papers, quoted in Fletcher, "The Negro Volunteer," 128.

82. Henderson H. Donald, *The Negro Freedman*, 5; Fleming, *Documentary History*, vol. 1, 359–60; Fleming, *Civil War*, 447–8. In some parts, the scheme went on until the turn of the twentieth century.

83. S. H. Mercher to General Clinton Fisk, December 12, 1865, RBRFAL Tennessee, quoted in Carter, "The Anatomy of Fear," 362.

84. Facsimile of military documents in Dennison, *Memoirs of James*, 39; National Park Service, *Civil War Soldiers and Sailors System*, James Mayors.

85. Dennison, *Memoirs of James*, 43. The information is contained in a Declaration for an Original Invalid Pension James filed in 1886.

86. The Civil War Archive.

87. Fletcher, "The Negro Volunteer."

88. Joseph T. Wilson, *The Black Phalanx: A History of the Negro Soldiers of the United States in the Wars of 1775–1812, 1861–'65*, 503–4.

89. *The Chicago Tribune*, January 18, 1864, quoted in Dudley Taylor Cornish, "The Union Army as a School for Negroes," 372. See also John W. Blassingame, "The Union Army as an Educational Institution for Negroes, 1862–1865."

90. T. D. Eliot, *Report of Hon. T. D. Eliot, chairman of the Committee on Freedmen's Affairs to the House of Representatives, March 10, 1868*, 22.

91. Berlin et al. *The Black Military*, 794–9.

92. *The African Repository* 6 (April 1830), 60; Terry Alford, *Prince Among Slaves: The True Story of An African Prince Sold Into Slavery in the American South*, 184.

93. Carl Bernhardt Wadstrom, *An Essay On Colonization*, part 2, 16.

94. *The Royal African: Or Memoirs of the Young Prince of Annamaboe*, 44–5, 47, 51.

95. Snelgrave, *A New Account*, 67–72; Robin Law, "King Agaja of Dahomey, the Slave Trade, and the Question of West African Plantations: The Mission of Bulfinch Lambe and Adomo Tomo to England, 1726–32," 137–63.

96. Archibald Dalzel, *History of Dahomy, An Inland Kingdom of Africa* (London: Frank Cass, [1793] 1967), 181.
97. James H. Sweet, *Recreating Africa: Culture, Kinship, and Religion in the African-Portuguese World, 1441–1770*, 31.
98. Rawick, *The American Slave*, Georgia Narratives, vol. IV, part 3, 200. The census takers recorded Shade's father as being born in Georgia, which, however does not mean that he was. U.S. Federal Census, 1870, Pike County, Georgia, 199; 1880 Census, District 592 Pike County, Georgia, 58.
99. Richard Madden, *A Twelve Month's Residence in the West Indies*; Carlton Robert Ottley, *Slavery Days in Trinidad*, 58; Carl Campbell, "John Mohammed Bath and the Free Mandingos in Trinidad: The Question of their Repatriation to Africa 1831–38."
100. "News of the Week"; "The Slaver Wanderer."
101. Antonio McDaniel, " Extreme Mortality in Nineteen-Century Africa: The Case of Liberia Immigrants," 585. Statistics on age of the freed Africans culled from 1870 and 1880 censuses.
102. James Saxon Childers, "From Jungle to Slavery."
103. Article published in the *Weekly Times* of Lagos concerning a meeting held on August 16, 1890, between the representatives and British colonial officers, quoted in Verger, "Retour des Brésiliens au Golfe du Bénin," 20–1.

CHAPTER SEVEN   **African Town**

1. John Josselyn, *An Account of Two Voyages to New England Made During the Years 1638, 1663*, 26; John R. Beard, *The Life of Toussaint L'Ouverture: The Negro Patriot of Hayti*, 24; Mederic Louis Elie Moreau de Saint-Mery, *Description topographique, physique, civile, politique et historique de la partie française de l'isle Saint Domingue*, 1797, I, 30.
2. Romeyn, "Little Africa," 16.
3. Hurston, *Barracoon*, 68.
4. Ibid.
5. Ibid.
6. Roche, *Historic Sketches*, 115–6. See also Hurston, *Barracoon*, 69–70.
7. Roche, *Historic Sketches*, 116; Hurston, *Barracoon*, 70.
8. Pettaway, *Africatown, U.S.A.*, 3; Frank Sikora, "Groups Tracing History of Last Slaves to Arrive"; Chris McFadyen, "Legacy of a 'peculiar institution.'"
9. "The Slave Ship Wanderer."
10. Roche, *Historic Sketches*, 117; Hurston, *Barracoon*, 70.
11. Land Sale. Thomas Buford to Jabez Chase, Horace Ely, Charley Lewis, Maggie Lewis, Matilda Ely, Lucy Wilson and Polly Shay. April 5, 1870. Deed Book 70, 242–4.
12. The 1860 Slave Schedules indicate that Buford owned a thirty-eight-year-old man and a twenty-seven-year-old woman who might correspond to the couple. In the 1880 Federal Census (Mobile, Kosters, 110) Horace Ely's year of birth was given as 1825, and Matilda's as 1836.
13. Deed Book 30, 601. *Mobile Directory 1872*, 238. A few years later, Wilson became one of three commissioners charged with handling Mobile's huge debt; his wife was the first American woman writer who made over $100,000 in royalties.

14. Deed Book 30, 643, 655.
15. Hurston, *Barracoon*, 71, 21; Romeyn, "Little Africa," 16.
16. Emma Roche, "Last Survivor of Slave Ship Deeply Grateful to God, Man." Description by Motley, one of Cudjo and Abile's grandsons, Pettaway, *Africatown USA*, 27.
17. The shipmates from Dahomey, like Gumpa, had been living in rectangular dwellings before their deportation.
18. Hurston, "The Last Slave Ship," 351; Henry C. Williams, Sr., September 21, 2002.
19. Hurston, *Barracoon*, 71.
20. Sundiata Keita Cha-Jua, *America's First Black Town: Brooklyn, Illinois, 1830–1915*. After the end of Reconstruction in 1877, about eighty black towns were created in the West, mostly by white speculators who had acquired undeveloped land and sold it to black brokers and settlers. See Kenneth L. Hamilton, *Black Towns and Profit: Promotion and Development in the Trans-Appalachian West, 1877–1915*.
21. See Cha-Jua's discussion of the criteria, *America's First Black Town*, 221.
22. "The Slaver Wanderer."
23. Pettaway, *Africatown*, 12.
24. Facsimile of receipts in Dennison, *A Memoir of Lottie*.
25. Sikora, "Groups"; Pettaway, *Africatown*, 15–7; Thomas D. Weise, "The Voyage of the Clotilde: A Short History of the Facts and Fiction Surrounding the Last Slave Ship to America and its Passengers," 7; Robertson, "The African Ancestry," 75.
26. Roger L. Ransom and Richard Sutch, *One Kind of Freedom*, 34–6; Rabinowitz, *Race Relations*, 61–96.
27. Serpos Tidjani, "Notes sur le mariage au Dahomey," 1, 56; Forde, "The Nupe," 31; Khaleel, "The Hausa," 49.
28. Tidjani, "Notes sur le mariage au Dahomey," 1, 52.
29. Scott, "Affika Town."
30. Roche, *Historic Sketches*, 126.
31. Clarke, *Travels and Explorations*, 245.
32. Ibid.
33. Roche, *Historic Sketches*, 117–8; Hurston, *Barracoon*, 70–1.
34. Roche, *Historic Sketches*, 117.
35. Ibid., 118.
36. Dennison, *A Memoir of Lottie* and *Memoirs of James*.
37. Dennison, *A Memoir of Lottie*, 50–2.
38. Roche, *Historic Sketches*, 126.
39. Tombstone, Plateau Graveyard. The headstone was bought by Kanko on December 9, 1891, for $8.35, facsimile of receipt in Dennison, *A Memoir of Lottie*, 35.
40. *Acts and Resolutions*, 99.
41. Report of J. W. Alvord, one of the founders of the Freedman's Bank, January 1866, quoted in Fleming, *Documentary History*, 1, 383.
42. Freedman's Bank Records, CD-Rom Library, Family History Resource File. The Dennisons' bank booklet is in the possession of their granddaughter Mable.
43. Frederick Douglass, *Life and Times of Frederick Douglass by Himself*, 409; Fleming, *Civil War and Reconstruction*, 453–5.
44. Douglass, *Life and Times*, 411.
45. Fleming, *Civil War and Reconstruction*, 455.
46. Naturalization Records. October 24, 1868. City Court Minutes, 8, 47.

47. Naturalization Records. October 22, 1868. City Court Minutes, 8, 42.

48. Amnesty Oath #80, September 14, 1868, File 37, 293. James had taken the oath on August 30, 1865 (#702, File 36, 2713) and again on September 11, 1868 (# 71, File 37, 291).

49. His name does not appear in the list of Alabamians who asked for a pardon in 1865. Case Files of Applications from Former Confederates for Presidential Pardons ("Amnesty Papers"), 1865–1867.

50. Jonathan M. Wiener, "Planter Persistence and Social Change: Alabama, 1850–1870," 235–60.

51. U.S. Federal Census, 1870, Mobile, Beat 3, 315.

52. United States. Naval War Records Office and United States Office of Naval Records and Library. *Official Records of the Union and Confederate Navies in the War of Rebellion. Series I—vol. 22: West Gulf Blockading Squadron (January 1, 1865–January 31, 1866); Naval Forces on Western Waters (May 8, 1861–April 11, 1862)*, 263–4.

53. *Mobile Daily Register*, January 3, 1869, quoted in Kolchin, *First Freedom*, 45. "Capt. Tim Meaher."

54. Rawick, *The American Slave*, Texas Narratives, vol. XVI, part 1, 135.

55. Ibid., part 3, 213.

56. Hurston, *Barracoon*, 71.

57. Eva Allen Jones, *History of the Union Baptist Church*, quoted in Pettaway, *Africatown, USA*, 5.

58. Litwack, *Been in the Storm*, 462–71; Kolchin, *First Freedom*, 107–27, 113.

59. Dennison, *Memoirs of James*, 47; Kolchin, *First Freedom*, 114.

60. Kolchin, *First Freedom*, 109; Fleming, *Documentary History*, 2, 245.

61. Frederick Douglas Richardson, *The Stone Street Baptist Church—Alabama's First, 1806–1982;* Charles Octavius Boothe, *The Cyclopedia of the Colored Baptists of Alabama*, 22–3. U.S. Federal Census 1870, Mobile, Ward 7, 306. Reverend Burke could read and write, and he owned $800—almost $6,000 today—in real estate. Until 1871, the church was located at Springhill Avenue and Ann Street before it moved to its present location on Tunstall Street.

62. Roche, "Last Survivor."

63. Weise, "The Voyage," 17.

64. Henry C. Williams, Sr., September 21, 2002. Roche, *Historic Sketches*, 114.

65. Chapter 145, 901.

66. "Religion of the Dahomans."

67. Henry C. Williams, Sr., September 21, 2002.

68. "Applications," 39.

69. "More Want to Go," 97. One letter explained the "condition is at best *but one remove from slavery*," "Three Thousand Applicants," 65. In May three hundred people from the Dallas County Emigration Society of Selma had declared they wanted to leave by November, Letter from Joseph Blake, Selma, May 9, 1872, *The African Repository*, 48, 6 (June 1872), 162.

70. "Of Present Interest"; "An Interesting Statement," 350.

71. "Colonization."

72. Twenty-seven left between 1878 and 1885 and sixteen in 1891; see *The African Repository*, 62, 4 (April 1885), 62, and 67, 6 (July 1891), 95.

73. Letter from Henry Russell, Greenville, November 30, 1874, *The African Repository*, 51, 4 (April 1875), 38.

74. Hurston, *Barracoon*, 71.
75. Old Landmark Baptist Church is the name given by Cudjo to Zora Neale Hurston. Descendants called it Old Baptist Church. The name was changed in 1903 to Union Missionary Baptist Church.
76. Federal Census, 1870, Mobile, Beat 5, 383.
77. Clarke County *Journal*, October 18, 1866, quoted in Kolchin, *First Freedom*, 118.
78. Fleming, *Civil War and Reconstruction*, 636–52; Litwack, *Been in the Storm*, 469; Kolchin, *First Freedom*, 120–1.
79. Romeyn, "Little Africa," 17.
80. Jefferson Hamilton, Preacher in charge to the Mayor and Board of Aldermen of the City of Mobile, April 11, 1840, quoted in Richardson, *The Stone Street*, 41–2.
81. Fleming, *Civil War and Reconstruction*, 272.
82. Avary, *Dixie After the War*, 203–4.
83. McFadyen, "Legacy"; Pettaway, *Africatown, USA*, 5; Jonathan Evan Maslow, "Africatown, Alabama: The Past Still Breathes," 14.
84. Hurston, "The Last Slave Ship," 558.
85. Romeyn, "Little Africa," 117.
86. Kirk Munroe, "Mobile, Alabama."
87. Hurston, *Barracoon*, 17; "The Last Slave Ship," 558.
88. "Honoring Cudjo Lewis: America's Last Piece of African 'Black Ivory.'"
89. Montgomery *Advertiser*, February 19, 1874, quoted in Fleming, *Civil War*, 780. William Warren Rogers et al., *Alabama the History of a Deep South State*, 263.
90. Fleming, *Civil War*, 773.
91. *Advertiser and Mail* (Montgomery) August 23, 1874; quoted in Lucille Griffith, *Alabama: A Documentary History to 1900*, 493.
92. *The Mobile Daily Register*, July 4, 1874, quoted in Henry M. McKiven, Jr., "Secession," 124–5.
93. Roche, *Historic Sketches*, 119–20.
94. United States Congress. House Select Committee on Affairs in Alabama. (43d Congress, 2nd Session) Report no. 262. *Affairs in Alabama*.
95. Loren Schweninger, "Black Citizenship in the Republican Party in Reconstruction Alabama," 103.
96. McKiven, "Secession," 124.
97. Kolchin, *First Freedom*, 98.
98. McKiven, "Secession," 117.
99. Kenneth B. White, "The Alabama Freedmen's Bureau and Black Education: The Myth of Opportunity," 107–24; Elizabeth Bethel, "The Freemen's Bureau in Alabama," 61; Kolchin, *First Freedom*, 79–106.
100. 39th Congress, January 1, 1866, House documents, quoted in Kolchin, *First Freedom*, 85. New York *Daily Tribune*, December 12, 1865, quoted in Kolchin, *First Freedom*, 85–6.
101. Civis, *The Public School in Its Relations to the Negro*, 10.
102. Kenneth B. White, "The Alabama Freedmen's Bureau and Black Education: The Myth of Opportunity," 118–23; Alvord, *Sixth Semi-Annual Report*, 31.
103. White, "The Alabama Freedmen," 118.
104. John Watson Alvord, *Fourth Semi-Annual Report on Schools for Freedmen, July 1, 1867*, 42; Fleming, *Civil War and Reconstruction*, 461; White, "The Alabama Freedmen's Bureau," 122; Writers' Program of the Work Projects Administration in the State of Alabama. *Alabama: A Guide to the Deep South*, 98.
105. Hurston, *Barracoon*, 75.

106. Ibid.
107. Howard N. Rabinowitz, "Half a Loaf: The Shift from White to Black Teachers in the Negro Schools of the Urban South, 1865–1890," 565–94.
108. Alvord, *Eighth Semi-Annual Report*, 38.
109. Rabinowitz, "Half a Loaf," 578–82.
110. Romeyn, "Little Africa," 16.
111. Litwack, *Been in the Storm*, 241–4.
112. Roche, *Historic Sketches*, 79; see also Hurston, *Barracoon*, 20–2.
113. Roche, *Historic Sketches*, 79.
114. Hurston, *Barracoon*, 73.
115. Marriage License, Cudgo Louis and Cecilia Louis, Mobile, March 15, 1880; Marriage License, Polle Alen [sic] and Rosa Allen, Mobile, March 15, 1880; Marriage License, Arci Kibbe and Annie Kibbe, Mobile March 15, 1880; Marriage License, Clara Aunspaugh and Samuel Turner, March 6, 1880; Marriage License, Lucy Lee and Luke Winters, April 14, 1880.
116. Marriage License, John Livingston and Zena Livingston.
117. Booker T. Washington, "Negro Four Years Hence."
118. Paul C. Boudousquie, Reference Map of Mobile and Vicinity.
119. Byers, "The Last Slave-Ship," 743; Roche, *Historic Sketches*, 123, 125; Hurston, *Barracoon*, 53.

CHAPTER EIGHT   **Between Two Worlds**

1. "Death of an Old Steamboatman"; "Last Cargo of Slaves."
2. "Death of Captain Tim Meaher, The Venerable Steamboat Man."
3. "Last of the Slave Trader."
4. "The Funeral of Captain Timothy Meaher."
5. U.S. Census Bureau, *Negro Population*, 105. In 1910 out of 22,763 African Americans (44.2 percent of the total population), 11,262 lived in ward 7; 3,950 in ward 6; and 1,387 in ward 5. Don H. Doyle, *New Men, New Cities, New South*, 302.
6. Daniel T. Williams, ed., "The Lynching Records at Tuskegee Institute; With Lynching in America: A Bibliography," 8. See also Glen Feldman, "Lynching in Alabama, 1889–1921," 118–9. Louisiana followed Alabama with 156 lynchings. Overall, between 1889 and 1918, Georgia was the leading state (386), then came Mississippi (373), Texas (335), Louisiana (313), and Alabama (276), NAACP, *Thirty Years of Lynching in the United States 1889–1918*, 35, 43–5. Of the 3,446 African Americans lynched between 1882 and 1968, 539 died in Mississippi, 492 in Georgia, 352 in Texas, 335 in Louisiana, 299 in Alabama, and 257 in Florida; Williams, "The Lynching Records," 6–7.
7. Hurston, *Barracoon*, 76.
8. Elisée Soumonni, March 26, 2006.
9. Hurston, *Barracoon*, 76.
10. See Jules Poirier, *Campagne du Dahomey, 1892–1894*; François Michel, *La campagne du Dahomey, 1893–1894: la reddition de Béhanzin*; Cornevin, *Histoire du Dahomey*, 339–58.
11. Figures for 1900, nonfarm homes, U.S. Bureau of the Census, *Negro Population*, 469.
12. Romeyn, "Little Africa," 16.

13. Diouf, "Introduction," *Fighting the Slave Trade*, xiv–xv.

14. Fulbert-Dumonteil, *Jardin Zoologique d'acclimatation, Guerriers dahoméens*, 25.

15. "Dahomey King." Newspapers such as *The New York Times, Houston Telegraph, Desert News* (Utah), *Pittsfield Sun* (Massachusetts), *Flake's Bulletin* (Texas), *Farmer's Cabinet, New Orleans Times* reported regularly on Dahomey's human sacrifices.

16. Romeyn, "Little Africa," 16.

17. M. L. d'Albéca, administrateur du cercle de Whydah to General de brigade à Porto-Novo, Whydah, January 7, 1893 in *Mémoire du Benin*, 81–4; Harry Alis, *Nos Africains*, 436.

18. Marriage License, Alexander Lewis and Mary Woods.

19. U.S. Federal Census 1870, Beat 4, Mobile, 329; Census 1880, Whistler, Mobile, 104B.

20. Hurston, *Barracoon*, 90.

21. U.S. Federal Census 1900, Whistler, Mobile, 7B.

22. Christopher MacGregor Scribner, "Progress Versus Tradition in Mobile, 1900–1920," 166.

23. Herb Jordan, "Eva Jones Remembers Her Heritage"; Jonathan Evan Maslow, "Africatown, Alabama: The Past Still Breathes," 14.

24. Chris McFadyen, "Legacy of a 'Peculiar Institution'"; see also Weise, "The Voyage," 7.

25. Frank Sikora, "Group Tracing History of Last Slaves to Arrive."

26. McFadyen, "Legacy."

27. Dennison, *A Memoir of Lottie*, 72.

28. Weise, "The Voyage," 6.

29. McFadyen "Legacy"; Weise, "The Voyage," 8.

30. Hurston, *Barracoon*, 74.

31. Ibid., 75.

32. U.S. Federal Census, 1880, Mobile, Whistler, 102A. Marriage License, Cudjoe B. Lewis and Louisa Thomas.

33. Cudjo did not mention the incident to Zora Neale Hurston—or if he did, he clearly asked her not to reveal it—and the few people alive who knew Cudjo are not aware of it.

34. Edward M. Robinson to Joseph F. Johnston, Mobile, July 25, 1900. Application for pardon or parole for Cudjoe Lewis. Applications for Pardons; Petition to Joseph F. Johnston to grant Cudjo Lewis a pardon or parole; Jabez J. Parker and Samuel B. Browne to Joseph F. Johnston, Mobile, July 25, 1900; Pardon or parole for Cudjoe Lewis.

35. Claim of Sheriff Charles E. McLean for fees and allowances for January 1900 to the Board of Revenue and Road Commissioners; Claim of Sheriff Charles E. McLean for fees and allowances for February 1900 to the Board of Revenue and Road Commissioners.

36. *In the matter of the special venire in the case v. Cudjoe Lewis*, Wednesday January 17, 1900. City Court Criminal Minute Book 18 (1899–1902), 112–3.

37. *The State of Alabama v. Cudjoe Lewis*, Tuesday January 23, 1900. City Court Criminal Minute Book 18, (1899–1902), 118. Insolvent Convictions March 12, 1900, claim by Sheriff Charles E. McLean to Board of Revenue and Commissioners, Mobile County. Cudjo owed $19.35 in fees for the clerk, and $28 for the sheriff.

38. For convict labor, see in particular, Robert Louis Cvornyek, "Convict Labor in the Alabama Coal Mines, 1874–1928"; Mildred C. Fierce, *Slavery Revisited: Blacks and the Southern Convict Lease System, 1865–1933*; Alex Litchtenstein, *Twice the*

Work of Free Labor: The Political Economy of Convict Labor in the New South; Matthew J. Mancini, *One Dies, Get Another: Convict Leasing in the American South, 1866–1928*; Mary Ellen Curtin, *Black Prisoners and their World, Alabama, 1865–1900*; Brian Kelly, *Race, Class, and Power in the Alabama Coalfields, 1908–21*; Alfred Lewis, "African American Convicts in the Coal Mines of Southern Appalachia"; Douglas A. Blackmon, "From Alabama's Past, Capitalism Teamed With Racism to Create Cruel Partnership." For an overview of the literature, see James S. Day, "The Convict-Lease System in Alabama, 1872–1927."

39. Female prisoners, youngsters under fifteen, and handicapped males worked in the farms, the lumber mills, and the turpentine industry. Mine work was reserved for the men, although the Joint Committee of the General Assembly of Alabama noted as late as 1900 the presence of "mere boys" in the prisons and mines "side by side with hardened criminals" and recommended that they be taught some trade. See *Report of the Joint Committee*, 22–3. For revenues, see Allen Johnston Going, *Bourbon Democracy in Alabama, 1874–1890*, 86.

40. Malcolm Charles Moos, *State Penal Administration in Alabama*, 6.

41. *Fourth Biennial Report of the Board of Inspectors of Convicts to the Governor From September 1, 1901 to August 31, 1902*, 59.

42. Going, *Bourbon Democracy*, 176; Lewis, "African American Convicts," 272; *Third Biennial Report of the Board of Inspectors of Convicts to the Governor From September 1, 1898 to August 31, 1900*, 44.

43. The Ninth Atlanta Conference, "Negro Crime," 50.

44. Descriptive List and Court History, Cudjoe Lewis. State Convict Records.

45. Lewis, "African American Convicts," 273; *Third Biennial Report*, 45.

46. These quotas were fixed in 1884, after the 1883 allotments of one ton more for each category was judged too high. Descriptive List and Court History, Cudjoe Lewis, State Convict Records; Statement of Sentence, Cudjoe Lewis, Montgomery, July 31, 1900, Convict Bureau, State Convict Records.

47. Alabama General Assembly Joint Committee, *Report of the Joint Committee Upon the Convict System*, 17–21. *Third Biennial Report*, 13.

48. As mechanization improved, the convicts were forced to produce higher output, from ten to fourteen tons a day in the 1910s.

49. George G. Korson, *Coal Dust on the Fiddle*, 167.

50. "Southern Convict Camps: A Crying Disgrace to American Civilization."

51. *Fourth Biennial Report*, 42.

52. Korson, *Coal Dust*, 168; Moos, *State Penal Administration*, 17.

53. Cvorniek, "Convict Labor," 177.

54. James Seay Brown, ed., *Up Before Daylight: Life Stories from the Alabama Writers' Project, 1938–1939*, 111.

55. Curtin, *Black Prisoners*, 68; Mancini, *One Dies*, 106–7; Cvornyek, "Convict Labor," 179; Lewis, "African American Convicts," 274; Moos, *State Penal Administration*, 18.

56. Moos, *State Penal Administration*, 18; Korson, *Coal Dust*, 170.

57. Brown, *Up Before Daylight*, 111.

58. *Second Biennial Report*, XVII; Moos, *State Penal Administration*, 15–6. As late as 1942, although these rates were not excused, they were racially "explained," "it should be noted that between 50 and 60 per cent of these deaths were caused by tuberculosis, that during this period approximately 85 per cent of the penal population was composed of negroes, and that the mortality rate from tuberculosis is much higher among Negroes than among whites. Despite the prevalence of tuberculosis among Negroes, the fact remains that the death rate was alarmingly high."

59. *Third Biennial Report*, 30–5.

60. Ibid., 39–41; Cvorniek, "Convict Labor," 199.

61. Copy of a receipt for five dollars, for legal services dated February 4, 1893, in Dennison, *Biographical Memoirs*, 60.

62. Thomas McAdory Owen, *History of Alabama and Dictionary of Alabama Biography*, vol. 3, 238.

63. Jabez J. Parker and Samuel B. Browne to Joseph F. Johnston, Mobile, July 25, 1900. Applications for Pardons. Edward M. Robinson to Joseph F. Johnston, Mobile, July 25, 1900. Applications for Pardons.

64. Petition by citizens of Mobile County to Joseph F. Johnston for pardon or parole of Cudjo Lewis. The deputies were W. Murphy, a fireman; Frank Cazalas; M. J. Goldsmith; J. E. Norton; and Ernest L. Wimberly, deputy sheriff and assistant jailor. *Mobile City Directory*, 1900.

65. *Report of the Joint Committee*, 23.

66. Elected governor in 1896, Joseph F. Johnston created a state Mine Inspector charged with enforcing safety regulations, and he sponsored a bill to put an end to convict leasing, to parole prisoners for good behavior, and to speed trials for severe crimes as a measure to reduce lynching. It was defeated. Although he was trying to abolish the convict-lease system, he was also accused of benefiting from it. The corruption that reigned in the prisons, combined with the sale of land belonging to the University of Alabama to the Sloss Steel and Iron Company, contributed to his downfall. See Louis R. Harlan, ed., *The Booker T. Washington Papers*, vol. 4, 245–6; Michael Perman, *Struggle for Mastery: Disfranchisement in the South, 1888–1908*, 171–7; Harvey H. Jackson III, "White Supremacy Triumphant: Democracy Undone," 19–21.

67. *Third Biennial Report*, 44.

68. Moos, *State Penal Administration*, 15.

69. Copy of letter from Burch, September 21, 1882, in Dennison, *Memoirs of James*, 40. Copy of declaration, ibid., 43.

70. Copy of Treasury Department letter to James Mayors, December 27, 1907, ibid., 41.

71. United States War Department, *Bounties of Colored Soldiers*, 1–2.

72. Donald R. Shaffer, *After the Glory: The Struggles of Black Civil War Veterans*, 119–42.

73. The National Archives have only two boxes of documents on the ex-slave pension movement, RG15 Ex-Slave Pension Movement, 21A. The fraud case against the National Ex-Slave Mutual Relief Bounty and Pension Association is in RG 28 Ex-Slave Pensions, Office of Postmaster General, Fraud Order Case Files 1912–1947.

74. Facsimile in Dennison, *Memoirs of James*, 29.

75. Facsimile in Dennison, *A Memoir of Lottie*, 34; James's certificate in Dennison, *Memoirs of James*, 20.

76. "Fight Freedmen Pension Bill."

77. *Omaha Daily Democrat*, July 20, 1890, quoted in Walter R. Vaughan, *Vaughan's "Freedmen's Pension Bill,"* 183.

78. Vaughan, *Vaughan's Freedmen*, 32.

79. Poster titled "A Secret Order" dated Chicago, 1892 quoted in Senate Report 75, 56th Congress, 1st session, January 16, 1900, "Pensions for Freedmen, etc. Adverse Report," 3.

80. Facsimile of letter from Harrison to Vaughan, August 17, 1883, in Vaughan, *Vaughan's Freedmen*, 34.

81. Facsimile of letter from Douglass, in Vaughan, *Vaughan's Freedmen*, 183–4.

82. For attitude of the black middle class, see Mary Frances Berry, *My Face is Black Is True: Callie House and the Struggle for Ex-Slave Reparations*, 143–4, 189–90.
83. Vaughan, *Vaughan's Freedmen*, 113.
84. *U.S. Department Eagle*, January 7, 1900, quoted in Senate Report, "Pensions for Freedmen," 2.
85. Walter B. Hill, Jr., "The Ex-Slave Pension Movement: Some Historical and Genealogical Notes."
86. Facsimile in Dennison, *Memoirs of Lottie*, 34.
87. Mary Frances Berry, *My Face is Black*, 82, 91–2, 131.
88. Department of Interior, Bureau of Pensions, Record Group 15, Ex-Slaves Pensions, 1902, quoted in Mary Frances Berry, "Reparations for Freedmen, 1890–1916," 224.
89. "Pensions for Freedmen, etc. Adverse Report." Senate Report 75, 56th Congress, 1st session, January 16, 1900; Walter L. Fleming, "Ex-Slave Pension Frauds."
90. "Ex-Slave Pension Scheme."
91. "Ex-Slaves in Mass Meeting."
92. Berry, *My Face is Black*, 171–87. RG15 Ex-Slave Pension Movement, 21A.
93. U.S. Attorney, Southern District of Alabama, Alexander R. Pitts to Attorney General Thomas Gregory, February 28, 1916, quoted in Berry, *My Face is Black*, 191.
94. She died of cancer in 1928 at sixty-seven. Dickerson had died in 1909.
95. Fleming, "Ex-Slave Pension," 3.
96. Quoted in Berry, *My Face is Black*, 83.
97. Will of William Foster, November 8, 1900.
98. U.S. Federal Census 1900, Whistler, Mobile, 17A.
99. "Capt. WM. Foster Commander of Last American Slave Vessel Buried Yesterday."

CHAPTER NINE **Going Back Home**

1. For studies on the Constitutional Convention and the 1901 Constitution and its impact, see in particular Joseph H. Taylor, "Populism and Disfranchisement in Alabama"; Malcolm Cook McMillan, *Constitutional Development in Alabama, 1798–1901: A Study in Politics, the Negro, and Sectionalism*; Michael Perman, *Struggle for Mastery*, 173–94; Bailey Thomson, ed., *A Century of Controversy: Constitutional Reform in Alabama*; Glenn Feldman, *The Disfranchisement Myth: Poor Whites and Suffrage Restriction in Alabama*.
2. Wayne Flint, "The Aftermath of the 1901 Constitution," in Thomson, ed., *A Century of Controversy*, 36.
3. *Official Proceedings of the Constitutional Convention of the State of Alabama*, May 21, 1901 to September 3, 1901, I, 12, quoted in McMillan, *Constitutional Development*, 303.
4. "The Pity of It."
5. *Official Proceedings* I, 191; McMillan, *Constitutional Development*, 303.
6. "The Pity of It."
7. Several organizations had swindled would-be emigrants out of their money, and the Back to Africa movement lost much credibility. In 1894, four white men founded the International Migration Society, headquartered in Birmingham, as a business venture. Rev. Jeremiah R. McMullen, an African American who was vice president of the African Steamship Company, was its president. The society held a large convention in Birmingham in September, and announced that it would

transport three hundred people from Mobile and New Orleans the following month. South Alabamians were said to be selling their crops in preparation for leaving. Only two trips were organized. The ships *Horsa* and *Laurada* brought 518 migrants to Liberia. See "Direct Communication With Africa Established," 2; "Negroes Will Go To Liberia"; Will M. Clemens, "Negroes Sail for Liberia"; Redkey, *Black Exodus*, 195–7.

8. *Official Proceedings* I, 190, quoted in McMillan, *Constitutional Development*, 303.
9. Montgomery *Advertiser*, June 27, 1901.
10. McMillan, *Constitutional Development*, 352–3.
11. August Meier and Elliott Rudwick, "The Boycott Movement Against Jim Crow Streetcars in the South, 1900–1906." David E. Alsobrook, "The Mobile Streetcar Boycott of 1902: African American Protest or Capitulation?"; Christopher MacGregor Scribner, "Progress Versus Tradition in Mobile, 1900–1920," 167–8.
12. Monroe Nathan Work, *Negro Year Book: An Annual Encyclopedia of the Negro 1925*, 292. The length of the school year was also unequal: 140 days for white children and 110 for blacks. Only Florida, with 147 and 106 respectively, did worse.
13. *The Alabama Negro, 1863–1946*, unpaged.
14. Marriage License, Isaac Green and Sarah Keeby, December 23, 1897; Henry C. Williams, *A History of Mobile County Training School*.
15. Work, *Negro Year Book, 1937–1938*, 211.
16. Hurston, *Barracoon*, 79–81.
17. U.S. Federal Census 1900, Mobile, Ward 1,12B; Hurston, *Barracoon*, 82.
18. *Cudjo Lewis vs. The Louisville and Nashville Railroad Company*. Instructions to Jury. Handwritten note to jury, pages 5 and 6.
19. Circuit Court of Mobile County, Civil Minutes, no. 31, 553–4; Hurston, *Barracoon*, 82–3; *Lewis vs. L&N RR*, Bill of Costs.
20. Claim for fees, Dr. H. P. Hirshfield, Coroner, October 13, 1902, for Peter Lee.
21. U.S. Federal Census 1880, Mobile, Whistler, 46; U.S. Federal Census, 1900, Mobile, Whistler, 8A.
22. Nick Caffey's application for Letters of Administration. Estate of Peter Lee.
23. Hurston, *Barracoon*, 76–7.
24. According to Henry C. Williams, Sr., the shooting was accidental. In this version, Cudjo was involved in a barroom fight, and rolled under a billiard table with his opponent. He was always on top of his adversaries, and Powe shot at the man on the floor. For once, Cudjo was the one at the bottom. Henry C. William, Sr., September 12, 2002.
25. Hurston wrote one page about her inquiry as a potential note. It is not included in the final version. The note is in the handwritten draft of *Barracoon*.
26. Hurston erroneously calls it Hays and locates it in Plateau. Samuel H. Powe remained the minister of Hay Chapel until his death on June 13, 1943, Death Certificate 11907, volume 24.
27. Hurston, *Barracoon*, 78.
28. Ibid., 83.
29. The Supreme Court of Alabama, November Term, 1904. Certificate of Reversal. "Plateau Negro."
30. Pettaway, *Africatown, USA*, 8. As the town grew, other churches were established, such as Yorktown Baptist Church (1884), Hopewell Baptist Church (1901), Little Bethel Baptist Church, and Our Mother of Mercy (Catholic) Church in 1926.
31. Weise, "The Voyage," 6.

32. Pettaway, *Africatown, USA*, 10.
33. Weise, "The Voyage," 17.
34. NAACP, *Thirty Years of Lynching*, 46.
35. "Mob Wounds A Negro."
36. Feldman, "Lynching in Alabama," 126. Most lynchings occurred in the Black Belt. According to Feldman, because whites were so outnumbered by blacks, they "felt the need to overawe" them. In contrast, "In Jefferson and Mobile counties mob violence probably developed from the acute job competition between working-class blacks and whites."
37. Hurston, *Barracoon*, 84–9. According to Henry C. Williams, Sr., Cudjo was said to have tried to hop on the train. September 25, 2002.
38. Hurston, *Barracoon*, 88–9.
39. Ibid., 89.
40. Coroner's bill for $5.40, November 17, 1905. His symptoms point to diphtheria.
41. Hurston, *Barracoon*, 92.
42. Death Certificate, Celie Lewis, November 14, 1908.
43. Roche, *Historic Sketches*, 122–3; Hurston, *Barracoon*, 93.
44. Roche, *Historic Sketches*, 121–2; Hurston, *Barracoon*, 93–4.
45. Land Sale, Hauser to Lewis, April 18, 1887; Cudjo Lewis deed to Eddy W. Cawthon.
46. Aleck died on December 9, 1908.
47. James Saxon Childers, "From Jungle to Slavery and Freedom: Aged Mobile Negro African Native Keeps Church."
48. Hurston, *Barracoon*, 92.
49. Pettaway, *Africatown, USA*, 8; Roche, "Last Survivor."
50. 1930 Federal Census, Whistler and Plateau, Mobile, 4A.
51. Marriage License, Joseph Lewis and Eugenia Davis, January 9, 1890; U.S. Federal Census 1880, Mobile, Kosters, 10.
52. Autrey et al., "Information Compiled."
53. Marriage License, Joseph Lewis and Mary Lewis, December 20, 1916; U.S. Federal Census 1920, Mobile, Whistler, 21A.
54. Autrey et al., "Information Compiled."
55. Marriage License, Alex West and Angeline A. Lewis. July 12, 1917. U.S. Federal Census 1920, Mobile, Whistler, 20A.
56. Roche, *Historic Sketches*, 120–1. Roche made mistakes in the number of survivors and their names. She stated there were three men alive: Pollee, Cudjo, and Oluale (Charlie Lewis.) But she drew the portraits of a fourth one. She called him Olouala and gave his original name as Orsey Kan. The fourth man in fact was Ossa Keeby.
57. "Last Slave Ship Sunk Here Raised."
58. Washington, *The Story of the Negro*, 104; Roche, *Historic Sketches*, 121.
59. Death Certificate, Chamber Wigfall, May 18, 1912, death certificate, Chas Lewis, November 29, 1912.
60. Roche, *Historic Sketches*, 118.
61. Roche mentioned that the person she called Charlee had died in 1914. Charlie Lewis, however, died in 1912. As she misidentified him with Ossa Keeby, there is reason to believe that she was actually referring to Keeby.
62. Will of James Dennison, March 30, 1914.
63. Facsimile of lawyer receipt, Dennison, *Memoirs of James*, 61; Death certificate, James Dennison, October 17, 1915.

64. The insurance company was founded by Rev. T. W. Walker of Shiloh Baptist Church in 1900. Facsimile of receipt book in Dennison, *A Memoir of Lottie*, 50.
65. Facsimile of letter from Commissioner of Bureau of Pension, dated October 30, 1915, in Dennison, *A Memoir of Lottie*, 63.
66. Facsimile of letter from Commissioner of Bureau of Pension, dated December 1, 1915, in Dennison, *A Memoir of Lottie*, 64.
67. Death certificate, Lottie Dennison, April 16, 1917. Facsimile Commissioner Bureau of Pension to Napoleon Dennison, August 9, 1917, in Dennison, *A Memoir of Lottie*, 66.
68. Ibid., 35–6, 41.
69. Death certificate, Katie Cooper, October 10, 1919; U.S. Census Bureau, *Negro Population*, 350.
70. Death certificate, Emmet Lewis, April 9, 1921; death certificate, John Levinston, Jr., November 16, 1923.
71. Death certificate, Polee Allen, August 19, 1922; Sikora, "Groups."
72. Work, *Negro Year Book: 1925–1926*, 385.
73. Kenneth T. Jackson, *The Ku Klux Klan in the City, 1915–1930*, 83.
74. Emmett J. Scott, "Letters of Negro Migrants of 1916–1918," 329, 306.
75. Work, *The Negro Year Book 1937*, 250–1.
76. Marriage License, Henry Lawson and Martha Lewis, July 26, 1899; U.S. Federal Census 1900, Kosters, Mobile, 15A; Kimberly M. Caldwell, "From Africatown to 'Out Stickney': Reminiscences of a Toledo, Ohio African-American Community 1919–1960," 51.
77. George Aspiotes, "Homewood Woman Recalls Growing Up in Africatown."
78. Roche, "Last Survivor."
79. Work, *Negro Year Book 1925*, 362, 370.
80. Land Sale, Cujo Lewis to Thomas Dawson, July 23, 1920. Recorded September 8, 1920; U.S. Federal Census, Whistler, Mobile, 37A; Land Sale, Cujo Lewis to Thomas Dawson, December 20, 1920; Land Sale, Cujo Lewis to Earl Amos Hill, January 12, 1922; U.S. Federal Census, Whistler, Mobile, 19A.
81. Land Sale, Cudjo Lewis to Mobile County, November 24, 1926.
82. Zora Neale Hurston, "Cudjo's Own Story of the Last African Slaver." For an account of the discovery and scope of the plagiarism, see Robert E. Hemenway, *Zora Neale Hurston: A Literary Biography*, 96–8. A document entitled *Voyage of the Clotilda* is held at The Museum of Mobile. It is a version of William Foster's trip narrative, which says nothing of the Africans' own story.
83. On Hurston's 1928 field trip, see Hemenway, *Zora Neale Hurston*, 109–15; Lynda Marion Hill, *Social Rituals and the Verbal Art of Zora Neale Hurston*, 61–73.
84. Handwritten note on back of page in second manuscript of *Barracoon*.
85. The photographer is unknown but is probably not Hurston. Everything she collected was Mason's property and Hurston never published any photograph of Cudjo. A drawing of Lewis, sitting barefoot with a dark suit, is also extant.
86. National Film Preservation Foundation, " Zora Neale Hurston's Fieldwork Footage (1928)." This footage is part of fifteen 16mm short films shot by Hurston during her 1928 trip. Only nine have survived. They were in the Margaret Mead/South Pacific Ethnographic Archives Collection, and were acquired by the Library of Congress in the 1980s.
87. Cudgo Lewis to Charlotte Osgood Mason, September 4, 1930.
88. Hurston to Mason, Maitland, Fla., May 26, 1932.
89. "Cudjoe's Celebration Attracts Large Crowd." If others from the group, outside of Mobile, had survived it is likely that their existence would have come to light.

The woman Zora Neale Hurston met in 1928 was older than Cudjo and may have been dead by 1935.

90. "Celebration for a Former Slave."
91. "Cudjoe's Celebration."
92. Honoring Cudjo Lewis: America's Last Piece of African 'Black Ivory'"; Roche, "Last Survivor."
93. Facsimile of program in John H. Smith, *Africatown, USA: A Pictorial History of Plateau and Magazine Point, Alabama*, 44. Glennon's daughter, Rosemary, wrote a fictional manuscript, "Kudjo," after having met with Cudjo several times. The manuscript has been published by her nephew, Robert M. Glennon, *Kudjo: The Last Slave Voyage to America*.
94. Childers, "From Jungle."
95. Roche, *Historic Sketches*, 124.
96. Clarke, *Travels and Explorations*, 245.
97. Childers, "From Jungle."
98. Ibid.
99. Roche, "Last Survivor."
100. Ibid.
101. Ibid.
102. Death certificate, Cudjo Lewis, July 26, 1935.
103. Roche, *Historic Sketches*, 123.
104. Roy Hoffman, "Search for a Slave Ship." Recollection of Martha West Davis, one of Cudjo's twin great-granddaughters, who was twelve at the time.
105. The only description of Cudjo's funeral was published by journalist Merlin N. Hanson, who stressed he was the only writer present. His article "Burial of the Last Slave" appeared in *Globe*. The Mobile *Press-Forum Weekly* published photographs but did not report on the funeral itself. It only touched on generalities about Cudjo's life.
106. Hanson, "Burial," 57.
107. "Famous Ex-Slave Dies Here With Ambition Unrealized"; "Ex-Slave is Dead at 105"; "Last of U.S. Slaves Born in Africa Is Dead At Mobile," 105.
108. Estate of Cudjoe Lewis, indebted to Mary Lewis, June 30, 1936.
109. Roche, "Last Survivor."
110. Affidavit by Mary Lewis, June 7, 1939; Land Sale, Estate of Cudjo Lewis to J. F. Pate, June 30, 1939; *Mobile City Directory* 1935, 517.
111. Byers, "The Last Slave-Ship," 743; Roche, *Historic Sketches*, 123, 125; Hurston, *Barracoon*, 53.
112. Paraphrase of Luiz Antonio de Oliveira Mendes 1812 comment, "With good reason, then, we may speak of these black Africans, who resist so much and survive so many afflictions, as men of stone and of iron." Quoted in Conrad, *Children*, 22.

Epilogue

1. Richard Lake, "Cudjoe Bust Found in Daphne"; "Bust of Slave Ship Survivor Recovered."
2. Henry C. Williams, Sr., September 23, 2002.
3. Russ Henderson, "Ongoing Disagreement Over Fate of Cudjoe Lewis Bust Flares Up."

4. The settlement was essentially independent and had no municipal service. In the 1920s, a fire devastated three blocks and could not be contained with only water from the wells and a few buckets. The residents organized themselves to ask for services but it was only in 1945 that they gave a structure to their movement by forming the Plateau Community Civic Association. They first approached the mayor of Prichard, hoping to be incorporated into the city; when their effort failed, they turned to Mobile. A referendum was held, and African Town (Plateau and Magazine Point) was finally annexed to Mobile. See John H. Smith, *Africatown, U.S.A.: A Pictorial History of Plateau and Magazine Point, Alabama*, 40.
5. Smith, *Africatown*, 48.
6. Diane Freeman, "Mobile Given Plaque Honoring Noted Slave."
7. Kendal Weaver, "Last Slave Ship to America Docked in Mobile."
8. Sikora, "Groups"; Cammie East, "Africatown Works Toward Its Future, Honors Its Past."
9. "AMPART Examines Twinning of Cities."
10. Carnell E. Davis, "Looking Back at Africatown."
11. Ron Colquitt, "Story of Clotilde Slaves Told as Mobile Arrival re-Enacted"; Barbara Drummond, "Scuttling of Clotilde Re-Enacted."
12. Bill S. 345 introduced by Senator Howell Heflin, and bill H.R. 1246 by Representative Jack Edwards ; Randy Quarles, "'AfricaTown' Bill is Offered."
13. Scott Paper has since closed. Garry Mitchell, "Firms Fear Designation of Historic Slavery Area"; Maslow, "Africatown," 14.
14. Roy Hoffman, "Search For a Slave Ship."
15. HB682, by Representatives Clark and Ford (J) RFD Boards and Commissions, May 6, 2003.
16. "AfricaTown, USA."
17. Henry Willett, "Mobile Community Holds On to Unique African Heritage."
18. Maslow, "Africatown," 14.
19. Hoffman, "Search for a Slave Ship."
20. "Slavery, Clotilda in 1860."
21. "Last Slave Ship Sunk."
22. Roy Hoffman, "Mobile's Infamous Slave Ship: Voyage of the Clotilda."
23. Ibid. Along with the piece of wood comes the 1931 *Literary Digest* article, and a photograph of what is said to be Cudjo's old house.
24. *Mobile City Directory* (1935), 401.
25. Casandra Andrews, "Descendants of Clotilde Survivor Heading Here by the Hundreds"; Patricia Keeby Howard, June 27, 2006.
26. Autrey, et al., "Information Compiled."
27. B. L. Johnson, "Lewis Quarters: Original Africatown Settlement"; Lorna Woods, February 28, 2006.
28. Dr. Dorothy Ford, February 26, 2006.
29. George Aspiotes, "Homewood Woman Recalls Growing Up in Africatown."
30. Maslow, "Africatown," 14.
31. Mable Dennison, February 26, 2006.
32. Matt Irvin, "Descendents of Settlers Stress Africatown's Place in History."
33. In February 2006, PBS aired a four-hour documentary, *African American Lives*, during which celebrities such as Oprah Winfrey, scholar Henry Louis Gates, Jr., Whoopi Goldberg, and Chris Tucker were tested and their DNA "matched" to various African populations. It is estimated that more than 100,000 African Americans have used DNA to trace their ancestry back to Africa. However, the sample

African populations are very small, and many geneticists have warned that it is not possible yet to link African Americans to specific ethnic groups in Africa.

34. February 22, 2004, Union Baptist Church.

Appendix

1. Wish, "The Revival," 582.
2. W. E. B. Du Bois, "Enforcement of the Slave-Trade Laws," American Historical Association *Annual Report* (1891), 173 quoted in Lewis C. Gray, *History of Agriculture in the Southern United States to 1860*, 2, 649–50; Winfield H. Collins, *The Domestic Slave Trade of the Southern States*, 16.
3. Noel Deerr, *History of Sugar*, vol. 2, 284.
4. Don E. Fehrenbacher, *The Slaveholding Republic*, 200–204.
5. Philip D. Curtin, *The Atlantic Slave Trade: A Census*, 72–5, 234.
6. David Eltis, *Economic Growth and the Ending of the Transatlantic Slave Trade*, 249; David Eltis, "The Nineteenth-Century Transatlantic Slave Trade: An Annual Time Series of Imports into the Americas Broken Down by Region," 136.
7. Gwendolyn Midlo Hall, *Slavery and African Ethnicities in the Americas*, 76–9.
8. According to *The Statistics of the Population of the United States Compiled from the Original Returns of the Ninth Census* (336), the number of Africans in 1870 was 1,984. Contemporary electronic transcriptions of that census give slightly different results. Ancestry.com's count is 1,690 while Heritage Quest in its *World Migration Series, African Americans in the 1870 Census* puts the number at 1,768. It is interesting to note that although almost everyone gave their country of birth as a generic Africa, twelve people specified Congo, thirty-four Guinea (including four Upper Guinea), two Madagascar and one Zanzibar. Those who mentioned Liberia were generally returnees, born after emancipation. When the 1880 census returns are added, the precise origins given to the census takers by Africans are: Guinea, forty-nine (largest concentrations in Louisiana, fifteen and Georgia, nine); Congo, seventeen (Louisiana, seven, Texas, six); Madagascar, five (five different states). What Guinea exactly represented for each individual is difficult to ascertain, since the name was given to a wide stretch of land. However, the twenty-four men and women from Louisiana and Georgia who identified their birthplace as Guinea may have meant the area just east of Senegambia, what is roughly Guinea today since numerous people from that particular zone are known to have been transported to these two states. Strangely, a Louise Congo from Saint James Parish, Louisiana, stated to the census taker in 1880 that she came from Guinea, Africa.
9. *Negro Population in the United States*, 18.
10. Warren S. Howard, *American Slavers and the Federal Law, 1837–1862*, 303 n.22.
11. Compiled from 1870 census.

An Essay on Sources

1. "News of the Week"; "The Slaver Wanderer—Recollections of Her Expedition—The Captured Africans Ask to be Returned to their Native Land." In addition to having the Africans arrive on the *Wanderer*, the second article also confuses that ship with the *Echo*. "Meeting of the New York Colonization Society. December 19, 1870."

2. "Applications," 39.

3. Henry Romeyn, "Little Africa," 14–17; also published as "Little Africa" in *The Times Democrat*.

5. Byers, "The Last Slave Ship."

6. Washington, *The Story of the Negro*, 103–4; "Negro Four Years Hence."

7. Roche, *Historic Sketches*. The book was written sometime before the end of 1912, as she sketched and photographed Charlie Lewis, who died on November 29.

8. Roche, "Last Survivor."

9. One early version of this tale was published in 1959 in "Ceremony Honors Cudjoe Lewis." It read, the "captain set fire to the ship and she burned to the water's edge. Meanwhile most of the Africans managed to reach the shore and they disappeared into the swamps area. . . . With the war between the States breaking out soon afterward, they were left pretty much to themselves."

10. As her letters indicate, Hurston was in Mobile from June to the end of July 1928, when she left for New Orleans, Kaplan, ed., *Zora Neale Hurston*.

11. Robert E. Hemenway, *Zora Neale Hurston*, 100–101.

12. She quotes Richard Francis Burton, *A Mission to Gelele*; Theophilus Conneau, *A Slaver's Log Book*; Frederick Edwyn Forbes, *Dahomey and the Dahomans*; and informants from the Gold Coast and Nigeria.

13. Hurston, "The Last Slave Ship"; *Dust Tracks*, 201.

14. Hurston, *Barracoon*, 47; "The Last Slave Ship," 353.

15. Hurston, "Cudjo's Own Story," 649; *Barracoon*, handwritten note; "The Last Slave Ship," 351; *Dust Tracks*, 201.

16. Hurston, "The Last Slave Ship," 356.

17. Hurston to Langston Hughes, in Kaplan, ed., *Zora Neale Hurston*, 123.

18. Foster, *Last Slaver*.

19. Ely Creek to the editor of the *Glasgow Weekly Herald*.

20. George Howe, M.D., "The Last Slave-ship," 113–28.

21. "Slavery, Clotilda in 1860." Donaldson, who seems to have been at the center of the affair, sent a letter to an acquaintance, William Woodberry in Boston, asking questions about dates and other issues. Some responses were found at the State Library, and Woodberry responded to Donaldson in October. The reason why Boston had become part of the story may be because George Howe, M.D., was living in Massachusetts. See U.S. Federal Census 1880, Framingham, Middlesex, Massachusetts, 229.

22. Augustine Meaher to G. Donaldson.

23. "Last Cargo of Slaves"; "The Last Slaver." There was a mistake on the date of the voyage: readers were informed that it had taken place in 1861.

24. "Capt. Tim Meaher's Sketch of His River History."

25. Howe, "The Last Slave-ship," 128.

Bibliography

PRIMARY SOURCES

Archival Material

POLLEE AND ROSE ALLEN

Naturalization Records, October 24, 1868. City Court Minutes, 8, 47. State of Alabama, City Court of Mobile.

Land Sale, Meaher to Allen. October 21, 1872. Deed Book 30, 643. Mobile County Probate Court.

Marriage License, Polle Alen [sic] and Rosa Allen, Mobile, March 15, 1880. CML 6, 438. Mobile County Probate Court.

Death Certificate, Polee Allen, August 17, 1922. Alabama Center for Health Statistics, Montgomery.

BUREAU OF REFUGEES, FREEDMEN, AND ABANDONED LANDS

Wager Swayne to Colonel George D. Robinson, Superintendent of the District of Mobile, Montgomery. September 18, 1865. Letters Received, Records of the Field Offices for the State of Alabama, Bureau of Refugees, Freedmen, and Abandoned Lands, 1865–1872. National Archives and Records Administration.

J. D. Kinnay to Captain L. J. Whiting. Montgomery May 22, 1866. Letters Received, Mobile Bureau, Records of the Field Offices for the State of Alabama, Bureau of Refugees, Freedmen, and Abandoned Lands, 1865–1872. National Archives and Records Administration.

S. Moore to George H. Tracy, Eastern Shore, Baldwin. April 17, 1867. Letters Received, Mobile Bureau, Records of he Field Offices for the State of Alabama, Bureau of Refugees, Freedmen, and Abandoned Lands, 1865–1872. National Archives and Records Administration.

James Gillette to William Coppinger. Mobile, December 26, 1867. Letters Sent, Records of the Field Offices for the State of Alabama, Bureau of Refugees, Freedmen, and Abandoned Lands, 1865–1872. National Archives and Records Administration.

CLOTILDA

Registration of Clotilda, April 19, 1855. National Archives and Records Administration, Southeast Region (Atlanta). RG 36 U. S. Customs Service, Collector of Customs.

Alphabetical List of Sender—Attorney General—Register of Letters Received, 1809–1863. Vol. A. LOC 230/01/30/01. National Archives and Records Administration. Washington, D.C.

G 4597—C. M. Goldbold, U.S. Marshal Southern District to Attorney General Jeremiah S. Black, Reporting the arrival of the schooner Clotilde with African slaves on board.

S 4600—Sanford, Collector to Jeremiah S. Black, Rel. to the schooner "Clotilde" and Africans introduced by her.

L 4606—Lewis S. Lude Acting District Attorney to J. S. Black, Writ of habeas corpus issued for the seizure of negroes imported into Alabama.

S 4593—Sanford, Collector to Howell Cobb, Secretary of Treasury, Rel. to recent importation of negroes into Alabama.

United States vs. John M. Dabney. Case no 2621. RG 21, Records of the District Courts of the United States, Final Record Book for the Southern District of Alabama, 1859–1860 (S-23), 270–4, and Box 46, Mobile, Mixed cases, 1820–1860. National Archives Branch Depository, East Point, Ga.

KATIE (OMOLABI) AND RICHARD COOPER

Marriage License, Katie Thomas and Richard Cooper, June 5, 1872. CML 3, 587. Mobile County Probate Court.

Death Certificate, Katie Cooper, October 10, 1919. Alabama Center for Health Statistics, Montgomery.

JAMES AND LOTTIE (KANKO) DENNISON

Marriage License, James and Lottie Dennison, April 10, 1875. CML 4, 48. Mobile County Probate Court.

Will, James Dennison, March 30, 1914. Book 10, 546. Mobile County Probate Court.

Death Certificate, James Dennison, October 17, 1915. Alabama Center for Health Statistics, Montgomery.

Napoleon Dennison, Petition concerning James Dennison's will, October 25, 1915. Pigeon Hole 85, 17. Mobile County Probate Court.

Death Certificate, Lottie Dennison, April 16, 1917. Alabama Center for Health Statistics, Montgomery.

Napoleon Dennison, Executor, final settlement of James Dennison's estate. March 3, 1917. Mobile County Probate Court.

WILLIAM FOSTER

United States vs. William Foster. Case 2619. National Archives Branch Depository, East Point, Ga., RG 21, Records of the District Courts of the United States, Final Record Book for the Southern District of Alabama, 1859–1860 (S-23), 270–4, and Box 46, Mobile, Mixed cases, 1820–1860.

Naturalization Records, October 22, 1868. City Court Minutes, 8, 42. State of Alabama, City Court of Mobile.

Will, November 8, 1900. Will Book 11, 347–8. Mobile County Probate Court.

Petition for Probate Will, December 5, 1919. Administrative Account Book 131, 485. Mobile County Probate Court.

Probate of William Foster's Will. February 20, 1920. Will Book 11, 348. Mobile County Probate Court.

OSSA AND ANNIE KEEBY

Naturalization Records, October 24, 1868. City Court Minutes, 8, 47. State of Alabama, City Court of Mobile.

Land Sale, Meaher to Kebee, October 28, 1872. Deed Book 30, 655. Mobile County Probate Court.

Marriage License, Arci Kibbe and Annie Kibbe, Mobile March 15, 1880. CML 6, 440. Mobile County Probate Court.

Marriage License, Isaac Green and Sarah Keeby, December 23, 1897. CML 13, 148.

PETER LEE (GUMPA)

Marriage License, Lucy Lee and Luke Winters, April 14, 1880. CML 6, 468. Mobile County Probate Court.

Nick Caffey's application for Letters of Administration. October 2, 1902. Administrative Account 125, 152–3. Mobile County Probate Court.

Nick Caffey's application for Letters of Administration, October 2, 1902. Minute Book 39, 416–7. Mobile County Probate Court.

Nick Caffey's petition, October 2, 1902. Pigeon Hole 199, 11. Mobile County Probate Court.

Estate of Peter Lee. Minute Book 39, 416–7. Mobile County Probate Court.

Dr. H. P. Hirshfield, Coroner, claim for fees, October 13, 1902 for Peter Lee, railroad accident, Three Mile Creek, September 11. Mobile County Probate Court.

ALEXANDER IYADEJEMI LEWIS

Marriage License, Alexander Lewis and Mary Woods, October 8, 1891. CML 10, 781. Mobile County Probate Court.

ANGELINE A. LEWIS

Marriage License, Alex West and Angeline A. Lewis, July 12, 1917. CML, 27, 49. Mobile County Probate Court.

CHARLIE (OLUALE) AND MAGGIE LEWIS

Land Sale, Thomas Buford to Jabez Chase, Horace Ely, Charley Lewis, Maggie Lewis, Matilda Ely, Lucy Wilson, and Polly Shay, April 5, 1870. Deed Book 70, 242–4. Mobile County Probate Court.

Marriage License, Henry Lawson and Martha Lewis, July 26, 1899. CML 13, 671. Mobile County Probate Court.

Death Certificate, Chas Lewis, November 29, 1912. Alabama Center for Health Statistics, Montgomery.

CUDJO (KOSSOLA) AND CELIA (ABILE) LEWIS

Naturalization Records, October 24, 1868. City Court Minutes, 8, 47. State of Alabama, City Court of Mobile.

Land Sale, Wilson to Cujo Lewis, August 3, 1872. Deed Book 30, 601. Mobile County Probate Court.

Marriage License, Cudgo Louis and Cecilia Louis, Mobile, March 15, 1880. CML 6, 439. Mobile County Probate Court.

Land Sale, Hauser to Cudjo Lewis, April 18, 1887. Deed Book 55, 160. Mobile County Probate Court.

Cudjo Lewis vs. The Louisville and Nashville Railroad Company. Subpoena: Jesse Johnson, Henry Doles, Jessie Early, Willie Briggs. December 31, 1902. Mobile County Circuit Court. University of South Alabama Archives.

Cudjo Lewis vs. The Louisville and Nashville Railroad Company. Instructions to Jury. Judge Anderson written in margin. Handwritten note to jury, pages 5 and 6. In folder for Docket no 10154, folder 4097. University of South Alabama Archives.

Cudjo Lewis vs. The Louisville and Nashville Railroad Company. January 14, 1903. Circuit Court of Mobile County. Civil Minutes 31, 533–4. Docket no 10154, folder 4097. University of South Alabama Archives.

Cudjo Lewis vs. The Louisville and Nashville Railroad Company. Bill of Costs. University of South Alabama Archives.

Louisville and Nashville Railroad Company vs. Cudjo Lewis. Certificate of Reversal, November 21, 1904. The Supreme Court of Alabama. University of South Alabama Archives.

Louisville and Nashville Railroad Company vs. Cudjo Lewis. Certificate of Reversal, November 21, 1904. The Supreme Court of Alabama. 141 Ala. 466, 37 So. 587.

Death Certificate, Celie Lewis, November 14, 1908. Alabama Center for Health Statistics, Montgomery.

Cudjo Lewis deed to Eddy W. Cawthon, November 21, 1908. The Museum of Mobile.

Land Sale, Cujo Lewis to Thomas Dawson, September 8, 1920. Deed Book 188, 166. Mobile County Probate Court.

Land Sale, Cujo Lewis to Thomas L. Dawson, December 20, 1920. Deed Book 189, 418. Mobile County Probate Court.

Land Sale, Cujo Lewis to Earl Amos Hill, May 12, 1922. Deed Book 193, 419. Mobile County Probate Court.

Land Sale, Cujo Lewis to Mobile County, December 18, 1926. Deed Book 212, 424. Mobile County Probate Court.

Death Certificate, Cudjo Lewis, July 26, 1935. Alabama Center for Health Statistics, Montgomery.

Affidavit by S. P. Gaillard concerning Cudjo Lewis's property, June 9, 1939. Deed Book 285, 227. Mobile County Probate Court.

Affidavit by Mary Lewis, for claim on Cudjo Lewis's estate, June 7, 1939. Deed Book 285, 228. Mobile County Probate Court.

Affidavit by Thomas L. Dawson concerning Cudjo Lewis's property, June 12, 1939. Deed Book 285, 230. Mobile County Probate Court.

Affidavit by Harry M. Touart concerning Cudjo Lewis's property, June 6, 1939. Deed Book 285, 230. Mobile County Probate Court.

Affidavit by Sidney Lee concerning Cudjo Lewis's property, June 12, 1939. Deed Book 285, 234. Mobile County Probate Court.

Final Sale of Cudjo Lewis's property, June 30, 1939. Deed Book 285, 246. Mobile County Probate Court.

CUDJO FEÏCHITAN LEWIS

Marriage License, Cudjoe B. Lewis and Louisa Thomas, CML12, 579. Mobile County Probate Court.

Claim of Sheriff Charles E. McLean for fees and allowances for January 1900 to the Board of Revenue and Road Commissioners. Mobile County Probate Court.

Claim of Sheriff Charles E. McLean for fees and allowances for February 1900 to the Board of Revenue and Road Commissioners. Mobile County Probate Court.

In the matter of the special venire in the case v. Cudjoe Lewis, Wednesday January 17, 1900. City Court Criminal Minute Book 18 (1899–1902), 112–3. University of South Alabama Archives.

The State of Alabama v. Cudjoe Lewis, Tuesday January 23, 1900. City Court Criminal Minute Book 18 (1899–1902), 118. USA Archives.

The State of Alabama v. Cudjoe Lewis, Saturday February 3, 1900. City Court Criminal Minute Book 18 (1899–1902), 129. USA Archives.

Edward M. Robinson to Joseph F. Johnston, Mobile, July 25th, 1900. Application for pardon or parole for Cudjoe Lewis. Applications for Pardons. Alabama Department of Archives and History.

Petition to Joseph F. Johnston to grant Cudjo Lewis a pardon or parole. Applications for Pardons. Alabama Department of Archives and History.

Jabez J. Parker and Samuel B. Browne to Joseph F. Johnston, Mobile, July 25th, 1900. Pardon or parole for Cudjo Lewis. Applications for Pardons. Alabama Department of Archives and History.

Statement of Sentence. Cudjoe Lewis. Montgomery July 31, 1900. Convict Bureau. State Convict Records. Alabama Department of Archives and History.

Descriptive List and Court History, Cudjoe Lewis. State Convict Records. Alabama Department of Archives and History.

Application for Pardon. Pardon issued August 7, 1900, Robert P. McDavid, Secretary of State. Applications for Pardons. Alabama Department of Archives and History.

Insolvent Convictions March 12, 1900, claim by Sheriff Charles E. McLean to Board of Revenue and Commissioners, Mobile County. Mobile County Probate Court.

JAMES AHNONOTOE LEWIS

Coroner's bill for $5.40, November 17, 1905. Mobile County Probate Court.

JOSEPH LEWIS

Marriage License, Joseph Lewis and Eugenia Davis, January 9, 1890. CML 10, 254. Mobile County Probate Court.

Marriage License, Joseph Lewis and Mary Lewis, December 20, 1916. CML 47, 161. Mobile County Probate Court.

Affidavit of Joe Lewis concerning Cudjo Lewis's property, June 7, 1939. Deed Book 285, 232. Mobile County Probate Court.

ZUMA AND JOHN LIVINGSTON/LEVINSON

Marriage License, John and Zena Livingston. June 16, 1887. CML 9, 1922. Mobile County Probate Court.

Death Certificate, John Levinston Jr. November 16, 1923. Alabama Center for Health Statistics, Montgomery.

JAMES, TIMOTHY, AND BURNS MEAHER

Burns Meaher, Summons 2620, National Archives Branch Depository, East Point, Ga., RG 21, Records of the District Courts of the United States, Records of the District Courts of the United States, Final Record Book for the Southern District of Alabama, 1859–1860 (S-23) pages 1–4, box 46, Mobile, Mixed Cases, 1820–1860.

City Tax Books for J. M. & T. Meaher for property listed Square 313 and Square 336 (Orange Grove), 1860 and 1861. City of Mobile Bureau of Taxes. Mobile Municipal Archives.

Runaway Records. Andrew, ran away from JM & T Meaher. April 12, 1863. Record Book of Runaway Slaves 1 (08/24/1857–03/20/1865), 148. Mobile County Probate Court.

James M. Meaher, Amnesty Oath # 702, August 30, 1865. File 36, 2713. Mobile County Probate Court.

James M. Meaher, Amnesty Oath # 71, September 11, 1868. File 37, 291. Mobile County Probate Court.

Timothy Meaher, Amnesty Oath # 80, September 14, 1868. File 37, 293. Mobile County Probate Court.

Petition of James P. Kinney, Defendants James M. and Timothy Meaher. July 16, 1884. Pigeon Hole 185, 3. Mobile County Probate Court.

Settlement of Timothy Meaher' s Estate. Pigeon Hole 257, 4. Mobile County Probate Court.

JABA AND POLLY SHADE

Land Sale, Thomas Buford to Jabez Chase, Horace Ely, Charley Lewis, Maggie Lewis, Matilda Ely, Lucy Wilson, and Polly Shay. April 5, 1870. Deed Book 70, 242–4. Mobile County Probate Court.

CLARA (ABACHE) AND SAMUEL TURNER

Marriage License, Clara Aunspaugh and Samuel Turner. March 6, 1880. CML 6, 432. Mobile County Probate Court.

SHAMBA AND HAYES WIGFALL

Marriage License, Chamba Donizen and Hales Wigfall. June 29, 1876. CML 5, 172. Mobile County Probate Court.

Death Certificate, Chamber Wigfall. May 18, 1912. Alabama Center for Health Statistics, Montgomery.

UK Parliamentary Papers

Correspondence relating to the Slave Trade, 1 April–31 Dec. 1860.

Class B:

> Inclosure 1 in no.1: Messrs Townsend & others to Consul Brand, Abeokuta, 19 Feb. 1860.
>
> Inclosure 5 in no.1: Rev. H. Townsend to Consul Brand, Abeokuta, 19 Feb. 1860.
>
> Inclosure 17 in no.1: Messrs Townsend & others to Consul Brand, Abeokuta, 27 Feb. 1860.
>
> Inclosure 18, in no.1: Rev. H. Townsend to Consul Brand, Abeokuta, 27 Feb. 1860.
>
> Inclosure 19 in no.1: Rev. E. Bickersteth to Wesleyan Missionary Society, Abeokuta, 28 Feb. 1860.
>
> Inclosure 22 in no.1: Rev. H. Townsend to Consul Brand, Abeokuta, 6 March 1860.
>
> No. 2: Consul Brand to Lord J. Russell, Lagos, 9 April 1860.

Miscellaneous

Ex-Slave Pension Movement. RG15 Ex-Slave Pension Movement, 21A. NARA.

U.S. v. Gould, 25 F. Cas.1375, 8 Am. Law Reg. 525, No. 15, 239 (S. D. Ala.,1860).

Senate Report 75, 56th Congress, 1st session, January 16, 1900, "Pensions for Freedmen, etc. Adverse Report."

City of Mobile Directories—1850–1936.

Freedman's Bank Records, CD-Rom Library, Family History Resource File US Federal.

Slave Schedules—1850, 1860.

U.S. Federal Censuses—1820–1930.

Unpublished Letters and Documents

Anonymous handwritten page n. d. on *Clotilda* and William Foster. Mobile Public Library, Local History and Genealogy.

"Crew of the Clotilda." Undated manuscript giving names of crew members of the *Clotilda*. The Museum of Mobile.

Ely Creek to the editor of the *Glasgow Weekly Herald*. The Museum of Mobile.

Cudjo Lewis to Charlotte Osgood Mason, September 4, 1930. Alain Locke Papers 164–99, Moorland-Spingarn Research Center, Howard University.

Foster, William. "Last Slaver from U.S. to Africa. A.D. 1860." Mobile Public Library, Local History and Genealogy.

Foster to Mr. Donaldson, September 29, 1890. Letter transmitting his account of the voyage of the schooner *Clotilda*. Mobile Public Library, Local History and Genealogy.

Hurston to Mason, Maitland, Fla., May 26, 1932. Alain Locke Papers 164–99. Moorland-Spingarn Research Center, Howard University.

Meaher, Augustine to G. Donaldson, Mobile November 10, 1890. Letter containing names of Africans from the *Clotilda*. Mobile Public Library, Local History and Genealogy.

"Religion of the Dahomans." Undated, unsigned manuscript by contemporary giving original names of twenty-six Africans in Mobile. The Museum of Mobile.

"Slavery, Clotilda in 1860." Mobile Public Library, Local History and Genealogy.

Voyage of the Clotilda. Dated March 4, 1859. Unsigned manuscript. Written in the first person. The Museum of Mobile.

William H. Woodberry to Mr. Donaldson, Boston, October 20, 1890. Mobile Public Library, Local History and Genealogy.

Unpublished Manuscript

Hurston, Zora Neale. *Barracoon*. Unpublished typescripts and handwritten draft, 1931. Alain Locke Collection, Manuscript Department, Moorland-Spingarn Research Center, Howard University.

Film Footage

"Zora Neale Hurston's Fieldwork Footage (1928)." National Film Preservation Foundation, *More Treasures from American Film Archives 1894–1931*.

Books

Ade Ajayi, J. F. "Samuel Ajayi Crowther of Oyo." In *Africa Remembered: Narratives by West Africans From the Era of the Slave Trade*, ed. Philip D. Curtin, 289–316. Madison: The University of Wisconsin Press, 1967.

Aikin, John G. *A Digest of the Laws of the State of Alabama*. Philadelphia: Alexander Towar, 1833.

Alabama. General Assembly Joint Committee Upon the Convict System of Alabama. *Report of the Joint Committee Upon the Convict System*. Montgomery, Ala.: Brown Printing Co., 1901.

Alden, Carroll Storrs. *George Hamilton Perkins, Commodore, U.S.N.: His Life and Letters*. New York: Houghton Mifflin Company, 1914.

Alis, Harry. *Nos Africains*. Paris: Librairie Hachette, 1894.

Astley, Thomas. *A New General Collection Of Voyages And Travels*. London: Printed for T. Astley, 1745–47.

Alvord, John Watson. *First Semi-Annual Report on Schools and Finances of Freedmen, January 1, 1866*. Washington, D.C.: Government Printing Office, 1868.

———. *Second Semi-Annual Report on Schools and Finances of Freedmen, July 1, 1866*. Washington, D.C.: Government Printing Office, 1868.

———. *Fourth Semi-Annual Report on Schools for Freedmen, July 1, 1867*. Washington, D.C.: Government Printing Office, 1867.

———. *Fifth Semi-Annual Report on Schools for Freedmen, January 1, 1868*. Washington, D.C.: Government Printing Office, 1868.

———. *Sixth Semi-Annual Report on Schools for Freedmen, July 1, 1868*. Washington, D.C.: Government Printing Office, 1868.

———. *Seventh Semi-Annual Report on Schools for Freedmen, January 1, 1869*. Washington, D.C.: Government Printing Office, 1869.

———. *Eighth Semi-Annual Report on Schools for Freedmen, July 1, 1869*. Washington, D.C.: Government Printing Office, 1869.

American Anti-Slavery Society. *Annual Report of the American Anti-Slavery Society*. 1855–1859, 1860–1861.

American Anti-Slavery Society. *Slavery and the Internal Slave Trade in the United States of North America*. London: T. Ward, 1841.

Armstrong, Orland Kay. *Old Massa's People: The Old Slaves Tell Their Stories*. Indianapolis: Bobbs-Merrill, 1913.

Avary, Myrta Lockett. *Dixie After the War*. New York: Doubleday, Page & Co., 1906.

Ball, Charles. *Fifty Years in Chains*. 1837. Reprint, New York: Dover Publications, 1970.

Barrister of the Middle Temple. *Extracts from the Evidence Taken Before Committees of the Two Houses of Parliament Relative to the Slave Trade*. 1851. Reprint, New York: Negro University Press, 1969.

Barth, Dr. Henrich. *Travels and Discoveries in North and Central Africa, 1849–1855*. 1859. Reprint, London: Frank Cass & Co. Ltd, 1965.

Blassingame, John. *Slave Testimony: Two Centuries of Letters, Speeches, Interviews, and Autobiographies*. Baton Rouge: Louisiana State University, 1977.

Bodichon, Barbara Leigh Smith. *An American Diary 1857–1858*. Edited by Joseph W. Reed, Jr. London: Routledge and Kegan Paul, 1972.

Boothe, Charles Octavius. *The Cyclopedia of the Colored Baptists of Alabama*. Birmingham: Alabama Publishing Company, 1895.

Bosman, William. *A New and Accurate Description of the Coast of Guinea*. 1705. Reprint, London: Frank Cass, 1967.

Botkin, B. A., ed. *Lay My Burden Down: A Folk History of Slavery*. Chicago: The University of Chicago Press, 1945.

Botume, Elizabeth Hyde. *First Days Amongst the Contrabands*. Boston: Lee and Shepard, 1892.

Bouche, Pierre Bertrand. *La Côte des Esclaves et le Dahomey: sept ans en Afrique occidentale*. Paris: Librairie Plon, 1885.

Boudousquie, Paul C. *Reference Map of Mobile and Vicinity*. New Orleans: T. Fitzwilliams and Co., 1889.

Bowen, Thomas Jefferson. *Adventures and Missionary Labours in Several Countries in the Interior of Africa from 1849 to 1856*. 1857. Reprint, London: Frank Cass & Co. Ltd., 1968.

Brown, James Seay, Jr., ed. *Up Before Daylight: Life Stories from the Alabama Writer's Project, 1938–1939*. University: University of Alabama Press, 1982.

Buckingham, James Silk. *The Slave States of America*, 2 vol. London: Fisher, Son & Co. 1842.

Bureau of the Census. *Negro Population in the United States, 1790–1915*. Washington, D.C., 1918.

Burton, Richard Francis. *A Mission to Gelele, King of Dahome*. London: Tylston and Edwards, 1863.

———. *Wanderings in West Africa*. 1863. Reprint, New York: Dover Publications, Inc., 1991.

Cable, George Washington. *The Silent South Together With The Freedman's Case in Equity And The Convict Lease System*. New York: Charles Scribner's Sons, 1885.

Ca' da Mosto, Alvise. *Voyages en Afrique noire d'Alvise Ca' da Mosto (1455 et 1456)*. Paris: Editions Chandeigne/Unesco, 1994.

Civis. *The Public School in Its Relations to the Negro*. Richmond: Clemmit & Jones, 1877.

Clapperton, Hugh. *Journal of a Second Expedition into the Interior of Africa*. 1829. Reprint, London: F. Cass, 1966.

Clarke, Lewis G. *Narrative of the Sufferings of Lewis Clarke*. Boston: David H. Ela, Printer, 1845.

Clarke, William. *Travels and Explorations in Yorubaland, 1854–1858*. Ibadan: Ibadan University Press, 1972.

Conneau, Captain Theophilus. *A Slaver's Log Book or 20 Years' Residence in Africa*. 1854. Reprint, Englewood Cliffs, N.J.: Prentice-Hall, 1976.

Conrad, Robert Edgar. *Children of God's Fire: A Documentary History of Black Slavery in Brazil*. University Park: The Pennsylvania State University Press, 1984.

———. *In the Hands of Strangers: Readings on Foreign and Domestic Slave Trading and the Crisis of the Union*. University Park: The Pennsylvania State University Press, 2001.

Cugoano, Ottobah. "Narrative of the Enslavement of Ottobah Cugoano, a Native of Africa; Published by Himself in the Year 1787." In Thomas Fisher, *The Negro's Memorial; or, Abolitionist's Catechism; by an Abolitionist*, 120–7. London: Printed for the Author and Sold by Hatchard and Co., 1825.

———. *Thoughts and Sentiments on the Evil of Slavery and Other Writings*. 1787. Reprint, London: Penguin Books, 1999.

Curtin, Philip D. "Ayuba Suleiman Diallo of Bondu." In *Africa Remembered: Narratives by West Africans From the Era of the Slave Trade*, 17–59, ed. Philip D. Curtin. Madison: The University of Wisconsin Press, 1967.

Davis, Robert Ralph, Jr. "Buchanian Espionage: A Report on Illegal Slave Trading in the South in 1859." *The Journal of Southern History* 37, 2 (May 1971): 271–8.

Dean, Captain Harry. *Umbala: The Adventures of a Negro Sea-Captain in Africa and on the Seven Seas in his Attempts to Found an Ethiopian Empire*. 1929. Reprint, London: Pluto Press, 1989.

Delany, Martin Robison. *Blake or The Huts of America*. 1861. Reprint, Boston: Beacon Press, 1970.

Dennett, John Richard. *The South As It Is: 1865–1866*. Henry M. Christman, ed. Athens: The University of Georgia Press, 1986.

Deschamps, Hubert, ed. *L'Afrique occidentale en 1818 vue par un explorateur français Gaspard Theodore Mollien*. Paris: Calmann-Levy, 1967.

Documents of the First Session of the Fourth Legislature of the State of Louisiana. "Report of the Special Committee on the Importation of Free Black Laborers Within the State." Baton Rouge, 1858, no XLIV.

Douglass, Frederick. *Life and Times of Frederick Douglass by Himself*. Boston: De Wolfe, Fiske, 1895.

———. *My Bondage and My Freedom*. New York and Auburn: Miller, Orton & Mulligan, 1855.

Du Bois, W. E. B., ed. *Some Notes on Negro Crime Particularly in Georgia*. Atlanta, Ga.: The Atlanta University Press, 1904.

Dunbar, Rowland, ed. *Jefferson Davis, Constitutionalist, His Letters, Papers, and Speeches*. Jackson: Printed for the Mississippi Dept. of Archives and History, 1923.

Duncan, John. *Travels in Western Africa in 1845 & 1846, Comprising a Journey from Whydah, Through the Kingdom of Dahomey to Adofoodia*. London: Richard Bentley, 1847.

Dutertre, Révérend Père Jean Baptiste. *Histoire naturelle des Antilles habitées par les François*. 1677, 2 vol. Reprint, Saint Pierre, Martinique: Durieu et Leyritz, 1868–1869.

Eliot, T. D. *Report of Hon. T.D. Eliot, chairman of the Committee on Freedmen's Affairs to the House of Representatives, March 10, 1868*. Washington, D.C.: GPO, 1868.

Ellis, A. B. *The Yoruba-Speaking Peoples of the Slave Coast of West Africa, Their Religion, Manners, Customs, Laws, Language, Etc. 1894*. Reprint, Chicago: Benin Press, Ltd., 1964.

Equiano, Olaudah. *The Interesting Narrative of Olaudah Equiano: Or, Gustavus Vassa, the African / written by himself*. London: Printed for and sold by the author, 1793.

Extracts from the evidence delivered before a Select Committee of the House of Commons, in the years 1790 and 1791. London: Wayland, 1791.

Falconbridge, Alexander. *An Account of the Slave Trade on the Coast of Africa*. London, 1788.

Featherstonhaugh, George W. *Excursion Through the Slave States*. New York: Harper & Brothers, 1844.

Fleming, Walter L. *Documentary History of Reconstruction*. New York: McGraw-Hill, 1966.

Fletcher, James, and D. P. Kidder. *Brazil and the Brazilians Portrayed in Historical and Descriptive Sketches*. Boston: Little Brown Boston, 1866.

Foà, Edouard. *LeDahomey: Histoire, géographie, moeurs, coutumes, commerce, industrie, expéditions françaises (1891–1894)*. Paris: A. Hennuyer, 1895.

Fonssagrives, Jean. *Notice sur le Dahomey. Publiée à l'occasion de l'Exposition universelle*. Paris: Imprimerie Alcan-Levy, 1900.

Forbes, Frederick Edwyn. *Dahomey and the Dahomans: Being the journals of two missions to the king of Dahomey, and residence at his capital, in the year 1849 and 1850*. London: Longman, Brown, Green, and Longmans, 1851.

Fourth Biennial Report of the Board of Inspectors of Convicts to the Governor From September 1, 1901 to August 31, 1902. Montgomery: Brown, 1902.

Fox, William. *A Brief History of the Wesleyan Missions on the West Coast of Africa*. London: Aylott and Jones, 1851.

Fulbert-Dumonteil. *Jardin Zoologique d'acclimatation, Guerriers dahoméens*. Paris, 1891.

Fuller, Hiram. *Belle Brittan on a Tour, at Newport, and Here and There*. New York: Derby & Jackson, 1858.

Gollmer, Charles Henry Vidal. *Charles Andrew Gollmer: His Life and Missionary Labours in West Africa Compiled From His Journals and the Church Missionary Society's Publications*. London: Hodder and Stoughton, 1889.

Griffith, Lucille. *Alabama: A Documentary History to 1900*. University: University of Alabama Press, 1968.

———. *History of Alabama, 1540–1900 as Recorded in Diaries, Letters, and Papers of the Times*. Northport, Ala.: Colonial Press, 1962.

Harlan, Louis R., ed. *The Booker T. Washington Papers*, 14 vol. Urbana: University of Illinois Press, 1972.

Hayne, Isaac W. *Argument Before the United States Circuit Court by Isaac W. Hayne, esq., on the Motion to Discharge the Crew of the Echo. Delivered in Columbia, S.C., December, 1858*. Albany, N.Y.: Weed, Parsons, 1859.

Helper, Hinton Rowan. *The Impeding Crisis of the South: How to Meet It*. New York: Burdick Brothers, 1857.

Hepworth, George H. *The Whip, Hoe, and Sword, or the Gulf-Department in '63*. Boston: Walker, Wise and Co., 1864.

Holt, Thad Jr., ed. *Miss Waring's Journal: 1863 and 1865. Being the Diary of Miss Mary Waring of Mobile, During the Final Days of the War Between the States*. Chicago: The Wyvern Press of S.F.E. Inc., 1964.

Howard, Oliver O. *Autobiography of Oliver Otis Howard, Major General, United States Army*, 2 vol. New York: The Baker & Taylor Company, 1907.

Hungerford, James. *The Old Plantation and What I Gathered There in an Autumn Month* [of 1832]. New York: Harper & Brothers, 1859.

Hurston, Zora Neale. *Dust Tracks On A Road: An Autobiography*. Philadelphia: J. B. Lippincott Co., 1942.

Isert, Paul Erdmann. *Letters on West Africa and the Slave Trade: Paul Erdmann Isert's Journey to Guinea and the Caribbean Islands in Columbia*.1788. Reprint, New York: Oxford University Press, 1992.

Josselyn, John. *An Account of Two Voyages to New England Made During the Years 1638, 1663*. 1675. Reprint, Boston: W. Veazie, 1865.

Kaplan, Carla, ed. *Zora Neale Hurston: A Life in Letters*. New York: Doubleday, 2002.

Korson, George Gershon. *Coal Dust on the Fiddle: Songs and Stories of the Bituminous Industry*. 1943. Reprint Hatboro, Pa.: Folklore Associates, 1965.

Labat, Jean Baptiste. *Voyage du Chevalier Des Marchais en Guinée, isles voisines, et a Cayenne, fait en 1725, 1726 & 1727*, 4 vol. Amsterdam, aux dépens de la Compagnie, 1731.

Lambert, Sheila. *House of Commons Sessional Papers of the Eighteenth Century*. Wilmington, Del.: Scholarly Resources, 1975–76, vol. 68 to 73.

Lanman, Charles. *Adventures in the Wilds of America*. 2 vol. Philadelphia: J. W. Moore, 1858.

Lloyd, P. C. "Osifekunde of Ijebu." In *Africa Remembered: Narratives by West Africans From the Era of the Slave Trade*, 217–288, ed. Philip D. Curtin. Madison: The University of Wisconsin Press, 1967.

Long, John Dixon. *Pictures of Slavery in Church and State*. Philadelphia: The Author, 1857.

Lovejoy, Paul E., and Robin Law, eds. *The Biography of Mahommah Gardo Baquaqua: His Passage From Slavery to Freedom in Africa and America*. Princeton: Markus Wiener Publishers, 2001.

Lyell, Sir Charles. *A Second Visit to the United States of North America*. London: J. Murray, 1849.

Madden, Richard. *A Twelve Month's Residence in the West Indies*. Philadelphia: Carey, Lea & Blanchard, 1835.

Mandirola, Renzo, ed. *Journal de Francesco Borghero, premier missionnaire du Dahomey (1861–1865): Sa vie, son Journal (1860–1864), la Relation de 1863*. Paris: Karthala, 1997.

Mellon, James, ed. *Bullwhip Days: The Slaves Remember*. New York: Avon Books, 1988.

Michel, François. *La campagne du Dahomey, 1893–1894: la reddition de Béhanzin: correspondance d'un commissaire des colonies présentée par son petit-neveu/ François Michel*. Paris: L'Harmattan, 2001.

Moore, Francis. *Travels in the Inland Parts of Africa*. London: Edward Cave, 1738.

Moore, Samuel. *Biography of Mahommah G. Baquaqua, a Native of Zoogoo in the Interior of Africa*. Detroit: Geo. E. Pomeroy and Co., 1834.

Moreau de Saint-Mery, Mederic Louis Elie. *Description topographique, physique, civile, politique et historique de la partie française de l'isle Saint Domingue*. 1797. Reprint, Paris: Société de l'histoire des colonies françaises, 1958.

National Park Service. *Civil War and Sailors System*. www.itd.nps.gov/ewss/soldiers.htm. Accessed March 16, 2006.

Newton, John. *The Journal of a Slave Trader 1750–1754*. 1788. Reprint, London: Epworth Press, 1962.

Official Proceedings of the Constitutional Convention of the State of Alabama, May 21, 1901 to September 3, 1901. Montgomery: Brown, 1901.

Olmsted, Frederick Law. *A Journey in the Seaboard Slave States; With Remarks on Their Economy*. New York; London: Dix and Edwards; Sampson Low, Son & Co., 1856.

Ormond, John J., Arthur P. Bagby, and George Goldthwaite. *The Code of Alabama*. Montgomery: Britan and De Wolf, 1852.

Owland, Dunbar, ed. *Jefferson Davis, Constitutionalist, His Letters, Papers, and Speeches*. Jackson: Printed for the Mississippi Dept. of Archives and History, 1923.

Palfrey, John G. *The Inter-State Slave Trade*. New York: American Anti-Slavery Society, 1855.

Pennington, James W. C. *A Narrative of Events in the Life of J. H. Banks, an Escaped Slave, from the Cotton State, Alabama, in America*. Liverpool, Eng.: M. Rourke, Printer, 1861.

Poirier, Jules. *Campagne du Dahomey, 1892–1894: précédée d'une étude géographique et historique sur ce pays*. Paris: H. Charles-Lavauzelle, 1895.

Pollard, Edward Alfred. *A New Southern Policy: The Slave Trade as Meaning Union and Conservatism*. Macon?: 185?.

Rawick, George P., ed. *The American Slave: A Composite Autobiography*. 17 vol. Westport, Conn.: Greenwood Publishing Co., 1977.

———. *The American Slave: A Composite Autobiography*, Supplement, Series 1, volume 1, Alabama Narratives. Wesport, Conn.: Greenwood Press, 1977.

Reid, Whitelaw. *After the War, a Southern Tour: May 1, 1865 to May 1, 1866*. London: Sampson Low, Son & Marston, 1866.

Religious Society of Friends. *An Exposition of the African Slave Trade from the Year 1840 to 1850, Inclusive*. Philadelphia: J. Rakestraw, Printer, 1851.

Report of the Joint Committee of the General Assembly of Alabama Upon the Convict System of Alabama. Montgomery, Ala.: Brown Printing Co., Printers & Binders, 1901.

Report of the Trials in the Echo Cases, in Federal Court, Charleston, S.C., April, 1859. Columbia: R. W. Gibbes, 1859.

Robinson, Charles Henry. *Nigeria, Our Latest Protectorate*. London: H. Marshall and Son, 1900.

Roche, Emma Langdon. *Historic Sketches of the South*. New York: Knickerbocker Press, 1914.

Russell, William Howard, Sir. *My Diary, North and South*. Boston: T.O.H.P. Burnham, 1863.

Said, Nicholas. *The Autobiography of Nicolas Said, a native of Bornu*. Memphis: Shotwell, 1873.

Scarborough, William Kauffman, ed. *The Diary of Edmund Ruffin*, 3 vol. Baton Rouge: Louisiana State University Press, 1972–89.

Schurz, Carl. *Report on the Condition of the South*. 1859. Reprint, New York: Arno Press and *The New York Times*, 1969.

Second Biennial Report of the Board of Inspectors of Convicts, 1896–1898. Montgomery: State Printer, 1898.

Skertchly, J. Alfred. *Dahomey As It Is: Being a Narrative of Eight Month's Residence in That Country, With a Full Account of the Notorious Annual Customs, and the Social and Religious Institutions of the Fons*. London: Chapman and Hall, 1874.

Smith, H. F. C. D. M. Last, and Gambio Gubio. "Ali Eisami Gazirmabe of Bornu." In *Africa Remembered: Narratives by West Africans From the Era of the Slave Trade*, 199–216, ed. Philip D. Curtin. Madison: The University of Wisconsin Press, 1967.

Smith, Venture. *A Narrative of the Life and Adventures of Venture a Native of Africa: But Resident above Sixty Years in the United States of America, Related by Himself*. New-London, Conn.: A Descendant of Venture, 1835.

Snelgrave, William. *A New Account of Some Parts of Guinea and the Slave-Trade*. 1734. Reprint, London: Frank Cass, 1971.

Spratt, Leonidas W. *The Foreign Slave Trade: The Source of Political Power, of Material Progress, of Social Integrity, and of Social Emancipation to the South*. Charleston: Walker, Evans & Co., 1858.

Sterling, Dorothy, ed. *The Trouble They Seen: The Story of Reconstruction in the Words of African Americans*. New York: Da Capo, 1994.

Stroyer, Jacob. *My Life in the South*. Salem: Newcomb & Gauss, 1898.

The Royal African: Or Memoirs of the Young Prince of Annamaboe. London: W. Reeves, 1720.

Third Biennial Report of the Board of Inspectors of Convicts to the Governor From September 1, 1898 to August 31, 1900. Montgomery: Roemer, 1900.

Thirty-Eighth Congress, 2nd session. *Acts and Resolutions*. Washington, D.C., March 3, 1865.

Told, Silas. *The Life of Mr. Silas Told*. London, 1796.

Torrey, Jesse. *American Slave Trade; Or, An Account Of The Manner In Which The Slave Dealers Take Free People From Some Of The United States Of America, And Carry Them Away*. 1822. Reprint, Conn.: Negro Universities Press, 1971.

Turnbull, David. *Travels in the West with Notices of Porto Rico, and the Slave Trade*. London: Longman, Orne, Brown, Green, and Longmans, 1840.

United States Congress. House Select Committee on Affairs in Alabama. (43d Congress, 2nd Session) Report no. 262. *Affairs in Alabama*, 3 vol. Washington, D.C.: GPO, 1875.

United States Department of the Interior. *The Statistics of the Population of the United States Compiled from the Original Returns of the Ninth Census*. Washington, D.C.: GPO, 1872.

United States, Naval War Record Office and United States Office of Naval Records and Library. *Official Records of the Union and Confederate Navies in the War of the Rebellion, Series 1, vol. 20: West Gulf Blockading Squadron (March 15, 1863–December 31, 1863)*. Washington, D.C.: GPO, 1905.

———. *Official Records of the Union and Confederate Navies in the War of the Rebellion, Series 1, vol. 21: West Gulf Blockading Squadron (January 1, 1864–December 31, 1864)*. Washington, D.C.: GPO, 1906.

———. *Official Records of the Union and Confederate Navies in the War of the Rebellion. Series 1, vol. 22: West Gulf Blockading Squadron (January 1, 1865–January 31, 1866); Naval Forces on Western Waters (May 8, 1861–April 11, 1862)*. Washington, D.C.: GPO, 1908.

United States. War Department. *Bounties of Colored Soldiers*. Washington, D.C., 1868?

United States. War Dept. United States. Record and Pension Office. United States. War Records Office. *The War of the Rebellion: A Compilation of the Official Records of the Union and Confederate Armies. Series 1—vol. 48 (Part I)*. Washington, D.C.: GPO, 1896.

Vaughan, Walter R. *Vaughan's "Freedmen's Pension Bill."* Omaha, Neb.: Walter R. Vaughan, 1891.

Wadstom, Carl Bernhardt. *An Essay On Colonization*. London: Darton & Harvey, 1794.

Washington, Booker T. *The Story of the Negro: The Rise of the Race from Slavery*. 1909. Reprint, New York: Peter Smith, 1940.

Weld, Theodore D., ed. *American Slavery As It Is: Testimony of a Thousand Witnesses*. New York: American Anti-Slavery Society, 1839.

Wilks, Ivor. "Salih Bilali of Massina." In *Africa Remembered: Narratives by West Africans From the Era of the Slave Trade*, 145–51, ed. Philip D. Curtin. Madison: The University of Wisconsin Press, 1967.

Williams, James. *Narrative of James Williams, an American Slave*. Boston: Isaac Knapp, 1838.

Zincke, F. Barham. *Last Winter in the United States*. 1868. Reprint, Freeport, NY: Books for Library Press, 1970.

Articles

"The African Apprentice System." From the Augusta, Georgia *Constitutionalist* in *The Pittsfield Sun* (Massachusetts), May, 20, 1858.

"The African Slave Trade." *The National Era*, November 9, 1848.

"The African Slave Trade." *Provincial Freeman*, August 5, 1854.

"The African Slave-Trade." *The New York Times*, June 28, 1856.

"The African Slave-Trade: Extent of the Traffic." *The New York Times*, November 17, 1862.

"African Slave Trade in Texas." *The North Star*, July 13, 1849.

"The African Slave-Trade: New Parties Arrested." *The New York Times*, June 28, 1856.

"Africans Arrived." Macon *Daily Telegraph*, July 11, 1860.

"The Africans of the Slave Bark Wildfire." *Harper's Weekly*, June 2, 1860.

"'AfricaTown' Bill is Offered," *Mobile Press Register*, January ?, 1983. Mobile Public Library, Local History and Genealogy.

"Alabama Ends Convict Leasing." *The New York Times*, July 1, 1928.

"Alabama Gives Up Leasing Convicts." *The New York Times*, July 1, 1928.

"American Slave Trade Ended at Mobile in 1859 History Class is Informed." *The Springhillian*. December 18, 1836.

"AMPART Examines Twinning of Cities." *USIA World*, April 1982.

"A Nut for the Abolitionists." *Harper's Weekly*, September 8, 1860.

Andrews, Casandra. "Descendants of Clotilde Survivor Heading Here by the Hundreds." *Mobile Press Register*, August 13, 1998.

"A Pension Fraud Exposed." *The New York Times*, January 21, 1900.

"Applications." *The African Repository* 47, 2 (February 1871): 38–40.

"Approves Mr. Hanna's Bill. Ex-Slave Holder Says the Negroes Should be Pensioned." *The New York Times*, February 8, 1903.

"Arrival of Gunboat Massachusetts." *The New York Times*, February 15, 1862.

"Arrival of the Pony Express." *The Weekly San Joaquin Republican*, July 28, 1860.

Aspiotes, George. "Homewood Woman Recalls Growing Up in Africatown." *Pittsburgh Tribune Review*, February 9, 2003.

"The Brig Gen. Pierce Captured by a Portuguese Man-of-War." *The New York Times*, June 28,1856.

"Bust of Slave Ship Survivor Recovered." Reuters, January 23, 2002.

"Capt. Luck Wainwright Talks of His Steamboat Experience." *Clarke County Democrat*, May 22, 1890.

"Capt. Owen Finnegan Writes of His River History." *Clarke County Democrat*, June 19, 1890.

"Capt. Tim Meaher's Sketch of His River History." *Clarke County Democrat*, June 12, 1890.

"Capt. WM. Foster Commander of Last American Slave Vessel Buried Yesterday." *Prichard Herald*. February ?, 1901. University of South Alabama Archives, Mobile.

"Capture of the Slave-Ship Erie." *The New York Times*, October 4, 1860.

"The Case of Gordon." *The New York Times*, February 21, 1862.

"Case of the Slaver Erie." *The New York Times*, June 21, 1861.

"The Case of the 'Wanderer.'" *Staunton Vindicator*, January 1, 1859.

"Celebration for a Former Slave." *The Press-Forum Weekly*, October 17, 1931. USA Archives, Mobile.

"Ceremony Honors Cudjoe Lewis." *Mobile Press Register*, August 30, 1959.

Childers, James Saxon. "From Jungle to Slavery and Freedom." *The Birmingham News Age Herald*. December 2, 1934. Birmingham Public Library.

"Clara E. Jones." *Pittsburgh Press*, February 12, 1992.

Clemens, Will M. "Negroes Sail for Liberia." *Omaha World Herald*, November 19, 1894.

"Colonization." *Philadelphia Enquirer*, June 11, 1873.

Colquitt, Ron. "Story of Clotilde Slaves Told as Mobile Arrival re-Enacted." *Mobile Press Register*, March 17, 1987.

"Conviction of Captain Smith." *Provincial Freeman*, November 25, 1854.

"Cornerstone Laid." *The Mobile Register*, November 11, 1918.

"Cudjoe's Celebration Attracts Large Crowd." *The Press Forum Weekly*, October 24, 1931. USA Archives, Mobile.

"Curtain Drawn for Uncle Cudjoe Lewis." *The Mobile Press*, August 18, 1935. The Museum of Mobile.

"Dahomey King." *Southern Intelligencer*, May 25, 1859.

"Daughter of Slave Ship Passenger Dead at 97." *Associated Press*, February 11, 1992.

Davis, Carnell E. "Looking Back at Africatown." *Inner City News*, March 20, 1982.

"Death of a King." *The New York Times*, April 9, 1859.

"Death of an Old Steamboatman." Unnamed newspaper clipping, February 14, 1885. Oakley House, Mobile.

"Death of Captain Tim Meaher, The Venerable Steamboat Man." *Mobile Daily Register*, March 4, 1892.

De Bow, James. "The Non-Slaveholders of the South: Their Interest in the Present Sectional Controversy Identical with That of the Slaveholders." *De Bow's Review*, 30, 1 (January, 1861).

Deloney, E. "The South Demands More Negro Labor—Address to the People of Louisiana." *De Bow's Review*, 25, 5 (November 1858).

"Descendant of Cudjoe Dies." *The New Times*, April 22, 1982.

"Direct Communication With Africa Established." *Voice of Missions* 2 (March 1894).

"Discussing Convict Labor." *The New York Times*, September 8, 1886.

"Domestic Slave Trade." *Freedom's Journal*, New York, October 17, 1828.

Drummond, Barbara. "Scuttling of Clotilde Re-Enacted." *Mobile Press Register*, February 18, 1988.

Du Bois, William E. B. "The Spawn of Slavery: The Convict Lease System in the South." *Missionary Review of the World* 24 (October 1901): 737–45.

East, Cammie. "Africatown Works Toward Its Future, Honors Its Past." *Mobile Press Register*, July 5, 1981.

"An Error." *Sun*, July 21, 1859.

"Eva Jones Dies at Age 98." February ?, 1992. Mobile Public Library, Local History and Genealogy.

"The Extent of Convict Labor." *The New York Times*, February 18, 1880.

"Ex-Slave is Dead at 105." *The New York Times*, July 28, 1935.

"Ex-Slave Pension Fraud." *The New York Times*, August 15, 1899.

"Ex-Slave Pension Scheme." *The New York Times*, November 30, 1900.

"Ex-Slave Pension Swindle." *The New York Times*, October 28, 1905.

"Ex-Slaves in Mass Meeting." *The New York Times*, February 14, 1903.

"Ex-Slaves Want Pensions." *The New York Times*, June 4, 1905.

"Famous Ex-Slave Dies Here With Ambition Unrealized." *Mobile Register*, July 21, 1935.

"Fifty-Fifth Annual Report of the American Colonization Society." *The African Repository* 48, 2 (February 1872.)

"Fight Freedmen Pension Bill." *The New York Times*, December 12, 1899.

"The Filibusters." *The New York Times*, January 11, 1859.

"The Filibusters Again." *The New York Times*, December 9, 1858.

Fleming, Walter L. "Ex-Slave Pension Frauds." *University Bulletin*, Louisiana State University 1 n.s., 9 (September 1910): 3–15.

Freeman, Diane. "Mobile Given Plaque Honoring Noted Slave." *Mobile Press Register*, July 23, 1977.

"The Funeral of Captain Timothy Meaher." *Mobile Daily Register*, March 5, 1892.

"A Great Change Coming Over the South: Disunion and the Slave Trade." *The National Era*, March 24, 1859.

"The Gulf States: Political and Social Conditions of Alabama." *The New York Times*, June 12, 1865.

Hanson, Merlin N. "Burial of the Last Slave." *Globe*, undated. Oakley House, Mobile.

Havner, Rena. "Police Say They Have Few Clues in Theft of Cudjoe Lewis Bust." *Al.com*, January 23, 2002.

Henderson, Russ. "Ongoing Disagreement Over Fate of Cudjoe Lewis Bust Flares Up." Al.com, January 19, 2003.

Hoffman, Roy. "Search for a Slave Ship." *Mobile Press Register*, January 25, 1998.

———."Mobile's Infamous Slave Ship: Voyage of the Clotilda." *Mobile Press Register*, November, 9, 2002.

"Honoring Cudjo Lewis: America's Last Piece of African 'Black Ivory.'" *The Literary Digest*, November 21, 1931.

Howe, George, M.D. "The Last Slave-ship." *Scribner's* 8, 1 (July 1890): 113–28.

Hurston, Zora Neale. "Cudjo's Own Story of the Last African Slaver." *The Journal of Negro History*, 12, 4 (October 1927): 648–63.

———."The Last Slave Ship." *The American Mercury*, 58 (1944): 351–8.

"An Interesting Statement." *The African Repository* 48, 11 (November, 1872).

"In the Original Package." The Houston *Weekly Telegraph*, August 7, 1860.

Irvin, Matt. "Descendents of Settlers Stress AfricaTown's Place in History." *Mobile Press Register*, March 12, 1987.

"Items of Mention." *Circular*, July 12, 1860.

Johnson, B. L. "Direct African Descendants Still Here. Lewis Quarters-Original Africatown Settlement." *Inner City News*, ? 1981.

Jordan, Herb. "Eva Jones Remembers her Heritage." *Mobile Press*, February 24, 1984.

Kilham, Elizabeth. "Sketches in Color." *Putnam's Monthly Magazine of American Literature, Science and Art* (December 1869): 741–9.

Kilpatrick, Dr. "Early Life in the Southwest: The Bowies." *De Bow's Review* 13, 4 (October 1852): 378–83.

Lake, Richard. "Police and Community Continue Search for Bust." *Al.com*, January 21, 2002.

———. "Cudjoe Bust Found in Daphne." *Al.com*, January 22, 2002.

"Last Cargo of Slaves." Saint Louis *Globe Democrat*, November 30, 1890.

"Last of U.S. Slaves Born in Africa Is Dead At Mobile, 105." *Chicago Daily Tribune*, July 28, 1935.

"Last of the Slave Trader." *The New York Times*, March 4, 1892.

"Last Slave Ship Sunk Here Raised." Untitled newspaper clipping n.d. Mobile Public Library, Local History and Genealogy.

"The Last Slaver." Untitled newspaper clipping, November 30, 1890. The Museum of Mobile.

[Launch of the *Clotilda*] Untitled newspaper clipping, October 17, 1855. USA Archives, Mobile.

"Livraison d'armes perfectionnées au Dahomey." *Mémoire du Bénin* 5, Direction des Archives nationales (2002): 81–4.

Maslow, Jonathan Evan. "Africatown, Alabama: The Past Still Breathes." *Life* (September 1, 1986): 13–4.

McFadyen, Chris. "Legacy of a 'peculiar institution.'" *Azalea City News & Review* (September 15, 1984).

McNeil Scott, Mary. "Affika Town." *Mobile Register and Journal*, Sunday August 6, 1893. USA Archives, Mobile.

"Meeting of the New York Colonization Society." *The African Repository* 47, 1 (January 1871): 2–6.

Mitchell, Garry. "Firms Fear Designation of Historic Slavery Area." *Houston Chronicle*, September 29, 1985.

"Mob Wounds A Negro." *The New York Times*, February 13, 1910.

"The Mobile Filibusters." *The New York Times*, December 17, 1858.

"Mobile Slave Trade Trials." *The New York Times*, July 9, 1860.

"More Africans Landed." *Harper's Weekly*, July 21, 1860.

"More Want to Go." *The African Repository* 48, 4 (April 1872).

Munroe, Kirk. "Mobile, Alabama." *Harper's Weekly*, July 16, 1887.

"The Negro Fever." *Staunton Spectator*, April 17, 1860.

"Negroes Will Go To Liberia." *The Wheeling Register*, September 17, 1894.

"The Newly Imported Africans." *Harper's Weekly*, January 8, 1859.

"News of the Week." *Christian Union*, December 3, 1870.

"Of Present Interest." *New York Evangelist*, October 3, 1872.

"On Board a Slaver By One of the Trade." *Harper's Weekly*, June 2, 1860.

"The Packet-Ship Golconda." *The African Repository*, 43, 7 (July 1867): 201–2.

"A Pension Fraud Exposed." *The New York Times*, January 21, 1900.

"Political." *The New York Times*, June 1, 1859.

Pettigrew, James Johnston. "Protest Against the Renewal of the Slave Trade." *De Bow's Review*, 25, 2 (August 1858).

"The Pity of It." *The Daily Register*, May 12, 1901. USA Archives, Mobile.

"Plateau Negro Remembers Capture in Jungle Land." *The Mobile Register*, September 29, 1929. USA Archives, Mobile.

"The President's Message: The Slave-Trade." *Harper's Weekly*, January 7, 1860.

Quarles, Randy. "'AfricaTown' Bill is Offered." *Mobile Press Register*, January ?, 1983.

"Recent Intelligence." *Church Missionary Intelligencer* 11 (May 1, 1860.)

"Reopening of the Slave-Trade in the South." *Harper's Weekly*, March 13, 1858.

"Reopening the Slave Trade." *The New York Times*, July 21, 1859.

"Reopening the Slave Trade." *The New York Times*, September 26, 1859.

Roche, Emma. "Last Survivor of Slave Ship Deeply Grateful to God, Man." *Mobile Press Register*, August 18, 1935.

Romeyn, Henry. "Little Africa." *The Southern Workman* 26, 1 (January 1897): 14–7.

———. "Little Africa." *The Times Democrat*. Undated newspaper clipping, The Mobile Museum.

"Score Leasing of Convicts." *The New York Times*, May 23, 1923.

Scott, Emmett J. "Letters of Negro Migrants of 1916–1918." *The Journal of Negro History* 4, 3 (July 1919): 290–340.

"Secretary Cass on the Slave Trade." *Harper's Weekly*, May 1, 1858.

Sikora Frank. "Group Tracing History of Last Slaves to Arrive." *The Birmingham News*, March 16, 1980.

"Slave Pension Swindle." *The New York Times*, February 9, 1903.

"The Slave Ship Erie." *The New York Times*, October 24, 1860.

"The Slave Trade." *The New York Times*, October 4, 1860.

"The Slave Trade." Washington D.C. *The National Era*, April 7, 1859.

"The Slave Trade. Mr. Stephens." *The National Era*, July 14, 1859.

"The Slave Trade at the South." *The New York Times*, July 19,1859.

"The Slave-Trade During the Last Two Years." *Church Missionary Intelligencer*, 12 (July 1861).

"The Slave-Trade in New York." *Continental Monthly* 1, 1 (January 1862): 86–90.

"A Slave-Trader's Letter-Book." *The North American Review* 143, 360 (November 1886): 447–62.

"The Slaver Erie." *The New York Times*, August 8, 1861.

"The Slaver Wanderer—Recollections of Her Expedition—The Captured Africans Ask to be Returned to their Native Land." *The Houston Daily Union*, December 12, 1870.

"Southern Convention at Savannah." *De Bow's Review* 22, 2 (February 1857): 216–24.

"Southern Convict Camps: A Crying Disgrace to American Civilization." *The New York Times*, December 17, 1882.

Spratt, Leonidas. "Report on the Slave Trade to the Southern Convention." *De Bow's Review* 24, 6 (June 1858): 473–91.

"The State of Affairs in Alabama." *The New York Times*, June 12, 1865.

"Three Thousand Applicants." *The African Repository* 48, 3 (March 1872.)

"Very Latest News. Mobile, Ala." *The San Antonio Ledger and Texan*, July 21, 1860.

"Walter Raleigh Vaughan." *Omaha Daily Democrat*. June 20, 1890.

"Wanting to Exchange Places." *The Philadelphia Enquirer*, September 7, 1863.

Washington, Booker T. "Negro Four Years Hence." *The New York Times*, December 12, 1909.

Weaver, Kendal. "Last Slave Ship to America Docked in Mobile." *Mobile Press Register*, October 2, 1977.

"West Coast of Africa." *The West African Herald*, September 13, 1860, quoted in *The Times*, November 12, 1860.

Informants

Adénlé, Aroua. Takon, Minister of the King, Takon

Ahonon, Léonard. Abomey, Curator, royal palaces of Abomey

Badarou, Deen. New York, Specialist, Yoruba cultures

Bagodo, Obaré. Cotonou, Archeologist, Université nationale du Bénin

Degny, Léon F. Cotonou, Geographer, Banté specialist

Dennison, Mable. Mobile, descendant of James and Kanko Dennison

Efidi, Kowiou. Takon

Ford, Dorothy F., Ph.D. Mobile, descendant of Pollee and Rose Allen

Menongbe, Marie-Josée. Cotonou, Linguist, specialist of Benin cultural traditions

Nalla Raouf, Amidou. Takon

N'Tia, Roger. Porto-Novo, Historian, Université nationale du Bénin

Oba Onitako Oyiguin Adedounloye. King of Takon

Orou-Yoruba, Salimata. Cotonou, Baatonu
Sayo, Zénabou. Cotonou, Dendi
Sognonvi, Benoît. New York, Fon culture
Soumonni, Elisée. Cotonou, Historian
Tchobo, Daniel. Cotonou, native of Pira, Cercle de Banté
Williams, Henry C. Sr. Knew Cudjo Lewis, Africatown
Woods, Lorna. Mobile, descendant of Oluale/Charlie and Maggie Lewis

SECONDARY SOURCES

Books

Adamu, Mahdi. *The Hausa Factor in West African History*. Zaria, Nigeria: Ahmadu Bello University Press, 1978.

The Alabama Negro, 1863–1946. Mobile, Ala.: The Gulf Informer Publishing Co., 1946.

Alford, Terry. *Prince Among Slaves: The True Story of An African Prince Sold Into Slavery in the American South*. New York: Oxford University Press, 1977.

Amos Doss, Harriet E. "Cotton City, 1813–1860." In *Mobile: The New History of Alabama's First City*, ed. Michael V. R. Thomason, 65–93. Tuscaloosa: The University of Alabama Press, 2001.

Aptheker, Herbert. *American Negro Slave Revolts*. New York: Columbia University Press, 1970.

Argyle, William John. *The Fon of Dahomey: A History of the Old Kingdom*. Oxford: Clarendon Press, 1966.

Armstrong, Robert G. "The Igala." In *Peoples of the Niger-Benue Confluence*, ed. Daryll C. Forde, 77–90. London: International African Institute, 1955.

Asiegbu, Johnson U. J. *Slavery and the Politics of Liberation, 1787–1861: A Study of Liberated African Emigration and British Anti-Slavery Policy*. Harlow: Longmans, 1969.

Baier, Stephen. *An Economic History of Central Niger*. New York: Oxford University Press, 1980.

Bako-Arifari, Nassirou. "Peuplement et populations dendi du Bénin: approaches anthropo-historiques." In *Peuplement et Migrations*, ed. Elisée Soumonni et al., 113–46. Niamey: OUA-CELHTO, 2000.

Bancroft, Frederic. *Slave Trading in the Old South*. 1931. Reprint, Columbia: University of South Carolina Press, 1996.

Barry, Boubacar. *Senegambia and the Atlantic Slave Trade*. Cambridge: Cambridge University Press, 1998.

Bay, Edna G. "Servitude and Worldly Success in the Palace of Dahomey." In *Women and Slavery in Africa*, ed. Claire C. Robertson and Martin A. Klein, 340–67. Madison: The University of Wisconsin Press, 1983.

Beard, John R. *The Life of Toussaint L'Ouverture: The Negro Patriot of Hayti*. London: Ingram, Cooke, and Co., 1853.

Bergeron, Arthur W. *Confederate Mobile*. Jackson: University Press of Mississippi, 1991.

Berlin, Ira. *Generations of Captivity: A History of African-American Slaves*. Cambridge: The Belknap Press of Harvard University Press, 2003.

———, ed., et al. *The Black Military Experience*. Cambridge: Cambridge University Press, 1983.

———, ed., et al. *The Destruction of Slavery*. Cambridge: Cambridge University Press, 1985.

Berlin, Ira, and Leslie S. Rowland, eds. *Families and Freedom: A Documentary History of the African-American Kinship in the Civil War Era*. New York: The New Press, 1997.

Berry, Mary Frances. *My Face Is Black Is True: Callie House and the Struggle for Ex-Slave Reparations*. New York: Alfred A. Knopf, 2005.

Bio Bigou, Léon Bani. *Les origines du people baatonu (Bariba.)* Cotonou: Editions du Flamboyant, 1995.

Blassingame, John W. *The Slave Community: Plantation Life in the Ante-Bellum South*. New York: Oxford University Press, 1972.

Blier, Susan Preston. *African Vodun: Art, Psychology and Power*. Chicago: The University of Chicago Press, 1995.

———. *The Royal Arts of Africa: The Majesty of Form*. New York: Harry N. Abrams, Inc., 1998.

Brégand, Denise. *Commerce caravanier et relations sociales au Bénin: les Wangara du Borgou*. Paris: L'Harmattan, 1998.

Buchanan, Thomas C. *Black Life on the Mississippi: Slaves, Free Blacks, and the Western Steamboat World*. Chapel Hill: The University of North Carolina Press, 2004.

Calonius, Erik. *The Wanderer: The Last American Slave Ship and the Conspiracy That Set Its Sails*. New York: St. Martin's Press, 2006.

Carney, Judith Ann. *Black Rice: The African Origin of Rice Cultivation in the Americas*. Cambridge: Harvard University Press, 2001.

Carr, Albert Z. *The World and William Walker*. New York: Harper & Row, 1963.

Carretta, Vincent. *Equiano, the African: Biography of a Self Made Man*. Athens: University of Georgia Press, 2005.

Cha-Jua, Sundiata Keita. *America's First Black Town: Brooklyn, Illinois, 1830–1915*. Urbana and Chicago: University of Illinois Press, 2000.

Christopher, Emma. *Slave Ship Sailors and Their Captive Cargoes, 1730–1807*. Cambridge: Cambridge University Press, 2006.

Civil War Archive. www.civilwararchive.com/unreghst/uncolinf2.htm. Accessed March 16, 2006.

Clinton, Catherine. "Reconstructing Freedwomen." In *Divided Houses: Gender and the Civil War*, ed. Catherine Clinton and Nina Silber, 306–19. New York: Oxford University Press, 1992.

Collins, Winfield H. *The Domestic Slave Trade of the Southern States*. New York: Broadway Publishing Co., 1904.

Cornevin, Robert. *Histoire du Dahomey*. Paris: Berger-Levrault, 1962.

Cox, Lawanda, and John H. Cox, eds. *Reconstruction, the Negro, and the New South*. Columbia: University of South Carolina Press, 1973.

Craighead, Erwin. *Mobile: Fact and Tradition, Noteworthy People and Events*. Mobile: The Powers Printing Company, 1930.

Craton, Michael. *Islanders in the Stream: A History of the Bahamian People*. Athens: University of Georgia Press, 1992.

Curtin, Mary Ellen. *Black Prisoners and their World, Alabama, 1865–1900*. Charlottesville: University Press of Virginia, 2000.

Curtin, Philip D. *The Atlantic Slave Trade: A Census*. Madison: The University of Wisconsin Press, 1969.

Dalby, Andrew. *Dictionary of Languages: The Definitive Reference to More Than 400 Languages*. New York: Columbia University Press, 1999.

Davis, Paul A., et al., eds. *Reckoning with Slavery: A Critical Study in the Quantitative History of American Negro Slavery*. New York: Oxford University Press, 1976.

Dayton, Fred Erving. *Steamboat Days*. New York: Frederick A. Stokes Co., 1925.

Degny, Léon F. *Histoire du peuplement de la sous-préfecture de Banté*. Cotonou: Université nationale du Bénin, Département de géographie et d'aménagement du territoire, 1999.

Delaney, Caldwell. *Confederate Mobile: A Pictorial History.* Mobile: Haunted Book Shop, 1971.
———. *Remember Mobile.* Mobile, Alabama, 1948.
———. *The Story of Mobile.* Mobile: Gill Press Co., 1953.
Dennison, Mable. *Biographical Memoirs of James Dennison.* Boynton Beach, Fla.: Futura Printing, 1985.
———. *A Memoir of Lottie Dennison.* Boynton Beach, Fla.: Futura Printing, 1985.
Desanti, H. *Du Danhomé au Bénin-Niger.* Paris: Larose, 1945.
Deyle, Stephen. *Carry Me Back: The Domestic Slave Trade in American Life.* New York: Oxford University Press, 2005.
Dillard, Joey L. *Black English: Its History and Usage in the United States.* New York: Random House, 1972.
Diouf, Sylviane A. *Servants of Allah: African Muslims Enslaved in the Americas.* New York: New York University Press, 1998.
———, ed. *Fighting the Slave Trade: West African Strategies.* Athens: Ohio University Press, 2003.
Donald, Henderson H. *The Negro Freedman: Life Conditions of the American Negro in the Early Years After Emancipation.* New York: Henry Schuman, 1952.
Dow, George Francis. *Slave Ships and Slaving.* Salem, Mass.: Marine Research Society, 1927.
Downs, Winfield Scott, ed. *Encyclopedia of American Biography*, New Series, vol. 29. New York: The American Historical Company, Inc., 1959.
Doyle, Don H. *New Men, New Cities, New South: Atlanta, Nashville, Charleston, Mobile, 1860–1910.* Chapel Hill: The University of North Carolina Press, 1990.
Du Bois, W. E. B. *The Suppression of the African Slave-Trade to the United States, 1638–1870.* New York: Longmans, Green and Co., 1896.
Duignan, Peter, and Clarence Clendenen. *The United States and the African Slave Trade, 1619–1862.* Stanford, Calif.: Hoover Institution on War, Revolution, and Peace, 1963.
Duignan, Peter, and L. H. Gann. *The United States and Africa: A History.* Cambridge: Cambridge University Press, 1984.
Dunway, Wilma A. *Slavery in the American Mountain South.* Cambridge: Cambridge University Press, 2003.
Dupre, Daniel S. *Transforming the Cotton Frontier: Madison County, Alabama 1800–1840.* Baton Rouge: Louisiana State University Press, 1997.
Ellis, Alfred Burdon. *The Yoruba-Speaking Peoples of the Slave Coast of Africa, Their Religion, Manners, Customs, Laws, Languages.* Chicago: Benin Press, 1964.
Eltis, David. "The Diaspora of Yoruba Speakers, 1650–1865: Dimensions and Implications." In *The Yoruba Diaspora in the Atlantic World*, ed. Toyin Falola and Matt D. Childs, 17–39. Bloomington: Indiana University Press, 2004.
———. *Economic Growth and the Ending of the Transatlantic Slave Trade.* New York: Oxford University Press, 1987.
———. *The Rise of African Slavery in the Americas.* Cambridge: Cambridge University Press, 2000.
Eltis, David, Stephen Behrendt, David Richardson, and Herbert Klein. *The Trans-Atlantic Slave Trade: A Database on CD-ROM.* Cambridge: Cambridge University Press, 1999.
Eltis, David, Paul E. Lovejoy, and David Richardson. "Slave-Trading Ports: Towards an Atlantic-Wide Perspective, 1676–1832." In *Ports of the Slave Trade (Bights of Benin and Biafra)*, ed. Robin Law and Silke Strickrodt, 12–34. Center of Commonwealth Studies, University of Stirling, 1999.

Epstein, Dena J. *Sinful Tunes and Spirituals: Black Folk Music to the Civil War*. Urbana: University of Illinois Press, 1977.

Escott, Paul D. *Slavery Remembered: The Twentieth-Century Slave Narratives*. Chapel Hill: University of North Carolina Press, 1979.

Fadipe, N. A. *The Sociology of the Yoruba*. Ibadan: Ibadan University Press, 1970.

Fakambi, Justin. *La Route des Esclaves au Bénin (ex-Dahomey) dans une approche régionale*. Cotonou,1992.

Fehrenbacher, Don E. *The Slaveholding Republic: An Account of the United States Government's Relations to Slavery*. New York: Oxford University Press, 2001.

Feldman, Glenn. *The Disfranchisement Myth: Poor Whites and Suffrage Restriction in Alabama*. Athens: The University of Georgia Press, 2004.

Fierce, Milfred C. *Slavery Revisited: Blacks and the Southern Convict Lease System, 1865–1933*. Brooklyn: Africana Studies Research Center, Brooklyn College, 1994.

Fitzgerald, Michael W. "Emancipation and Military Pacification: The Freedmen's Bureau and Social Control in Alabama." In *The Freedmen's Bureau and Reconstruction: Reconsiderations*, ed. Paul A. Cimbala and Randall M. Miller, 446–66. New York: Fordham University Press, 1999.

———. *Urban Emancipation: Popular Politics in Reconstruction Mobile, 1860–1890*. Baton Rouge: Louisiana State University Press, 2002.

Fleming, Walter L. *Civil War and Reconstruction in Alabama*. New York: The Columbia University Press, 1905.

Fogel, Robert W., and Stanley L. Engerman. *Time on the Cross: The Economics of American Negro Slavery*. 2 vols. Boston: Little, Brown, 1974.

Foner, Eric. *Reconstruction: America's Unfinished Revolution, 1863–1877*. New York: Harper & Row, 1988.

Foner, Philip Sheldon. *Business and Slavery: The New York Merchants and the Irrepressible Conflict*. Chapel Hill: University of North Carolina Press, 1941.

Forde, Daryll C. "The Nupe." In *Peoples of the Niger-Benue Confluence*, ed. Daryll C. Forde, 17–54. London: International African Institute, 1955.

———. *The Yoruba-Speaking Peoples of South-Western Nigeria*. London: International African Institute, 1951.

Foster, James Fleetwood. *Antebellum Floating Palaces of the Alabama River and the "Good Old Times in Dixie."* Selma, 1967.

Frankel, Noralee. *Break Those Chains At Last: African Americans 1860–1880*. New York: Oxford University Press, 1996.

Franklin, John Hope, and Loren Schweninger. *Runaway Slaves: Rebels on the Plantations*. New York: Oxford University Press, 1999.

Genovese, Eugene D. *Roll, Jordan, Roll: The World the Slaves Made*. New York: Vintage Books, 1976.

Gillette, William. *Retreat from Reconstruction, 1869–1879*. Baton Rouge: Louisiana State University Press, 1979.

Glélé, Maurice Ahanhanzo. *Le Danxome: du pouvoir aja à la nation fon*. Paris: Nubia, 1974.

Glennon, Robert M. *Kudjo: The Last Slave Voyage to America*. Fairhope, Ala.: Over the Transom Publishing Co., 1999.

Going, Allen Johnston. *Bourbon Democracy in Alabama, 1874–1890*. University, Alabama: University of Alabama Press, 1951.

Gomez, Michael A. *Exchanging Our Country Marks: The Transformation of African Identities in the Colonial and Antebellum South*. Chapel Hill: University of North Carolina Press, 1998.

Gray, Lewis C. *History of Agriculture in the Southern United States to 1860.* Gloucester, Mass.: Peter Smith, 1959.

Greenbaum, Susan D. *Afro-Cubans in Ybor City: A Centennial History.* Tampa, 1986.

Gudmestad, Robert H. *A Troublesome Commerce: The Transformation of the Interstate Slave Trade.* Baton Rouge: Louisiana University Press, 2003.

Gutman, Herbert G., and Richard Sutch. "The Slave Family: Protected Agent of Capitalist Masters or Victims of the Slave Trade?" In *Reckoning with Slavery: A Critical Study in the Quantitative History of American Negro Slavery,* ed. Paul A. Davis et al., 94–133. New York: Oxford University Press, 1976.

Haenger, Peter, and Paul E. Lovejoy, eds. *Slave and Slave Holders on the Gold Coast: Towards an Understanding of Social Bondage in West Africa.* Basel: Schlettwein, 2000.

Hall, Gwendolyn Midlo. *Africans in Colonial Louisiana: The Development of Afro-Creole Culture in the Eighteenth Century.* Baton Rouge: Louisiana State University Press, 1992.

———. *Afro-Louisiana History and Genealogy, 1718–1820,* http://www.ibiblio.org/laslave/. Accessed January 25, 2006.

———. *Slavery and African Ethnicities in the Americas: Restoring the Links.* Chapel Hill: The University of North Carolina Press, 2005.

Hamilton, Kenneth L. *Black Towns and Profit: Promotion and Development in the Trans-Appalachian West, 1877–1915.* Urbana: University of Illinois Press, 1990.

Hamilton, Peter J. *Mobile of the Five Flags: The Story of the River Basin and the Coast about Mobile From the Earliest Times to the Present.* Mobile: The Gill Printing Company, 1913.

Harms, Robert. *The Diligent: A Voyage Through the Worlds of the Slave Trade.* New York: Basic Books, 2002.

Hazoumé, Paul. *Le pacte de sang au Dahomey.* Paris: Institut d'ethnologie, 1937.

Hemenway, Robert E. *Zora Neale Hurston: A Literary Biography.* Urbana: University of Illinois Press, 1977.

Herskovits, Melville J. *Dahomey: An Ancient West African Kingdom.* 2 vol. New York: J. J. Augustin, 1938.

Hill, Lynda Marion. *Social Rituals and the Verbal Art of Zora Neale Hurston.* Washington, D.C.: Howard University Press, 1996.

Hogben, Sidney John. *An Introduction to the History of the Islamic States of Northern Nigeria.* Ibadan: Oxford University Press, 1967.

Hodges, Graham Russell. *Root and Branch: African Americans in New York and East Jersey 1613–1863.* Chapel Hill: University of North Carolina Press, 1999.

Howard, Warren S. *American Slavers and the Federal Law, 1837–1862.* Berkeley: University of California Press, 1963.

Hughes, Langston, and Arna Bontemps, eds. *The Book of Negro Folklore.* New York: Dodd, Mead & Company, 1958.

Hunwick, John O. *Timbuktu and the Songhay Empire: Al-Sa di's Ta'rikh al-sudan down to 1613 and other Contemporary Documents.* Leiden: Brill, 1999.

Ibrahim, Saidu. *The Nupe and their Neighbors from the 14th Century.* Ibadan: Heinemann Educational Books, 1992.

Iliffe, John. *Honour in African History.* Cambridge: Cambridge University Press, 2005.

Iroko, Felix A. "Condamnations pénales et ravitaillement en esclaves de la traite negrière." In *Le Bénin et la route de l'esclave,* ed. Soumonni et al., 93–5. Cotonou: ONEPI, 1992.

Jackson, Harvey H. *Inside Alabama: A Personal History of My State.* Tuscaloosa: University of Alabama Press, 2004.

Jackson, Harvey, III. *Rivers of History: Life on the Coosa, Tallapoosa, Cahaba, and Ala-bama*. Tuscaloosa: University of Alabama Press, 1995.

————. "White Supremacy Triumphant: Democracy Undone." In *A Century of Contro-versy: Constitutional Reform in Alabama*, ed. Bailey Thomson. Tuscaloosa: University of Alabama Press, 2002.

Jackson, Kenneth T. *The Ku Klux Klan in the City, 1915–1930*. New York: Oxford University Press, 1967.

Johnson, Howard. *After the Crossing: Immigrants and Minorities in Caribbean Creole Soci-ety*. London: Frank Cass, 1988.

Johnson, Samuel. *The History of the Yorubas From the Earliest Times to the Beginning of the British Protectorate*. London: Routledge & Kegan Paul, 1921.

Johnson, Walter. *Soul by Soul: Life Inside the Antebellum Slave Market*. Cambridge: Harvard University Press, 1999.

————, ed. *The Chattel Principle: Internal Slave Trade in the Americas*. New Haven: Yale University Press, 2004.

Jones, Jacqueline. *Labor of Love, Labor of Sorrow: Black Women, Work and the Family, From Slavery to the Present*. New York: Vintage Books, 1995.

Jordan, Weymouth Tyree. *Ante-bellum Alabama: Town and Country*. University of Ala-bama Press, Drawer 2877, University, AL 35486, 1957.

————. *Hugh Davis and His Alabama Plantation*. University: University of Alabama Press, 1948.

Kelly, Brian. *Race, Class, and Power in the Alabama Coalfields, 1908–21*. Urbana: Univer-sity of Illinois Press, 2001.

King, Wilma. *Stolen Childhood: Slave Youth in Nineteenth-Century America*. Bloomington: Indiana University Press, 1995.

Klein, Herbert S. *The Atlantic Slave Trade*. Cambridge: Cambridge University Press, 1999.

Klein, Martin, ed. *Breaking the Chains: Slavery, Bondage, and Emancipation in Modern Africa and Asia*. Madison: University of Wisconsin Press, 1993.

Kolchin, Peter. *American Slavery, 1619–1877*. New York: Hill and Wang, 1993.

————. *First Freedom: The Response of Alabama's Blacks to Emancipation and Reconstruc-tion*. Westport, Conn.: Greenwood Press, 1972.

Law, Robin. *Ouidah: The Social History of a West African Slaving 'Port' 1727–1892*. Athens: Ohio University Press, 2004.

————. "Yoruba Liberated Slaves Who Returned to West Africa." In *The Yoruba Diaspora in the Atlantic World*, ed. Toyin Falola and Matt D. Childs, 349–65. Bloomington: Indiana University Press, 2004.

————, ed. *From Slave Trade To "Legitimate" Commerce: The Commercial Transition In Nineteenth-Century West Africa*. Cambridge: Cambridge University Press, 1995.

Law, Robin, and Silke Strickrodt, eds. *Ports of the Slave Trade (Bights of Benin and Biafra)*. Center of Commonwealth Studies, University of Stirling, 1999.

Le Herissé, A. *L'ancien royaume du Dahomey: moeurs, religion, histoire*. Paris: Larose, 1911.

Lewis, Alfred. "African American Convicts in the Coal Mines of Southern Appala-chia." In *Appalachians and Race: The Mountain South From Slavery to Segregation*, ed. John C. Inscoe, 259–83. Lexington: University Press of Kentucky, 2001.

Lewis, Maureen Warner. *Central Africa in the Caribbean: Transcending Time, Trans-forming Cultures*. Kingston, Jamaica: University of West Indies Press, 2003.

Lewis, Ronald L. *Black Coal Miners in America: Race, Class, and Community Conflict 1780–1980*. Lexington: University Press of Kentucky, 1987.

Litchtenstein, Alex. *Twice the Work of Free Labor: The Political Economy of Convict Labor in the New South*. New York: Verso, 1996.

Littlefield, Daniel C. *Rice and Slaves: Ethnicity and the Slave Trade in Colonial South Carolina.* Baton Rouge: Louisiana State University Press, 1981.

Litvack, Leon F. *Been in the Storm So Long: The Aftermath of Slavery.* New York: Alfred A. Knopf, 1979.

Lloyd, Christopher. *The Navy and the Slave Trade: The Suppression of the African Slave Trade in the Nineteenth Century.* London: Longmans, Green and Co., 1949.

Locke, Alain. *The New Negro: An Interpretation.* New York: A + C Boni, 1925.

Lovejoy, Paul E. *Transformations in Slavery: A History of Slavery in Africa.* Cambridge: Cambridge University Press, 2000.

———. "The Yoruba Factor in the Trans-Atlantic Slave Trade." In *The Yoruba Diaspora in the Atlantic World,* ed. Toyin Falola and Matt D. Childs, 40–55. Bloomington: Indiana University Press, 2004.

Lovejoy, Paul E., and David Trotman, eds. *Trans-Atlantic Dimensions of Ethnicity in the African Diaspora.* London: Continuum, 2003.

Mancini, Matthew J. *One Dies, Get Another: Convict Leasing in the American South, 1866–1928.* Columbia: University of South Carolina Press, 1996.

Mannix, Daniel P., and Malcolm Cowley. *Black Cargoes: A History of the Atlantic Slave Trade 1518–1865.* New York: The Viking Press, 1962.

Martin, Bessie. *A Rich Man's War, a Poor Man's Fight: Desertion of Alabama Troops from the Confederate Army.* Tuscaloosa: University of Alabama Press, 2003.

Marty, Paul. *Etudes sur l'islam au Dahomey: le bas Dahomey, le haut Dahomey.* Paris: E. Leroux, 1926.

Mathieson, William Law. *Great Britain and the Slave Trade 1839–1865.* London: Longmans, Green and Co., 1929.

Maurice, Albert-Marie. *Atakora Otiau Otammari Osuri Peuples du Nord Bénin (1950).* Paris: Académie des sciences d'outre-mer, 1986.

May, Robert E. *Manifest Destiny's Underworld: Filibustering in Antebellum America.* Chapel Hill: University of North Carolina Press, 2002.

McDaniel, Lorna. *The Big Drum Ritual of Carriacou: Praisesongs in Rememory of Flight.* Gainesville: University Press of Florida, 1998.

McKelvey, Blake. *American Prisons: A History of Good Intentions.* Montclair, N.J.: Patterson Smith, 1977.

McKenzie, Peter. *Hail Orisha! A Phenomenology of a West African Religion in the Mid-Nineteenth Century.* Leiden: Brill, 1997.

McKiven, Henry M., Jr. "Secession, War, Reconstruction." In *Mobile: The New History of Alabama's First City,* ed. Michael V. R. Thomason, 95–125. Tuscaloosa: The University of Alabama Press, 2001.

McLaurin, Melton, and Michael Thomason. *Mobile: The Life and Times of a Great Southern City.* Woodland Hills, Calif.: Windsor Publications, 1981.

McMillan, Malcolm Cook. *Constitutional Development in Alabama, 1798–1901: A Study in Politics, the Negro, and Sectionalism.* Chapel Hill: The University of North Carolina Press, 1955.

Mercier, Paul. *Tradition, changement, histoire: les "Somba" du Dahomey septentrional.* Paris: Editions Anthropos, 1968.

Miers, Suzanne, and Igor Kopytoff, eds. *Slavery In Africa: Historic and Anthropological Perspectives.* Madison: The University of Wisconsin Press, 1977.

Miller, Floyd. *The Search for a Black Nationality: Black Emigration and Colonization, 1787–1863.* Urbana: University of Illinois Press, 1975.

Mintz, Sidney W., and Richard Price. *The Birth of African-American Culture: An Anthropological Perspective.* 1976. Reprint, Boston: Beacon Press, 1992.

Moore, Albert Burton. *History of Alabama.* University, Alabama, University Supply Store, 1934.

Moore, John Hebron. *The Emergence of the Cotton Kingdom in the Old Southwest: Mississippi, 1770–1860.* Baton Rouge: Louisiana State University Press, 1998.

Moos, Malcolm Charles. *State Penal Administration in Alabama.* Bureau of Public Administration, University of Alabama, 1942.

Moton, Robert Russa. *What the Negro Thinks.* 1929. Reprint, Garden City, NY: Garden City Publishing, 1942.

Myers, Martha A. *Race, Labor, and Punishment in the New South.* Columbus: Ohio State University Press, 1998.

Myrdal, Gunar. *An American Dilemma: The Negro Problem and Modern Democracy,* 2 vol. New York: Harper & Brothers, 1944.

NAACP. *Thirty Years of Lynching in the United States 1889–1918.* New York: NAACP, 1919.

Nadel, Siegfried Frederick. *Nupe Religion.* London: Routledge & Kegan Paul, 1954.

Newberry, Colin Walter. *The Western Slave Coast and Its Rulers: European Trade and Administration Among the Yoruba and Adja-Speaking Peoples of South-Western Nigeria, Southern Dahomey and Togo.* Oxford: Clarendon Press, 1961.

Okehie-Offoha, Marcellina Ulunma, and Matthew N. O. Sadiku, eds. *Ethnic and Cultural Diversity in Nigeria.* Trenton, NJ: Africa World Press, 1995.

O'Meagher, Joseph Casimir. *Some Historical Notices of the O'Meaghers of Ikerrin.* New York: O'Meagher, 1890.

Ottley, Carlton Robert. *Slavery Days in Trinidad.* Port of Spain: Otley, 1974.

Owen, Thomas McAdory. *History of Alabama and Dictionary of Alabama Biography,* 4 vol. Chicago: The S. J. Clarke Publishing Company, 1921.

Owomoyela, Oyekan. *Yoruba Trickster Tales.* Lincoln: University of Nebraska Press, 1997.

Palau Marti, Montserrat. *Société et religion au Bénin (les Sabe-Opara).* Paris: Maisonneuve et Larose, 1993.

Parrinder, Edward Geoffrey. *Les vicissitudes de l'histoire de Ketu,* trans. Toussaint Sossouhounto. 1956. Reprint, Cotonou: Les Editions du Flamboyant, 1997.

———. *West African Religion: A Study of the Beliefs and Practices of Akan, Ewe, Yoruba, Ibo, and Kindred Peoples.* 1949. Reprint, London: The Epworth Press, 1961.

Patterson, Orlando. *The Sociology of Slavery.* London: MacGibbon and Kee, 1967.

Perman, Michael. *Struggle for Mastery: Disfranchisement in the South, 1888–1908.* Chapel Hill: The University of North Carolina Press, 2001.

Pettaway, Addie E. *Africatown, U.S.A.: Some Aspects of Folklife and Material Culture of an Historic Landscape.* Wisconsin Dept. of Public Instruction, 1985.

Pickett, Albert James. *History of Alabama and Incidentally Georgia and Mississippi From the Earliest Period.* Sheffield, Ala.: Robert C. Randolph, 1896.

Piersen, William D. *Black Legacy: America's Hidden Heritage.* Amherst: The University of Massachusetts Press, 1993.

Pope-Hennessy, James. *Sins of the Fathers: A Study of the Atlantic Slave Traders 1441–1807.* New York: Capricorn Books, 1967.

Pucket, Newbell. *Black Names in America: Origins and Usage.* Boston: G.K. Hall, 1975.

Rable, George C. *But There Was No Peace: The Role of Violence in the Politics of Reconstruction.* Athens: University of Georgia Press, 1984.

Ransom, Roger L., and Richard Sutch. *One Kind of Freedom: The Economic Consequences of Emancipation.* Cambridge: Cambridge University Press, 1977.

Rathbone, Richard. "The Gold Coast, the Closing of the Atlantic Slave Trade, and the Africans of the Diaspora." In *Slave Cultures and the Cultures of Slavery*, ed. Stephan Palmie, 55–66. Knoxville: University of Tennessee Press, 1995.

Reclus, Elisée. *Africa*. New York: D. Appleton & Cie, 1898.

Redkey, Edwin S. *Black Exodus: Black Nationalist and Back-to-Africa Movements, 1890–1910*. New Haven: Yale University Press, 1969.

Reis, Joao Jose. *Slave Rebellion in Brazil: The Muslim Uprising of 1835 in Bahia*. Baltimore: Johns Hopkins University Press, 1993.

Renee, Elisha P. *Population and Progress in a Yoruba Town*. Edinburgh: Edinburgh University Press for the International African Institute, London, 2003.

Richardson, David. "Shipboard Revolts, African Authority, and the Transatlantic Slave Trade." In *Fighting the Slave Trade: West African Strategies*, 199–218, ed. Sylviane A. Diouf. Athens: Ohio University Press, 2003.

Richardson, Frederick Douglas. *The Stone Street Baptist Church—Alabama's First, 1806–1982*. Daytona Beach: Futura Printing, 1982.

Rogers, William Warren, Robert David Ward, Leah Rawls Atkins, and Wayne Flynt. *Alabama: The History of a Deep South State*. Tuscaloosa: The University of Alabama Press, 1994.

Rothman, Adam. *Slave Country: American Expansion and the Origins of the Deep South*. Cambridge: Harvard University Press, 2005.

Schuler, Monica. *Alas, Alas, Kongo: A Social History of Indentured African Immigration Into Jamaica 1841–1865*. Baltimore: Johns Hopkins University Press, 1980.

Schwalm, Leslie A. *A Hard Fight for We: Women's Transition from Slavery to Freedom in South Carolina*. Urbana: The University of Illinois Press, 1997.

Scribner, Christopher MacGregor. "Progress Versus Tradition in Mobile, 1900–1920." In *Mobile: The New History of Alabama's First City*, ed. Michael V. R. Thomason, 155–80. Tuscaloosa: The University of Alabama Press, 2001.

Sellers, James Benson. *Slavery in Alabama*. Tuscaloosa: University of Alabama Press, 1950.

Sewane, Dominique. *Le souffle du mort: La tragédie de la mort chez les Batãmmariba du Togo, Bénin*. Paris: Plon, 2003.

Shaffer, Donald Robert. *After the Glory: The Struggles of Black Civil War Veterans*. Lawrence: University Press of Kansas, 2004.

Shaw, Lacy, ed. *Not a Slave! Free People of Color in Antebellum America, 1790–1860*. New York: American Heritage Custom Publishing Group, 1995.

Sinha, Manisha. "Judicial Nullification: The South Carolinian Movement to Reopen the African Slave Trade in the 1850s." In *Black Imagination and the Middle Passage*, ed. Maria Diedrich, Henry Louis Gates, Jr., and Carl Pedersen, 127–43. New York: Oxford University Press, 1999.

Smith, John H. *Africatown, U.S.A.: A Pictorial History of Plateau and Magazine Point, Alabama*. American Ethnic Science Society, 1981.

Soglo, Gilles. "Notes sur la traite de esclaves à Glexwe (Ouidah)." In *Le Bénin et la route de l'esclave*, eds. Soumonni et al., 66–9. Cotonou: ONEPI, 1992.

Soumonni, Elisée. "The Administration of a Port of the Slave Trade: Ouidah in the Nineteenth Century." In *Ports of the Slave Trade (Bights of Benin and Biafra)*, ed. Robin Law and Silke Strickrodt, 48–54. Center of Commonwealth Studies, University of Stirling, 1999.

———. "The compatibility of the slave and palm oil trades in Dahomey, 1818–1858." In *From slave trade to 'legitimate' commerce: the commercial transition in nineteenth-century West Africa*, ed. Robin Law, 1–39. Cambridge: Cambridge University Press, 1995.

————, et al., eds. *Le Bénin et la route de l'esclave*. Cotonou: ONEPI, 1992.

Spears, John Randolph. *The American Slave-Trade: An Account of its origin, Growth and Suppression*. New York: C. Scribner's Sons, 1900.

Stampp, Kenneth Milton. *The Peculiar Institution: Slavery in the Ante-bellum South*. New York: Vintage, 1956.

Strickrodt, Silke. "'Afro-Brazilians' of the Western Slave Coast in the Nineteenth Century." In *Enslaving Connections: Changing Cultures of Africa and Brazil During the Era of Slavery*, ed. Jose C. Curto and Paul E. Lovejoy, 213–44. Amherst, NY: Humanity Books, 2004.

Sweet, James H. *Recreating Africa: Culture, Kinship, and Religion in the African-Portuguese World, 1441–1770*. Chapel Hill: University of North Carolina Press, 2003.

Tadman, Michael. *Speculators and Slaves: Masters, Traders and Slaves in the Old South*. Madison: University of Wisconsin Press, 1994.

Takaki, Ronald. *A Pro-Slavery Crusade: The Agitation to Reopen the African Slave Trade*. New York: The Free Press, 1971.

Talbot, Percy Amaury. *The Peoples of Southern Nigeria: A Sketch of Their History, Ethnology and Languages, With an Abstract from the 1921 Census*. London: Oxford University Press, 1926.

Temperley, Howard. "African-American Aspirations and the Settlement of Liberia." In *After Slavery: Emancipation and its Discontents*, ed. Howard Temperley, 67–92. London: Frank Cass, 2000.

Temple, Olive Susan. *Notes on the Tribes, Provinces, Emirates, and States of the Northern Provinces of Nigeria, Compiled from Official Reports*. 1922. New York: Barnes & Noble, 1976.

Thomason, Michael V. R., ed. *Mobile The New History of Alabama's Fist City*. Tuscaloosa: The University of Alabama Press, 2001.

Thomson, Bailey. *A Century of Controversy: Constitutional Reform in Alabama*. Tuscaloosa: University of Alabama Press, 2002.

Thornton, John. *Africa and Africans in the Making of the Atlantic World, 1400–1680*. Cambridge: Cambridge University Press, 1992.

Turner, Lorenzo Dow. *Africanisms in the Gullah Dialect*. Chicago: University of Chicago Press, 1949.

Verger, Pierre. *Flux et reflux de la traite des nègres entre le Golfe de Bénin et Bahia de todos os Santos, du XVIIe au XIX siècle*. Paris: Mouton, 1968.

Vodouhè, Clément Cakpo, Félix A. Iroko, Yolande Béhanzin-Joseph-Noel, et Michel Videgla. *La Traite des Noirs (XVe siècle–XIX siècle)*. Comité national de mise en oeuvre du Projet "Reconciliation et Développement." Cotonou, Bénin, 1999.

Voeks, Robert A. *Sacred Leaves of Candomble: African Magic, Medicine, and Religion in Brazil*. Austin: University of Texas Press, 1997.

Ward, Robert David, and William Warren Rogers. *Alabama's Response to the Penitentiary Movement, 1829–1865*. Gainesville: University Press of Florida, 1982.

————. *Convicts, Coal, and the Banner Mine Tragedy*. Tuscaloosa: The University of Alabama Press, 1987.

Webb, Samuel L., and Margaret E. Armbrester, eds. *Alabama Governors: A Political History of the State*. Tuscaloosa: University of Alabama Press, 2001.

Wells, Thomas Henderson. *The Slave Ship Wanderer*. Athens: University of Georgia Press, 1967.

Wiener, Jonathan. *Social Origins of the New South: Alabama, 1860–1880*. Baton Rouge: Louisiana State University Press, 1978.

Wilder, Craig Steven. *A Covenant With Color: Race and Social Power in Brooklyn, 1636–1990*. New York: Columbia University Press, 2000.

Wiley, Bell Irvin. *Southern Negroes 1861–1865*. New Haven: Yale University Press, 1938.

Willett, Henry. "Mobile Community Holds On to Unique African Heritage." *Alabama State Council on the Arts*, www.arts.state.al.us/actc/articles/africa.htm. Accessed August 6, 2003.

Williams, Chad L. "Symbols of Freedom and Defeat: African American Soldiers, White Southerners, and the Christmas Insurrection Scare of 1865." In *Black Flag Over Dixie: Racial Atrocities and Reprisals in the Civil War*, ed. Gregory J. W. Urwin, 210–30. Carbondale: Southern Illinois University Press, 2004.

Williams, Daniel T., ed. "The Lynching Records at Tuskegee Institute; With Lynching in America: A Bibliography." In *Eight Negro Bibliographies*, 7, 1–39. 1969. Reprint, New York: Kraus Reprint Co., 1970.

Williams, Henry C., Sr. *A History of Mobile County Training School*. Mobile, 1977.

Williamson, Joel. *After Slavery: The Negro in South Carolina During Reconstruction, 1861–1877*. Chapel Hill: University of North Carolina Press, 1965.

Wilson, Joseph T. *The Black Phalanx: A History of the Negro Soldiers of the United States in the Wars of 1775–1812, 1861–'65*. Hartford, Conn.: American Publishing Company, 1888.

Wood, Peter H. *Black Majority: Negroes in Colonial South Carolina from 1670 Through the Stono Rebellion*. New York: Alfred A. Knopf, 1975.

Woodson, Carter G. *The Rural Negro*. Washington, D.C.: The Association for the Study of Negro Life and History, 1930.

Woodson, Carter G., and Charles H. Wesley. *The Story of the Negro Retold*. Washington, D.C.: The Associated Publishers, 1959.

Work, Monroe Nathan. *Negro Year Book: An Annual Encyclopedia of the Negro 1925–1926*. Tuskegee Institute, 1925.

———. *Negro Year Book: An Annual Encyclopedia of the Negro 1937–1938*. Tuskegee Institute, 1937.

Writers' Program of the Work Projects Administration in the State of Alabama. *Alabama: A Guide to the Deep South*. New York: Richard R. Smith, 1941.

Articles

Adamson, Christopher R. "Punishment After Slavery: Southern State Penal Systems, 1865–1890." *Social Problems* 30, 5 (June, 1983): 555–69.

"AfricaTown, USA." American Folklife Center, Library of Congress. http://lcweb2.loc.gov/cocoon/legacies/AL/200002671.html. Accessed August 1, 2002.

Alsobrook, David E. "The Mobile Streetcar Boycott of 1902: African American Protest or Capitulation?" *The Alabama Review* 56, 2 (April 2003): 83–103.

Barker, Eugene C. "The African Slave Trade in Texas." *Southwestern Historical Quarterly* 6, 2 (October 1902): 145–58.

Batty, R. Braithwaite. "Notes on the Yoruba Country." *The Journal of the Anthropological Institute of Great Britain and Ireland* 19 (1890): 159–64.

Bay, Edna G. "Protection, Political Exile, and the Atlantic Slave-Trade: History and Collective Memory in Dahomey." *Slavery and Abolition* 22, 1 (April 2001): 42–60.

Berlin, Ira, and Herbert G. Gutman. "Natives and Immigrants, Free Men and Slaves: Urban Workingmen in the Antebellum American South." *The American Historical Review* 88, 5 (December 1983): 1175–1200.

Bernstein, Barton J. "Southern Politics and Attempts to Reopen the African Slave Trade." *The Journal of Negro History* 51, 1 (January 1966): 16–35.

Berry, Mary F. "Reparations for Freedmen, 1890–1916: Fraudulent Practices or Justice Deferred?" *The Journal of Negro History* 57, 3 (July 1972): 219–30.

324 *Bibliography*

Bethel, Elizabeth. "The Freedmen's Bureau in Alabama." *The Journal of Southern History* 14, 1 (February 1948): 49–92.

Blackmon, Douglas A. "From Alabama's Past, Capitalism Teamed With Racism to Create Cruel Partnership." *Wall Street Journal*, July 16, 2001.

Blassingame, John W. "The Union Army as an Educational Institution for Negroes, 1862–1865." *The Journal of Negro Education* 34, 2 (Spring, 1965): 152–9.

"Book Recalls Last Slave Shipment to Port." *Mobile Press Register*, August 4, 1946.

Bovill, E. W. "Jega Market." *Journal of the Royal African Society* 22, 85 (October 1922): 50–60.

Boyd, Willis D. "The Ile a Vache Colonization Venture, 1862–1864." *The Americas* 16, 1 (July 1959): 45–62.

Brittain, Joseph M. "Some Reflections on Negro Suffrage and Politics in Alabama Past and Present." *The Journal of Negro History* 47, 2 (April 1962): 127–38.

Byers, Samuel Hawkins Marshall. "The Last Slave Ship." *Harper's Monthly*, 113 (1906): 742–6.

Campbell, Carl. "John Mohammed Bath and the Free Mandingos in Trinidad: The Question of their Repatriation to Africa 1831–38." *Journal of African Studies* 4 (1975–76): 467–95.

Carpenter, John A. "Atrocities in the Reconstruction Period." *The Journal of Negro History* 47, 4 (October 1962): 234–47.

Carter, Dan T. "The Anatomy of Fear: The Christmas Day Insurrection Scare of 1865." *The Journal of Southern History* 42, 3 (August 1976): 345–64.

Conrad, Alfred H., and John R. Meyer. "The Economics of Slavery in the Ante Bellum South." *The Journal of Political Economy* 66, 2 (April 1958): 95–130.

Cornish, Dudley Taylor. "The Union Army as a School for Negroes." *The Journal of Negro History* 37, 4 (October 1952): 368–82.

Day, James S. "The Convict-Lease System in Alabama, 1872–1927." *Gulf South Historical Review* 21, 2 (Spring 2006): 7–29.

Denzer, LaRay. "Yoruba Women: A Historiographical Study." *The International Journal of African Historical Studies* 27, 1 (1994): 1–39.

Du Bois, W. E. B. "Reconstruction and Its Benefits." *The American Historical Review* 15, 4 (July 1910): 781–99.

Durden, Robert F. "J. D. B. De Bow: Convolutions of a Slavery Expansionist." *The Journal of Southern History* 17, 4 (November 1951): 441–6.

Eltis, David. "Mortality and Voyage Length in the Middle Passage: New Evidence from the Nineteenth Century." *The Journal of Economic History* 44, 2 (June 1984): 301–8.

———. "The Nineteenth-Century Transatlantic Slave Trade: An Annual Time Series of Imports into the Americas Broken Down by Region." *The Hispanic American Historical Review* 67, 1 (February 1987): 109–38.

Evans, Robert Jr. "Some Economic Aspects of the Domestic Slave Trade, 1830–1860." *Southern Economic Journal* 27, 4 (April 1961): 329–37.

Feldman, Glenn. "Lynching in Alabama, 1889–1921." *The Alabama Review* 48, 2 (April 1995): 114–41.

Fitzgerald, Michael W. "'To Give our Votes to the Party': Black Political Agitation and Agricultural Change in Alabama, 1865–1870." *The Journal of American History* 76, 2 (September 1989): 489–505.

———. "Wager Swayne, the Freedmen's Bureau, and the Politics of Reconstruction in Alabama." *The Alabama Review*, 48, 3 (July 1995): 188–232.

Fletcher, Marvin. "The Negro Volunteer in Reconstruction, 1865–66." *Military Affairs* 23, 3 (December 1968): 124–31.

Foner, Eric. "Reconstruction Revisited." *Reviews in American History* 10, 4 (December 1982): 82–100.

Free, Joe Brayton. "Petitions to Become A Slave." *Gulf South Historical Review* 15, 2 (1999): 98–107.

Gavoy, Administrateur. "Note historique sur Ouidah, 1913." *Etudes dahoméenes* 13 (1955): 45–70.

Gbaguidi, Benjamin. "Chronique ethnographique-origine des noms de villages—Cercle de Savalou." *Etudes dahoméenes* 8 (1952): 65–80.

Graqy, Daniel Savage. "Bibliographical Essay: Black Views on Reconstruction." *The Journal of Negro History* 58, 1 (January 1973): 73–85.

Hardin, Stephanie C. "Climate of Fear: Violence, Intimidation and Media Manipulation in Reconstruction Mobile 1865–76." *Alabama Historical Quarterly* 2, 1 (Fall 1986): 39–52.

Harris, Carl V. "Reforms in Government Control of Negroes in Birmingham, Alabama, 1890–1920." *The Journal of Southern History* 38, 4 (November 1972): 567–600.

Harris, P. G. "The Kebbi Fishermen (Sokoto Province, Nigeria)." *The Journal of the Royal Anthropological Institute of Great Britain and Ireland* 72, 1–2 (1942): 23–41.

Hill, Walter B., Jr. "The Ex-Slave Pension Movement: Some Historical and Genealogical Notes." *Negro History Bulletin* 59, 4 (Oct.–Dec. 1996): 7–11.

Hurston, Zora Neale. "Cudjo's Own Story of the Last African Slaver." *The Journal of Negro History* 12, 4 (October 1927): 648–63.

Igue, Ogunsola John. "Sur l'origine des villes Yoruba." *Bulletin de l'I.F.A.N.* Série B 41, 2 (Avril 1979): 248–80.

Inscoe, John C. "Carolina Slave Names: An Index to Acculturation." *The Journal of Southern History* 49, 4 (November 1983): 527–54.

Jackson, Harvey H. "The Wreck and Recovery of the Orline St. John." *The Alabama Review* 46, 3 (July 1993): 180–98.

Johnson, Michael P. "Work, Culture, and the Slave Community: Slave Occupations in the Cotton Belt in 1860." *Labor History* 27 (Summer 1986): 325–55.

Jordan, Weymouth Tyree. "Ante-Bellum Mobile: Alabama's Agricultural Emporium." *The Alabama Review* 1, 3 (July 1948): 181–202.

Kellogg, John. "Negro Urban Clusters in the Postbellum South." *Geographical Review* 67, 3 (July 1977): 310–21.

Klein, Herbert S., Stanley L. Engerman, Robin Haines, and Ralph Shlomowitz. "Transoceanic Mortality: The Slave Trade in Comparative Perspective." *The William and Mary Quarterly* 58, 1 (January 2001): 93–118.

Kocher, Kurt Lee. "A Duty to America and Africa: A History of the Independent African Colonization Movement in Pennsylvania." *Pennsylvania History* 51: 2 (1984): 118–53.

Kolchin, Peter. "Reevaluating the Antebellum Slave Community: A Comparative Perspective." *The Journal of American History* 70, 3 (December 1983): 579–601.

Kotlikoff, Laurence J., and Sebastian Pinera. "The Old South's Stake in the Inter-Regional Movement of Slaves, 1850–1860." *The Journal of Economic History* 37, 2 (June 1977): 434–50.

Law, Robin. "King Agaja of Dahomey, the Slave Trade, and the Question of West African Plantations: The Mission of Bulfinch Lambe and Adomo Tomo to England, 1726–32." *Journal of Imperial and Commonwealth History* 19 (1991): 137–63.

———. "Slave-Raiders and Middlemen, Monopolists and Free-Traders: The Supply of Slaves for the Atlantic Trade in Dahomey c. 1715–1850." *The Journal of African History* 30, 1 (1989): 45–68.

Law, Robin, and Kristin Mann. "West Africa in the Atlantic Community: The Case of the Slave Coast." *The William and Mary Quarterly*, 3rd Ser. 56, 2 (April 1999): 307–34.

Lovejoy, Paul E. "Autobiography and Memory: Gustavus Vassa, alias Olauclah Equiano, the African." *Slavery and Abolition* 27, 3 (December 2006): 317–47.

———. "The Kambarin Beriberi: The Formation of a Specialized Group of Hausa Kola Traders in the Nineteenth Century." *The Journal of African History* 14, 4 (1973): 633–51.

McDaniel, Antonio. "Extreme Mortality in Nineteen-Century Africa: The Case of Liberia Immigrants." *Demography* 29, 4 (November 1992): 581–94.

McDaniel, Antonio, and Carlos Grushka. "Did Africans Live Longer in the Antebellum United States?" *Historical Methods* 28, 2 (Spring 1995): 97–106.

Meier, August, and Elliott Rudwick. "The Boycott Movement Against Jim Crow Streetcars in the South, 1900–1906."*The Journal of American History* 55, 4 (March 1969): 756–75.

Mercier, Paul. "L'habitation à étage dans l'Atakora." *Etudes dahoméennes* 11 (1954): 29–88.

———. "Mouvements de population dans les traditions Betâmmaribè." *Etudes dahoméenes* 1 (1948): 47–55.

———. "Notice sur le peuplement Yoruba au Dahomey-Togo." *Etudes dahoméenes* 4, (1950): 29–40.

Miller, William L. "A Note on the Importance of the Interstate Slave Trade of the Ante Bellum South." *The Journal of Political Economy* 73, 2 (April 1965): 181–7.

Montgomery, Charles J. "Survivors from the Cargo of the Negro Slave Yacht *Wanderer*." *American Anthropologist* 10 (1908): 611–23.

Montgomery, Margaret L. "Alabama Freedmen: Some Reconstruction Documents." *Phylon* 14, 3 (3rd Qtr. 1952): 245–51.

Morel, Alain. "Un exemple d'urbanisation en Afrique occidentale: Dassa-Zoumé (Dahomey moyen)." *Cahiers d'Etudes Africaines* 14, 4 (1974): 727–48.

Myers, John B. "The Alabama Freedmen and the Economic Adjustments During Presidential Reconstruction, 1865–1867." *The Alabama Review* 26, 4 (October 1973): 252–66.

———. "Reaction and Adjustment: The Struggle of Alabama Freedmen in Post-Bellum Alabama 1865–1867." *The Alabama Historical Quarterly* 32, 1&2 (Spring and Summer 1970): 5–22.

Nelms, Jack N. "Early Days with the Alabama River Steamboats." *The Alabama Review* 37, 1 (January 1984): 13–23.

Nelson, Bernard H. "Confederate Slave Impressment Legislation, 1861–1865." *The Journal of Negro History* 31, 4 (October 1946): 392–410.

Niane, Djibril Tamsir. "Africa's Understanding of the Slave Trade: Oral Accounts." *Diogenes*, no. 179, 45, 3 (Autumn 1997): 75–90.

The Ninth Atlanta Conference. "Negro Crime."1906. Reprint, *The Review of Black Political Economy* 16, 1–2 (Summer/Fall 1987): 47–61.

N'Tia Roger. "Géopolitique de l'Atakora précolonial." *Afrika Zamani*, nouvelle série 1, 1 (July 1993): 107–24.

Parkinson, John. "The Legend of Oro." *Man* 6 (1906): 103–5.

Parrinder, Edward Geoffrey. "Yoruba-Speaking Peoples in Dahomey." *Africa: Journal of the International African Institute* 17, 2 (April 1947): 122–9.

Piersen, William D. "White Cannibals, Black Martyrs: Fear, Depression, and Religious Faith as Causes of Suicide Among New Slaves." *The Journal of Negro History* 72, 2 (April 1977): 147–59.

Rabinowitz, Howard N. "Half a Loaf: The Shift from White to Black Teachers in the Negro Schools of the Urban South, 1865–1890." *The Journal of Southern History* 40, 4 (November 1974): 565–94.

Ralston, Richard D. "The Return of Brazilian Freedmen to West Africa in the 18th and 19th Centuries." *Canadian Journal of African Studies* 3, 3 (Autumn 1969): 577–93.

Reid, Robert D. "The Negro in Alabama During the Civil War." *Journal of Negro History* 35, 3 (July 1950): 265–88.

Ripley, Peter C. "The Black Family in Transition: Louisiana, 1860–1865." *The Journal of Southern History* 41, 3 (August 1975): 369–80.

Ritchie, Carson I. E. "Deux textes sur le Sénégal (1673–1677). *Bulletin de l'I.F.A.N.* 30, 1 (January 1968): 289–353.

Ross, David A. "The Career of Domingo Martinez in the Bight of Benin 1833–64." *The Journal of African History* 6, 1 (1965): 79–90.

———. "The Dahomean Middleman System, 1727–c. 1818." *The Journal of African History* 28 (1987): 357–75.

———. "The Fist Chacha of Whydah: Francisco Felix de Souza." *Odu* 2 (1969): 19–28.

Rouch, Jean. "Les Sorkawa pêcheurs itinérants du Moyen Niger." *Africa: Journal of the International African Institute* 20, 1 (January 1950): 5–25.

Salamone, Frank. "The Serkawa of Yauri: Class, Status or Party?" *African Studies Review* 18, 1 (April 1975): 88–101.

Schweninger, Loren. "Black Citizenship in the Republican Party in Reconstruction Alabama." *The Alabama Review* 29, 2 (April 1976): 83–103.

———. "James Rapier and the Negro Labor Movement, 1869–1872." *The Alabama Review* 28, 3 (July 1975): 185–201.

Shlomotvitz, Ralph. "'Bound' or 'Free'? Black Labor in Cotton and Sugarcane Farming, 1865–1880." *The Journal of Southern History* 50, 4 (November 1984): 569–96.

Souza, Roberto Francisco de. "Contribution à l'histoire de la famille de Souza." *Etudes dahoméennes* 13 (1955): 17–21.

Spencer, C. A. "Black Benevolent Societies and the Development of Black Insurance Companies in Nineteenth Century Alabama. *Phylon* 46, 3 (3rd Qtr. 1985): 251–61.

Steckel, Richard H. and Richard A. Jensen. "New Evidence on the Causes of Slave and Crew Mortality in the Atlantic Slave Trade." *The Journal of Economic History* 46, 1 (March 1986): 57–77.

Tambo, David C. "The Sokoto Caliphate Slave Trade in the Nineteenth Century." *The International Journal of African Historical Studies* 9, 2 (1976): 187–217.

Taylor, Alrutheus A. "The Migration." *The Journal of Negro History* 11, 2 (April 1926): 327–46.

———. "The Movement of Negroes from the East to the Gulf States From 1830 to 1850." *The Journal of Negro History* 8, 4 (October 1923): 367–83.

Taylor, Joseph H. "Populism and Disfranchisement in Alabama." *The Journal of Negro History* 34, 4 (October 1919): 410–27.

Tebeau, C. W. "Some Aspects of Planter-Freedman Relations, 1865–1880." *The Journal of Negro History* 21, 2 (April 1936): 130–50.

Tereau, Lt-Col. Med. and Dr. Huttel, "Monographie du Hollidjé." *Etudes dahoméennes* 3 (1950): 59–72.

Thomason, Michael V. R. "Researching a Legend." *Gulf South Historical Review* 15, 1 (Fall 1999): 102–6.

Tidjani, Serpos A. "Notes sur le mariage au Dahomey." *Etudes dahoméennes* 6 (1951): 28–107.

———."Notes sur le mariage au Dahomey II." *Etudes dahoméennes* 7 (1952): 5–81.

Verger, Pierre. "Retour des "Brésiliens" au Golfe du Bénin au XIXeme siècle." *Etudes Dahoméennes*, Nouvelle série 8 (October 1966): 5–28.

———. "Rôle joué par le tabac de Bahia dans la traite des esclaves au Golfe du Bénin." *Cahiers d'études africaines* 15 (1964): 349–70.

Vinson, Robert Trent. "The Law as Lawbreaker: The Promotion and Encouragement of the Atlantic Slave Trade by the New York Judiciary System, 1857–1862." *Afro-Americans in New York Life and History* (1996): 35–58.

Waters, Wendy W. "'One of Dese Mornings, Bright and Fair, Take My Wings and Cleave De Air'": The Legend of the Flying Africans and Diasporic Consciousness." *Melus* 22, 3 (Autumn 1997): 3–39.

White, Kenneth B. "The Alabama Freedmen's Bureau and Black Education: The Myth of Opportunity." *The Alabama Review* 4, 2 (April 1981): 107–24.

Wiener, Jonathan M. "Planter Persistence and Social Change: Alabama, 1850–1870." *Journal of Interdisciplinary History* 7, 2 (Autumn 1976): 235–60.

Wilentz, Gay. "If You Surrender to the Air: Folk Legends of Flight and Resistance in African American Literature." *Melus* 16, 1 (Spring, 1989): 21–32.

Wish, Harvey. "The Revival of the African Slave Trade in the United States, 1856–1860." *The Mississippi Valley Historical Review* 27, 4 (March 1941): 569–88.

———. "Slave Disloyalty Under the Confederacy." *The Journal of Negro History* 23, 4 (October 1938): 435–50.

Work, Monroe N. "Negro Criminality in the South." 1913. Reprint *The Review of Black Political Economy* 16, 1–2 (Summer/Fall, 1987): 63–9.

Yetman, Norman R. "Ex-Slave Interviews and the Historiography of Slavery." *American Quarterly* 36, 2 (Summer 1984): 181–210.

Dissertations

Caldwell, Kimberly M. "From Africatown to 'Out Stickney': Reminiscences of a Toledo, Ohio African-American Community 1919–1960." Ph.D. diss., Bowling Green State University, 2001.

Cvornyek, Robert Louis. "Convict Labor in the Alabama Coal Mines, 1874–1928." Ph.D. diss., Columbia University, 1993.

Michozounou, Romuald. "Le peuplement du plateau d'Abomey des origines à 1889." Ph.D. diss., Université Paris I Panthéon-Sorbonne, 1991–1992.

Reid, John. "Warrior Aristocrats in Crisis: The Political Effects of the Transition from the Slave Trade to Palm Oil Commerce in the Nineteenth Century Kingdom of Dahomey." Ph.D. diss., University of Stirling, 1986.

Robertson, Natalie Suzette. "The African Ancestry of the Founders of Africa Town, Alabama." Ph.D. diss., University of Iowa, 1996.

Shields, Francine. "Palm Oil and Power: Women in an Era of Economic Transition in 19th Century Yorubaland (South Western Nigeria)." Ph.D. diss., University of Stirling, 1997.

Unpublished Manuscripts

Autrey, Lilian Gary, Cordelia E. Dennis, Lorna Gail Woods. "Information Compiled by the Children and Offspring of Charlie Lewis." Mobile, 1991–1992.

Weise, Thomas D. "The Voyage of the Clotilde: A Short History of the Facts and Fiction Surrounding the Last Slave Ship to America and Its Passengers." Xavier University, Institute of Black Catholic Studies, April 26, 1991. University of South Alabama Archives.

Index

Abache. *See* Turner, Clara
Abbot Devereux (ship), 31
Abeokuta, 34, 35, 63
Abile. *See* Lewis, Celia
Abomey, 45–50, 185; *barracoon*, 49; sale ceremony, 50; stone pile ritual, 50; triage of captives, 50
Abram, 94–95
Adams, James Hopkins, 16, 254n 50
Adams, John Quincy, 16
Adissa (Brunston), 38, 132
Advertiser, 10
Africa: and children of African Town, 216; and emigration attempts, 138–41, 146–50, 170–71, 208, 286n 7; leaving, 58–59; marriage and family life in, 113, 137–38, 219–20; slavery in, 103; as surname, 134, 275n 37; villages and towns in, 42
Africa, Bettie, 134
Africa, Sarah, 134
Africa, William, 134
Africa Growth and Opportunity Act, 235
African Americans: Africans' relations with, 4, 96, 104–5, 106, 107–12, 185; and African Town, 157; and Church, 167–69, 172–73; Colored Troops, 144–46; and convict-leasing system, 192–99, 232, 284n 39, 285n 66; disenfranchisement, 207–9; and domestic slave trade, 12–13; and education, 176–77; emigration efforts, 139–41; family structure, 160; fictive kinship, 107; land for, 143, 152, 154–55, 159, 186; lynching of, 183, 215; and marriage, 112; migration after emancipation, 126–29; in Mobile, 223; and names, 133, 136; patriarchy, 142, 161; plantation history, 107, 113–14; in prison, 193–94; ratio of Africans to African Americans, 109; women's work, 141–42

African Labor Supply Association, 18
African Methodist Episcopal Church, 167–68
African Methodist Episcopal Zion Church, 167–68
Africans: *See also* African Town; savage stereotype of Africans; shipmates; age of Africans, 149, 162; capture of, 186–87; and citizenship, 165–66; degradation of, 61, 70, 77, 78, 81–82, 95–96; descendants of, 104–5, 109; distribution of population, 110; and emigration attempts, 138–41, 146–50, 170–71, 208, 286n 7; emotional expression of Africans, 96–98, 102, 117, 189; and families (*see* families of Africans); and honor, 47, 61, 66; humiliation of, 61, 70, 77, 78, 81–82, 95–96; identity as, 111–12, 232; and marriage, 112; and names, 132, 134–36 (*see also* names of Africans); perceptions of, 106, 108; on "racial" distinctions, 110; ratio of Africans to African Americans, 109; reaction to enslavement, 102–5; reaction to humiliation, 96; redemption of family members, 52, 147–48; relationships with African Americans, 4, 96, 104–5, 106, 107–12, 185; resistance of, 52, 100–102, 175–76, 269n 45; on whites, 53–54, 110–11
African Squadron, 23, 28–29, 78
African Town (now Africatown): *See also* shipmates; annexation of, 291n 4; cemetery, 184, 221, 222, 230; and citizenship, 165–66, 175–76; construction of houses, 155–56; and cultural preservation, 190–91; and descendants of Africans, 5; and education, 178, 209–10; establishment of, 2, 3, 154; family structure in,

Timothy Meaher. From *Encyclopedia of American Biography*, n.s., vol. 29 (New York: The American Historical Company, 1959). Milstein Division of United States History, Local History and Genealogy, The New York Public Library, Astor, Lenox and Tilden Foundations.

William Foster. The Museum of Mobile Collections.

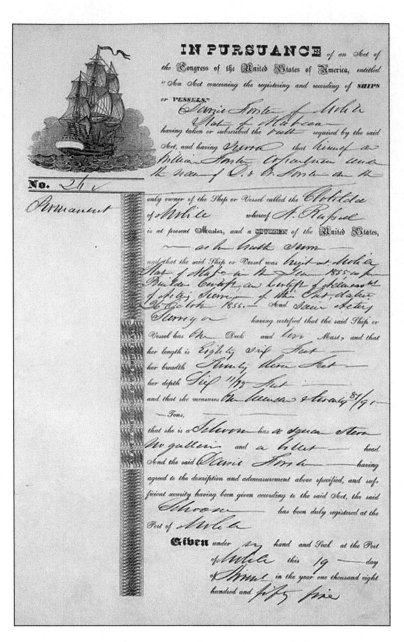

Registration of the *Clotilda*, April 19, 1855. National Archives and
Records Administration, Southeast Region (Atlanta).

William Foster's account of the
Clotilda's voyage, November 1890.
Page 1: List of trade items; page 8:
The departure from Ouidah.
Courtesy of the Mobile Public
Library. All rights reserved.
Reprinted with permission.

Benin and Nigeria. Rutgers University Cartography.

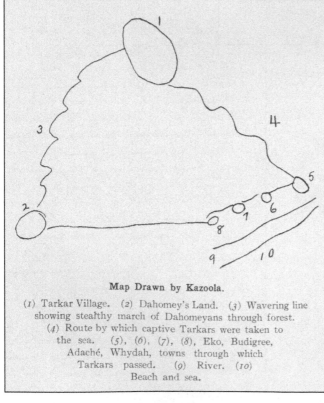

Map Drawn by Kazoola.

(1) Tarkar Village. (2) Dahomey's Land. (3) Wavering line showing stealthy march of Dahomeyans through forest. (4) Route by which captive Tarkars were taken to the sea. (5), (6), (7), (8), Eko, Budigree, Adaché, Whydah, towns through which Tarkars passed. (9) River. (10) Beach and sea.

Map of alleged route to Ouidah. From Emma Langdon Roche, *Historic Sketches of the South* (New York: Knickerbocker Press, 1914). General Research and Reference Division, Schomburg Center for Research in Black Culture, the New York Public Library, Astor, Lenox and Tilden Foundations.

Wreck of the *Clotilda*, ca. 1912. From Emma Langdon Roche, *Historic Sketches of the South* (New York: Knickerbocker Press, 1914). General Research and Reference Division, Schomburg Center for Research in Black Culture, the New York Public Library, Astor, Lenox and Tilden Foundations.

Abache/Clara Turner and Kossola Cudjo Lewis, African Town, ca. 1912. From Emma Langdon Roche, *Historic Sketches of the South* (New York: Knickerbocker Press, 1914). General Research and Reference Division, Schomburg Center for Research in Black Culture, the New York Public Library, Astor, Lenox and Tilden Foundations.

Oluale/Charlie Lewis, African Town,
ca. 1900. Courtesy of Lorna Woods,
University of South Alabama
Archives.

Pollee Allen, African Town, ca. 1912.
From Emma Langdon Roche,
Historic Sketches of the South (New
York: Knickerbocker Press, 1914).
General Research and Reference
Division, Schomburg Center for
Research in Black Culture, the New
York Public Library, Astor, Lenox
and Tilden Foundations.

Ossa Keeby, African Town, ca. 1912.
From Emma Langdon Roche,
Historic Sketches of the South (New
York: Knickerbocker Press, 1914).
General Research and Reference
Division, Schomburg Center for
Research in Black Culture, the New
York Public Library, Astor, Lenox
and Tilden Foundations.

Zuma Livingston, African Town, ca.
1905. Viola Allen's collection, courtesy
of Dr. Dorothy Ford, with permission
from the Wisconsin Department of
Public Instruction.

The first Old Landmark Baptist Church built by the Africans. The trees on the right are on Cudjo Lewis's property. Viola Allen's collection, courtesy of Dr. Dorothy Ford, with permission from the Wisconsin Department of Public Instruction.

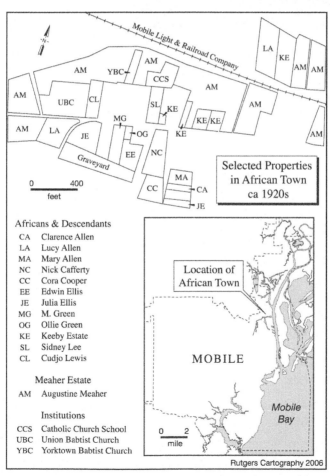

African Town. Rutgers University Cartography.

THE STATE OF ALABAMA,
MOBILE COUNTY. *Know all Men by these Presents, That we,*

Cudgo Lewis & *Polee Allen*

are held and firmly bound unto the State of Alabama, in the penal sum of
TWO HUNDRED DOLLARS, for the payment whereof, we bind ourselves, our heirs,
executors and administrators, jointly and severally, firmly by these presents.

Sealed with our seals, and dated this *15* day of *Mch* A. D. 187

The Condition of the above Obligation is such, That whereas the above
bounden *Cudgo Lewis* has obtained
License to intermarry and be joined together in the Bonds of Matrimony with
Cecilia Lewis, over 18 years of age, NOW, if there
be no lawful cause why such marriage should not be celebrated, then this obligation to be void, otherwise to remain in full force and effect.

Cudgo his + mark Lewis (SEAL)
Polee Allen (SEAL)

THE STATE OF ALABAMA,
MOBILE COUNTY. Before me, PRICE WILLIAMS, Jr., Judge
of Probate in and for said County and State, personally appeared
and the said
being first duly sworn, deposes and says, that the within named
is over twenty-one years of
age; that within named is
over the age of eighteen years; and is residing in this County, and that there
is no lawful cause why the contemplated Marriage within referred to, should
not be celebrated, so far as affiant knows or has any reason to believe.

THE STATE OF ALABAMA, To any of the State Judges, or to any Ordained Minister of the Gospel
MOBILE COUNTY. or to any Justice of the Peace of said County—Greeting:

Know Ye, That you are hereby authorized and Licensed to join together
in the Bonds of Matrimony *Cudgo Lewis*
with *Cecilia Lewis, over 18 years of age,*
Given under my hand and seal, this *15* day of *Mch* 1880
P. Williams Jr (SEAL)
JUDGE.

THE STATE OF ALABAMA, To the Judge of Probate of said County.
Mobile County.
I Hereby Certify, That I this day solemnized the rites of Matrimony,
between *Cudgo Lewis* and *Cecilia Lewis*
who are within named, at *Residence*
in said County.
WITNESS my hand this, the *15th* day of *March* 1880
Benj Burke M.G.

Marriage Certificate of Cudjo and Abile/Celia Lewis, with Pollee Allen's signature.
Mobile County Probate Court.

First, second, and third generations in African Town, ca. 1887. Back row, left to right: Julia Ellis, Kattie Allen, and Mary (daughters of Pollee and Rose Allen); Martin (Zuma's son); Rose Allen holding her grandson, Leonard Ellis. Front row: Mary Jane (Zuma's daughter) and Martha (daughter of Pollee and Rose). Viola Allen's collection, courtesy of Dr. Dorothy Ford, with permission from the Wisconsin Department of Public Instruction.

Julia, daughter of Pollee and Rose Allen, with Alabama-born husband, William Ellis. Married in 1886, they had eleven children. William was a ship carpenter. Courtesy of Dr. Dorothy Ford.

Zuma and her grandchildren, African Town, ca. 1912. From Emma Langdon Roche, *Historic Sketches of the South* (New York: Knickerbocker Press, 1914). General Research and Reference Division, Schomburg Center for Research in Black Culture, the New York Public Library, Astor, Lenox and Tilden Foundations.

To His Excellency, Jos. F. Johnston, Governor of Alabama:-

we the under-

signed, citizens of Mobile County, respectfully petition your Excellency

to grant to CUDJO LEWIS a Pardon or parole. He has always been a man of

most excellent character, and has stood well with all the people who

knew him, white or colored. The circumstances under which he killed

the deceased were such as to leave some doubt of his guilt of manslaugh-

ter, and there certainly was some provocation for the act.

We believe the purposes of justice have been subserved.

Petition for Cudjo Lewis's pardon, Mobile, July 1901. Alabama Department of
Archives and History, Montgomery.

Tomb of Aleck Iyadjemi Lewis, Cudjo and Abile's first child. Old Plateau Cemetery, 2006. Photo by Sylviane A. Diouf.

Cudjo Lewis and his great-granddaughters, twins Mary and Martha, African Town, ca. 1927. Mary now lives in Philadelphia, and Martha in Mobile. Erik Overbey Collection, University of South Alabama Archives.

Oluale/Charlie Lewis's death certificate, November 29, 1912, with parents' "American names." Alabama Center for Health Statistics, Montgomery.

James Dennison's will, March 30, 1914. Mobile County Probate Court.

Above Viola, Pollee and Rose Allen's granddaughter, with trunk made by Pollee, Africatown, 1985. With permission from the Wisconsin Department of Public Instruction.

Right Cudjo Lewis, barefoot, in front of his house. McGill Studio Collection, University of South Alabama Archives.

Cudjo Lewis at home, ca. 1927. Erik Overbey Collection, University of South Alabama Archives.

1111

Dear friend you may
Have seen in the Papers
about my History But
this Has Been over
three years since I
Has let any one take it
off to Coppy from it
I only Did that so they
Would Help me But there
is no one Did for me
as you Has OThe lord
Will Bless you and will
gave you a long life

Where there no more
Parting yours in Christ

Cudjo Lewis

Cudjo Lewis to Charlotte Osgood Mason, September 4, 1930. Alain Locke Papers, Moorland-Springarn Research Center, Howard University.

Cudjo Lewis's death certificate, July 26, 1935. Alabama Center for Health Statistics, Montgomery.

Gumpa/Peter Lee's chimney, Africatown, 2006. Photo by Sylviane A. Diouf.

Above, left Dr. Dorothy Ford, great-great-granddaughter of Pollee and Rose Allen, Mobile, 2006. Photo by Sylviane A. Diouf

Above, right Lorna Woods, great-great-granddaughter of Oluale/Charlie and Maggie Lewis, near the river, in Africatown, where her ancestors arrived, 2006. Photo by Sylviane A. Diouf

CPSIA information can be obtained at www.ICGtesting.com
Printed in the USA
BVOW06s2135121115

426780BV00007B/19/P